PEASANTS, LANDLORDS AND PRINCES IN EAST PUNJAB STATES (1920—1956)

PEASANTS, LANDLORDS AND PRINCES IN EAST PUNJAB STATES (1920—1956)

S.D. Gajrani

Peasants, Landlords and Princes in East Punjab States (1920—1956)

First Published : 2009

ISBN 978-81-311-0107-0

Published by :
COMMONWEALTH PUBLISHERS PVT. LTD.
4831/24, Prahlad Street,
Ansari Road, Darya Ganj,
New Delhi - 110002
Ph. : 23272541, 23257835
Fax : 91- 011- 23257835
e-mail : campusbooks@hotmail.com
commonwealthbooks@gmail.com

Laser Typesetting by :
Stylish Laser Typesetter
Delhi - 110053

Printed at :
Roshan Offset Printers
Delhi

PREFACE

An attempt has been made to bring to light some neglected aspects of the agrarian structure, agrarian unrest as well as peasants'/tenants' movements in the East Punjab States during the period between 1920 to 1956. We are fully aware at this stage of research. Our knowledge regarding agrarian conditions and class struggle constitute only approximations towards infinitely complex phenomena which are not yet adequately explored. We are also aware that several myths have been built around the agrarian upsurges in this part of the Punjab; general aspects have yet to be explored and numerous essential sources yet to be adequately explored. Hence, we shall try to focus our attention on the issues like the type of peasants' organization; the detailed history of the various peasants'/tenants' movements, their socio-economic base or the involvement of various sections of the peasantry; the role of castism and communalism; the ideological aspects and strategic perspective as well as the form of struggle in the peasants' movements; the method and nature of mass mobilization; leadership of these movements and finally their achievements and failures.

Though the centre of the INC, which had been directing the nationalists' struggle, was confined to what was known as British India, the people of the Indian states did not lag behind. They also contributed towards the achievements of this goal. In the states, the struggle was, however, two fold and more complex. In the states the rulers were autocratic and they had denied even those elementary civil rights which the citizens of the British India as a rule and right enjoyed.

One of the main objectives of this study is to investigate the grievances and demands of the agriculturists. This will help us to determine the social contents of this movement. What was its social base in the Punjab States? What was the involvement of the different sections of the agriculturists in this struggle? What was the participation of various political groups in it? Some more issues such as leadership of the peasants'/ tenants' movements and structural relationship among peasants, *biswedars* and the government have also been raised here. The failure that was faced by the radical leadership of different political groups related to this struggle has also been narrated in the later part of the second as sell as in the eight chapters. The approach and attitude of these groups towards this struggle is also cited.

Another important set of questions relating to the structure and strategy of this struggle has also been raised. We shall be in chapters IV, V and VI, the form that the Punjab States' tenants' struggle adopted was basically agitational and it was not different from the form adopted by the peasants' movements in the British Punjab, in U.P., in Andhra, in Bengal and Bihar and also by the national movement. However, there is inadequate relationship between the two. The Punjab Congress, which favoured the Urban groups and the moneylenders, failed to win over the peasantry in the certain imperialist struggle. Consequently, it remained week. The government policy towards the peasants' demands, grievances, unrest and struggle has been discussed at length. At the same time British Indian Government was able to bring into operation some countervailing forces against the Congress, the communists, the *Praja Mandal,* etc. It followed two fold policy-suppressive on the one hand and conciliatory towards some rural strata on the other. The continuation of repressive and reformist policies have been traced in the 7th chapter as well as in the three preceding chapters. However, it does not mean that the people of the British Punjab were happy. They were equally exploited and suppressed by the British imperialists, the Indian *zamindars, banias* and agriculturist moneylenders. Their economic lot was not even some what better. The agriculturists had been fighting for their rights against the British repressive policies since 1907 when agrarian unrest broke out. To substantiate this point we may even refer to the peasants' movements in the *Nili Bar* area in Lahore and also several other parts of the central Punjab.

The peasants' struggle in this region was against autocratic princely rule as much as against British imperialism. Moreover, this struggle was the product of the internal and external factors which are thoroughly discussed in the second chapter. Here, an attempt has been made to trace the economic background to the agrarian unrest characterizing the Punjab States in the period under review. To have a more vivid picture the nature of agriculture land revenue and land tenure have been discussed in the very first chapter. The approach and attitudes of the different political groups towards the peasants' struggle and thereafter rise of communalism are discussed and analysed in the third chapter. In brief, this chapter has two main objectives : firstly, to present the facts about the activities of the major political parties and the interest they displayed in connection with agrarian problems and secondly, to measure the strength of each political organization in the Punjab States. This chapter also covers the development of party politics and the involvement of the major political parties in this part of the Punjab. Also, an effort has been made to highlight the impact of party politics on the realities in particularly.

As stated in the main text of this work, the objectives of the states' governments and that of the British Indian Policy was complex. As the nationalist movement gathered momentum and the left wingers began to make their presences felt, the government had to go beyond law and order measures. To political manipulation to keep these forces in check, structural relationship among peasants, *biswedars* and the government is discussed at length in the 9th chapter of this study. In the last chapter, an attempt has been made to prepare the balance sheet of the achievements as well as the week points of the peasants' struggle during the period of our study.

The scholars in Punjab working on the history of Punjab, especially the East Punjab States, are placed under numerous constraints. There does not exist a single book on the subject which could be used for the necessary background of some of the issues discussed in this work. Even so, an attempt has been made to build up an account of the agrarian unrest piece by piece, with the help of the available contemporary writings, newspapers, journals, the government files and various other sources lying scattered in different Libraries, archives and private collections.

I studied in original the proceedings of the Home Department (Political) 1917-1945; Proceeding of the Home Department 1917-45; Proceedings of the Department of Revenue and Agriculture 1894-1910; Punjab State Agency Records (Patiala) 1920-39; Punjab State Agency Records (General) : 1920-37; These proceedings are available in the National Archives of India and Central State Library, Patiala. I also consulted the Patiala State Records—Prime Minister office files and the files of Nabha, Kalsia, Kapurthala, Faridkot, Malerkotla States which are at the PSA, Patiala. In these files I found many pamphlets in *Panjabi* language which helped me in building up my account of the peasants unrest and problems in the East Punjab states.

I have also consulted papers of Linlithgoed, Montagu, Zetland, Hailey, Ereking, Hune, etc. in Microfilm at NMML, New Delhi. I had to sit at the Punjab State Archives, Patiala for almost 3 years to study in original some of the valuable sources, such as Chamber of Princes Records, Proceedings of the Punjab States' Council Meetings held at Lahore in 1940, Simla in 1942 and in Patiala in 1943; Faridkot State Records : Political Movement Files, Kalsia State Records (Confidential) files; Kapurthala and Nabha States Records files, etc. I also made use of Annual Administration Reports of PNKKP and Jind States for the year 1911-1939, at Central State Library, Patiala (Reference Section). Other important sources I have made use of are the *Kirti* and the *Kirti Lehar* from February 1926 to November 1939. This paper particularly tells us at length about the condition of the workers and peasants. It also exposes the exploitation of the poor peasants in the hands of the *zamindars* and moneylenders; various articles published in its different issues in *Panjabi* language have been very useful. Some more

Panjabi source material in-forces of pamphlets and books are also used. For instance, *Praja Malerkotla Di Dard Kahani* by Giani Kehar Singh; *Aap Biti* by Sahib Singh, *IKK Jiwan-IKK Itihas* by Jagjit Singh Aulakh, etc. I have also made use of the private papers of Sardar Sunder Singh Majithia, Dr. Chaman Lal, Prithvi Singh Azad, etc. as well as the transcripts of nearly 30 freedom fighers oral testimonies which are available at NMML, New Delhi.

In search of material, I had to contact persons who could give over the requisite information about the peasants' problems and their struggle. I collected information through interviews with Sardar Jagir Singh Joga, Sardar Hira Singh Pathal, Sardar Sohan Singh Josh, Master Hari Singh, Shri Brish Bhan, Shri Chhajju Mal, Pandit Kishori Lal, Sardar Ishar Singh Majhail and some more freedom fighters and activists who were closely connected with the agrarian movement in the Punjab East Punjab States as well as in the British Punjab. In the beginning I was cold shouldered by some of them but my going to them time and again made them realize that I was a genuine seeker of information regarding their participation in the agrarian movement in the East Punjab States as well as in the British Punjab.

The conclusions arrived at in this study are only such as primary and contemporary evidence has yielded. In case of oral information, I have tried to compare that with the contemporary documentary evidence. I have no allowed my judgement to be influenced by the reverence and the esteem in which the people in India in general and that of the Punjab states in particular had held the leadership.

ACKNOWLEDGEMENT

My indebtedness to my supervisor Dr. A.C. Bose—Professor of History, Jammu University, Jammu for his generous help and keen interest in my work is too deep for words. I am really grateful to him for his very kindly and scholarly suggestions during the course of the writing of my D. Lit. Thesis. That in spite of the constant and valuable criticism and suggestions given by my advisor many errors still have crept is in entirely due to my imperfection. I am also beholden to Dr. Sabyoschi Bhattacharya, Professor of History, Jawaharlal Nehru University, New Delhi. It was entirely due to his encouragement I first undertook this study.

I take this opportunity of expressing my gratitude to the custodian of Archives of India, Punjab State Archives, Patiala, Archives of Contemporary History of India, J.N.U. New Delhi; Dwaraka Dass Library, and such of the libraries as I often visited in search of material.

Contents

ABBREVIATION

AICC : All India Congress Committee

AIKS : All India *Kisan Sabha*

AISPC : All India States People's Conference

CPI : Communist Party of India

CENSUS : Census of India Report

CSP : Congress Socialist Party

CWR : Confidential Weekly Reports

HH : His Highness

IGP : Inspector General of Police

NAI : National Archives of India

NMML : Nehru Memorial Museum and Library

NPR : Native Papers Report (Journals and Periodicals published in the Punjab Reports of the Government of India)

PAR : Administration Report of the Punjab and its dependencies (Annual)

PSCP : Punjab Council Socialist Party

PEPSU : Patiala and East Punjab States Union

PHC : Punjab History Conference

PKC : Punjab *Kisan* Committee

PM'S : Prime Ministers'

PMOF : Prime Minister's Office File

PPCC : Punjab Provincial Congress Committee

PPA	:	Punjab Press Abstracts
PPP	:	Punjab Past and Present
PROGS	:	Proceedings
PSA	:	Punjab State Archives
PSR	:	Patiala State Records
SGPC	:	*Shiromani Gurdwara Parbandhak* Committee
SVNP	:	Selections from the Vernacular Newspapers published in the Punjab.
WPP	:	Workers and Peasants' Party

GLOSSARY

Abi	: Irrigated land
Abiana	: Water Rate
Abwab	: Cesses paid by a cultivator to State in addition to land revenue
Acre	: A measure of land equal to 4840 square yards
Ahalkar	: An official; a functionary of the Government; an agent
Ain-ul-mal	: Land revenue papers, the receipts of which went to State exchequer, See, '*Khalsa*'.
Akali	: Literally meaning 'immortal'; a member off the Akali Party
Anna	: A coin representing 1/16 of a rupee
Asami	: A tenant; a cultivator without a proprietary claim
Bandobast	: Settlement of the revenue payable
Banjar	: Barren land; cultivable waste; land fallen out of cultivation
Barani	: Unirrigated Land depended on rain
Batai	: Share cropping; the system of cropping where revenue is a certain portion of the produce
Betawas	: An official who divide the crop for purpose of land revenue
Begar	: Compulsory forced labour, unpaid, a cess in lieu of unpaid labour

Benami : Illegal transfer of land in the names of relatives or servants

Bhaichara : A land tenure in which land was held in soverality by different proprietors whose shares were regulated by the revenue payable, and not by ancestral or customary shares. Also see *Siradari.*

Bikrami : Sambat, which is about 57 years behind the Christian era

Bigha : A measure of land generally considered equal to 20 biswas or 113/19 kanals; also ½ of a ghumaon, the actual size varying from region to region

Bir : Forest reserve

Biradari : Kinship

Biswa : Fifty square yards, also see *bigha* above

Biswedar : Absentee Landlord (In the beginning, he was, literally, possession of the land; holder of a right over a 1/20th part or 5% in the produce from land, and as such, also called *Malik-i-ala*).

Chahi : Land irrigated by well.

Chakla : Denoting an administrative division in Mughal times covering a number of parganas

Chaudhari : A traditional leader of a community back to Mughal times, when they were appointed in petty positions of authority in the countryside

Cho : A stream

Dakilkars : Erstwhile Malerkotla state tenants having equivalent rights to those of occupancy rights

Dami Sharhni : A cess payable by a proprietor of land to the state

Dastora : A due payable by a tenant to a *biswedar,* which was four *sers* per *maund*

Deh : A village as revenue unit

Dhaia : A loamy assessment circle of land

Dharna : A form of protest through continuous squatting

Durbar : Court of a ruler

Firman : A decree

Firman-i-shahi : A royal decree

Ghair Marusi : Non-hereditary, tenant-at-will

Ghair-maurusi muzara : Non-occupancy tenant

Ghair mustsgil : Fluctuating assessment

Ghallughara : Holocuast

Ghumaon : A measure of land varying in different parts of the Punjab, and consisting of eight kanals, also equal to two *bighas* or about an *acre* (in *Manjha*)

Girdawar : Revenue official

Girdawari : See *Khasra Girdawri*

Goonda : Bad character of Ruffians

Gora Deh : A residential place in villages, used by visiting State officials

Hag serins : A tax farmers' remuneration, over and above the dues to the State

Hag Tehsil : A cess levied on account of he tehsil staff

Hathail : Handle of a plough

Hidayat	:	Ordinance
Hal	:	Plough
Ijlas-i-khas	:	Royal Secretariat
Illaqa	:	Area
Jagir	:	An assignment of land revenue in recognition of some service to State or a status
Jagirdar	:	A person who got an assignment of land revenue in lieu of salary or some other reason like a meritorious service
Jamna	:	The aggregate revenue assessed
Kabuliat	:	Agreeing to pay rent or written agreement
Kamin	:	A village Menial, literally inferior, such as sweepers, potters, cobblers, barbers and water drawers etc.
Kachh Batai	:	Kind assessment
Kachhu	:	An official who measured sown area by pacing the sides
Kankut	:	A method of assessment based on the appraisement of standing crop by measurement of land and inspection of crop
Kanungo	:	A revenue official supervising the work of Patwaris
Karam	:	One Karam equals to two steps, approximately five and half feet. One square karam is equal to one sarsahi. Nine sarsahi is equal to one marla
Kashtwar	:	An agriculturist
Kharif	:	Summer crop-sown in April-May-June before the commencement of the rains and reaped in October-November

Khasra : Description of land or a record

Khasra : A record

Khasra girdawari : A field book containing record of cultivators specifying their status

Khud kast : Self cultivated

Khus hasiyat : A cess payable by all agriculturists of the state which was three annas per bigha

Khwanin : Muslim landlords

Kiara : A small piece of land, forming a part of a large field

Kisan : A farmer

Lakh : A hundred thousand

Lambardar : The headman of a village, or part thereof called patti; Lambardari; 5% of the revenue paid to him by the tenants in his capacity as a zamindar

Mahant : A head of a Gurdwara (Sikh temple)

Mafidar : Depositer of revenue

Mai baap : Parents, the state people considered the ruler as their parents

Majha : The Central portion of the Bari Doab, covering the region roughly from Amritisar to Qasur and from Lahore to Bhairowal on the Beas

Malba : Fund out of which village expenses were defrayed; also Debris

Malguzar : Revenue officer

Malik-i-adna : Literally, inferior proprietor, secondary owner, like adhlapi, chakdar and Sildar

Malik Ala : Literally, a superior proprietor, he had a

		recognized right over land, and claim to a certain share in the produce usually ranging 1.5 to 10 per cent; primary owner
Malikana	:	The proprietary dues paid by the tenant to the proprietor, the amount generally ranging between 1½ to 25 per cent of the land revenue
Malik qabas	:	Ownership possession
Maurs	:	Exemption from payment of land revenue
Maurusi	:	Literally, hereditary; an occupancy tenant
Maufidar	:	Holder of revenue free grant
Muktar	:	A manager of a large estate
Muzara	:	A tenant who cultivated the land of others on certain conditions
Muzarian Bardash Jadid	:	Meritable tenancy on fixed rates introduced to encourage the cultivation of Inferior lands
Muzarian Bardash Sabaq	:	Meritable tenancy since early settlement and renewable with permission of the government
Muzarian Bashara parta	:	Meritable tenants in possession of lands for considerable period, paying fixed rates
Mizarian Bila Tayan sift	:	Tenants unprotected by Act 1907 but having privileges of the above mentioned tenants
Muzarian Chakotar Nautor	:	Tenants of government land paying cash rent at varying within situated individual holdings
Muzarian chakrote-dari khas	:	Having all the rights of shartiya according to Act IV 1907 of erstwhile Faridkot state
Muzarian Darbandi	:	Tenants paying cash rent for a stipulated period, meritable with the permission of the government and renewable

Muzarian Shartiya	:	Tenants with hereditary rights, paying cash rents, who could alienate rights with permission of the government
Muzarian Tabia Marni Malik	:	Tenants paying rent in addition to land revenue
Nazar	:	An offering a present, also ceases charged for paying salaries to various officials
Nazrana	:	Gift (either cash or kind) made out by tenants to their landlords to retain or secure leases
Nazim	:	Executive head of a district
Nehri	:	Land irrigated by canal
Noonia	:	A gift in cash, given on occasion of a weddings on reciprocatory basis
Pakka bigha	:	Twenty biswas are equal to one pakka bigha, also three kacha bighas make one pakka bigha
Patta	:	A deed of lease; a document given to the revenue-payer, indicating the sum payable by him
Pattidar	:	Holder of an ownership deed
Pattidari	:	A system of land tenure in which land was supposed to be divided and held in severalty by different proprietors according to ancestral or customary shares which also determined the revenue payable
Patwari	:	The village account—the customary remuneration of the Patwari amounting to 1½ anna of a rupee or ¼ to ½ seer of a mound
Powadh	:	Indicative of rich agricultural land, which had a loamy soil

Rabi	:	Winter crop; the spring crop generally sown in October-November and reaped in April-May
Rasad	:	Maintenance allowance
Raznomcha	:	A diary kept by a Patwari keeping a record or notable occurrences with a hearing on agriculture
Sahukar	:	Merchant
Sailab	:	Irrigated by monsoon overflow of a water court
Sanad	:	A royal ordinance or any deed or grant or certificate from one authority
Shamlast	:	The village common land
Sufedposh	:	One holding a respectable position
Sufedposhi	:	A cess charged by State to remunerate those holding positions of respect
Talukdar	:	Lord or owner of a taluka, *i.e.* a group of several villages
Taqavi	:	Literally, strengthening or assisting; the money advanced to cultivators for implements, seeds, digging wells, etc.
Talluga	:	An administrative unit next to the province, during the Sikh rule in the trans-Satluj Punjab
Tappa	:	The sub-division of a talluqa or the pargana
Tehsil	:	An administrative sub-division of a district
Thana	:	A police post
Thanedar	:	In charge of a police post
Thikripehra	:	A system under which villagers performed the duties of watchman

Tikka Sahib	:	Heir-apparent
Vakil	:	Agent
Wazir	:	Prime Minister
Zabti	:	Assessment of land revenue in cash; To give land on lease on fixed terms/money
Zaildar	:	A village chief above a Lambardar
Zilledari	:	Unit of canal administration
Zanana	:	Morom
Zamindar	:	Literally, possessor of the land; a peasant proprietor also, the holder of a right over a certain share in the produce from land, and as such, also produce from land, and as such, also called malik-i-ala or ta' alluqdar

1 HISTORICAL BACKGROUND

A brief survey of the nature of state and its administrative structure became imparative as the agrarian system and the peasant struggle in this region of the Punjab was closely allied to the administrative set up of the state. The former, therefore, can not be studied apart from the latter. So an attempt has been made to trace out briefly the history of the administrative structures and socio-economic life of the people of this region to have a vivid picture of the agrarian system and causes responsible for the rise and growth of the peasants movement. Now the existing Patiala state territory was once part of the Mughal *Sarkar* of Sirhind. The Maharajas of Patiala had no earlier administrative traditions of their own. So they retained most of the Mughal administrative system. Maharaja Ranjit Singh, however, introduced some modifications into the Mughal system. His rule extended to trans-Satluj Punjab.

No administrative reforms were introduced in the Patiala state till the middle of the 19th century. The first two rulers, Ala Singh and Amar Singh were busy in fighting against their enemies and conquering new territories. Sahib Singh was good for nothing. Maharaja Karam Singh, of course, introduced some administrative reforms. His well-informed Prime Minister, Barkat Ali Khan, set up different administrative departments in the Patiala state. He introduced Persian as the court language. Law courts began to function properly. Soldiers were paid cash salaries.[1] Karam Singh's successor Narinder Singh was attracted by the British glitter. He wanted to introduce administrative reforms on British lines. But he died before he could fulfil his dream. Even then during his life time the Grand Trunk Road

1. Giani Gian Singh, Twarikh Guru Khalsa (Patiala : 1970-reprint), 600.

passing from Ambala to Ludhiana was completed. He divided state into four districts. The first summary settlement, was effected in 1861-62. The criminal and revenue suits began to be decided properly.[2] His successor Mohinder Singh established the educational and medical departments in the state. The construction, of Sirhind canal was begun in his life-time. Mahindra College was founded in 1876.[3] The work on the Sirsa Branch of the Western Yamuna Canal began during the regime of Maharaja Rajinder Singh, Mohinder Singh's successor. A railway line from Rajpura to Bhatinda became operational during Rajinder Singh's time. He wanted to modernize the state police force and to eradicate corruption,[4] but all his schemes remained unfulfilled due to his sudden death. His minor son Bhupinder Singh succeeded him after his death. In the early part of his regime (1900-1909) the Regency council introduced many British inspired reforms in the state. During this period the political control of the states was taken over directly by the Punjab government. Curzon, the viceroy, through his initiative and keen efforts, re-established political agency for the three Phulkian states. The political agent was entrusted with the duty of guiding and advising the Regency council of Patiala, the headquarters of the agent being located at Patiala. Regular settlement of the state was completed under the stewardship of Major Popham Young[5] an officer on deputation from the

2. *Ibid.*, 612; Sarkar, K.M., *The Grand Trank Road in the Punjab* (Patiala : 1971), 31.
3. PSR, File No. H 263, PSA, Patiala.
4. *Akhbar-i-Am* (Lahore), March 7,1900, *SVNP for 1900*,119; *Khalsa* Bahadur (Lahore), February 26,1900, 105-05, NAI, New Delhi.
5. Young was an ICS Officer, had specialized in revenue affairs. After completing his work in Patiala he returned to his parent cadre and on his retirement he was knighted. *Vide., Foreign Department Proceedings Internal*-A, February, 1902, No. 33; also of October, 1903, Nos. 38-48, 99; *Foreign Department Proceedings* Establishment-B, July 1909, Nos 275-276, NAI, New Delhi; Barbara, Ramusack, The Princes of India in the Twilight empire Disolution of a Patron client system : 1914-1939 (Columbus : 1978)

British Punjab. J.P. Warburton a British officer overhauled the state police force.[6] T.S. Biddulph, a British Finance expert, improved and restored the economy of the state.[7] Maharaja Bhupinder Singh took over the direct rule of the state after the Regency period. He realized the need of introducing some reforms in the state. During his rule the administrative structure experienced change from mediaeval to modern. Bhupinder Singh's English education influenced his outlook and attempt for administrative reforms on the pattern of secretary-system existing in Britain, the state ministers were designated as secretaries.[8] But in 1921, the old arrangement was resumed,[9] as the new system was not found to be suitable. In 1927 the Cabinet system was introduced with the Maharaja as the President, the Prime Minister as the Vice-President and other ministers as its members.[10] Revenue and civil administration was stream lined. Judiciary and law-courts were reformed.[11] As a result of the efforts of the commission headed by P.L. Newman, the recruitment, training and working conditions of the police were improved. But all these reforms meant nothing but a show in

---

6. *Administration Report of Punjab and Its Dependencies for 1900-1901,* Akhbar-i-Am (Lahore), March 16,1900 in *SVNP for the Year* 1900, 143-44, NAI, New Delhi.
7. *Foreign Department Proceedings,* Internal-A, February, 1902, No. 33; also of October, 1903, Nos, 38-38, 99-100.
8. Foreign Department, Secret, January, 1907, No. 67, NAI, New Delhi, *Administration Report of Punjab and its Dependencies for 1920-21,* 3, PSA, Patiala (For further details about Maharaja's early education and the British impact, see *The Tribune* (Lahore), November 13,1900, 2.
9. *Official Guide to the working of Administration of His Highness's* Government Patiala (Patiala : 1927), 141 : *The Daily Jathedar* (Amritsar), September 23, 1928.
10. *Administration Report of Punjab and Its Dependencies* : *1920-21,* 3 (In the absence of elected assembly, the cabinet or responsible system of Government introduced in the state was a more comouflaged.
11. *Report of the Ministry of Law and Justice of Patiala for 1935-36,* 24.

Bhupinder Singh's feudal personal rule.[12] The efforts of the agriculture department to reform agrarian system were not massbased.[13] It was no secret that the Maharaja was licentious, dissolute-given to the pleasures of the flesh. The state budgets were running into deficit year after year. Six Fredrick, an experienced financier was appointed as the finance Minister of the state in order to restore the economy of the Patiala state.[14]

The political movement in the state gained momentum with the emergence of the *Riyasti Praja Mandal* in 1928. There was an outcry for administrative and constitutional reforms. The Maharaja Bhupinder Singh died before the commission appointed by him could make head way. The people of Patiala state had high hoped from his successor, the young prince Yadvindra Singh. He displayed his generosity by throwing open private roads of the rulers for public use. Cruel *shikar* (game) and *nazool* laws were repealed. *Begar* was abolished.[15] The work of constitutional reforms was hampered by the world war-II. Some administrative and constitutional reforms were introduced on the insistence of the Chancellor of Chamber of Princes to bring about liberal reforms in the state. Public service commission to make appointments to gazetted posts was set

---

12. *Patiala Gazette* (Patiala), November 9,1919, 612; Borpara, Ramusack, *op.cit.*
13. *Patiala Gazette* (Patiala), November, 7, 1924,11.
14. PSR *Ijlas-i-khas,* File No. 1377 (Bhupinder Singh contributed lavishly to all causes dear to the British possibly as the guid pro quo the British were soft on him) Vide., *Administration* Reports of Punjab and Its Dependencies for *1910-21,* also see *Foreign Department Proceedings* Secret, 1930; File No. 522-p; (*) *Foreign Department Proceedings,* 1934, File No. 145-P, NAI, New Delhi. (*) *Foreign Department Proceedings* Secret, 1930, File No.646.
15. *Administration Report of the Patiala state fore 1938-39,* 13; *Patiala Gazette* (Patiala) June 6 and 8, July 13,1938; Chamber of Princes, File on Internal Reforms and Beneficial Activities in the states, 176, PSA Patiala : Ganda Singh, *Patiala and East* Punjab States Union (Patiala 1951), 53.

up. In order to subdue agitations, the police force of the state was overhauled.[16]

From the above discussion about the administrative set-up in the Patiala state it can be inferred that the Maharaja of the state at all times was at the helm of the state affairs : He was the master of internal and external policies. The ministers danced to his tune. He was the supreme commander of the armed force. He could grant capital punishment and had the pre-rogative of pardon and mercy.[17] Though he had full authority and power, theoretically, yet in practice he sought advice of wise counsellors and public opinion. The Paramount Power exercised control over the authority of the Maharaja and the affairs of the state in general. Interference from the political agency showed itself in the form of British inspired administrative reforms. Maharaja Bhupinder Singh for example, had to accept the advice of the political department of India to appoint Sir Fredrick Gauntlet as the finance Minister in order to restore the economy of the state.[18]

---

16. *Census Report of Patiala State for 1941,* 34, *Patiala Gazette* Extra-ordinary (Patiala), July 9, 1947; *Patiala Gazette,* Jan. 28, 1945, 697; Chamber of Princes File on Internal Reforms and Beneficial Activities in the States, 167 and 175; *Administration Report of Patiala state for 1939-40,* 26, PSA : Patiala.
17. *Administration Report of Patiala State for 1929-30,* 2; PSR, File No. R 114 B, PSA, Patiala (Most of the State appointments were made in an arbitrary manner. It was only at the later stages of Yadvindra Singh's regime to make gazetted appointments. However, the final appointing authority still remained with the Maharaja. For instance, D.K. Sen, the foreign minister was dismissed in 1932, but Yadvindra Singh re-appointed him in 1939) *Vide., Patiala Gazette* (Patiala), December 7, 1932, 141, and also of April 9, 1939, 2.
18. Panikar, K.M. *An Autobiography* (Madras : 1977), 101, Jarmani Das, *Maharaja* : *Lives and Loves and Intrigues of India Princes* (Bombay : 1969), 63-64.

It would not be wrong to say that there was communal harmony in the state. The Maharajas were broad-minded and secular in their outlook.[19] The Maharajas had matrimonial alliance with Rajpur Princes. In fact, the royal family originated from the Bhatti Rajputs.[20] The first cabinet of Maharaja Bhupinder Singh comprised Hindus, Sikhs and Muslims.[21] Sir Liaqat Hayat Khan had been the Prime Minister of the Patiala state for a long time.[22] Sardar P.M. Pannikar was the foreign Minster of the Patiala state for sometime. The Maharajas of Patiala contributed liberally towards the funds of Aligarh Muslim University, Benaras Hindu University and Khalsa College, Amritsar. Rupees one lakh and forty thousand was contributed for construction of a gurdwara in London by Maharaja Bhupinder Singh. Bhupinder patronized Muslim sportsmen and musicians.[23] But all his actions were not inspired by philanthropy and benevolence. His sympathy towards the British during the World War-I had political undertones.[24] This

---

19. It was only on the indication of Publications that communalism raised its head in the state in early 1940s.
20. Even Yadvindra Singh was first married to a Rajput princess of Sarai Mela see Rosita Perias, *India of Princes* (London : 1939), 61.
21. The Tribune (Lahore), May 27, 1910 and February 22, 24,1911.
22. (The Sayyid family had a long and distinguished tradition of serving the House of Patiala. Syid Barkat Ali Khan, Khalifa Syed Muhammad Hussain and Khalifa Syed Hamid Hussain of this family served in Patiala) see Giani Gian Singh, *Twarikh Guru Khalsa* (Patiala : 1970-reprint) 598, 619, *Paisa Akhbar* (Lahore) February, 1911, PSR, File No. H. 14 B, H27 B, PSA Patiala) Panikar, K.M., *An Autobiography* (Madras : 1977), 94-95.
23. *Khalsa Advocate* (Amritsar) September 8,1911; PSR, File Nos. H 5B H 21 B, PSA, *Patiala*; Fauja Singh, *Patiala and Its Historical Surroundings*, 27-30.
24. (Bhupinder Singh even offered his services to the British to combat the Indian Freedom Movement. There was a wide outery in the native press against the lavish hospitality of Bhupinder Singh for the British, which was thought to be motivated by self-interest) *Vide., Foreign Department Proceedings*, Political File No.33-P of 1929; Home Department, Political- A May 1917, File No.124-28, NAI, New Delhi.

was prompted by need to remain in good books of the British. The All India States Peoples Enquiry Committee of 1929, laid bore a misanthrope in Maharaja Bhupinder Singh.[25] The Maharaja Bhupinder Singh was almost a despot and his rule was not inseparable from the evils of despotism. He, for example, could call upon the subjects of the state to render free service for him or for the people. This right of *begar* could be of labour, or of services like transport or of goods. [26] Condolence tax levied on the people at the death of a Maharaja was another evil effect of despotism. This had to be deposited in cash in the state treasury. Maharaja Yadvindra Singh, of course, repealed it.[27] Again, some roads were kept for their private used by the Maharajas. While the people of the state, in general were poor and miserable, the Maharajas led a luxurious life. A private lake and navigational channel were constructed for the exclusive use of the rulers.[28] The royal *shikars* were a nuisance for the public. The *birs* (reserves) were a menace to the forming class as the wild animals like the pigs and bears played havoc with the crops. The agriculture lands lying around the *birs* were the worst hit in this regard. Even the villagers of surrounding villages were called upon to act as bearers and supply rations to the haunting parties.[29] The ministers were selected and appointed by the Maharaja and their decisions were also subject to his will.

---

25. *Foreign Department Proceedings Ge-n.* October 1916, No. 43-Deposit, NAI, New Delhi; For further details also see *Indictment of* Patiala (Bombay : 1930).
26. *Indictment of Patiala,* (Bombay : 1930), para 76; *Foreign Department Proceeding Gen.*, October 1916, No. 43-Deposit, NAI, New Delhi.
27. *Administration Report of Patiala State for 1938-39,* 13; *Patiala Gazette* (Patiala), July 18, 1938, 46 (At the time of Maharaja Bhupinder Singh's death, it was calculated to the rupees 44,969; *Indictment of Patiala,* (Bombay : 1930), para 67.
28. *Patiala Gazette* (Patiala) July 6, 1938,21; *Indictment of Patiala,* (Bombay : 1930), para 67.
29. *Indictment of Patiala* (Bombay : 1930), para 70.

As regards the cabinet the Prime Minister (*wazir*) was over all in-charge of the administration next to the Maharaja. Apart from giving advice to the Maharaja, the *wazir* took up some important portfolios. For example, Liaquat Hayet as Prime Minister held the portfolios of Police, CID and publicity. The Home Minister forwarded appeals to the *Ijlas-i-khas.* He supervised and controlled the districts of the state. The foreign Minister (*Mohar Munshi*) conducted the external correspondence of the state and he was in charge of political affairs. He prepared and despatched communications of the Maharaja to the British and informed *Ijlas-i-khas* of all the corresponding replies. The finance Minister was in charge of the financial matters of the state. He supervised the office of the Accountant General prepared the annual budget of the state, and made monetary allocations to other ministeries.[30] The British interfered in the financial matters of the state. When Maharaja Bhupinder Singh was a minor, an Englishmen, Mr. Biddulph was thrust upon the state as the Finance Minister. Sir Fredrick Gauntlet headed the ministry till the death of the Maharaja.[31] The Minister of Law and justice was incharge of judiciary. He was the chief judge of the chief court. He advised the Maharaja on legal implications of important cases.[32] The *Sardar Sahib Deori Maulla* (the officer incharge of the Royal household), the commander-in-chief of the state Armed Forces and Inspector-General of the State Police were other important functionaries of the state.

In 1927 the cabinet became an organized body. It met at regular intervals. It was presided over by the Maharaja with

---

30. *Patiala Gazette* (Patiala), April 12, 1942, 148; Barque, A. H., *Eminent Sikhs of Today,* Vol. I(Lahore : 1942) 69; *Administration Report of Patiala State for 1939-40;* 27 and also *for 1940-41,* 27; PSR Prime Ministers' Office File No. 3648, PSA; Patiala; *Official Guide to the Working of His Highness' Government* Patiala, 3.
31. *Administration Report of Patiala State for 1932-33,* 70 and also for 1938-39, 108.
32. *Administration Report of Patiala State for 1932-33,* 47; Barbara *Ramusack, The Princes of India in Twilight of Empire,* (Columbus : 1978) 6.

the Prime Minster as its vice-President and with other ministers as its members. The cabinet advised the Maharaja on matters of high policy or emergency[33]. But the Maharaja was not found to accept its advice.

The Patiala state consisted of six *nizamats* (districts), Barnala, Bassi Pathana, Kandaghat, Narnaul, Patiala and Sunam. A *naib nazim mal* assisted the *nazim* who was an administrative head of a district.[34] There were twelve *tehsils* (sub-divisions or *nizamats*) at Barnala, Bhatinda, Bhawanigarh, Dhuri, Kandaghat, Mansa, Narnaul, Narwana, Patiala, Rajpura, Sirhind and Sunam.[35] A *tehsildar* was an administrative head of a *tehsil.* Though he was subordinate to the *nazim,* yet he was overall incharge of land revenue of a *tehsil.*[36] The *lambardars* and *zaildars* were the village headmen. Originally, they were appointed by the government but later these headships became hereditary. Only a few villages of the state had *panchayats.* Later the Government introduced *dehat sudhar* committees to some villages on experimental basis.[37]

The state revenue was treated as a personal purse of the Maharaja. When the chamber of princes was founded, it instructed the princes not to keep more than ten per cent of the revenues as their privy purses. Maharaja Bhupinder Singh, however, ignored these instructions. The people of the state led a miserable life while the Maharajas indulged in vulgar and wild enjoyments.[38] Maharaja Bhupinder Singh, in particular owned a fleet of costly cars and private planes. He patronized

---

33. *Official Guide to the working of His Highness's Government Patiala,* 1.
34. *Ibid., Administration Report of Patiala State for 1932-33,* 47.
35. *Census, Report of Patiala State for 1941,* 9.
36. A detailed account of the land revenue administration is given little later in this very chapter.
37. For details and criticism see *Kripan Bahadur* (Amritsar) August 8, 1928, 3; theesa (Amritsar), June 4, 1928, 4-5.
38. *Ibid.*

artists for his personal *entertainment.*[39] No scientific and systematic reforms were carried out in the financial machinery of the state which despite the appointment of some highly competent financiers, continued to remain far from satisfactory in 1929-30, the annual income of the state stood at rupees 15,892,052 in which the commerce and industry contributed a paltry sum of rupees one lac.[40] The financial machinery was far from modern. Till 1921, there were only seven co-operative societies in the state. By 1941, however, there were 420 co-operative societies in the Patiala State. The credit benefits from the co-operative societies went to the landlord class. The first bank in the state, the bank of Patiala, came into existence in 1917 with the state supplying the total capital. Its main function was to supply short-term credit to grain dealers and other traders. Maharaja Yadvindra Singh tried to put the economy in proper shape. He reduced his privy purse and did away with unnecessary expenditiure.[41] Retrenchments were affected and number of *jagirs* which did not have a solid basis were resumed.[42] But these economic measures were inadequate and as such they failed to satisfy the people, especially the peasants who were woefully exploited by the *biswedars* and state officials. Schools, roads, hospitals and postal services were levied. Revenue and water rates were very high. Landlords charged heavy rents from their tenants. Partials, of course, was one of the leading states that took up the cause of education. Mahindra College, Patiala, for example, was founded in 1876. Even then the literary rate of the state as compared to other

39. Chudgar, P.L., *Indian Princes under British Protection* (London : 1929 173, Fauja Singh, *Patiala and Its surroundings,* 30 Irving Wallace, *The Sunday Gentleman* (New York : 1958-reprint) 290; also see Ganda Singh's 'Obituary' Maharaja Yadvindra Singh in *Punjab Past and Present,* Vol. VIII-II, October, 1974, Patiala.
40. *Administration Report of Patiala State for 1929-30,* 75.
41. *Census Report of Patiala-State for 1941,* 41; Dr. Ganda Singh *op. cit.,* 576.
42. Barbara Ramusock, *People, Princes and Paramount Power,* 191-92; *Firman-i-shahi* No.2, November 21,1940, see *Patiala Gazette* (Patiala), 25.

states in Punjab was very low. The high rate of illiteracy in princely times had left its mark. As compared to Ludhiana district which had 57-69% literary rate-the highest in the state-the literary rate of Bhatinda was 28-30% which was below the general state literary rate of 40.74%[43]. In 1941 the per square mile literacy rate of the state in comparison to some other Punjab states was : [44]

Name of the State	*Literate per square mile*
Patiala	69
Kapurthala	112
Nabha	89

Owing to financial stringency no new roads were constructed or metalled. The Rajendra Hospital, Patiala was the only one worthwhile hospital in the whole state. It is noteworthy to state that the average tax burden on every state subject in 1926-27 was twelve rupees and eight *annas* while just three *annas* per head on education and two *annas* per head on medical relief and sanitation were spent by the state. The Patiala state had no legislature which could involve the masses in the administration;[45] while some of the progressive states, like Mysore, Trevancore, Baroda, Hyderabad and Kashmir, constituted Legislatures.[46] The word of the Maharaja was the

43. *Ibid., The Tribune* (Chandigarh), March 24, 1981, 2.
44. *Census Report of Patiala State for 1941,* 290. For more details see details of Land Revenue Administration; *Administration Report of Patiala State for 1920-21,* 16, Statement of S. Jagir Singh Joga, whom I interviewed personally and also File No. 20-Oral History Cell, Punjab Historical Studies Department Panjabi University, Patiala.
45. Chudgar, P.L. *Indian Princes under British Protection* (Chandigarh : 1976-reprint) 173.
46. *All India State People Conference (AISPC) Papers,* File No. 225 NMML. New Delhi; Barbara Ramusack, *the Princes of India in Twilight of the Empire* (Columbus : 1978), 6; Handa, R.L. *History of Freedom Struggle in Princely States* (New Delhi : 1968), 60; Popham Young, *Final Report of the Settlement of the Patiala State* (A.D. 1900-1908) (Ajmer : 1909), 97; *AISPC Papers* File No. 261 NMML, New Delhi.

final law. As such there were no rules and regulations of law. Some codes of law like those in British Indian were introduced in the Patiala state but they were not followed in practice. At the same time there were many laws in the Patiala State which did not exist in British India.[47] These laws were based on British models and on personal whims of the Maharaja.[48] There was no freedom of the press in the state. All government organizations and officials subscribed to the *weekly Gazette*, the Patiala *Gazette*. It propagated the cause of autocracy.[49] The boundaries of the Patiala State were not well-defined during 1900-1948. Its territories were scattered unevenly from the mountains of lower area of the present Himachal Pradesh to the fertile plains of the present Patiala district of East Punjab and to semi-desert area of the Narnaul district of the Existing Haryana. The state had 3607 villages and 11 towns; [50] and , this state was spread over an area of 5980 square miles.[51]

As regards population in 1941, the Sikhs formed 46.20% the Hindus 30.85%, Muslims 22.55% and the rest only 32% of the total population which ranged from 15,195,692 to 19, 36,239

47. *AISPC Papers*, File No. 261, NMML, New Delhi.
48. Barbara Ramusack, *The Princes of India in the Twilight of Empire* (Columbus : 1978), 6; For further details also see Nehru, J.L., *An Autobiography* (New Delhi : 1962-reprint), 109-16.
49. *Kirpan Bahadur* (Amritsar), August 8, 1927, 3; *Swadhinta* (Calcutta) August 1,1928 in Foreign and Political File No. 323F of 1929, NAI, New Delhi ; *Patiala Gazette* (Patiala) August 21 and December 23, 1910.
50. Banerjee, S.N. *History of Patiala* (n.p.n.d.) 10 and 13; (The irregular boundaries of the state were a perpetual source of headache to the state administration so far as the law and order problem was concerned. Criminals and political offenders took asylum in adjoining territories lying outside the state. This factor was also exploited by political dissenters) Also see *Report on settlement of Patiala*; 11 *Census Report of Patiala for 1931*, 1-2 *Census Report of Patiala State for 1911*, 3-4, Also part II of this Report, 5; *Census Report of Patiala State for 1941*, 295.
51. *Census Report of Patiala State for 1911*, 2.

during 1900-1948.[52] About 87% people lived in villages; of which 71% was directly dependent on agriculture and pursuits allied to it.[53] In 1931, 66.3% of the total population depended on agriculture. The proportion in British India was 72% in the same years.[54] *Jats arain, Rajput, Kamboj, mali, saini, pathan, sikh Mughal, Biloch, Machhi, qhirit, kanot, khokhar, ahir, dogara* and *qujjar* were mainly agricultural casts.[55] Out of these the *jats* of Malwa were considered the best peasants in India.[56] *Atwal, Bhullar, Chail* Chaliwal, Dhillon, Dindsa, Chuman, Gill, Grewal, Mann, Sandhu, Johl Sidhu and Tiwana, etc.; were sub-castes of *Jats*.[57] The *Arain* or *Rain* specialized in vegetable farming. They were mostly Muslims. *For example, out* of their total number of 47,431 in 1931, only 720 were Hindus and 67 were Sikhs. Majority of these Rain lived in Sirhind, Patiala and Rajpura *tehsils*[58]. The Rajputs were mostly Muslims and Hindus[59] in the region; they were inferior to the *jats* in farming.[60] The *Kambohs* numbering about 24,310 in 1931 mainly resided in Dhuri, Rajpura, Bhawanigarh, Sunam and Patiala.[61] They were from among the Muslims, Hindus and Sikhs and were

---

52. *Census Report of Patiala State for 1941*, 252, 295.
53. *Ibid.*, 252.
54. *Ibid.*, 248-252.
55. *Census Report of Patiala State for 1921*, 232, 241-42; *Census Report of Patiala State for 1931*, 202, Crooke, W., *Races of* Northern India (Delhi : 1973), 93.
56. Banerjee, S.W. *History of Patiala* (n.p.n.d.) 21-22.
57. *Punjab States Gazetteer*, 61-64; For more details see Ibbetson D; *Punjab Castes* (Patiala : 1970-reprintt), 97-131; Rose, H.A.; Glossary *of the Tribes and Castes of Punjab and North West Frontier Province*, Vol. II (Patiala : 1970-reprint) 11-12.
58. *Census Report of Patiala State for 1931*, 193, *Punjab States Gazetteer*, 67; Ibbetson, D., *Punjab Castes* (Patiala : 1970-reprint) 189-95.
59. *Census Report of Patiala State for 1921*, 248.
60. *Punjab States Gazetteer*, 65; Crooke, W., *Races of Northern India* (Delhi : 1973) 92.
61. Ibbetson, *Punjab Castes* (Patiala : 1970-reprint) 201-02; Bedi Sohinder Singh, *Folklore of Punjab* (Delhi ; 1973) 6-7.

petty landholders.[62] The *Malis* (gardners) a class of cultivators were scattered all over of state except, Sirhind and Dhuri. They were mostly Hindus, a few Sikhs and nominally Muslims.[63] The *Sainis,* market-gardeners were also scattered all over the state except Mansa.[64] The *pathans,* a Muslim tribe, mainly resided in Narnaul and Patiala *tehsils.*[65] The *Sheikhs,* on elite Muslim caste, numbering 16,860 were spread all over the state. Mughal, Bolich, Khokhar Moes, etc. were very small in number. Ghirit was a Hindu agricultural caste, while Kanet and Machni were of mixed castes of Hindus, Sikh and Muslims.[66] The *Ahirs* who were known as industrious cultivators numbering about 50,581 in 1931 lived mostly in Mohindrgarh district.[67] The *Dogars* were an exclusively muslim pastoral class; their social status was the same as that of Gujjars.[68] They were found throughout the state. The *Gujjars* were an important agricultural and pastoral tribe. They were mostly Hindus and Muslims with a small number of Sikhs. The Hindus *Gujjars* lived mostly in Narnaul, Kandaghat and Patiala *tehsils,* the Muslim *Gujjars* in Dhuri and the Sikh *Gujjars* in Sunam.[69]

In social order the landlords and *biswedars* were at the top. They owned vast tracts of land which they did not cultivate themselves, but rented out; they were so to say the rural elite. The middle class peasants came second in social order. They owned small tracts of land. These cultivating owners or peasant proprietors unlike landlords, cultivated their land themselves. The largest portion of land in this region was under their

62. *Census Report of Patiala State for 1921,* 243; also 1931, 198-205.
63. *Census Report of Patiala State for 1921,* 245.
64. *Punjab States Gazetteer,* 68; Ibbetson, *Punjab Castes* (Patiala : 1970-reprint) 188-89.
65. *Census Report of Patiala State for 1921,* 197-98.
66. Ibbotson, *Punjab Castes* (Patiala : 1970-reprint), 38-96, 178-81 and 195-200.
67. *Census Report of Patiala State for 1931,* 197-98.
68. *Census Report of Patiala State for 1921,* 240.
69. *Census Report of Patiala State for 1921,* 241; Crooke, W., *Races of Northern India* (Delhi : 1973) 116-18.

cultivation. They were really a hard working and an ambitious class. They were, in fact, the main support of the agrarian economy. The lower peasants came third in social order. They had no land of their own but cultivated land of the landlords or *biswedars* on rent. The tenancy was of two kinds-occupancy tenants (*maurusi muzaras*) and tenants-at-will (*qhoir maurusi muzaras*). The occupancy tenants were tenants of long standing while the tenants-at-will were at the mercy of the landlords. The agricultural labourers—servants and menials—were the last in social order. Some of the labourers were from the strata of poor peasantry. Carpenters, blacksmiths, oil pressers, weavers and barbers were included among manials. In addition to labour chores in agricultural operations, they performed a host of other services earmarked for them.

Of the 3,607 villages in the Patiala State, 1057 were in the hilly areas, and the remaining in plains; about 80 villages were *Se-chirag i.e.* uninhabited.[70] In hilly areas a village consisted of a few houses, may be even one or two, built at the top of a hillock. Water for cattle and for drinking purposes was obtained from small *bawris i.e.* ponds, for streams and springs.[71] The villages, were self-sufficient in the plains. A village generally contained a pond, one or two wells for drinking water. Here and then a *pakka* house owned by a *Sahukar* or a *biswedar* stood out amidst huts of mud. Of course, a *mandir*, a *gurdwara* or a *masjid* or all the three existed in each village. Generally the villages were surrounded by hedges of thick bushes.[72] Different communities lived in different localities; the sweepers and low caste people generally lived in mud-houses on the outskirts of the villages. At the entry of a village there was generally a residential building meant for visiting state officials or some other casual visitors or travellers. Even the elders of the village also assembled at or near this common place to smoke *huqqa* in order to while away their time in gossip or playing crude

70. *Census Report of Patiala State for 1931,* 30.
71. *Census Report of Patiala State for 1941,* 45.
72. *Census Report of Patiala State for 1931,* 32.

country games.[73] Ordinary people in villages ate *chapatis* in winter, which were made of ground *makki, jowar* or *bajra* while *mung, moth, urd*; green *sarson* and gram were cooked as vegetables. Sometimes for a change *khichri* made of rice / *bajra, moth* or mung was also eaten. In summer chapatis made of wheat were eaten with *dal*. The regular meals were taken at mid day and in the evening. Farmers mostly ate left-over chapatis of the past day with biller-milk (*lassi*) because they had to go to fields early in the morning. The *Chapatis* eaten by villagers were generally thicker than those made in towns. Muslim and Sikhs generally relished goat-meat on festivals and marriages. *Rabri* made of barley, gram or *bajra* flour with *chhachh* was relished by the people of Mohindergarh *nizamat*. *Sattu* made from flour of parched grain and *sharbat* was taken throughout the state. *Sattu* generally formed the breakfast meal particularly in the Pinjore *tehsil*. Parched grain-gram, maizy, barley, *jowar* were also eaten. Punjab rock-salt was mostly used in the state except in Mohindrgarh where the samber lake salt was taken.[74]

The simple dress of a villager consisted of a shirt (*kurta*) a waist cloth (*dhoti* or a *bhotha*), a turban (*safa* or *pagri*) a cloth carried over shoulders (*chaddar*) and a pair of shoes made by the village, *chamar*. Some landlords wore English dress. Muslims wore *tehbend* or *lungi* instead of a *dhoti*. In winter they had a *khes* (a cotton or woollen blanket). A woman wore *Suthan* (*Salwar*) a *kurta*, a *chaddar* and a *phulkari*. When going out a woman wore a *ghagra* (petticoat). The Muslim woman wore *pyjama, kurta* and *chaddar* but not a petticoat. The *jangal jats* wore very long turbans. In the hills men wore a *topi*. On fairs, festivals and marriages etc., men women were colourfully dressed.[75]

The peasants because of their dependence on nature for success of agricultural operations were, in general, religious-

---

73. *Census Report of Patiala State for 1941*, 45; Crookes, W., Races of Northern India (Delhi : 1973) 153-55.
74. *Punjab State Gazetteer*, 80,.85-86.
75. *Punjab State Gazetteer*, 87.

minded but superstitious. *Sitla* the goddess of small pox was worshipped by all Hindus and Muslims. *Guga Pir,* a snake god was also worshipped throughout the Malwa region.[76] Another diety the *Lalanwala Pir* was worshipped for his power to restore animal health.[77] Animals were sacrificed to appease the river god. The Maharaja of Patiala used to offer a golden ring, a coconut and grass to the river diety whenever there was a flood in the Ghaggar a small stream. It is said that after the ritual, the flood water receded.[78] There were rustic games and means of wild enjoyments in villages. *Mirasis* (jesters) entertained the villagers by their crude jokes and skits. Boys played *kabaddi gulli danda* and *lukan miti* (hide and seek). Kite flying was popular with men and boys. In hot weather men and boys used to swim in ponds. Wrestling matches were very common. Wandering acrobats (nats) and jugglers were very popular.[79] There were many fairs and festivals, shared by Hindus and Muslims. The first eight days of *asuaj* (September-October) and *Chet* (March-April) were considered very auspicious, for then the various gods were believed to be in animation.[80] Cattle fairs were held at different places of the state throughout the year. The *Jhakari* festival was celebrated for the longevity of huabands.[81]

Before the western ways of living crept in, each village was self-sufficient and independent. Its *chamaras* supplied the villagers with shoes; local carpenters made their ploughs;

76. For details see Rose, M.A. *Glossary of the Tribes and Castes of Punjab and North West Frontier Provinces,* Vol. II (Patiala : 1970-reprint) 350-56; Crooke, W., *Religion and Folklore of Northern India* (New Delhi : n.d), 87, 118-19.
77. For more details see Rose, M.A. *op. cit.,* 143-47 and 171-82;Crooke, W., *op. cit.,* 163-64 and 392.
78. Bedi, Sohinder Singh, *Folklore of Punjab* (Delhi : 1973), 35-36.
79. *Punjab States Gazetteer,* 92.
80. For more details see Randhwa, Mohinder Singh (ed.) Punjab (Patiala : 1960), 193-214.
81. *Administration Report of Patiala State for 1939-40,* 186; *Patiala Gazette* (Patiala) August 10, 1927, 28; *Punjab States Gazetteer,* 84 and 92.

blacksmiths (*lohars*) their plough-shares; potters (*kumhars*) their utensils and weavers (*julahas*) their cotton cloth. There were family barbers (*nai*) the washermen (*dhobi*) and the blacksmith (*lohars*) who received yearly salaries in the form of harvest. This system of interdependence was known as *jajmani*.[82] Thus, the self-sufficient nature of the village did not permit the political awakening to reach the people easily and early. The process was delayed.

This traditional system underwent some change with the emergence of modern trends in agriculture and commercialization during 1900-1948. The caste system was also weakened and began to loose its hold over professional matters. The villages slowly began to witness transformation for many disintegrating influences were at work in breaking down the solidarity of rural life. The western influences infused spirit of individualism among villagers. Now they demanded cash payment for the actual work done by them. They aspired for higher and more dignified pursuits. People began to migrate to cities in search of better jobs. Cheap European goods and factories swallowed village industries. In advanced parts of the state the old village organization was disintegrating. The economic life of the Patiala ruralities viewed as a whole, presented a contrast of poverty and prosperity. The lower peasants and the menials led a miserable life in unhygenic surrounding.[83] On the other hand, the *biswedars* and land lords led a luxurious life. Their houses were more spacious and

---

82. A European Clergyman Mr. wiser wrote at length about Jajmani system prevalent in a villages in the then united provinces of British India. The latest research about this system holds that the system has disappeared almost in whole of India. But it will not be wrong to say that some villages of the system are still visible in the rural India (For more details in this regard, see wiser, W.H., *The Hindu Jajmani system* (Lucknow : 1969-reprint).
83. For further details, Godgil, D.A., *The Industrial Evolution of India in recent time* (Delhi : 1973), 157-84, Desai, A.R. *Social Background of Indian Nationalism*, (Bombay : 1976) 37-50; *Census Report of Patiala State for 1921*, 267; also for 1931, 267.

comfortable amidst hygienic surroundings. Their fields provided them with ample food. Their women owned costly ornaments and jewellery.[84] The lower peasants were shut out from the outside world and deprived of all the amenities and chance of a civilized life.[85] This section of peasantry neither had the time nor money to improve their lot. Their social life had become of an ending drugery. Most of their time was spent in agricultural operations but their income from agriculture was bare minimum by minimum by which they could hardly make both ends meet. But the state authorities did not care to improve their miserable condition. Popham Young, the settlement commissioner opined that the *Panchayat* system was well-suited to the circumstance of this country. The state, however, paid little attention to this suggestion. Only 85 village *panchayats* were functioning in the state in 1938-39.[86]

In order to improve the condition of some villages, a rural uplift Department under the supervision of commissioner of Agriculture was created. In all 17 villages were selected for this purpose. Five to seven influential members of a village were nominated as members of *Dehat Sudhar* committee. These committees were entrusted with the work of supervising paving of lanes, construction of drains and living conditions of the villages.[87] They were also to encourage progressive farming and social reforms in the villages. They also helped villagers to utilize their leisure gainfully by popularizing traditional games.[88] The different village committees followed following

84. *Census Report of Patiala State for 1941,* 46-47.
85. *Ibid.*
86. *Foreign Department Proceedings,* Internal B., July 1907, Nos. 570-77; *Report on Settlement of Patiala,* 57 (Note on the *Panchayat* System greatly impressed upper section of British bureucracy of British Government of India. It was, therefore, printed every week and circulated throughout the country); *Administration Report of Patiala State for 1938-39.*
87. *Administration Report of Patiala State for 1939-40,* 192-93 Harchand Singh's Rural Uplift in Patiala State, in *Patiala Post,* December 1943, January 1944, 29.
88. *Administration Report of Patiala State for 1939-40,* 94-96.

sources of income for *Dehat Sudhar* fund :[89] 1/4th of the *malba* fund; collection of grain in *kharif* and *rabi* cropsl subscriptions by members; subscription on happy occasions, such as marriages or the birth of a child; fee for compromises in cases; voluntary subscriptions, and fines imposed on persons who violated rules passed by the committees. This programme was extended to 208 villages of the state.[90] Had the *panchayat* system been encouraged, this programme could have come under its control and then all the villages would have been benefited. But this was not so. Thus during 1900-1948 socio-economic changes were taking place; emergence of three significant factors has to be taken note of. Firstly, the traditional society was giving way to changes both in social and economic fields. Secondly, the gulf between the upper classes and middle and lower peasants was widening. Thirdly, the masses were being alienated from the state because of the apathetic attitude of the authorities. These factors contributed towards the genesis of public discontent expressed itself through socio-religious reforms and peasant movements; which we have discussed, of course, in brief in the second chapter of this work. However, it is to be noticed that the shortcomings in various walks of life were responsible for the rise of economic and political unrest in this region and ultimately these unrests became responsible for the peasants' movements during the period of our study.

89. *Ibid.*, 94.
90. Harchand Singh, 'Rural Uplift in Patiala State', *Patiala Post*, December, 1943-January 1944, 29.

2 NATURE OF AGRICULTURE, LAND REVENUE AND TENURES

The agrarian system of a country depends, to a large extent, on its agriculture. So in order to study the agrarian system of the East Punjab states, which ultimately became responsible for the agrarian unrest and peasants' movements, it is essential to examine its agriculture with reference to the soil conditions, the irrigation system and some other relevant features of agriculture.

The topography of the Patiala state—Himalayan, Sub-Himalayan and the Western Indo-Gangetic plains—had its influence on soil conditions, quantum of rainfall and population which are, of course, related to agriculture. In the Himalayan region the soils were *Changar, Katual* and *Kul*, the first meant unirrigated and the latter two stood for irrigated land.[1] The Himalayan region in the Patiala state was the Pinjore *tehsil*. It had a cold climate and thick growth of natural vegetation. In this hilly area the natural conditions were not conducive to the development of agriculture. Only 26% of the total area was cultivable.[2] Even then 824 persons per thousand depended upon agriculture as their main source of libelihood,[3] the highest for any division of the state.

The sub-Himalayan region comprised *tehsils* of Rajpura, Sirhind and Patiala and this part of the region was known as *powadh*.[4] Overall good soil conditions helped agricultural

1. *Punjab States Gazetter*, 93.
2. *Census Report of Patiala State for 1911*, 26; *Report on settlement of Patiala*, 5; also see *census Report of Patiala state for 1921*, 27 and for 1941, 9.
3. *Census Report of Patiala State for 1921*, 263.
4. *Census Report of Patiala State for 1921*, 26.

development. So this region had prosperous agriculture in the state. The density of population was the highest for any natural division of the state.[5] Only 55.4% of the total population of this region lived on agriculture, the rest adopted industry and commerce as profession.[6]

The Indo-Gangetic region of the Patiala state comprised *tehsils* of Narwana, Bhawanigarh, Sunam, Dhuri, Barnala, Mansa, Bhatinda and Narnaul. As regards area and population, this was the largest part of the state. On the whole the land of this area was fertile.[7] Among the soils of this (*jangal*) region was loam of Patiala sub-division, known as *rausli* and *bhur*. *Rausli* was capable of retaining moisture and was the best soil for *barani* cultivation. *Bhur* was a very poor land; it required little ploughing as the sub soil retained whatever moisture it received. Jangal, at best, was indicative of lowly developed agriculture in the region. As Young opines : "This (*jangal*) is singular misnomer in English ideas since the tract in question is peculiarly devoid of trees, or, indeed, of anything in the way of natural vegetation. Rolling sand hills are the distinctive features, and at first sight it is difficult to credit this tract with the fertility which it possesses."[8]

Portions of Dhuri and Bhawanigarh *tehsils* were covered with *powadh* tract. The *bangar* was the high land tract lying to the south-east of *Ghaggar*.[9] This tract also contained the rich *loam* land known as *dakar*.[10] The Narwana *tehsil* and few villages attached to Sunam *tehsil* were a part of this treat and this region had an annual rainfall ranging between 12 to 16

---

5. *Report on Settlement of Patiala*, 4-6, *Punjab State Gazetteer*, 92; *Census Report of Patiala State for 1911*, 26 and also *for 1921*, 263.
6. *Census Report of Patiala State for 1921*, 263.
7. *Ibid.*, 33-35; *Census Report of Patiala State for 1911*, 26; *Punjab State Gazetteer*, 140-41.
8. *Report on Settlement of Patiala*, 4; *Punjab State Gazetteer*, 92.
9. Punjab State Gazetteer, 140-41.
10. *Punjab States, Gazetteer*, 93; *Census Report of Patiala State for 1911*, 26.

inches. Though this area supported the largest population in the state but it had the average of 324 persons per square mile.[11] Over 8% of its total area was cultivable and about 65% of its population were occupied in agriculture.[12] This region was benefited from the canal irrigation system.

The Patiala state did not have even one perennial river passing through its territory. Ghaggar was the main stream flowing through the state. It first ran from north east to the south west direction through the *powadh* and then taking westerly course separating *powadh* from *bangar* finally leaving the state territory. Its bed was narrow and ill-defined near Rajpura and Banur, but in Ghanaur region its banks were low causing floods.[13] Some more mansoon streams passed through the state. The Sirhind *cho* flowed through Fatehgarh, Bhawanigarh and Sunam *tehsils*. It probably followed the alignment of the canal which was cut in about 1361 by Feroz Tuglaq when he created Sirhind as a separate district.[14] The Jhambowali *cho* which rose near chinarthal, running through Bhawanigarh and Karamgarh *thanas,* joined the Ghaggar near Bharni.[15] The third stream was the Patialawali *nadi,* rising near Manimajra and carrying with it the water of several other streams. It flowed past Patiala, falling into Ghaggar near Patarsi.[16] In the Mohindergarh *nizamat* the two chief streams, were Dohan and Krishnawali.[17] In the Pinjore *tehsil* irrigation was effected from some perennial springs. Here the land was irrigated for some three months of the year from springs which ran only for a short time after monsoons.[18] Thus the Patiala state was not lucky as regards the natural drainage. Only some mansoon streams ran through the state. These streams generally

---

11. *Census Report of Patiala State for 1911,* 26; and also *for 1941,* 9.
12. *Census Report of Patiala State for 1921,* 263.
13. *Punjab Stats Gazetteer,* 2.
14. *Ibid.*
15. *Ibid.*
16. *Ibid.*
17. *Ibid.*
18. *Census Report of Patiala State for 1911,* 26.

flooded rich agricultural plains during the monsoon. Even the Ghaggar the most prominent stream was channelised to serve a limited irrigational purpose.[19]

The people in the Patiala State mainly depended on agriculture for their livelihood. Natural irrigation was, however, insufficient. So as network of artificial irrigation was required to sustain its agriculture. Wells being an important and traditional source of irrigation that protected the state from the possibility of serious famines. The excavation of wells in turn depended upon the level of sub-terranean water and texture of water. There were *kacha* and *pakka* wells. A single bucket well could irrigate four to five *kacha bighas* in one day. *Jats* generally used the *charas*. Persian wheels (*rahat*) were generally used in the villages where sugarcane was largely grown. A Persian wheel irrigated a small area than bucket well did, but was less troublesome.[20] Some *kambohas* and *Sainis* of Banur region used the *dhingli*,[21] a modification of the *charas* system. In areas of Sirhind, Payal and Amargarh water was plentiful and wells numerous. However, in the rest of the sub-Himalayan region extending westward to Patiala, soil was stiff and water-level was deep. So here, there were very few wells. Thus, in the north-west of Patiala territory well-irrigation was common and successful. In the east and south, along the Ghaggar Valley and beyond it in *bangar*, it was not successful. In the west it was almost non-existent. In the Mohindergarh district although the water bed was low, yet well-irrigation was fruitful.[22]

However, the most significant source of irrigation in the state was the canal system. Three canal systems irrigated about 1/6 of the total area of the state. These were Sir-hind, canal, Sirsa branch of the western Jamuna canal and the Banur

---

19. *Punjab States Gazetteer*, 105.
20. *Ibid.*, 104.
21. *Ibid.*, 104-05.
22. *Census Report of Patiala State for 1911*, 26 *Report on Settlement of Patiala State*, 6.

Inundation canal.[23] In 1879 a branch canal office was opened under a *nazim nohar* but the department as such actually came into existence in 1885 when the services of an Executive Engineer were secured from the Punjab Irrigation Department. There were at that time only two sub-divisions under the Executive Engineer with seven *zilladari* sections.[24] Since then the department had gradually expanded. In 1938-39 it was headed by a Chief Engineer who had under his control, five sub-divisional officers, two Deputy Collectors, seventeen *zilledari* sections, twenty-eight work subordinate sections and 148 *patwaris.* In *rabi* 1885, there were only 4,342 *acres* under irrigation. During 1938-39, total irrigated area came upto 6,85,257 *acres.*[25] The Maharaja Narinder Singh first thought of constructing the Sirhind canal in 1861 and a survey was carried out by Captain Crofton in 1862.[26] The project was however then shelved considering the prohibitive cost involved in irrigating such a limited area.[27] An estimate for a combined British and Native States system was submitted by Captain Robert Home in 1869 and received the British Government's sanction in 1870.

In 1873 an agreement was reached between the British Government and the three Phulkian states, which laid down shares in cost of construction and in the canal water.[28] The canal was to command 5,322 sq. miles of British territory and 2,998

---

23. *Administration Report of Patiala State for 1938-39,* 57; and also *for 1939-40,* 65.
24. *Administration Report of Patiala State for 1929-30,* 34.
25. *Administration Repot of Patiala State for 1938-39,* 201.
26. *Punjab States Gazetteer,* 105.
27. *Punjab Administration Report for 1920-21,* 168, Arora, A.C. 'British, Government and Cannals in the Phulkian State'. *Punjab Past and Present,* Vol. XV-I, April, 1981, Patiala 96.
28. *Punjab Administration Report of r1920-21,* 168; *The Land of Five Rivers* (Being Volume I of the *Punjab Administration Report 1921-22*), Punjab Government Publication (Lahore : 1923) 168; Foreign Department Revenue Irri. A. April 1873, Nos. 1-10 Foreign Department Proceedings, Internal, October, 1904, Nos. 20-21, para 57; also, of 1928, File No. 176-R; and also of 1931, File No. 155-R, NAI New Delhi, PSR, File No. H5B, PSA, PSA Patiala.

sq. miles in the Phulkian states which accounted for 64% and 36% of the total command area respectively.[29] The cost was to be debited accordingly. East Phulkian state bore the cost of construction of its own tributaries. Other charges were shared amongst the states in this ratio : Patiala 83.6% Nabha 8.8% and Jind 7.6%. The 36% of the canal water was the share of the Phulkian states out of the total was to be distributed among the three states according to the said ratio. This work of distribution was done by the British Executive Engineer known as canal agent who was posted at Patiala. The total construction cost falling in the Patiala state share up to the end of 1901 was rupees 1,14,61,277.[30] The canal was originally designed for a full supply discharge of 4,500 cusecs, rising on occasions to 6,000 cusecs. The *rabi* supply was expected to be 3,000 cusecs. By 1929-30, the canal was capable of carrying as much as 9,040 cusecs during *kharif*, while its authorized discharge during *rabi* was 8,430 cusecs. The supply authorized of the Phulkian feeder was 3,130 cusecs in *kharif* and 2,920 cusecs in rabi. It was to be distributed between the states of Patiala, Nabha and Jind in the proportion as stated above, by the British Executive Engineer known as canal agent. The headworks of the canal were at Ropar. The main canal flowed in the south-westerly direction for 39 miles, then dividing into two brances. One of these branches belonged to the British Government and the other to the three Phulkian states. The British branch split into two branches, the Abohar branch and the Bhatinda branch. A lot of irrigation was done in the Patiala state from the Bhatinda branch. Its charges were collected by the state and credited to the British Government. The Phulkian states branch curved in a south-easterly direction to Patiala. It had three lare distributaries—the Kotla branch, the Ghaggar branch and the Choa branch.[31]

From the first feeder of the main canal Lisra *rajbaha* took off at Bharthala, and end of the first feeder, the Kotla Branch

29. Punjab Administration Report for 1920-21, 168.
30. *Punjab States Gazetteer*, 106
31. *Administration Report of Patiala State for 1929-30*, 35; *Land of Five Rivers*, 169.

took off which was about 98 miles and ended in a reservoir at Desu. There was British rajbaha at tail entitled to the escape water. The Patiala distributaries on that branch were Mahorana, Sheron, Barnala, Longowal, Kot Dunna, Bhikhi, Saini, Ghuman, Talwandi, Jodhpur, Bangi, Raghowala and Pakka. At the beginning of the second feeder the *rajbaha* Bhagwanpur took off and at the end at Rohti, the Ghaggar Branch. On the Ghaggar Branch the Patiala state *rajbahas* were the Bhawanigarh, Newoda, Nidhampur, Ladbanjara, Kharial, Sunam, Kolra, Dialpura, Arkbas and Boha. This branch tailed into the Ghaggar *nala*. At Rauni the end of the third feeder, the Choa Branch the working *Rajbahas* of the Patiala state were Samana and Karamgarh. This branch also tailed into the Ghaggar Nala. The navigation channel had one *rajbaha* flowing into the Patiala baradari.[32]

The importance of this scheme of irrigation to the Patiala state could not be overestimated. Its distributaries covered almost the whole of the wide *jangal* region where the rainfall was scarce. The headworks of the Sirsa branch of the Western Jamuna canal were at Tejewala which had been constructed between 1889-1892. The Patiala state bore the entire cost of its headworks.[33] Patiala share of the cost of construction amounted to about Rs. 11,00,000.[34] The share of the water, to which the state was entitled was put at 27.66 per cent of the supply in the branch.[35] The project provided for commanded area of 2,43,204 *acres* but the actual culturable commanded area was later determined at 1,79,060 *acres* with a proposed annual irrigation of 59,301 acres.[36] As against the posed annual irrigation of 59,301

32. *Punjab States Gazetteer*, 107.
33. PSR, File No H. 53, PSA, Patiala; Foreign Department Proceeding Internal—A, September 1893, Nos. 75-81; Foreign Department Proceedings, 1926, 1926, File No 336-I; Aitchison, C.U.; *A collection of Engagements and Sanads*, Vol. III (Calcutta : 1931) 239-8.
34. *Land of Five Rivers*, 166; *Administration Report of Punjab and Its Dependecies* : 1893-94, 159.
35. *Administration Report of Patiala State for 1929-30*, 35-36.
36. *Administration Report of Patiala State for 1938-39*, 202.

acres the actual figures went upto 90,000 acres.[37] The irrigation from the state tributaries on the Sirsa branch started in 1892 and the control remained with the British government till 1908 when the state assumed its charge.[38] The soil of the *tehsil* of Narwana was stiff and here rain was scarce. It was saved from famine by this canal and its tributaries.

A canal started from the right bank of river Ghaggar at Village Chatt, nearly five miles above the old town of Banur. It was constructed in the time of Maharaja Karam Singh, and was improved during the reign of Maharaja Mohinder Singh. It was maintained by Patiala Irrigation Department.[39] During the times of heavy flood, this canal ran upto the fort of Bahadurgarh, about 25 miles from Banur. Sometimes it did not run beyond the twelfth year. During the summer the supply of water was sudden and depended on rain in the hills. In the *kharif* little irrigation was done because the country was mostly flooded even with ordinary rainfall. In the *rabi* the supply of water was so little that the crops did not mature properly.[40]

During 1938-39, the total irrigated area of the state was 60,71,501 *pakka bighas* of which 47,14,177 or roughly 77% was under cultivation.[41] To make the point more clear a table is prepared : (given below).

37. *Administration Report of Patiala State for 1932-33*, 35-36.
38. *Administration of Patiala State for 1938-39*, 202-03.
39. *Administration of Report of Patiala State for 1929-30*, 36; and also *for 1932-33*, 36.
40. *Ibid.*
41. *Administration Report of Patiala State for 1938-39*, 37.

Table : 1

Class of Land	*Area in the year under report in pakka bighas*	*Area at the time of settle-ment in pakka bighas*		*Increase or decrease in pakka bighas*
'A' Irrigated	4,97,149	3,57,616	+	1,39,533
(i) By wells	10,55,585	8,51,676	+	2,03,909
(ii) By canals	13,986	25,052	-	11,066
(iii) Abi	-	-		-
Total	15,66,720	12,34,344	+	3,32,376
Unirrigated				
(i) Sailab	76,737	73,287	+	4,450
(ii) Barani	30,70,720	33,25,623	-	2,54,903
Total	31,47,457	33,98,910	+	2,50,453
G. Total	47,14,177	46,33,254	+	81,923

It may be noted that the headworks and the distribution of water in the Phulkian states was under the control of the British officers. The Patiala state had to pay to the British four *annas* per *acre* irrigated from the water supplied by both the Satluj and Jamuna rivers.[42] The table given here gives a detailed particulars about the expansion of irrigated area and net canal revenue from 1900 to 1939 :[43]

42. In contrast to the stagnation in irrigation facilities during the British period, there was rapid expansion in the irrigation network in the aftermath of freedom vide; *Report on Administration of Pepsu, April, 1951 to March, 31, 1952,* 71-72.
43. Punjab States Gazetteer, 109; *Administration Report of Patiala State for 1929-30,* 39; and also *for 1938-39,* 205-10.

Table : 2

Year	*Irrigated area in acres*	*Gross Revenue collections*	*Working Expenses*	*Net Revenue*
1900-01	1,99,081	11,48,244	3,94,527	7,53,717
1929-30	5,75,088	33,86,288	8,32,972	29,62,316
1938-39	6,85,357	41,17,907	9,43,357	32,95,730

Thus, the irrigated area from 1900 to 1939 grew three times, while the net revenue collection grew about four and a half times. Different revenue rates were charged for different crops. For example, in 1924 sugarcane on *rabi* channels was charged rupees three and *annas* two per *kacha bigha,* wheat on *rabi* rupee one per *kacha* bigha and rice rupee one and twelve *annas* per *kacha bigha.*[44] The Patiala peasants criticized the Government for charging higher water rate from them than that being charged in the Punjab. For instance, during 1934-35, Patiala rate on the average was one rupee eight *annas* while the rate in the British territory was one rupee.[45] Reduction of water-rate was one of the main demands of the peasantry when the peasant movement was launched 1/6 of the state area was under canal irrigation. But even then it was not free from droughts. For example, in 1939-40 there was a widespread drought in the state. The state agriculture depended largely on monsoons. The twelve crop seasons extending over the years 1915 to 1921, seven harvests failed due to deficient monsoons. The eighth harvest, that of *kharif* in 1917, was seriously damaged by successive and excessive rainfall.[46] Thus the irrigation system, particularly the canal irrigation system, of the state was inadequate. Old system like the Persian wheelcontinued in lands irrigated by wells. Poor peasants could not afford the high cost of sinking *pakka* wells.

44. For details see Appendix-I.
45. *Administration Report of Patiala State for 1938-39,* 208.
46. *Administration Report of Patiala State and Its Depedencies for 1915-16,* 2; *Administration Report of Punjab and Its Dependencies* : 1916-17, 2. and also *for 1918-19,* 2; and also *for 1920-21,* 3.

Another worth nothing point is that the difference in topography, soils, rainfall and irrigation facilities in the Patiala state and their impact brought about variety in the methods of agriculture. In the beginning of the 20th century the rulers realized that the general prosperity of the state depended on agricultural prosperity. Earlier the state's interest did not go beyond the collection of land revenue and very little interest was taken in the general development of agriculture. During 1890-1905 when Lord Curzon was the Viceroy, special stress was laid on the modernization of Indian agriculture. It had effect on the Indian states also. Now, Indian council of Agricultural Research was founded.[47] In 1905 Imperial college of Agriculture was set up at Poone.[48] With the appointment of Directors of Agricultive in all the provinces, Sardar Harchand Singh was appointed Agricultural Expert in the Patiala state in 1913.[49] On his advice Bhupendra Agricultural Farm was set up with an area of 520 *kacha bighas,* in 1917.[50] In 1923 an Agricultural school was founded in the state which developed into the Bhupendra Agriculture Institute. This institute followed the syllabus and courses of Punjab Agriculture College, Lyallpur.[51] Sardar Harchand Singh was appointed as Director of the Newly created Agriculture Department of the state in 1919.[52] Later in 1936 he was promoted as commissioner of Agriculture and Rural upliftment. A.H. Sadiq was appointed Director in his place.[53] Both of them continued working in these capacities till inclusion of Patiala with Pepsu in 1948.

47. For further details see Randhawa, M.S., *A History of Agriculture in India,* Vol. III (New Delhi : 183), 262-81.
48. *Patiala Gazette* (Patiala) May 7, 1924, 11, Randhawa, M.S., *op. cit.,* 271-72.
49. *Ibid.*
50. (Principal motive behind the Bhupendra Agriculture Farm was demonstration, experimentation and seed multiplication) vide., *Administration Report of Patiala State for 1939-40,* 181.
51. *Administration Report of Patiala State for 1932-33,* 31.
52. Harchand Singh, 'Rural Uplift in Patiala State' in *Patiala Post,* December 1943 and January 1944, PSA, File No. Hemant 95 B, PSA, Patiala.
53. *Patiala Gazettee* (Patiala) April 24, 1946, 976.

The Agriculture Department, though looked into the improvement of agriculture, had special powers to control *mandis* (markets) of the state. Its work was divided into the following sub-section[54] : *(i)* Bhupendra Agriculture Farm and Institute; *(ii)* District work; *(iii)* well-boring; *(iv)* Veterniary; *(v)* Bhupendra Diary Farm, and *(v)* Cattle Fairs.

In a year, there were two agricultural seasons; *rabi* crops were sown in the month of *Assuj* (September-October) and *kharif* harvest was threshed in the month of *Katak* (October-November) and cotton picking began. The main *kharif* crops were rice, maize, *bajra, jowar* and pulses. The main *rabi* crops were wheat, barley and gram. Rice was sown throughout the state but the best rice came from the hills. *Bajra* was the most important crop in the sandy *bangar* tract of the state. It was very popular in Mohindergarh *nizamat. Jowar* was also a *kharif* crop sown in the Mohindergarh *nizamat.* The cultivation of wheat was wide-spread. A number of varieties of wheat were sown in the state. Barley was sown later and ripened earlier.[55]

Cotton was mostly grown in irrigated lands in the *bangar* and *jangal* regions. It was also sown in unirrigated lands of the *powadh. Dakar* and *rausli* soils were most suited to its cultivation.[56] Sugarcane was largely cultivated where irrigation was done by wells, but in the bet it was sown in *sailab* and also in *barani* lands. Indigo was grown in Bhawanigarh, Patiala, Narwana and Sirhind *tehsils.* In some parts of Sirhind, Banur and Payal, poppy was grown. Tobacco was grown in lands irrigated by wells. Garlic, onions, aniseed, coriander and *ajwain* were popular with the Arains. Potatoes and *arabi* were mostly grown in the hills. Ginger and tumoric were grown in Kulu. *Bathu Kulthi, Mandwa* were also grown from whose sees poor people made chapattis.[57]

---

54. Official Guide into the working of His Highness's Government Patiala, 178. *Administration Report of Patiala State for 1939-40,* 181.
55. For details see *Punjab States Gazetteer,* 95.
56. *Ibid.,* 100-02.
57. *Ibid.,* 100.

A horticulture department existed in the Patiala state, as the Patiala ruler evinced keen interest in horticulture. Its principal interest was fruit farming. There were seventeen gardens in Patiala and eight at other places with area of 59,880 *acres*, in 1938-39. The popular fruits in the state were almonds, apples, apricots, grapes, peaches, mangoes, pears, persimmons, plums and pomegranates. This department first identified and then took proper measures to isolate the fruit diseases. The department also organized flowers and fruit shows. Landscaping was its special interest.[58]

For wheat and maize the fields were ploughed after four or five watering and for sugarcane after six or seven, but sugarcane fields were generally ploughed after the winter rains. After ploughing the surface was levelled so that the land may retain the moisture.[59] Hoeing (*gudai*) was done by hand. It was done with *khurpa*, but in the *bangar* and Mohindergarh it was done standing with a *kasola*. The irrigated crops were generally hoed after every watering. The cotton and sugarcane required repeated hoeings. Hoeing increased productivity of crops. It was mostly done in the irrigated lands but in the hills land was hoed for all *kharif* crops.[60]

The harvesting was done in a sitting posture. The thresher (*phala*) was drawn round and round by two bullocks driven by a man. In this way the straw was broken up and grain separated from the husk. The mixed straw and grain was tossed in the air with a *tangli*, separating grain from the straw. Every kind of grain except maize was treated in this manner. In case of maize *kukris* or *challies* were broken and piled and ten beaten with rods and thus the grain was separated from the cobs.[61]

58. *Ibid.*, 102-03, *Administration Report of Patiala State for 1938-39*, 193.
59. *Administration Report of Patiala State for 1939-40*, 186-90.
60. For details see Bedi, Sohinder Singh, *Folklore of Punjab* (Delhi : 1971), 145.
61. *Ibid.*

Though animal waste was the main source of manure, people did not realize its full manure value. Mostly it was used as fuel. As early as 1911 the state advised the farmers to adopt green manuring because of its productive value. Only the bigger *zamindars* and *biswedars* followed this advise, but in general this advice had fallen on deaf ears.[62] Besides, deficiency of rains often led to failure of crops and in turn to famines in the state Locust (tiddi) brought havoc in the month of *bhadon* (August-September). *Sundi,* a caterpillar attacked the gram and mustard stalks. Wild animal caused the greatest damage to the crops. Black buck, wild pig and jackals were specially active in the countryside.[63]

The traditional plough was used throughout the state. Very simple implements were used in agricultural operations. *Datri* (sickle) was used for reaping the crop *tanali* for winnowing, *gandasa* or *gandasi* (chopper) for chopping fodders; *kahi* for making irrigation channels; *ramba* or *khurpa* with a crooked handle for hoeing.[64] Farm hands (kamas) were employed by big land proprietors. They got wages both in cash and kind. A *siri* (sharer) was a grade above the *kama*. These two categories were returned as agricultural labourers in the census reports.[65] However, at the time of sowing and reaping additional farm labourers were employed. Landless *Jats Rangars, Chuhras* and *Chamars* generally looked for such seasonal jobs. Such field jobs were done by women in the hills, even in the plains women were employed for picking cotton, etc.

The number of people depending on agriculture rose from 64% to 70% during 1931-41. The Patiala State appeared to be a land of cultivating owners. At the time of the census of 1941, there were 2,58,381 earners and 6,30,647 dependents. Next to them were *batai* share croppers followed by cultivating

62. *Punjab State Gazetteer,* 96.
63. *Patiala Gazette* (*Patiala*), May 31, 1911, 8.
64. *Punjab State Gazetteer,* 103.
65. *Ibid.,* 97.

proprietors. The following table gives details of status of those dependent on agriculture.[66]

Table : 3

Group	*Principal Earners*	*Dependents*
Non-cultivating proprietors taking rent in cash or kind.	43,195	49,579
Batai (share-croppers)	76,709	1,69,986
Estate Agents and managers or owners	10	53
Estate Agents and Manager of Government	7	20
Rent collectors	8	3
Cultivating owners	2,38,301	6,30,647
Tenent cultivators	26,978	58,640
Agricultural labourers	25,865	96,613

The veterinary section and cattle fairs were under the supervision of the Directorate of Agriculture. There were four veterinary hospitals at Patiala, Bhatinda, Bassi and Bhawanigarh. Each of these hospitals was placed under the control of duly qualified veterinar and assistant surgeon.[67] This displays the state's interest in creation of healthy and standard livestock. Organizations of cattle fairs was an important function of the Directorate of Agriculture. Wrestling matches and other interesting rural games and amusements were organized in order to attract villagers. The biggest attractions at the cattle fairs were the cattle, agricultural implements and improved crop seeds exhibitions. During the year 1939-40 no fewer than forty-nine cattle fairs were held. In these fairs farmers

66. *Punjab States Gazetteer,* 99; *Census Report of Patiala State for 1941,* 249.
67. *Administration Report of Patiala State for 1938-39,* 192-96; also *for 1939-40,* 186.

were educated on how to improve the health and quality of their livestock.[68]

Census of 1941 shows that 15,151 persons were engaged in occupation of stock raising. They had 32,812 persons as their dependents. These could be further classified into four categories : *(i)* herdsmen, shepards and breeders of other animals; *(ii)* breeders of transport animals, *(iii)* breeders and keepers of cattle and buffeloes for milk production; and *(iv)* breeders and keepers of cattle buffeloes for other purposes.[69] There was a sharp rise in those engaged in this subsidiary agricultural occupation. This may possibly be the result of state encouragement non-existent in the state.

In the agriculturally rich *powadh* region of Sirhind, farmers could afford larger number of cattle. Consequently the animals had less work burden and were healthy. Agriculture was far less renumerative in the *jangal tehsil* of Bhatinda than in the *powadh*. Bullocks were generally used for ploughing throughout the state but in some parts of *jangal* and in the Mohindergarh district camels were also used. The following table vividly describes the regional variation in ploughing burden of agricultural cattle in the state.[70]

Table : 4

Tehsil	*Number of Agricultural cattle*	*Cultivated land in bighas*	*Area cultivated per one agricultural cattle per bigha*
(1)	*(2)*	*(3)*	*(4)*
Patiala	28,352	2,66,582	9
Rajpura	24,970	2,27,857	9
Sirhind	84,647	2,67,790	3
Kandaghat	76,734	57,326	8

(Contd....)

68. *Patiala Gazette* (Patiala), August 16, 1927, 86; *Administration Report of Patiala state for 1939-40,* 186.
69. *Census Report of Patiala State for 1941,* 251, 310.
70. *Ibid.*

(Contd...)

(1)	*(2)*	*(3)*	*(4)*
Bhawanigarh	28,350	3,27,320	11
Sunam	24,638	4,35,316	17
Dhuri	35,927	12,20,430	34
Narwana	20,371	5,18,580	25
Bhatinda	30,471	8,20,155	27
Barnala	18,169	3,08,420	17
Mansa	24,940	8,18,844	23
Narnaul	1,09,357	4,55,237	4

For the sale of farmers products the state had a lot of *mandis* (markets). The district *nazims* were responsible for the management of these *mandis* and octroi towns. The income to the state from Octroi during 1938-39 was Rs. 4,01,215 as against Rs. 3,82,041 in 1939-40.[71]

Variation in the prices of agricultural products depended on the position of demand and supply in the state. Therefore, seasonally the price of a single crop varied, but prices in one *tehsil* did not vary drastically from those in another.[72] From 1920 to 1940, the prices of almost all these goods doubled but for sugar and rice.[73] The state had no sugar mill, and whatever sugarcane was sown was boiled into *gur* for domestic consumption and the state *gur* did not possibly have an external market. As for rice, it was produced in the state in larger quantity than it could be consumed and this factor kept down its price.

Most of the peasants in the state were leading a very poor and miserable life. When rains failed and drought conditions prevailed, a system of agricultural credit was arranged to help the farmers. Besides, the *sahukars tagavi* and co-operative societies were the two main government sponsored credit

71. *Administration Report of Patiala State for1939-40,* 72.
72. *For details regarding prices in 1940,* see Appendix-II.
73. See Appendix II and III.

sources. However, there sources were not very helpful as both were not very responsive to the needs of the cultivators. This fact clearly emerges from the Administration Report of the state for the year 1932-33, which clearly states, "Owing to introduction of the cooperative societies system in the state no fresh loans were advanced during the year 1932-33.[74] Consequently rural indebtedness became a widespread evil of the countryside. The peasants were compelled by circumstances to have recourse to traditional sources of credit. The *sahukars* were very cruel in their financial dealings with the farmers. As a consequence, the peasants were caught in the vicious circle of lifelong indebtedness. In turn, the existence of crushing debt was one of the major causes of the peasant's miserable condition. According to an enquiry conducted during the census operation of 1941, 3,20,603 land-holders (as compared with 51,205 land-holders during the cenus of 1931) were indebted to the total extent of rupees 12.42 *crores*. Out of this, loan of rupees 7,76,87,581 or 62 per cent was secured on land whereas rupees 4,65,16,880 or 32 per cent was unsecured. The land involved in mortgage against the secured debt was 12,96,297 *bighas*, whereas the total land involved was 57,60,072 *bighas*, which was assessed to the tune of rupees 47,86,969. The remaining land *viz.*, 44,63,775 *bighas* represented the area of land which was held by indebted proprietors but did not cover the loan. In all, only a sum of rupees 3.15 *crores* or 25 per cent of the total debt was incurred for productive purposes, *viz.*, purchase of land, implements and towards liquidation of previous debts.[75] Deducting this sum from the total debt the net debt which was contracted for social engagements such as marriages, death and litigation comes to rupees 9.27 *crores*, that gave an incidence of about rupees 282 per person and rupees 14 per *bigha*. The highest incidence of indebtedness was found in Kohistan (Pinjore) district. There the women folk lived in expensive style. Social customs and marriage among the hill people were also expensive. The total debt in Kohistan district

74. *Administration Report of Patiala State for 1932-33*, 38.
75. For details see Appendix-IV.

was Rs. 58,99,143 out of which a little less than 50% was due to marriages alone. The Patiala and Bassi districts came next to the Kohistan district in indebtedness. The agrarian condition of these districts was good and so money-lenders readily advanced money to the agriculturists. Regarding the Bassi district it may be said that the majority of the *zamindars* were muslims who were far from frugal. The incidence of indebtedness was the lowest in the Narnaul district.[76] Here the land was less productive and agriculturists had small holding, and so money-lenders were not tempted to advance money to them. According to random survey of 17 villages in 1943, the villagers were under a debt of Rs. 2,25,000, 51% of this debt was incurred on social functions, such as marriages and deaths; 9% on litigation; 18% on intoxicants and only 22% for productive agriculture purposes.[77] Another noteworthy factor is that large proprietors had more borrowing proclivities than the small ones and the small proprietors more than the tenants, because a large proprietor had more security to offer than a small proprietor and a small proprietor had more to offer than a tenant and from this it may be deducted "debt followed credit."[78]

The state, under the British influence tried to modernize agriculture. The Department of Agriculture, a model farm and an agricultural training institute were set-up. The cultivators were encouraged to improve the quality of their implements and livestock. Despite all these efforts, the state of agriculture in this region remained backward; and the quality of agricultural inputs did not go much beyond the medieval standard. The facilities of loan and credit were available only to the influential *zamindars.* An average cultivator became a victim to the moneylender for his credit needs. Most of the agriculturists especially the lower and middle peasants, were head over ears in debt and poverty. The state Census Report of 1941 blames the peasant for his miserable lot. He never made

76. *Census Report of Patiala State for 1941,* 37-39.
77. Harchand Singh, 'Rural Uplift in Patiala State' in *Patiala Past,* December 1943, January 1944, 26.
78. *Census Report of Patiala State for 1941,* 37.

efforts to increase his income and resources but remained content if he could make both ends meet. In his mode of living, in his way of cultivating and earning, the peasant was static.[79] The peasants lost all faith in the government because it was opposed to their legitimate rights and interests. Gradually, the discontent of the lower peasants grew because of increasing burdens imposed upon them under the feudalistic regime and insecurity of the tenure particularly for the lower peasantry. This gave rise to the peasant movement which gained momentum with the passage of time, culminating in their violent revolt against the repressive princely regime, existing feudalistic system as well as imperialism.

Land Revenue Administration was the most important ingredient of the agrarian system. To examine the agrarian system of the East Punjab States during the period under review, here an attempt has been made to study the land revenue administration in the light of its revenue functionaries, revenue units and state demand.

The *diwan* of the state was in charge of the land revenue administration, but he danced to the tune of the ruler who was the supreme head of the administration edifice including the land revenue system.[80] All reforms in connection with land revenue had to receive his sanction; only he could grant relief and remit revenue and other cesses.[81] However, the final appeal in cases pertaining to revenue lied with the *Ijlas-i-khas.*[82] In 1918

79. *Ibid.*, 248.
80. *Official Guide to the working of Administration of His Highness : Government Patiala* (Patiala : 1927), 2; *Administration Report of Patiala State for 1938-39*, 55.
81. *Patiala Gazettee* (Patiala) July 18, 1939, 46; *Administration Report of Patiala State for 1938-39*, 13.
82. (The peasants approached the *Ijlas-i-khas* for a number of reason by virtue of its being the final arbitrator of justice. It was Maharaja's court and had a special secretariat) vide., PSR, *Ijlas-i-khas,* file Nos. 1263, 1968, PSA, Patiala; also see Report or Supplement to Punjab Tenuary Act, VII of 1887 in *Report on Settlement of Patiala*, 71-73.

the revenue department was separated from finance. Now, the revenue secretary looked after this department. But after 1922 the revenue secretariat was merged with the Revenue Commissioner's office and the Revenue Commissioner was made the ex-office Secretary. The designation of the revenue commissioner was changed to Revenue Minister in 1925. Kahan Chand was the first revenue minister of the state.[83] He decided all matters regarding revenue in consultation with the ruler. He had the pore for sale of land upto fifty *bighas* for non-payment of revenue. He could acquire land and grant compensation upto Rs. 1000.[84] Interestingly enough prior to the first summary settlement of 1861-62, next to the *diwan* was the *tehsildar* who headed each *pargans*.[85] At the time of *batai*, the *Kuchhus* were the land appraisers. The *batawas* fixed the state-share on the basis of measurement by the *Kachhus*. The *muharries* or the *likharis* were the revenue clerks. They took down the figures for record; in other words they compiled the *khasra*. The *muhassals* or the watchmen were appointed in each village to keep guard before the division of the crop.[86] Thus a team of *kachhus, batawas* and *likharis* was appointed for a group of villages to supervise *batai* operations. For the each group of villages there were two *kachhus*, two *batawas* and *likharis*. It is important to note that one in each pair was an appointee of the *diwan* and the other that of the *tehsildar*. This procedure had evidently been conceived with the object that their mutual jealousy, rivalry and dependence on two separate superiors might serve as a check on dishonesty.[87] All these

83. *Administration Report of Patiala State for 1929-30*, 23; also *for 1932-33*, 24.
84. *Official Guide to the working of Administration of His Highness Government, Patiala*, 3.
85. The major parts of the Patiala state when it come to be formed constituted of the *sarkar* of Sirhind which comprised of many *parganas* (a unit which was hierarchically next to *sarkar* in the Mughal administrative set up) *vide.*, Abul Fazl, *Ain-i-Akbari* (trans) Vol. II, 301-01.
86. *Punjab States Gazetteer*, 150.
87. *Ibid.*, 150-51.

revenue officials except the *tehsildar* were appointed seasonally who were to supervise the batai operation. As a consequence corruption among them was rampant. To check the corrupt practices which were prevalent in the system of kind assessment, the ruler introduced cash assessment in 1862. But the reforms appeared foredoomed as it came in for severe opposition from the official class. As a result, the Maharaja Narinder Singh dismissed the diwan of the state. A *munsarim diwan* with limited powers was appointed in his place. Now, the state was divided into four divisions. A *nazim*, who was first known as *munsarim-i-hadbast* and later *mohitman bandobast*, was appointed for each division of the state.[88] *Patwaris* were introduced as new village officials. The lambardars helped them in the collection of state dues in the villages.[89] However, at the end of the 19th century it was found that this system of revenue collection was not successful.[90]

In order to streamline the land revenue system, Major Popham F. Young was appointed the settlement commissioner of the state in 1900 A.D. He invited some trained officials from the British Punjab on deputation.[91] A *tehsildar* along with a *naib-tehsildar* was appointed for each *tehsil*. The *tehsil* staff in the whole state consisted of 18 *tehsildars*, 17 *naib-tehsildars*, 71 *kanungoes* and 810 *patwaris*.[92] Young found that the *lambardars* had become ineffective; he, therefore, on the basis of existing pattern in the Punjab, suggested the appointment of

88. *Ibid.*, 152.
89. Popham Young, *Report on Settlement of Patiala*, 35.
90. For more details see *Ibid.*
91. Foreign department proceeding's internal-B, October, 1902, Nos. 187-88; also Internal-B, September, 1902, 8-9; Internal-B, June, 1902, 164-65; also see Foreign department proceedings, General-B, November, 1909, No 142.
92. Administration Report of Patiala state for 1938-39, 55; *Popham* Young, Report on settlement of Patiala, 23; (The Pinjore *tehsil* had a *naib-tehsildar* prior to Young's reform) *vide*; *Punjab States Gazetteer*, 141.

zaildars which was done. By 1913, there were 9,491 *lambardars* to 3,707 villages in the state; which meant that on the average there were 2.6 *lambardars* per village. The total number of *zaildars* for the state was 257. Thus, there were fourteen village to a zaildar.[93] By 1940 the Revenue Department was further overhauled on the pattern prevailing in the British Punjab.[94] The Revenue Minister was given the powers of Financial Commissioner and Revenue Commissioner those of the commissioner.[95] A *nazim* had the powers of a collector. He was empowered to dispose cases under land revenue and tenancy acts. He could bear appeals regarding cases decided by his subordinantes.[96]

Three *naib nazims mal* helped the *nazim* in his work. The *tehsildars* of Narnaul and Kundaghat performed the duties of *naib-nazims mal* as well. A *naib nazim* was also called a *mal* officer. A *tehsildar* was responsible for proper maintenance of village records of his *tehsil*. A *tehsildar* was as important to his *tehsil* as a *nazim* was to his district. He was helped by *naib-tehsildar*. A naib-tehsildar carried a small scale sketch map displaying village boundaries, main roads and canals while he was on tour

93. For complete details regarding many land revenue officers see Appendix-V.
94. (Undoubtedly, Punjab was the Model for the Phulkian states to emulate), vide., *Administration Report of Patiala State for 1938-39*, 55.
95. *Administration Report of Patiala State for 1938-39*, 54; also *for 1939-40.*, 65 (Besides the Revenue Department proper revenue minister looked after several other related departments, such as Income Tax, Excise, Registration, Octroi and mandis, development, rural uplift and consolidation of Holdings departments. Sometimes, other subsidiary departments were also attached to the ministry. For instance, the irrigation department was transferred under the change of Revenue Minister for one month in 1938).
96. PSR File No. 4B, PSA, Patiala : Douis, J.M., *Punjab Land Administration Manual* (Lahore : 1908), 100-03.

with the tehsildar.[97] The field *kanungo* was to tour his circle and inspect the work of *patwaris* on the spot. The office *kanungo* was the revenue clerk of the *tehsildar*. He preserved all records sent by the *patwaris*. The district *kanungo* maintained all records received from the *kanungoes* and the *patwaris*. A well maintained kanungo's office was assest in ensuring the efficiency of revenue system.[98] The district *kanungo* ensured the efficiency of both the office and field *kanungoes*. He maintained all records received from the kanungoes and the *patwaris*.[99] The district *patwar* fund was under his charge. He also kept copies of prescribed statistical registers for each assessment circle, *tehsil* and district.

In the land Revenue Act (Punjab Act, XVII of 1887), the term village officer was used for *patwari, lambardar* and *zaildar*. Of these the *patwari* was the most important functionary in revenue matters.[100] He kept a dairy known as *roznamcha*, which was renewed seasonally, and contained a record of notable occurrences pertaining to the cultivation of land. He was supposed to keep the *tehsildar* informed of happenings which were likely to have a direct or indirect effect on agricultural operations. He inspected the crops seasonwise and informed the *nazim* about the conditions and prospects of each state. Preparation of *khasra girdawari*,[101] jamaban di[102] and a register of mutations were his main jobs.[103] The *lambardar*

97. Boden Powell, *The Land Systems of British India*, Vol. II (Delhi 1974), 731-38 (The Punjab Tenancy and Revenue Acts of 1887 were introduced in the state in to except for some minor changes introduced here and there to suit the local conditions. These Acts, therefore, can be relied upon for reference so far as revenue administration and tenancy conditions were concerned) *vide., Punjab States Gazetteer*, 146-49.
98. Baden Pawell, *op. cit.*, 738-39 Douie, J.M., *op cit.*, 113.
99. *Ibid.*
100. Baden Powell, *op. cit.*, 733.
101. A field book containing a record of cultivators, specifying their status.
102. A roll showing both revenue and rent dues in a village.
103. Baden Powell, *op. cit.*, 734-38.

and the *zaildar* were paid from revenue collections. The *lambardar* was paid *pachotra,* five per cent of the total demand of the particular area under his charge. He acted on behalf of the landowners, tenants and other residents in their relations with the state. It was his duty to collect revenue from the agriculturist and deposit it with the *zaildar.*[104] He also helped in carrying out harvest inspections, surveys and other revenue business. He was, however, not accountable for any revenue arrears due from agriculturists, nor was he required to file suits against the actual defaulters; at the most he was expected to approach higher authorities to take appropriate action in such cases. Also, was his duty to keep the *tehsildar* informed of death of any assignee of any encroachment on government property. The *zaildar* supervised the work of *lambardars* and *patwaris.* He was required to assist in conducting surveys, crop inspections and preparation of records and assessments in his *zail* and to exert his influence in securing within the *zail* adherence to government orders. He was paid one per cent of the total demand of his zail.[105]

Competent and qualified staff was required for proper functioning of the settlement. Soon after Young took over as the settlement, commissioner, several old hands who had no knowledge of the revenue work were sent for practical training and for passing certain examination.[106] Fresh recruits also had to undergo training. The salary of *tehsildars* was increased from Rs. 55 to Rs. 80 to 100, while that of *patwaris* from Rs. 8 to Rs. 11 to 15.[107] Even *Patwaris* began to be impartd training, both in theory and practice. During the course of Young's settlement operations 65 *kanungoes* and 767 *patwaris* passed the *kanungo* and *patwar* examinations, respectively.[108] Vacancies as a rule were to be filled up either by promotion from the next lower

104. *Ibid.,* 740 Douie, J.M., *op. cit.,* 61.
105. Baden Powell, *op. cit.,* 740-41.
106. Young Popham, *Report on Settlement of Patiala,* 23.
107. *Ibid.,* 24.
108. *Ibid.,* 23-24.

grade or by giving appointment to the senior most candidates on the list. Regular registers of candidates for posts of *tehsildars* and *kanungoes* were maintained in accordance with the forms prescribed in the office of the Financial Commissioner of the Punjab. Every candidate was required to pass the prescribed departmental examination.[109] Even then persons with influence continued to jump the line as far as the selections to the service were concerned.

Personality of the state revenue units started taking shape during the regime of Maharaja Karam Singh. It further crystallized during the period of Maharaja Narinder Singh, who ruled from 1845 to 1862. It was in his times that the first summary settlement of the Patiala state was completed in 1862. Although Maharaja Ranjit Singh's rule at Lahore was young, as compared to the Patiala state, yet it had a better system of revenue units. The largest revenue units in Ranjit Singh's kingdom were the *subas.* Next were the interchangeable *telluqas* and *paraganas,* which were analogous to districts. The sub-divisions of *pargana* were the *tappas,* while the smallest unit of revenue administration was the village (*mauza or deh*).[110]

In Patiala State the earliest land revenue units were *parganas* roughly corresponding to *tehsils.* Each *pargana* had a *tehsildar* who headed the land revenue administration. A *tehsildar* at the time of harvest divided his *tehsil* into a number of suitable circles.[111] Each of these circles comprised of a number of villages. And temporary staff was appointed to supervise *batai* operations there in at each harvest. Another practice prevalent before the introduction of each assessment in 1862 was that of revenue farming. According to this practice, the contracting parties after a certain payment to the state were left free to collect revenue. Such collectors were known as *Ijaraders* and were not unoften high officials of the state. It was

109. *Administration Report of Patiala State for 1938-39,* 56.
110. Banga, Indu, *Agrarian System of the Sikhs* (New Delhi : 1978) 63-71.
111. *Punjab States Gazetteer,* 150-51.

a singularly pernicious system form the point of view of revenue payers, as after clearing the state dues, the tax-farmers tried to extort the maximum from the peasants.[112] It was during Ranjit Singh's rule that the Patiala state was divided into *nizamats* which were the most important land revenue segments to the state. These nizamats corresponded to the districts of the British Punjab. The *nizamat* boundaries and headquarters continued to be changed from time to time. In 1920 there were five *nizamats* in the state with their headquarters at Bhawanigarh, Bassi Pathana, Barnala, Pinjore and Mohindergarh.[113] By 1931, the *nizamat* headquarters were Patiala, Bassi Pathana, Sunam, Barnala and Narnaul. The Kohistan (Pinjore) district which earlier had its headquarters at Pinjore was amalgamated with Patiala.[114] However, later it was again separated to form an independent *nijamat* with a new district headquarters at Kandaghat.[115] There was no uniformity regarding the area of the *nizamats* or the number of villages coming under their jurisdiction. For example, the area of Barnala District was 1836 square miles but that of Mohindergarh was 576 square miles. Barnala District had 462 villages whereas Mohindergarh had only 287 villages.[116] Each *nizamat* was divided into *tehsils*. In 1911 there were, in all sixteen *tehsils* in the Patiala state. While the *nizamats* of Bhawanigarh and Pinjore had four tehsils each, Barnala and Bassi had three each. The *nizamat* of Mohindergarh had just two *tehsils*. For administrative convenience by 1941, the number of tehsils was reduced to twelve. Sunam and Barnala districts had three *tehsils* each, Patiala and Bassi districts had two *tehsils* each, while Kohistan (Pinjore) and Mohindergarh districts had one *tehsil* each.[117] The area and number of villages that fell under each *tehsil* also varied. In 1911 Bathinda *tehsil* with an area of 868 square miles was the

112. Banga, Indu, *op. cit.,* 104.
113. *Administration Report of Patiala State for 193-40.*
114. *Census Report of Patiala State for 1941,* 9.
115. *Ibid.*
116. *Census Report of Patiala State for 1911,* 2-3.
117. *Ibid.*

largest and Rajura *tehsil* with an area of 868 square miles was the largest and Rajpura *tehsil* was an area of 141 square miles was the smallest.[118] Mohindergarh *tehsil* with an area of 299 square miles had 120 villages and Pinjore hilly *tehsil* with an area of 342 square miles consisted of 1074 villages.[119] The *tehsils* were further split up into kanungo circles. Each such circle was directly under the charge of field kanungo. The *kanungo* circle were subdivided into *Patwars* which were directly under the charge of the *Patwaris*. A patwar was composed of a few villages, depending on land area of the villages composing it and the resultant work land on the *Patwari*. *Lumbardar* and *Zaildars* directly collected revenue from the peasantry.

The state flourished on the land revenue and other cesses from the peasants. The 'Kind' share was fixed at one-sixth to one-third of the produce.[120] In the reign of Ala-ud-din Khalji, it was raised to one-half of the produce.[121] Sher Shah and afterwards the Mughal Emperors fixed this at one-third.[122] During Ranjit Singh's rule over the Punjab the rate of land revenue varied from one-sixth of half of the gross produce.[123] In the Patiala state the land revenue rate varied from one-fifth to one half and was on the average one-third of the produce.[124]

118. *Census Report of Patiala State for 1941*, 9.
119. *Census Report of Patiala State for 1911*, 2-3.
120. Sharma, R.S., *Ancient India* (Delhi : 1977), 78; Thaper, Romilla, History of India, Vol. I, (Aylesberg : 1976-reprint) 245, Dutt, R.P. *India Today* (Bombay : 1947) 223.
121. Moreland, W.H. *The Agrarian System of Muslim India* (Cambridge, 1929), 17; Lal, K.S., *History of the Khaljis : 1290-1320* (Delhi : 1967), 181-82.
122. Marland, W.H., *op. cit.*, 82-83 (The end of the Mughal rule and the anarchy that it offset encourage the local chieftains to increase the land revenue, vide., Dutt, T.P. *op. cit.*, 223.
123. (Indu Banga has estimated the revenue rate to range from 1/3 to 2/5 of the produce while Fauja Singh estimates a wider range as referred above) *vide.*, Banga Indu, *op. cit.*, 110; Fauja Singh, *Some Aspects of State and Society under Ranjit Singh* (Delhi : 1982), 176.
124. *Imperial Gazetteer of India : Provincial Series Punjab*, Vol. II (Calcutta : 1908), 269.

The share of the state from the harvested crop was called *mal.* Besides this the state used to extort money in the name of *Kharach, nazrat, begari, roz sipahi, lipai kot, sarafi, nira sarkar* and *nira tehsildar* etc.[125] The land revenue was collected in kind till 1862.

Ijardars and seasonally appointed officials were corrupt. The erratic and severe nature of revenue exactions by them has already been referred to. But Maharaja Narinder Singh streamlined the process of land revenue and other taxes. The assessment was made in cash and all the afore mentioned cesses were commuted into a cash rate and fixed at twenty-five per cent on land revenue proper. The collections on this account equalled to one-fifth of the whole demand and were known as the *abwaba.*[126] To begin with, a settlement for one year based on an estimate of existing capabilities of a village and the average collection of the last 22 years was made. The yearly average of 22 years was about rupees 23 lakhs and the new assessment amounted to rupees 30,87,000.[127] In the Barnala District constituting of three *jangal tehsils* of Bhatinda, Bhikhi and Barnala, new settlements were effected in 1862-63, 1865-66, 1868-69, 1878-79 and 1890-91. In the Narnaul district there were fresh settlements in 1864-65, 1868-69, 1880-81 and 1890-91. In the districts other than these, excluding the Himalayan *tehsil* of Pinjore, settlements were renewed in 1862-63, 1865-66, 1875-76 and 1887. The assessments were made in a rough manner. The chief basis for formulating the state demand was the rate fixed at the settlement of 1861-62 and this was raised or lowered practically at the discretion of local officers, who

---

125. *Naz-rat* was cess which was in account of nazars in name of various officials. *Jagari* was cess in lieu of free service which the cultivators were supposed to perform for the state *Rozsipahi* was defence cess. *Lipaikot* was a cess charged for the maintenance of villages. *Sarafi* was a coinage cess, *nira sarkar* and *nira tehsildar* were charged for Government and *tehsildar.* vide., Poham Young, *Report on settlement of Patiala.*, 34.
126. *Ibid.*
127. Griffin, *The Rajas of the Punjab* (Patiala : 1970-reprint), 150.

were mainly guided by the comparative case or difficulty with which the revenue was collected. When Young started his operations, the state demand stood at Rs. 43,68,294. From 1861-62 to 1900 there was 40 to 50% increase in the land revenue. Besides the *mal* (the pure land revenue) and the *abwabs* fixed by the cash settlement of 1862, some new taxes came to be charged. The *patwar* cess was introduced in 1862; the road and school cesses in 1871; the hospital cess in 1873 and the postal cess in 1892. Over and above these taxes, numerous other petty cesse were levied.[128] In the Mohindergarh *nizamat* the following extra cesses were also levied :

(i) Bar-i-Doh : A cess dating from the time of the *nawab* of Jhajjar, which was levied at the rate of one to two per cent; *(ii) Itlaq :* An old cess, the origin of which is not clearly ascertainable beyond the fact that *itlaq navis* (desp atcher) and *chaprasi* used to draw their pay from this fund before the area was merged with the Patiala State; *(iii) Begar cess :* In the old times the villagers were required to supply a certain number of collies, of course in turn, to the officer in charge of the district. This custom was discontinued long ago and was replaced by a cash cess amounting to one to two per cent of the land revenue; *(iv) Lambardari :* This cess had been levied at the rate of four per cent on the *mal* in *tehsil* Mohindergarh and at three per cent in *tehsil* Narnaul since the *illaga* came into possession of the Patiala Chief. A similar cess of five per cent was levied from Bhadaur (situated in *tehsil* Barnala), Payal and Sirhind. In other part of the state a small allowance known as *panchai* was given to the *lambardars* of the state, out of the state revenue; *(v) Sarafi :* A cess at the rate of *annas* two per 100 rupees was levied to remunerate the money testers, working at the treasuries of Mohindergarh and Narnaul; *(vi) Maskirat :* This cess was apparently introduced by the Patiala State in 1880 in lieu of leasing the vends of liquor and intoxicating drugs. Although later such sales were prohibited, except under a licence, the cess continued to be levied at eight annas to rupees two per

---

128. *Report on Settlement of Patiala*, 1892-93; *Punjab States Gazetteer*, 152.

annum per village; *(vii) Nankar :* A cess under the head *nankar* was levied in lump sum from a few villages in Narnaul in addition to their revenues, and was paid to *kanungoes, chaudharies* and few *lamberdars* as *sufedposhi* after deducting one-tenth share, which went to the State treasury; *(viii) Mandir Haridas :* A cess at the rate of rupee one to rupees two per annum was levied in Narnaul *tehsil* for the maintenance of Haridas Mandis; *(ix) Gaushala :* A cess at eight annas per cent was recovered for the protection of cows, but money was not credited to the treasury; and *(x) Bhet Gurdwara :* A bi-annual cess of rupee one per estate was levied from Narnaul villages in the name of Gopi Nath Brahmin of Jhajjar in the Nawab's time but as soon as the Patiala State took over, this was converted to Gurdwara cess.[129]

Besides the foregoing cesses *nazars* had to be paid to the following officers at the rates mentioned against each :[130] *(i)* to *diwan* at rupees two-per estate per harvest; *(ii)* to *nizam* at rupees one (in Mohindergarh) only; *(iii)* to *tehsildar* at rupee one; *(iv)* to *thanedar* at rupee one. This meant that a cess of rupees ten in Mohindergarh *nizamat* and rupees eight elsewhere per annum was due from each estate, irrespective of their *jammas.*

The land revenue and other cesses were not realized uniformly from different parts of the state. These shortcomings in the land revenue system continued till 1900. The corrupt revenue officials caused considerable difficulties to the peasants as well as loss to the state. However, Popham Young was appointed settlement Commissioner in 1900, who was to consolidate the state demand by fixing revenue rates of each class of land,[131] in order to end harassment to the *zamindars* and also lessen the account working of the revenue officials. The consolidated demand that young fixed was in theory equal

129. *Punjab States Gazetteer,* 152-54.
130. *Ibid.*
131. Young Popham, *Report on Settlement of Patiala,* 55-56.

to 62½% or the 5/8th of net assets,[132] including all the cesses. Hence, the new rate was fixed in concurrence with the existing rate in the British Punjab.[133] For every rupees 100 realised as land revenue comprised of following items :[134]

(a) *Khalsa* (Ain-ul-mal) : Money that goes to the State exchequer.		Rs. 80%
(b) Rates and cesses :		
(i) local rate, Roads, Schools, Hospitals, Post-offices		Rs. 11%
(ii) *Patwar*		Rs. 4%
(iii) *Lambardari*		Rs. 4%
(iv) *Zaildari*		Rs. 1%
	Total	Rs. 20%
	G. Total	Rs. 100%

For instance, in the agricultural year 1939-40 as per the above standard the following was the break up of state demand under the various heads :[135]

132. (The gross income from an estate was technically called ('gross estate' and 'net assets' was estimated average annual surplus produce of each estate or group of estates remaining after deduction of the ordinary expenses of cultivation as ascertained or estimated. The Governments share was called standard of assessment. It meant that the Government claimed 5/8th of net assets as its share) *vide.*, Mohan Lal, *Punjab Land Revenue Act., XVII of 1887* (Delhi : 1975), 385-94.
133. Popham Young, *Report on Settlement of Patiala*, 55-56.
134. *Administration Report of Patiala State for 1929-30*, 29.
135. This table has been compiled on the basis of statistics given in *Administration Report of Patiala State for 1939-40*, 68-69.

(a) Land Revenue proper (*Khalsa*)		Rs. 36,03,727
(b) Rates and Cesses :		
(i) Local Rate		Rs. 5,84,405
(ii) Patwar		Rs. 2,12,450
(iii) Lambardari		Rs. 2,09,959
(iv) Zaildari		Rs. 55,558
	Total	Rs. 10,62,372
(c) Miscellaneous		Rs. 3,62,297
	G. Total	Rs. 49,76,396

For the fixation of revenue rates all land was divided into two main categories—irrigated and unirrigated. The irrigated land was split into ten heads ranging from *nahri* to *sailab*. The non-irrigated land was split into twelve heads ranging from cultivated to *dakar*. The *tehsils* were divided into different circles according to the type of soils in each, for instance, *jangal, maili, bangar, seoti*, etc. In all there were 37 assessment circles. The highest revenue rates were fixed on lands irrigated by well in *dhaia* assessment circle of the Sirhind *tehsil* which was rupees three and twelve *annas* per *pakka bigha*; in Amargarh circle of Dhuri *tehsil* rupees three and nine *annas* per *pakka bigha*; in Payal circle of Payal *tehsil* rupees three and nine *annas* and six *paisa* per *bigha*; in the Narnaul circle of Narnaul *tehsil* rupees three and eight *annas* per *bigha* in the *pahar* circle of *tehsil* Pinjore, the lowest rates on well irrigated lands were fourteen *annas* per *bigha*; in *naili-bangar* of Bhawanigarh, and in *naili* of Sunam eleven *annas* and eight *annas* three *paisa* in two assessment circles of Bhiki *tehsil*, eight *annas* and nine *paisa* in Sunam *bangar*, and seven *annas* six *paisa* in Bhatinda *tehsil*. The highest *barani* rate was rupees two and one *anna* per *bigha* in *scoti*-circle of Ghanaur *tehsil*. The lowest *barani* rate was three *annas* on sandy soil in Bhatinda circle. The rate by all means would always stick to the general standard of 62% of net produce. In the canal irrigated areas the standard demand was made according to the category of land.[136] A special charge of canal irrigation advantage was left to be charged in the shape of an irrigation levy on the pattern of the British Punjab.[137] At the time of regular settlement, the *banjar* lands were left unassessed. But in later settlements if some owners brought their *banjar* tracts under cultivation those were assessed according to categories of soil which they began to constitute.[138] Assessment on *banjar* lands was light. Those patches of land which become *banjar* later on, were granted remission from land revenue.[139] For instance, as a result of reassessment of Dhuri and Payal *tehsils* in 1937-38, an extra income of rupees 1,05,462 accured to the State.[140]

The cultivators of inferior soil were poor. So Young introduced fluctuating assessment in such areas. Initially twenty *naili* villages came under this scheme. These villages were irrigated by river Ghaggar, a source which was not dependable.[141] During 1929-30 it was still in operation in the *naili* Sunam *tehsil*.

Despite his protections of an equitable assessment and awareness that the '*biswedari*' estates were responsible for the shortfall in assessment.[142] Young appeased the *biswedars* by giving concessions to them. He was made to believe that it was a practice for the *biswedars* to get concessions from the ruler. Later, however, it was found, the assessment of the very large number of *biswedari* estates existing in certain *tehsils* constituted an important but a difficult problem. He devised a formula which he endeavoured to apply impartially to all alike. He fixed the initial *biswedari* concession at 10% in case of resident, and 15% in case of absentee landlords. Behind Young's special favour to the *biswedars* and landlords were the blessings

136. For details of assessment, see Appendix-VI.
137. *Report on Settlement of Patiala*, 32-34.
138. *Administration Report of Patiala State for 1929-30*, 29-30, 59.
139. *Ibid.*
140. *Ibid.*
141. *Report on Settlement of Patiala*, 45.
142. *Ibid.*, 27.

of the Maharaja of Patiala and the British policy of appeasing the landlords. He designed a sliding scale for a further concessions to be granted in consideration of the increase on the past demand to be made after deducting the *biswedari* concession from his assessment of a full and fair assessment.[143] The peasant proprietors of lower rung and tenants did not receive adequate attention from Young; rather he ignored them. This injustice done to both the classes *i.e.* peasant proprietors and tenants by Young later proved to be a source of tremendous strength to the tenants movement. Even Young feared that his report and his endeavours could create more problems than it would solve and problems it did create.

It will not be out of the way to compare assessments of Ludhiana and Ferozepur districts in the British Punjab and that of Patiala state. Both these areas were irrigated by the Sirhind Canal. The total area of the Patiala State was 37,92,598 acres, that of Ludhiana and Ferozepur combined, was 34,92,576 *acres.* In the Patiala State 28,98,242 *acres* were under cultivation. In Ludhiana and Ferozepur the cultivated area was 30,09,042 *acres.* The population of Patiala state was returned at the census of 1901 as 15,97,092 that of the two British districts was 16,31,169. The Patiala state was a little larger than the two districts but had a smaller cultivated area. But in the former the cultivated

---

143. *Ibid,* 39 (The concession formula for *biswedari* estimates for example in case of an absentee landlord whose net assets worked out to Rs. 2400 and whose past revenue demand was Rs. 400, the assessment worked out as follows : Full fair assessment minus *biswedari* concession equals X% increase over past demand. The increase concession justified by x% increase amounts to 4%. The maximum increase concession justified by an enhancement of 200% over 20%.

= 5/8 of Rs. 2,400	= Rs. 1500
Biswedari concession = 15%	= Rs. 225
F.F.A. = 155-225	= Rs. 1275
Rs. 1275 = Rs. 400 (Past Demand)	= Rs. 875
Increase = 218%	= Rs. 175
Increase concessions =	= Rs. 1100

Assessment Rs. 1500 Rs. 225 Rs. 175.

area equalled approximately 1.81 *acres* per head of population, while in the latter the cultivated area per head was 1.88 *acres.*[144] But the state demand in the Patiala state was much higher than that of Ludhiana and Ferozepur district. The land revenue and cesses collected by the Patiala state amounted to Rs. 44,51,806, whereas those demanded by the British authorities in the above districts were only Rs. 26,00,591.[145]

In the mid-thirties fresh assessment was made even after Young's settlement had been made for thirty years. Accordingly, revised assessments of *powadh, jangal* and *seoti* circles of *tehsil* Patiala and sub *tehsil* was also fixed from the same date. The term of land revenue assessment of *tehsil* Kandaghat fixed at the regular settlement also expired in 1938-39. As it was not considered necessary to undertake any revision of settlement of this *tehsil* like other *tehsils* the settlement was extended by ten years.[146] In these assessments, the standard set by Young was adopted. The table given below indicates the extension of cultivation as also the state demand.[147]

Table : 5

Total area of the state in pakka bighas	*Year*	*Cultivated area in pakka bighas*	*State demand in Rs.*
60,71,480	1861-62	35,06,000	38,00,000
	(first settlement)	46,20,861	44,51,006
	1909-10		
	(regular settlement)		
	1929-30		52,39,779
	1939-40	30,26,613	53,13,494

144. Popham Young, *Report on Settlement of Patiala,* 46.
145. *Ibid.*
146. *Ibid.*
147. The following sources have been used to prepare this table : *Administration Report of Patiala State for 1929-30,* 30; *for 1932-33,* 26; *For 1938-39,* 58-59; *For 1939-*40, 65; Popham Young, *Report on Settlement of Patiala,* 8-9, 19, 32; *Patiala Gazettee* (Patiala), July 11, 1934, 150-51. (1939-40 was a draught year, therefore the cultivated area decreased in comparison to the preceding year).

But in collecting the revenue coercive methods were used. In the revenue year 1939-40, thirty-seven defaulters were sent to prison. Movable property worth Rs. 11,285 was attached and some property was actually sold. These coercive methods yielded only Rs. 16,842; but Rs. 1,36,839 could not be recovered.[148] For about a century since its foundation, the land revenue administration of the Patiala state remained at once anomalous and unscientific. The *parganas* or *tehsils* were the highest revenue units, for each of which the only regular officer was a *tehsildar,* though many other functionaries were appointed at the time of *batai.* The assessment being in kind, when it was weighed at the time of sale it was often found to be under weight. In such cases the cultivators were forced to make good half of the State's losses as they were held equally guilty along with the officials for the shortage. The second practice of giving revenue forming rights to influential persons was equally deplorable, for the contractors tried to extract the maximum from the peasants.

In the absence of any scientific system, the revenue rate almost depended on the capacity of the peasants to pay and that of the collectors to collect. However, in the second half of the 19th century, some reforms were introduced in the revenue system. Instead of the *tehsil, nizamat* or district was made a new unit of revenue administration. A uniform cash rate was introduced. Later the Punjab Land revenue Act of 1887 was introduced in the state. The uniform cash rate became meaningless because other taxes were also charged over and above the uniform rate. Young carried out regular settlement in the state from 1900 to 1908. He fixed the units of revenue administration. He introduced three categories of officials—the Revenue Assistant, *naib-tesildars* and *kanungoes.* In villages he introduced *zaildars* instead of *lambardars.* Of course, cash rate was introduced.

---

148. *Administration Report of Patiala State for 1939-40,* 68; and also for 1938-39, 59-60; Dutt, Ramesh, *The Economic History of India,* Vol. I, (Delhi-1976-Reprint), 55-56.

The above discussion highlights the loopholes in the revenue administration of the Patiala state. Young's special favour to the *biswedars* and the creation of *zaildars* as village officers instead of *lambardars* were objectionable and condemnable. From the point of view of topography, area, irrigation facilities and average holdings, the Patiala state and the British districts of Ludhiana and Ferozepur were quite similar. But the revenue charged in the Patiala state was far higher than that in the said British districts. The Patiala state did not feel any sympathy for the poor revenue payers. Even in 1939-40 when the state was hit by drought, the revenue demand of the state was increased by over one lakh rupees, whereas the cropped area went down by about 17 lakh *pakka bighas*. The high revenue and water rate, cruelty in collecting revenue and above all the partiality shown to the agrarian elite or *biswedars*, brought about agrarian crisis which ultimately led to unrest among the lower and middle peasants and tenants. This sense of injustice and exploitation gave birth to the peasant Movement in this region of the Punjab.

The Land Tenures in another important feature of the agrarian structure. Keeping in view the importance of land to human society as well as to the state the British gave top priority to the land problem. The introduction of Permanent Settlement in Bengal (1793) also known as the *zamindari* system was the first major reform of the British in India. Later it was extended to Bihar and Orissa. This reform was the result of the British desire to have certainty of land revenue and creation of a dependable class of agriculturists to guarantee it. This settlement led to creating landlords out of hereditary tax-prayers.[149] In Madras, Thomas Munro introduced the *ryotwari* system in 1820,[150] which was later extended to Bombay, Sindh, Barar and some other areas.[151] The *ryotwari* was a settlement with *ryots* or petty cultivators of land, changing them into

149. Desai, A.R. *Social Background of India Nationalism* (Bombay : 1975), 38.
150. Dutt, Romesh, *op. cit.*, 105.
151. Desai, A.R., *op. cit.*, 40.

owners of land which they cultivated. The *mahalwari* system was introduced in the Punjab and it was extended over most of Northern India. According to this system, settlements were made with village communities and village headmen were made responsible for collection of land revenue. In the Punjab, one and the same man was generally owner as well as cultivator, though he was free to lease out few fields to tenants.[152] Of the three land system, the *ryotwari* and the *mahalwari* system protected better the interests of the actual cultivators. The Punjab Land Alienation Act of 1901 was enforced to save the petty peasants and tenants from being exploited by money-lenders and landlords.[153] Land laws passed in the late 19th and early 20th century tried to give some kind of security to the peasant proprietors and tillers of the soil. Indian National Congress also favoured the cause of the tillers of the soil.[154]

Things were different in the Indian Princely states. The well entrenched feudalistic order was fighting hard to perpetuate itself on the one hand and on the other the feudal lords were exploiting the poor peasants here. In some of these states, like Faridkot and Malerkotla, the rulers by virtue of their being '*ala-maliks*' claimed to be superior owners of most of the land of the state.[155] In other states including Patiala, the rulers, despite general acceptance of proprietary bodies, at least on theory, clung to their right as receivers of both land revenue and rent. Besides artificial landlords—henchmen of the rulers

---

152. Dutt, Romesh, *op. cit.*, Vol. II, 69.
153. (Part of such reforms were the Tenancy Act of 1868 and 1887. These sought to protect the tenants) *vide.*, Dutt, Romesh, *op. cit.*, Vol. II, 342.
154. In 1935 a congress party resolution stated : "....There is only one fundamental method of improving village life, namely the introduction of a system of peasant proprietorship under which the tiller of the soil is himself the owner of it..." Chester Bowles, *Who owners the land*? (New Delhi : 1964), 6.
155. Walia, Romesh, *Praja Mandal Movement in East Punjab State* (Patiala 1972), 48; Statement of Wazir Singh Daftriwala, Oral History Cell, File No. 41, Punjab Historical Studies Department, Punjabi University, Patiala.

were imposed on the tillers of the soil. To understand fully the agrarian system of the Punjab state it is imperative to examine various tenures current there. Indeed, the land tenures are of pivotal importance to our subject of study, because the settlement of tenures led to the agrarian unrest in the state. In the absence of adequate records in this respect,[156] we have to bank heavily on British accounts—a source which should be carefully shifted before being put to use. The settlement operation of Major Popham Young in Patiala was of course, the first scientific attempt in this direction.

It is wrong to say that the proprietorship of land rested with the ruler alone. Before the British rule the land did belong to the peasantry and the government received revenue in proportion to the fertility of the soil.[157] Popham Young also does not agree to the wrong view of some European writers that land belonged to the ruler only.[158] This way the proprietorship was subject to the sovereign rights in as much as the owner was expected to pay land revenue. There was no question of free alienation. The right to abandon or dispose of the land as its holder might choose, which is the essential feature of modern proprietary right. If in one sense the land belonged to the peasant in another the peasant belonged to the land. He would not leave it or refuse to cultivate it.[159]

The rulers of Patiala state had no direct heritage from the predecessor government. After the disintegration of the Mughal administration, several, families and tribal groups usurped or

---

156. *Punjab States Gazetteer*, 93 (Evan Infan Habib in his work. *The Agrarian System of the Mughals : 1526-1707*, states both the agriculture and agricultural statistics and census are often incomplete, especially in the earlier years in respect of the princely states. See page 9).
157. (The prominent among the writers who travelled to Indian in the 16th and 17th centuries and wrote their accounts were J. Xavier, Thomas Roe, Barnier, Fryer and Manucci) *vide.*, Irfan Habib, *op. cit.*, 111; Dutt, R.P., *India Today* (Bombay : 1947), 221.
158. Popham Young, *Report on Settlement of Patiala*, 17.
159. Irfan Habib, *op. cit.*, 115.

occupied lands. As a result, sovereign protection in lieu of payment of land revenue became meaningless. Most of the Malwa villages voluntarily sought protection under strongmen like Ala Singh of Patiala. The Patiala ruler became both the landlord and the sovereign.[160] But with the passage of time this dual control disappeared as the sovereign waxed and the landlord waned.[161] The vast areas of land and its ownership were passed on to their traditional owners.[162] The dual control was, however, maintained in some of the *khalsa* tract, which included hamlets initially taken by the ancestors of the Patiala rulers, or it was forced on tracts in the vicinity of their seat of power, which they wanted to possess as their personal estate.[163] At other times the compatriots of the rulers which included their relatives and kinsmen secured land on payment of minor *nazranas*. Sometimes, as in the earlier phase of the rule, in the face of internal or external crises, liberal land grants were made to men of influence to win them over. From the revenues accruing to them they were expected to maintain their contingents ready for service. Certain other factors were also responsible for effecting grants of land.[164] In short, it was a

160. Popham Young, *Report on Settlement of Patiala*, 16.

161. Ibid.

162. With regard to this we can drawn parallels to the fact brought out by two very interesting and informative agrarian studies on Trans-Satluj, Punjab, namely. *Vilyatpur : 1848-1968* and *Agrarian Society of the Punjab*. In these two studies there is a mention that at the end of the Mughal rule new peasants' bodies with same rights like collection of rent on land were imposed on the existing one. While the older *Jagirdars* and *zamindars* kept alive their proprietary claims, which some of them did manage to reacquire, at the time of British settlements. See Tom G. Kissinger, *Vilyatpur : 1948-1964* (New Delhi : 1979), 30-35, 38-40, Banerjee Himadri, *Agrarian Society of the Punjab* (New Delhi : 1982), 3.

163. For instance, the Bahadurgarh estate which is just 8 kilometers from Patiala, was owned as personal estate until recently by the erstwhile ruling family, See PSR, PM Office File No. 847, PSA, Patiala.

164. Punjab State Gazetteer, 144; Griffin, Lepal, *The Rajas of the Punjab* (Patiala : 1970-reprint), 125-26.

favourite plan of the Sikh government to carve out new estates, regardless of existing rights, and plant new settlements on cultivated land. Sometimes the object in view was to reward faithful service, sometimes replace thriftless cultivators, sometimes to plant a hostile colony in the neighbourhood of a powerful feudatory.

Resourceful men from within or without the village were deputed to collect the revenue; and for this he was given *inam naugiari*—definite share from the revenue collected.[165] In many villages, however, a landlord or a *biswedar* was imposed upon the cultivating community by the will of the ruler.[166] These were colonized when peace and order was established; many villages were founded in waste lands by men who were in a position to impose upon those desirous of cultivating lands such terms as were economically practicable. These men were given *sanads* to this effect.[167]

Before the regular settlement there was no formal record of tenants or *biswedars*. Both the tenants and proprietors were entered as *asamis* in the records of the summary settlement of 1875.[168] Before the regular settlement of 1908, the Chief of Patiala state besides collecting the land revenue never gave up his claim over full rental or in other words landlords' profits. All the

---

165. It is believed that at the time of introduction of cash assessments, an extra payment of eleven (giara) per cent of the revenue was realized from the villages and nine percent was repaid to the *biswedars* (collectors) in recognition of their states. The right descended from father to son and the person receiving this *inam* was acknowledged as a *biswedar*. However small the amount was it was greatly prized. Slowly the receipt of *inam naugiari* came to be considered as the test of full ownership, carrying with it a share in the village common gland. Young recommended its abolition. However later of its own, while various rights in land were articulated by the settlement, the value of *inam* as a measure for ownership diminished.
166. Popham Young, *Report on Settlement of Patiala*, 17.
167. Griffin, Lepel, *op. cit.*, 157.
168. *Punjab State Gazetteer*, 93.

occupants of the land called owners or tenants were liable to pay the rent. The position of the so-called owner was little better than that of a priviledged or superior tenant or a tenant-in-chief.[169]

Rights of the tenants were not formally laid down before the regular settlement. Some trends, though hazy, did begin to emerge after the summary settlement of 1862, but they became clear only when the Punjab tenancy laws began to be applied in the State in the last decade of the nineteenth century.

The land in Patiala state was cultivated by village communities whose members though in legal terms did not have any claim to proprietary rights, yet cultivated the lands in their occupation on almost the same terms as recognized proprietors, and they had done so far long periods.[170] Some of them had been the first to bring under cultivation the land in their possession by reclaiming the *multar* (or waste land) customarily; they paid a share of their land produce direct to the State whereas else paid rent in revenue rates.[171] Regarding the existence of occupancy tenancies in the State, Young held : "Prior to this settlement the existence of a right of occupancy on the part of tenants of old standing had been recognized both by the public opinion and authority. But there was no clear understanding either how these rights were acquired or what they amounted to".[172]

Even in the absence of a 'clear understanding' the tenants of longstanding referred to above were not liable to ejectment. Till the summary settlement of 1862 no distinction between occupancy and non-occupancy tenants was made; and it was

169. In fact, *asami,* and *kashtkar* are the words interchangeably used which according to *Punjab States Gazetteer* stand for a tenant (*muzara*). They may be put closer to a cultivator. See *Punjab State Gazetteer,* 146.
170. PSR, PM's Officer File No. 1103, PSA, Patiala; Papham Young, *Report on Settlement,* 19.
171. *Punjab State Gazetter,* 146.
172. PSR, *Ijlas-i-khas.* File No. 1266, PSA, Patiala.

not till 1867 that the word *maurusi*[173] gained popularity in the state.

In 1867 a royal decree was issued that no person cultivating land with a proprietary right be declared a *maursi muzara* (tenant). But in 1872, in line with the Punjab Tenancy Act of 1868, the state ordered that any tenant cultivating a piece of land for thirty years be recognized as *maurasi* tenant.[174] This rule, however, was never carried out in practice. Sometimes tenants with over thirty years of possession were not confirmed as maurasi muzaras and at other times twenty-five years of possession was enough to secure proprietary rights.[175] At one time it was decided to enforce the Punjab Tenancy act in the State in Toto which never meterialised. But when certain tenancy disputes arose the provisions of the Act were referred to. Most of the illiterate and ignorant tenants never cared to assert their claims of occupancy. The *biswedars* also never thought in terms of ejecting them as long as they paid their rent.[176] But on the commencement of regular settlement, fearing that the tenants might be declared *maurusis,* the *biswedars* started ousting them without legal process and without regard to the proper time of ejectment. On the other hand, some cultivators who had been long out of possession took advantage of the weakness of the landowners and forcibly occupied fields which they had seldom or never cultivated. There were sudden violent clashes between the tenants and landlords. To unnecessarily harass the tenants, even those with legitimate claims, were dragged to courts by *biswedars* on frivolous grounds. A great majority of 17,706 cases, that were fought in the appelate courts of the settlement were concerned with tenant's rights and liabilities.[177]

In order to prevent these violence, the Punjab Tenancy Act of 1887 was introduced in the Patiala State. It was enforced

173. For details see *Young, Report on Settlement of Patiala,* 27.
174. *Punjab State Gazetteer,* 146.
175. *Ibid.*
176. *Ibid.*
177. *Ibid.*

with slight modifications, necessitated by local conditions from 15th September 1901. But this Act did not check litigation. There were disputes for proprietary title between cultivating residents and descendants of the founder of the village. He claimed that his admitted right as *majidars* covered proprietary title as well.[178] There was a strong alliance between the *ahalkar* (officers) and *biswedars*. Sometimes shall proprietors with official connections became occupancy tenants; and old tenants in *biswedari* estate became mere tenants-at-will.[179] Under the above circumstances no system could be better devised to give rise to disputes leading to litigatin.[180] Sometimes even descendants of the founders of a village were force to share equally with tenant cultivators. However, Young's efforts to display fair play and justice also proved futile.

According to the final settlement report of 1908, 700 villages of the state were marked as biswedari villages.[181] The *biswedars* did not cultivate lands themselves in these villages. The so-called tenants of the villages were in possession of land that they cultivated for long duration. In Patiala the *biswedari* tenures ranged from nineteen to twenty-one per cent, and these to were concentrated in a few *tehsils*, those of Mansa, Sunam and Barnala, whereas no where else in the region of the Sikh rulers did the proportion appear to have been even 10% of the total.[182]

In addition to the biswedars, there were jagirdars, who were feudatories of Patiala rulers. The chief *jagirs* were those of Bhadaur[183] and Khamanon.[184] While the *Sardars* of Bhadaur

178. Young, *Report on Settlement of Patiala*, 28.
179. *Ibid.*, 27.
180. *Ibid.*
181. *Ibid*, 25
182. The number of biswedari villages grew with passage of time. By 1948, they stood at 784, See PSR, PM's Office File Nos. 5804, 6157 and *Ijlas-i-khas* File No. 2077, PSA, Patiala.
183. The averages have been worked out on the basis of *census Report of Patiala State from 1911 to 1941*; also see Walia Romesh, *op. cit.*, 96; Banga, Indu, *op. cit.*, 171.
184. For more details see Grifin, Lepel, *op. cit.*, 27-99.

received rupees 70,000 per annum, those of Khamanon got rupees 90,000. In addition, they were landlords of some villages that came under them and were in effect *biswedars* of those tracts. The *jagir* of Payal[185] constituted the only remaining *jagir* of note. The value of this jagir amounted to about rupees 18,000 per annum.[186]

A vast majority of the villages of Patiala state, like those of the Punjab,[187] were under the cultivation of peasant proprietors. Out of the total number of recorded holdings of 337,555 in 1931, 256,033 or 75.85 per cent of the recorded holdings belonged to the peasant proprietors. Likewise of 40,5343 recorded holdings in 1941, 258,381 or 63.74 per cent of the recorded holdings belonged to peasant proprietors.[188]

A vast majority of the villages of Patiala state were under the cultivation fo peasant proprietors. One from among the community in these villages had been given *malguzari* rights and he performed the functions of a *lambardar*. After the regular settlement when the proprietors were given *pattas* or ownership deeds, the division of land began to be governed by ancestral shares. This gave rise to pattedari system.[189] It was the peasant proprietor villages that generally spearheaded the political dissent in the state, specially in the nascent stages of its growth. Later they vigorously supported the tenants cause.

Under the regular settlement affected by Young, there were two types of tenants : *(a)* the *ghair maurusi* or the tenants-at-will; *(b)* the *maursi* tenants or occupancy tenants under Sections 5,6 and 8 of Punjab Tenancy Act. The tenancy claims were

---

185. For further details see *Ibid.*, 228-31.
186. *Imperial Gazetteer of India Provincial Series Punjab*, Vol. II (Calcutta : 1908), 295.
187. M.L. Darling in his monumental work has described the British Punjab as the land of peasant proprietors. For details see Darling's *Punjab Peasant in Prosperity and Debt* (London : 1925).
188. *Punjab States Gazetter*, 155-56; *Imperial Gazetter Punjab*, 294-95.
189. *Census Report of Patiala State for 1941*, 249.

hereditary. The former could be easily ejected from land, while the latter had permanent occupancy rights. The regular settlement recorded 34,394 occupancy holdings, comprising a total area of 503,602 *pakka bighas,* of these tenancies 23,479 were closed under section 5 of Tenancy Act, 2,879 under section 6 and 8,036 under section 8. In 1910-11, 11,42,244 *acres* of land were under occupancy and non-occupancy holdings. It comprised 39,18% of total cultivable land in acres.[190] There were 35,318 holdings of non-occupancy tenants which extended over 2,01,573 *acres* of land and there were 3,00,826 holdings of occupancy tenants spread over 9,33,312 *acres* of the state land.[191] The vague idea on the subject of land tenure prevailing in the British India seems to have been hurriedly applied to Patiala. Young seems to have become a prey to the machinations of the unholy alliance between the *biswedars* and *ahalkars* of the Patiala state. Any type of *biswedari* imposed on settled villages had no justification.[192] For example, with the state beginning to pay cash salaries, the *jagirs* of army should have automatically lapsed. The mafidars or the holders of *inam naugiari* who were confirmed as *biswedars,* we know, were in early stages' only tax-farmers. As Young himself admitted :[193]

> Generally speaking, the landlord, in ambryonic stage of his existence..., was allowed to recover from the cultivators a small cess over and above the payment which had to be made to the state. This in its original simplicity was the *'hag serina'*, which was limited to one *ser* in a *maund* of produce raised. Eventually the state itself contributed something to the support of the landlord in the shape of drawback from the revenue. Finally, when contract

190. *Punjab State Gazetteer,* 144 (For details regarding Land Tenures in Patiala State also see *Imperial Gazetteer Punjab,* 288.
191. According to one estimate 1/5th of the State's population comprised of the tenants. For this see AISPC-Papers, File No. 133-A (ii), NMML, New Delhi.
192. PSR, PM's Office File No. 1103, PSA, Patiala (See in this file the report of Sardar Nathu Lal, Settlement Officer), Popham Young, *Report on Settlemnt of Patiala,* 17.
193. Griffin, Lepel, *op. cit.,* 250-51.

settlements on case basis were introduced, those who had acquired the *biswedari* status were in a position to retain for themselves the old state share of the produce, plus the *serine,* plus a number of other cesses, which had gradually been introduced on pretext or another, and also the whole of the drawback from the revenue, or *inam,* allowed to those who were classed as responsible *malguzars,* or revenue payer.

Young, the Settlement Officer, in his report said that sometimes the claims of the tenants were not inferior to those of *biswedars.* Even then the State courts often delivered judgement in favour of the *biswedars* because they were men of influence and could get things done. For example, in the *muzara-biswedar* dispute of Kishangarh Pherwahi the tenants submitted that they were in possession of Kishangarh land since 1743, while the biswedars were imposed only in 1829. For some time the *biswedars* and the tenants used to pay *batai* on equal footing. It was only in the settlement of 1870 that *biswedars* exercising their influence got themselves recorded as *maliks* and the tenants as *muzaras.*[194] In fact, the Patiala state was not interested in safeguarding the interest of the actual cultivators.

Probing further for example according to the revenue statement of financial year 1868-69 out of the gross revenue receipts of rupees 38,18,309 only rupees 10,000 was left back (on some plots of land, generally 2-4 ploughs) as allowance to *biswedars* 'for distinction and maintenance'. There is no mention in the statement of proprietary right of *biswedars* over certain villages.[195]

Where the *sandas* were granted in exchange of minor *nazranas* say presenting of a horse to the ruler, Sardar Nathu Ram the Settlement Officer in his report of 1928 strongly suggested revision of their rights.[196] Even in the case where villages were settled by *biswedars,* the tenants claims were quite

194. PSR, PM's Office File No. 1103, PSA, Patiala.
195. PSR, *Ijlas-i-khas,* File No. 1264.
196. PSR, *Ijlas-i-khas,* File No. 1968, PSA, Patiala.

solid for in those early days it was certain that the competition between the landlords was not for land but for tenants.[197]

The peasantry in the Patiala state could be divided into three categories—*biswedars,* peasant proprietors and tenants. The state had a soft corner for the *biswedars* and they continued to be imposed upon the tenants, though their proprietary claims had no legitimate basis. A majority of villages in the Patiala state had peasant proprietary tenure and there was agragian peace and harmony. The peace and harmony of these village was, however, distributed by growing peasant unrest in the neighbouring Punjab. Now, there was some activity in this class and men from among this class provided the first political leadership cadre in this region. The peasant proprietors had a natural relationship with the lower peasants or the tenants. They fought shoulder to shoulder with the lower peasants when the peasant movement gained momentum. But the tenants especially the non-occupancy tenants were the most miserable. The tenancy laws having been enforced, the landlords wanted that none in future could claim to be a *maurusi* tenant. Hence, the *bisw-edars,* therefore, would change the pieces of land that the *Gair maurusi* tenants cultivated, after every one or two years. The chief grievance of the *maurusi muzaras* was that their proprietary claim was no less legitimate than that of the *biswedars* in accordance with Tenancy Laws, while the *ghair-maurusis* felt cheated because many a time tenants with influence, though with no better claims than their's were, recognized a *maurusis.* The core of the agrarian crisis in the Patiala state was that the occupancy tenants aspired for full proprietary rights and the non-occupancy tenants wanted the *maurusi* status. These were some of the grievances that the peasant movement aired and assured the tenantry to get

197. This impression one gathers after going through the relevant documents pertaining to tenant movement in the states. The issue of the abolition of *batai* was raised from the very start of the peasant's movement.

redressed at later stages. Even the much vaunted settlement of Young fell flat when it came to treating the tenants with regard to payment of land revenue.

The tenants continued to pay land revenue in kind to landlords and this remained an irritant in agrarian social relations.[198] Though in 1861-62 cash rates were introduced, *kankut* system continued for the tenantry. In fact, in 1872 kind rates were fixed for tenants by a special decree. Though they were finally abolished at the time of the enforcement of regular settlement, yet they continued till 1948. Even no attempt was made to regularize the *batai* system and it continued to be exacted at the fear of *biswedars* whip and at arbitrary local rates. The system of *kankut* made the tenants all the more miserable. While the crops still stood, rates were fixed. The rate once fixed was unchangeable. Actually at the time of a harvest a field might yield much less than the crop determined for *batai*.[199] Besides the cruel *batai* there were arbitrary taxes imposed on the tenantry; one such tax was known as, '*khush hasiyat*' tax or cheerfulness tax which was three *annas* per *bigha* and had no reasonable basis.[200] *Abiana* or water tax was far higher than that which was charged in the British territory.[201]

Young's successor Nathu Ram as the state settlement office bitterly criticized Young's tenurial arrangement. He ordered a complete revision and amendment of the settlement but nothing worthwhile was done in practice.[202] The helpless peasants were a picture of abject misery. Their patience was more in practice.[203] The helpless peasant were a picture of abject misery. Their patience was monumental. But everything has its limit. The excessive land revenue, numerous taxes, the cruel *batai* system,

198. State of Daftriwala, *op. cit.*, 1.
199. PSR, PM's Office File No. 6157, PSA, Patiala.
200. For details see statement of Daftriwala, *op. cit.*, 45.
201. AISPC-Papers, File No. 138-A(ii), NMML, New Delhi.
202. *Indictment of Patiala*, para-89.
203. PSR, PM's Office File Nos. 1155, 1860, 4516, PSA, Patiala.

insecurity of tenures and lack of minimum civic amenities condemned an average peasant to a cesspool of misery? drudgery and frustration.[204] The conditions noticed in the states were reminiscent of the pre-revolutionary France. And this situation led to the peasant revolution.

204. PSR, PM's Office, File No. 1103, PSA. Patiala.

3 AWAKENING AMONG PEASANTS : CAUSES

At the very outset of the twentieth century princely states of the Punjab were integrated with the rest of the British Punjab and the rest of the country from the economic view point. But, if we take the country as a whole in respect of internal developments, there were great variations among the native states of India. While some like Baroda and Mysore had made remarkable progress in the fields of Industry and education, etc. Others like Hyderabad, Bhawalpur (now in Pakistan) and the East Punjab states (Patiala, Nabha, Malerkotla, Faridkot, Kapurthala and others) lagged behind.[1] Historical factors and the economic and administrative policy of the Government in each state had bearing on the political attitudes and movements associated with it. It will be worthwhile to study the conditions prevailing in the East Punjab states during the period of our study.

It is well known fact that since 1809 the relations of these states with the British continued to be friendly and the unbroken record of loyal and faithful service reached its zenith in 1914 when the states mobilized their total resources in support of the war effects. Their contribution in cash and material was Rs. 1.2 *crore* or a sum nearing its total revenue for a whole year. More than 28,000 recruits were supplied by these states which gave a staggering proportion of one out of every ten male

1. Home Department, File No. 17/6/1939-Political, NAI, New Delhi; *The National* (Lahore), 13th April, 1923; *Reports on the Native Newspapers Punjab* : 1923, 267; File No. G-35-AICC (A letter from Mr. R.S. Azad to Mahatma Gandhi), 3, NMML, Teen Murti, New Delhi.

persons of the fighting age.[2] But the Punjab came to be very harshly treated during war and harsh methods were applied by the British bureaucrats in the mater of conscription and forcible realization of war funds.[3]

During the period under review, the policies of the rulers of princely states; their personal style or mode of functioning and centralisation of power in one individual or at least a group of persons made decision-making either too protracted or too rough as also ready and abrupt a process. Again, the administration in most of the states lacked the bureaucratic efficiency of the Government in British India, allowing situations to reach a crisis point in the former much oftener than in the latter.[4] There were areas like Mohindergarh, Bawal and Dadri possessed by Patiala, Nabha and Jind respectively bordering on United provinces, Rajasthan and Delhi, where

---

2. *Some Confidential Papers of the Akali Movement,* Dr. Ganda Singh (*ed*)., Amritsar : *Sikh Itihas Research Board,* S.G.P.C., 1965, 175-89. (The services which the Malerkotla rendered to Great Britain during the Great War can never be forgotten. From 1914 to the last days of the war this force was constantly on active service and suffered heavy casualities which were made good by reinforcement from the state. The total number of subjects who served during the war was over 31 per cent of the eligible male population, surpassed only by two British districts). Vide., File On. 32-AICC (Indian states and Round Table Conference), NMML, Teen Murti, New Delhi.
3. File No. 32-AICC, NMML, Teen Murti, New Delhi, Ramesh Walia *A Study of the Praja Mandal Movement in the East Punjab States,* Punjabi University Publication, Patiala : 1974-56.
4. File No.60, State Proceedings of the Second Conference of the *Punjab Riyasti Praja Mandal* held at Ludhiana on 11, 12 and 13 October, 1930, (Fore further details see File No. G-35-AICC (long unheeded and unbearable *zulum* by the Maharaja of Patiala); Basta No. 13, Proceedings of the 4th Patiala Conference held at village Tungwali, P.S., Nathana, District Ferozepur; Serial No. 595, Case No. 485/13 of 1929; Serial No. 138, File No. 25 of 1938 *Records of the Kalsia State* : Punjab State Archieves, Basta No. 18, case No. 224 of 1928, PSA : Patiala.

people, particularly the ruralties as well as the lower officials were subjected to harassment from the states' administration. The peasants/tenants in these areas were subjected to an arbitrary and oppressive administrative machinery of the Punjab states.[5]

Absence of timely and impartial justice and other such things were very common which disappointed the masses, particularly the tenants and peasants. They were annoyed and dissatisfied with the utter lack of efficiency in the administration of the princely states and the Government machinery, which contrasted with the bureaucratic efficiency and morality in the Government of the British Punjab. At the same time, the liberty that the people enjoyed in the British Punjab had not been discernible in the Punjab States at this time and nor were there any kind of representative institutions. Besides, the rulers and their *ahlkars* had adopted a repressive policy and there was absolutely no check on them. Owing to this policy, on one hand, inefficiency and instability crept into the administration of these states and on the other, the already provocative situation deteriorated further. With it developed the feelings of disappointment and opposition among he masses and the rebellious instinct got strengthened. This also pushed the peoples' agitation and resistance into different forms from those in the neighbouring British districts. However, these ways were quite different from those adopted in the regions of the British Punjab.

---

5. File No. G-35 (A letter from Mr. R.S. Azad to Mahatma Gandhi dated 25th Septemebr, 1938); Ramesh Walia, *A Study of the Praja Mandal Movement in the East Punjab States,* Patiala : 1974, 56; Handa, R.L., *History of Freedom Struggle in Princely States,* Central News Agency : Delhi, 1968, 138-39; File No. 565/C of 1939-PSR, PM's Office Files, Basta No. 179 Case No. (Welcome address made by Harnam Singh of Dharmgarh-Kisan Conference held at village Chau near Mansa); Serial No. 138, File No. 25 Of 1938-*Kalsia State Records*; Case No. 377/C of 1930; PSA, Patiala.

At the very outset let it be noted, while the Haryana and the hilly areas (then the parts of Punjab) were predominantly Hindu with a sizeable number of Muslims, they had practically no Sikh population except some men in the Government service,[6] whereas these states were, mainly inhabited by Sikhs; it was a matter of special significance to these states. Sikh were generally agriculturists and they had a large share of the jobs in the armed forces. Sikhs were also dominating among the landed aristocracy particularly in the states of Patiala, Nabha, Kalsia and Faridkot.

To all intents and purposes, the economy of these states represented all that was backward and conservative in India as a whole. Practically no effort was made to assess and evaluate the mineral resources or to set up any industry in this region of the Punjab. A vast majority of the population lived in villages. According to the 1931 census, only 10.4% of the total population in Patiala state lived in urban areas.[7] Agriculture was the mainstay of the people. Out of a population of 16,25,520 more than 10 lacs directly depended on agriculture. A large majority of about 2.5 lakhs of artisans and about a lakhs of traders also indirectly depended on it.[8] The Punjab Government was, however, callous and careless and did absolutely nothing for the progress of agriculture; while in the Punjab the situation was changing fast with the colonisation of vast areas in the *Bari-Doab* districts, provision of relief against rural indebtedness, popularization of better methods of cultivation and consolidation of holdings, in the states agriculture continued suffering under the debt weight of an unchanging exploitative system. But for the provision of certain irrigational facilities which too came as a by-produce of the development of the canal

---

6. *Census Report of Patiala State* : 1931., printed at Civil Military Gazette Limited : Lahore.
7. *Ibid.*
8. *Ibid.*

system in British Punjab the princes did nothing for ameliorating the lot of the peasants.[9]

The rulers and their courtiers were concerned only with the revenue of the states and the chief criterion of efficiency of an administrator was the state of revenue under his control. The states existed for the pleasures of the princes. The Kapurthala Maharaja, for example, had a reputation of spending most of his time abroad and was rarely available in his own statte.[10] Every thing was done to satisfy the whims of the individual ruler. Consequently, the people, particularly the peasants and tenants, at large suffered utter neglect. A glance at the budget of these states will be helpful to understand the economic grievances of the peasantry in particular and others in general. Let us take for instance, the situation in Patiala.[11] The first administration report was published in 1920-21 which showed an annual income of Rs. 135 *crores* which continued rising despite the steep fall in the prices of agriculture produce, till it stood at Rs. 1.59 *crores* in 1929-30. Out of this, commerce and industry contributed a meagre sum of Rs. 1 lac. The report for 1932-33 admitted the effect of abnormal fall in the prices of agricultural produce on the agriculturists, but did not suggest any relief measures. Instead it treated he whole mare as a simple

---

9. Handa, R.L., *History of Freedom Struggle in Princely States,* Delhi : 1968, 271; Nehru, Jawaharlal, *An Autobiography,* 113; Ramesh Walia, *A Study of the Praja Mandal Movement in the East Punjab States,* Patiala : 1974, 58; File No. 60-Prime Minister Office Files, PSA : Patiala; Personal interview with Master Hari Singh, Communist Office, Chandigarh on December 19th & 20th 1978; File No. 139, *AISPC Papers;* Part I, *Partap* (Lahore), June 26th, 1921; Report on the native Newspapers, 1921, 69, NAI, New Delhi.
10. The *Liberal,* 22nd June, 1921; *Bande Mataram,* 28th June, 1921 Dewan Raj Kumar, *Modern* Kapurthala *and Its Maker,* A Kapurthala State Government Publication, (For more details see Fortnightly reports of the year 1921, Home Department Political, NAI, New Delhi).
11. *Patiala State Administration Report for 1932* : also see Sr. No. 138, File No. 25 of 1938, State Kalsia, PSA, Patiala.

law and order problem which had led to dacoities and other crimes. According to the official report, "political unrest, economic depression and heavy unemployment combined to promote the spirit of lawlessness and various gangs of dacoits sprang up".[12] The Revenue Department with the help of police, on the other hand was resorting to more and more coercive measures in realising the land revenue. He following figures speak for themselves : [13]

	1929-30	*1932-33*
No. of writ demands and *Dastaks*	870	1250
Warrants and Arrests issue	117	479
Cases of imprisonment	3	118

Thus the peasants were crushed under a heavy load and had been reeling under miseries and atrocities for a long period. Actually the rates of land revenue and *abiana* were quite high. If these rates are compared to those in the neighouring British Punjab region, it becomes evident that injustice was being meted out to the peasants in the states. So, the demand to reduce these rates was a common and justified one and it too caused unrest among the peasants and tenants.

Further, while the state was extracting every peny due from the peasants, it was doing absolutely nothing for them. No *taccavi* advances were granted in the years 1929-30 and 1932-33. The outstanding of the old *taccavi* at the beginning of the year was Rs. 2158.[14] Similarly, the disposal of the cases for compensation for land acquired by the state had been much in arrears. There was a balance of 201 cases of the previous year

---

12. Memorandum submitted by the members of the Patiala War Council, Patiala, *Patiala State Records* : Prime Minister's Office, File No. 565/C-1939 (*Biswedar Hakumat Da Namuna*-an article in Punjabi); Dewan's letter dated 20th November, 1939, *Kalsia State Records,* File No. 164; File no. 182, Ramesh Walia, *A Study of the Praja Mandal Movement in the East Punjab States,* Patiala : 1974, 69.
13. *Patiala State Administration Report for 1929-30 and 1932-33.*
14. *Ibid.*

and 50 new cases were instituted in the year 1932-33. There was thus a total of 251 cases and 7 out of these had been finally settled.[15] There were only seven co-operative societies working in the Patiala state, four of them were agricultural and here non-agricultural. Their total working capital was just Rs. 75 thousand.

The report of 1920-21 admitted that no new road had been built since 1907-08. There could be no expansion of irrigational facilities because of the stringency of funds caused by the financial equilibrium having been seriously disturbed during the first world war. In 1924, even Nabha town had no metalled roads.[16] About any cut being applied to the privy-purses of the prices or any economy affected in their levish expenses, the reports are absolutely silent. Moreover, the budgetary policies, heavily loaded in favour of the rulers, attached little importance to the welfare of the peasants/tenants and the expenditure on public welfare agencies was negligible. It was, therefore, quite natural for any political movement to demand restrictions on the privy-purses and to have more funds shifted to the construction of roads, hospitals and schools in the countryside.[17]

---

15. Typed copy of an article by Singh, G.B. of Nabha, available in the Library, S.G.P.C., Amritsar; Home Department, File No. 79/ 1931-Political, 19, NAI, New Delhi; Sr. No. 1546, Prime Minister's Office, Files, PSA : Patiala.
16. *Patiala State Adminsitration Report for 1920-21,* PSA : Patiala; Vaid, Chhajju Mal, '*Pepsu Ch MuzariariDa Ghol Ten* communist Party (in Panjabi), *Souvenir,* issued by the Communist Party in January, 1976.
17. File No. 138, Part-I, AISPC-Papers, NMML, New Delhi. 42.2% was being spent on administration and army and just 2.7% on education and 2.5% on medical facilities in Patiala State. The same was true of Kapurthala and Faridkot. In Faridkot in 1910-11, the state spent 5 lacs out of 12 lacs on the ruler's marriage. *Vide.* Joginder Dayal, '*Riyasti Lokan Da Ghol Ten* Communists', *Souvenir,* issued on 26th January, 1976 by the GPI; Handa, R.L., *History of Freedom Struggle in Princely State,* Delhi : 1968, 70;

(Contd...)

Another important aspect of these policies was that they were not at all conducive to increase in agricultural production or reduction of rural indebtedness.[18] Though banking institutions made their appearance quite early, yet it was more or less a Government agency and its main function was to provide short term credit to grain dealers and other traders. It did nothing practically for the economic advancement of the states. To rural co-operative societies, for example, the bank advanced a sum of Rs. 20.8 thousand in the year 1926-27 in Patiala State. In fact, the bank was merely co-operative in name; it was a joint stock concern with effective control, in the hands of the Government. Consequently, peasantry in the state was not benefited by this institution at all.[19]

All the state services were monoplised by the landed aristocracy or the urban Hindu traders and immigrants from British India. Only the army had a handful of jobs to provide to the common village folk. It was purely through the favour of the prince or his ministers that one could get a job or retain it. Corruption was rampant and in some states, the posts were openly auctioned.[20] Efforts were made to recruit only such persons as were close relatives or co-religionists of the state

---

(17. Contd...)

Ramesh Walia, *A Study of the Praja Mandal Movement in the East Punjab States,* Patialal : 1974, 63; For more details about the expenses of the ruler See "*Indian Princes as the People see Them*".

18. File No. 138, part-I, AISPC-Papers, NMML, New Delhi; Ramesh Walia, *A Study of the Praja Mandal Movement in the East Punjab States,* Patiala : 1974 : 63, Vaid, Chajju Mal, "Tenant Struggle in *Pepsu* Area", *Souvenir,* issued on the eve of 21st National Confernece, All India *Kisan Sabha,* Bhatinda : 1973; Sr. No. 4756, Case No. 1025 of 1892 Sambat/611-C; Basta No. 51 file No.565/ C and 1017/C. PSA : Patiala.
19. Ramesh Walia, *A Study of the Praja Mandal Movement in the East Punjab States,* Patiala : 1974, 67-68.
20. Personal meeting with Giani Kartar Singh of village Chak Malerkotla : January 15-16, 1976; interview with Sewa Singh Bapla, Malerkotla : January 17-18, 1976; Interview with Ishar Singh Majhail at Patiala on July 20-21, 1976; Basta No. 20, Case No. 485, PSA : Patiala.

officials or favourites of the ruler. An aggrieved employee could hardly secure justice if he had no influence over some ahalkar.[21]

With the introduction of Minto-Moreley reforms in 1909 a strong people's movement represented by the Indian National Congress (hereafter INC), backed the cause of legislative assemblies in British India. The steadily growing political consciousness of the people never allowed the British rulers to retrace a step once it had been taken, but in the states, the people were deprived of such assemblies, reforms and political awareness.[22] Moreover, the local-self Government institutions which became in British Punjab an effective instrument for the spread of political ideas and provided training facilities for budding leaders, did not play any such role in the states. Another agency which could have played a positive role in imparting consciousness among the peasants and tenants was the village school, but educationally the states were backward. In 1933, Patiala, the biggest of the East Punjab States, was sending 1.24 students to schools per hundred of population as against 4.44% in the British Punjab.[23] It was no wonder then

---

21. Puri, Sahib Chand, *Ahlkari Sazshen,* Pulkian Samachar Publications : Patiala; Every Minister had his own clique and there were plots and counter plots to gain access to the ruler. *Vide.,* Diwan, Jermani Dass, *Maharaja* (A number of interesting incidents have been related by the authors of *Ahlkari Sazshen.*
22. The Kapurthala State Assembly, for instance, never met after 1931 as some of the members were putting embarrassing questions to the Ministers. *Vide* Sr. No. 639, His Highness Government : Patiala, Home Ministry Case No. 347 of 1930/1987, PSA : Patiala (See this file also for the detailed information regarding the denial of elementary political rights. This view is also supported by Master Hari Singh-Personal meeting at Chandigarh.
23. Basta No. 50, File No. 565/C-Prime Minister's Office Files, PSA : Patiala; *Vaid,* Chhajju mal, 'Tenants' Struggle in *Pepsu* Area, Souvenir, issued on the eve of 21st National Conference All India *Kisan Sabha,* Bhatinda : 1973; Ramesh Walia, A Study of the *Praja Mandal Movement in the East Punjab States*, Patialal : 1974, 72.

that the average literacy rate in the states was 4.1% as compared to the average rate of 6.2" in he neighbouring districts of Ludhiana, Hoshiarpur, Jalandhar, Ferozepur and Ambala.[24] Further, the states followed the policy of insulating their people from the influence of the press in British Indian territory. Undesirable printed matter was not allowed entry and political literature was often confliscated.[25] Thus, the contemporary circumstances had become a significant factor in giving impetus to the agrarian unrest and the peasant's/Tenants' movement because these circumstances had some problems of their own and it came out with some effects of its own.

Before tracing the history of the relationship between the tenants and *biswedars* (which was the local term for the *zamindar*) in these states, which is the history of exploitation of the tillers of the soil by a group of people, who happened to be favourites of the rulers of the Punjab states, it would be relevant to define the terms 'tenant' and '*biswedar*'. Tenant means a person who holds land under another person and, but for a special contract, is liable to pay rent for that land. It will be of great use if we study, of course, in brief the meaning, origin and evolution of the *biswedari* system because its role in the social, economic and political life of this region promoted agrarian unrest which culminated in the rise of various peasants movements. The word *biswedari*. It is composed of two words, *biswa* and *dari*. *Biswa* means a unit of land, and *dari* means possession or ownership. Thus *biswedar* is the holder of land. But the institution of *biswedari* is not as simple as its literal meaning is. It is rather a complicated system relating to the agrarian structure of the mediaeval age. Land was, generally, granted to the persons who served the state. Like the term

24. The literary rate has been derived from the 1931 census figures (for further details see Basta No.22 Case No. 66 of 1931/1988-PSR, PM's Office Files).
25. For detail see a report of the District Magistrate of Faridkot State, Confidential diaries of the district Magistrate No. 2920-21 Faridkot State Records File No. 23, PSA : Patiala; Pattabhai Sitaramayha, *History of the Indian National Congress*, Vol. I, 10.

talukadari prevalent in Oudh, it was very much akin to the *jagirdari*. Under this system of substantial part of the land revenue, states, villages and some administrative rights were granted to the state officials as rewards for the services they rendered to the state.[26] Generally the grant of land came to be the normal way of securing the services.

The terms *Biswedari* and *jagirdari* are synonymous in as much as they represent feudalism in one form or the other, in its nature and ideology.[27] Feudal system dominated before the modern socio-economic, political and administrative system came into being. In this system, *biswedars* and *jagirdars* were agents of the upper strata of feudal hierarchy in collecting land revenues from the peasants. In fact, the privileged feudal elite class of *biswedars* and *jagirdars* was non productive, collaborationist having parasitic acquired and retained its privileged land holding status through unjustifiable ways.[28]

In India *biswedari* was an institution in itself. It had its own administration, programmes and plans for exploiting the poor peasant class. The *biswedars* were a middle feudal elite class. They acted as a liason between the feudal—state lord and the peasants. The feudal lords, to run the administration

26. Indu Banga, *Agrarian System of the Sikhs* (Delhi : Manohar Publications, 1978), p. 190.
27. The feudalism in the context of Indian agrarian structure is used only as a generic term because some historians are of the opinion that in India feudalism in a specific sense never prevailed in India. Their argument is based on the fact that the character and nature of the institution of slavery did not correspond to the medieval Europe. Moreover, due to flourishing trade during the medieval period money economy was very much prevalent in the medieval Indian state. The absence of money economy is considered as one of the important features of feudal economy. For further details, see *Encyclopedia of the Social Sciences* (New York : the Macmillan Company, 1931), 14th printing in 1962.
28. For details, see Ronald J. Merrug, *Land to the Tiller: The Political Economy Agrarian Reforming South Asia* (Delhi : Oxford University Press, 1983), p. 127.

smoothly and to control the subject, used to confer the *jagirs* upon the persons who also, had political, economic and administrative rights.[29] From this precise discussion, this may be safely stated that the political essence of feudalism lay in the organization of the whole administrative structure on the basis of land and its economic essence lay in the poor peasants who were attached to the soil by the landed intermediaries like biswedars placed between the state chief and the actual tillers, with his vague rights of middlemanship. He was essentially more for a ruler for the purpose of collection of the state revenue and for supporting him in all other matters. In other words, the *biswedar* who with the local *ahalkar*, wielded the biggest stick, is the direct ancestor of the present landlord.

From the above deliberations, we come to the conclusion that the *biswedari* was an oriental method, as well as a strategy of the Sikh governments to carve out new estates at the cost of the peasants.[30] In the beginning the highly organized powerful rural communities had full, traditionally inalienable, rights in the land which they cultivated and so this cultivable area was inhabited by these cultivators. But with the passage of time when the states' Chiefs became powerful, they aimed at establishing new settlements on cultivated land. They wanted to set up a rival colony in the vicinity of a powerful feudal state. From this stand-point, the state chiefs started offering *jagirs* with special rights at the cost of the peasants. The objective

---

29. It was a favourite plan of the Sikh Governments to carve out new estates, regardless of existing rights, and plant new settlements on cultivated land. Sometimes the object in view was to reward faithful service, sometimes to replace thriftless cultivators, sometimes to plant a hostile colony in the neighbourhood of a powerful feudatory. Hence, there were many villages in Patiala State the property of single owners or single families. It may be mentioned here also that *jagirs* were not only conferred upon the persons to create a class defending the feudal overlord but were also granted to the religious institutions under the item of *daramarth* grants.
30. H.H. Baden Powell, *The Land Systems of British India*, Vol. II, (Delhi : Oriental Publishers, 1974), p. 257.

of such a scheme was to 'plant new settlements on cultivated land' and set up a hostile colony in the neighbourhood of a powerful feudatory.[31] Consequently a large number of *zamindari* or *biswedari* villages sprang up. These villages constituted a power block subordinate to the state ruler and owing its allegiance to it. This power block subordinate regulated its economic structure keeping in mind its own benefits and of the rulers as well.

Now, the *biswedars* were almost owners of 784 villages out of the total of 3580 villages in the Patiala State.[32] They usurped the land that originally belonged to the cultivators. Under the new scheme the *biswedars* were authorized by the government to collect share of the produce as revenue.[33] These *biswedars* were either relations of the rulers of Patiala or secured *biswedari* by virtue of their services to he state. The revenue records point to the origin or the *biswedari*. "*Biswedari*" had its origin in the brotherhood relationship of the royal family and in matrimonial alliance. The biswedari villages in relation to brotherhood were Bhadaur, Rotduma, Jound, Rampura and Pagoara, etc. In case of marriage ties the villages were Tamkot, Dalalsaingh Wala, Kishangarh, Rajomajra. The system of *jagiradari* or *biswedari* also came into existence when the villages were given as gifts on the occasions pertaining to births, deaths or other ceremonial functions of the ruling family.[34] Such villages were Dharamgarh, Gonindgarh, Dayalgarh and Bishanpur. Some persons got the rank of *biswedari* in lieu of the services to the state.

Some got these rights in lieu of the payment made to the state in some way or the other. In village Daska the *biswedari* had such origin. In some cases the escheat property was declared *nazul*[35] and was given over to the favourtie persons

31. Punjab State Gazetteers, *op. cit.,* p. 144.
32. File No. 10189, Prime Minsiter's Office, *Patiala State Records,* Punjab State Archieves (Hereafter P.M., PSR, PSA).
33. *Ibid.*
34. For details, see Appendix VII.
35. Property which falls to the State from default of heir.

of the state. In some cases the shrewd *nambardars* or *zaildars* who used to pay land revenue on behalf of the whole village played false with the poor peasants by getting the ownership of the land transferred in their own favour with the help of revenue department.[36]

The rise of *biswedari* reduced the peasants, the real owner of the land, to the level of occupancy tenants or tenants-at-will.[37] In fact, the revenue department itself was responsible for the birth of *biswedars* and the *biswedari* system. The government made the peasants dependent upon the influential and well-to-do persons, the so-called *biswedars* by demanding from the peasants the state share of the produce in cash. Generally, the peasants were deficient in cash and so they had to fall back upon the wealthy and well-off persons, connected with the officials for help. These well-off persons realized produce in kind from the peasants and deposited equivalent amount in the treasury on behalf of the peasants. In the process these crafty persons made a good deal of profit. Moreover, in this way they developed connections with the state bureaucrats and finally they utilized these connections in securing proprietary rights.[38] These very persons became *biswedars* as well as the part of the ruling elite by registering lands in their names on one pretext or the other. As the Patiala State sided with the British during the revolt of 1857, the imperialists favoured the cause of the ruling elite at the cost of the poor peasants. Thus, the British rulers of India helped in further strengthening the *biswedari* system.[39]

The death of Maharaja Narinder Singh gave an impetus to the growth of *biswedari* system. The successor to the Chiefship of the Patiala State, Maharaja Mohinder Singh, was a minor. So on November 13, 1862 a Council of Regency was set up in order

---

36. File No. H-38 B (H.is for His Highness and B for Bhupinder Singh PSR, PSA.
37. File No. 10189, P.M., PSR. PSA; and File No. H 135, B, PSR, PSA.
38. File No. 5804, P.M., PSR, PSA.
39. *Punjab States Gazetteer*, 50, 73; Foreign Department Proceedings, July, 2, 1858, Nos. 169, 187-88, NAI, New Delhi.

to run the administration of the State.[40] The royal relations and officials fully availed themselves of these circumstances. Some of them committed the henious and fraudulent act of depositing the revenue of some villages in their own name. They realized *batai* from the land proprietors of these villages. Thus the feudal elite and the ruling class robbed the tillers of the soil of their proprietary rights by fraudulent and treacherous means. All these things conspired to hasten the development and consolidation of the tyrannical *biswedari* system. Such a fraudulent attempt to consolidate this *biswedari* system was made for the first time under the *gadmi bandobast* in 1877.[41] The proprietary rights were snatched away from the original owners of the land and were given to the *biswedars*.[42] The regular settlement of 1903 further encouraged *biswedars* and

---

40. It was decided in 1859 in response to the Phulkian Chiefs 'Paper of Request', that in the event of an infant heir, a council of Regency consisting of three of the old and trusted and most capable ministers of the state might be selected by the commissioner (British Resident) with the advice of other two surviving chiefs. On November 13,1862 after the death of Maharaja Narinder Singh a council of Regency was set up which carried on the administration of the state till His Highness Maharaja Mohinder Singh assumed power in 1870. The members of the council were Jagdish Singh, Rahim Bux and Udey Singh. Maharaja Mohinder Singh was again succeeded by his minor son Maharaja Rajinder Singh. Consequently the administration of the State was run by a council of Regency with its members Sardar Dewa Singh, Charat Ram and Namdar Khan, which ceased in 1890. A minority administration followed again for the third time in succession in 1900, after the death of Maharaja Rajinder Singh. To run the administration during the minority of Maharaja Bhupinder Singh a Regency Council, was set up under the Presidentship of Sardar Gurmukh Singh, which carried on the administration of the State till 1909. The other two members of the regency council were Khalfa Saiyyid Muhammad Hussain and Lala Bhagwan Dass.
41. Means measurement by Qadmi-distance between one foot and the other while walking.
42. *Muzarian da Ghol Te Tuhada Farz,* a pamphlet published by the Secretary of *Muzara* Committee *Riast* Patiala (n.d.), p.3.

expanded the scope of *biswedari*. The proprietary rights in land were transferred fraudulently under this settlement in favour of the royal relatives and elites, who were courtiers.[43] The *biswedars* bribed the settlement commissioners to get the thumb impressions of the peasants to the statements favourable to the *biswsedars* and determental to the welfare of the peasants. This way the tenants could not comprehend that they had been made liable to pay *batai*.[44]

The division of the tenants into occupancy tenants and tenants-at-will weakened the cause of the tenants and strengthened the case of the biswedars to secure proprietary rights. This division burdened the peasants in as much as they were made to pay one *seer* per *maund* as privilege charges to the biswedar.[45] The peasants were also required to pay *maunds* of grain from every harvest to craftsmen and community servants such as water carrier, *dhobi*, barbar, watchmen, etc. The *biswedar* also could demand one-fourth or one-third from the remaining stock. The peasants bore the burden to giving free labour and other cesses like *neoda* on the occasions of marriages, etc. In the *biswedars* house, all expenditure concerning the entertainment of government officials visiting the villages and staying with the *biswedar* as his gests was borne by the tenants. The members of the tenants' families were treated as menials in as much as they rendered beggar free forced labour to the landlord family.[46]

The *biswedars* multiplied and flourished during the reign of Maharaja Bhupinder Singh. The Maharaja patronized new *jagiradars* known as *biswedars* by granting *jagirs* to his relatives, kith and kins of his over 300 ranis. The consolidated feudalism following on the foot steps of British imperialism in

43. Kishangarh, The Peasant's Heroic Defence of His land published by *Pepsu Kisan Sabha*, Bhatinda.
44. H. 138, B, PSR, PSA.
45. Kishangarh, *op.cit.*, p.13.
46. Chhajjumal Vaid, "Tenant Movement" in Master Hari Singh, Punjab Peasants in Freedom Struggle, Vol. II (New Delhi : People's Publishing House, 1984), p. 241.

order to appease the British imperialists. The villages and peasants in these areas gifted to the *biswedars* were almost under the command of these feudal lords. There were 784 tenant villages with occupancy rights and thousands of villages with tenants-at-will.[47] Under these circumstances, the condition of the peasants deteriorated from bad to worse. They were scarcely left with enough grain for their families, sometimes for even the time until the next harvest.[48] Besides, the biswedars thrived and fattened on the hard labour of the peasants. They got strengthened. The large portion of money went in their pockets which enabled them to impart good education to their children and also to enjoy luxurious living.[49] Table given below shows the land possessed by the biswedars in Patiala State.

Hence the table showing areas occupied by *biswedars* in tehsils such as Patiala, Rajpura, Bhawanigarh, Sirhind, Sunam, Dhuri, Mansa, Narnaul, Kandaghar and Bhatinda indicate that

47. In addition to the biswedars there were jagirdars who were feudatories of Patiala rulers. The chief *jagirs* were those of Bhadour and Khamanon, which the Sardar of Bhadaur received Rs. 70,000 per annum, those of Khamanon got Rs. 90,000. In addition they were landlords of some villages which came under them and were effect biswedars of those tracts. The jagir of Payal valued Rs. 18,000 per annum.
48. Kishangarh, *op.cit.*, p. 14.
49. It is worth nothing that the *biswedars* who enjoyed so many material advantages of all kinds, who fill all the state offices with their relatives and friends continually quarrelled with and frequently oppressed their tenants. The miserable condition of the peasants has been vividly explained in the Census Report of 1941 : "The ploughman has practically no social life but a mere drudgery. He has got no idea of marry making or enjoying life. From early morning till late in the evening, he works in the fields or does other type of labour in order to make both ends meet. In short he is shut out from the outside world and was deprived of all the amenities and charms of civilization. His implements of agriculture are so primitive as to be dated back to the book of Genesis. In certain cases he is an embodiment of misery and melancholy. It is the tide and not the eddy of reforms that will ameliorate the conditions of the peasant".

Table 1. Showing the Land Possessed by the Biswedars in Patiala State

Name of the Tehsil	*Land under the Biswe-dars Bighas/ Biwas*	*Revenue paid Rs - A - .pie*	*Female Biswe-dars*	*Land under Female Biswedars*	*Hindu*	*Muslim*	*Sikh*	*Jat*	*Non-Jats*
					Number of Biswedars				
Barnala	92118 - 1	-	4	3528 - 8	-	1	44	44	1
Bhatinda	219622 - 4	36650-5-4	5	13194 - 5	1	-	65	65	1
Bhawanigarh	256821 - 0	-	6	10758 - 3	21	32	78	24	107
Dhuri	104385 - 4	-	13	11998 - 4	13	33	63	50	59
Kandaghat	49780 - 5	6816-10-0	5	4674 - 6	30	4	8	7	35
Mansa	313855 - 8	-	12	22117 - 18	3	10	177	177	13
Narnaul	29959 - 17	-	15	6566 - 4	56	27	58	5	136
Narwana	185738 - 3	-	4	9246 - 1	85	15	39	36	103
Patiala	228647 - 0	57129-0-0	17	20390 - 0	26	46	81	73	80
Rajpura	74948 - 12	21136-8-2	7	13296 - 8	13	17	37	18	49
Sirhind	80451 - 9	-	3	6694 - 4	4	14	39	8	47
Sumam	132182 - 8	-	5	4614 - 4	5	35	63	23	80
Total	17885090 - 11	121731-24-0	94	127078 - 5	257	234	752	530	711

Source : File No. 645 Ijlas-i-khas office, Patiala State Records Punjab State Archieves, Patiala.

the *biswedars* dominated. In *tehsils* such as Mansa, Bhatinda, Dhuri, Bhawanigarh, Sunam and Patiala, the *biswedars owned* maximum possible land. It is estimated that 66% of the total land was under the *biswedars.* That is why there was an atmosphere of ill-will against the *biswedars* in these areas. The Sikh *biswedars* far out-numbered the Hindu *biswedars* or Muslim *biswedars.* The Sikh *biswedars* swelled in number because they had the blessings of the Maharaja of the Patiala, especially because they had matrimonial alliance with the Maharaja. The Hindu *biswedars* numbering 257, had land mostly in Narnaul, Narwana and Kandaghat, and the Muslim *biswedars* numbering just 235, had land mostly in Patiala, Sunam, Dhuri and Bhawanigarh tehsils, but they were scattered all over the state in small numbers. The Sikh *biswedars,* mostly *jats,* on the other hand, numbered 752 and they had land in Mansa, Bhatinda, Dhuri, Bhawanigarh, Sunam, and Patiala. An area of land measuring 1,27,078 *bighas* and 5 *biswas* was under the possession of 96 female biswedars by virtue of their being once members of the Maharaja's herm or being somehow, related to him. Some of these female *biswedars* were widows. In *tehsils* like Dhuri, Bhatinda, Barnala, Mansa and Patiala, the *jat biswedar* numbering 530 predominated, whereas in *tehsils* like Narnaul, Bhawanigarh, Patiala, Sunam and Dhuri, the non-*jats* numbering 711 owned land. No doubt, the Sikh *biswedars, jats* and non-*jats,* were in a majority, but there were *biswedars* in almost every other community.

The origin of the problem cropped up even before the First Regular Settlement was reached at in Patiala in the beginning *of the twentieth* century.[50] A demand in the report of this settlement read that the conflict and controversy regarding the proprietary right existed even before the conclusion of this settlement and its implementation.[51] It seems that the biswedars,

50. AISPC-Papers, File No. 133A, 1946-48, Folio. 253-257, Patiala State Records, Prime Minister's Office File 556 1929-30, PSA : Patiala.

51. "The relations between the *biswedars* and *muzaras* were strained and bitter, long before the settlement commenced". *Vide Final Report of the Settlement of the Patiala State A.D. 1909-8* (Hereafter *Settlement Report*), 26.

who had previously some *maufi*-rights or revenue rights, because of their increasing influence in the administration demanded hereditary rights or proprietary status. The attitude of the courts at this time was that these rights should be conferred upon the tenants and the self-farming cultivator should be given the status of occupancy tenants.[52] But as a result of this settlement, the conflict between the tenants and the Government increased all the more.[53] This settlement roused the fears of conflict where there was no conflict and germinated the seeds of conflict where they existed already. And, it is interesting to note, though the Settlement Commissioner knew it before hand that the revenue officials were leaving a lacuna owing to which there was full fear of the intensification of conflict in the future, yet he did not take any step regarding it.[54] However, far from remedying the inequitable court decisions, the settlement merely accepted and gave further sanction to the status-quo, granting absolute proprietary status to biswedars; and no benefit had accrued to the peasant/tenants from the Punjab Tenancy Act of 1885.[55] In fact, the Settlement Commissioner showed haste while submitting the report. The motive behind this action was to pacify the peasants/tenants but they had become so rebellious that the Settlement could not have been implemented in a practical way without resorting to any stringent measure, while the right to take any strong step did not fall in the jurisdiction of the officials of the Settlement Department. Thus, the situation not only took a

52. The tendency was for the small proprietors, who happened to be share holders in a village in which some one connected with the official class was an assignee of revenue or the owner of a predominant interest therein, to become occupancy tenants, and for old tenants in a *biswedari* estate to sink to the level of mere tenants-at-will. *Ibid.*, 26.
53. *Settlement Report*, 26-27.
54. *Ibid.*, 27.
55. (This Report also pointed out that "the great majority of the 17,706 cases, which have been fought in the appellate courts of the Settlement, have been concerned with tenants' rights and tenants' liabilities". *Vide Ibid.*, 28.

critical and serious turn but there appeared a great fear of quarrels and murders and with it appeared the fear of intensification of the peasant's unrest as well as the movement. Of course, this danger was averted for some time.[56]

With the passage of time, the exploitation of the tenants grew, whereas, in the adjoining British territory, there were the peasants, who enjoyed ownership of land which they cultivated. This made them strive for a recognition of better status, which would entitle them to own their land and pay revenue direct to the state and thus get rid of the *biswedars*, whose dominance was imposed on the cultivating community, by the will of the ruler. It was indeed ironical that a tenant after hard toil of the whole day, could not make both ends meet.[57] He had to depend upon the village moneylender to take loan from him for emergency needs. The rate of interest was so high that generations after generations, he could not get rid of the money once taken on loan and the moneylender always sucked their blood.[58]

The peasantry had been suffering ruthless repression and hardships at the hands of the *biswedars*.[59] During the second half of the 19th century the land was under the cultivation of occupancy-tenants known as *muzara maurusi*. As the Punjab states were not under the direct control of the British

56. File No. 2193, PSA : Patiala, 39; Poster published in October, 1938 and Jagan Singh's pamphlet '*Dukhee Janta ka Ubaal*', Ferozepur City, Amrit Electric Press : 1939.
57. File No. 138, Part-I, *AISPC-Papers*, NMML, New Delhi; Salana Sahib Singh, *Aap Biti* (Panjabi), 134; File No. 2193; File No. 135 of 1931-Prime Minister's Office files, PSA : Patiala.
58. Patiala State tenants File No. 6, PSA : Patiala, 151; File No. 565/ C-Basta No. 50-Prime Minister's Office Record; *AISPC-Papers*, File No. 138, NMML, New Delhi; Giani Kehar Singh, *Praja Malerkotla Di Dard Kahani*, printed and published by Joga, Jagir Singh, Amritsar : *Desh Dardi* Press, Introduction, 1-2.
59. *Rajomajra Enquiry Committee Report*, PSA, Patiala, Walia, Ramesh, *A Study of the Praja Mandal Movement in the East Punjab States*, Panjabi University, Patiala, 1974, 58.

Government, the problem of the land was different from the one in other parts of India. The rulers enjoyed a free had in regard to the distribution of land and they always preferred to give the lands to their own proteges. So, the landlords got the land from the state. When the land was allotted to the *biswedars* they were not in position to cultivate whole of the land. So they had to get help from the tenants who cultivated the land. The *biswedar* was to take profit which was due to him.[60]

There was another type of *biswedars* also. They were from the persons who were playing the role of middlemen between the Government and the peasantry. They collected the land revenue like *batai* from the peasants and deposited it with the Government.[61] With the passage of time, the absentee landlords began to dominate and according to the law prevailing at that time in the state, the land belonged to the absentee landlords, not to the occupancy tenants.[62] The latter had to pay a share of the crop (*batai*) at every harvest to the former. If the tenant failed to pay the *batai* he could be evicted out of the holdings. The occupancy tenants who had been attached to the land for many generations were resentful of their position as such. The fact was that many of them were the landlords and real proprietors, but had been deprived to their rights by the cunning landlords at the time of land settlement.[63]

In 1901-03, through quinquennial land Settlement the *biswedari* system was further strengthened.[64] The *muzaras* were further differentiated into occupancy-tenants and tenants-at-will. Moreover, in the same village some land was recorded as

60. *Patiala State Records*, Prime Minister's Office File No. 578, PSA : Patialal; Also File No. 595.
61. *Patiala State Administration Report for the year 1924-25*, PSA : Patiala.
62. Popham Young, *Settlement Report*, 1904, 26-28.
63. Vaid., Chhajju Mal, '*Pepsu Muzarian De Ghol Ten* Communist Party' (An article in Panjabi), Published in a *Souvenir*, Issued by the C.P.I. on January 26, 1976, 73.
64. *Patiala State Administration report for the year 1904-05*, PSA : Patiala; Popham Young, *Settlement Report*, 1904-29.

maurusi and some *gair-maurusi*.[65] In this land-settlement, the occupancy-tenants even when they had enough documentary evidence in their possession in support of their claim as proprietors, failed to prove or establish their rights. They deemed themselves the proprietors and protested against all inequalities. Hence, there arose a struggle against the *biswedari* system. The occupancy tenants now wanted to get rid of the vicious system of landlordism;[66] but they were very much conscious of their rights to the land. They made many attempts to get rid of the yoke of the absentee landlords.

Forced by the agitation and clamour for reform an official commission was appointed on 24th July, 1939, to enquire into the respective positions of the tenants and the landlords on the basis of evidence and to suggest reforms. The Commission completed its report in 1942, but the Report never saw the light of the day as it had hinted at certain reforms in favour of the peasants. Thus the position of the tenants remained the same.

Further, it is evident that the condition of self-cultivating peasants was not very good nor were they safe because they had got land for a stipulated period; in other words, all they got was fixity of tenure and were not provided with any protection against rack-renting. It was clearly told in the settlement report that "the capacity of the tenants to resist extortion, and to maintain their hold on lands which they had brought under cultivation, rested upon their own strength or obstinacy and upon the weakness or the good feeling of their landlords, rather than upon any legal basis.[67] The landlords had also succeeded in getting a *hidayat* in 1872 making it incumbent upon all occupancy tenants to pay rent in cash. Besides, the amount of *batai* or share rent was decided by the *kankut* system which meant that standing crops were assessed before each harvest by a *kankut* committee consisting of state

---

65. *Patiala State Records*, Prime Minister's Office file No. 710, PSA : Patiala; Interview with Sardar Hari Singh, Chandigarh.
66. Patiala State Records, File Nos. 2177 : P.S.A., Patiala.
67. *Settlement Report*, 27-29.

functionaries and the amount to be given to the *biswedars* fixed accordingly.[68] The *muzaras* of roughly 800 *biswedars* villages (comprising about 1/6th of the total number in the Patiala State only) had grievances chiefly related to three issues : *(a)* The loss of proprietary right and reduction in their position in the tenurial structure; *(b)* the consequential increase in their obligations to the *biswedars*; and *(c)* the *kankut* system, in which over assessment of crop was a constant cause of complaint coupled with the uncertainty of the exact amount to be paid at each harvest. Thus, the grievances of the tenants/peasants had been gaining strength since the time of settlement. As a result, they agitated against the callousness of the state. The only means left with them was to refuse the share of the crops *i.e. batai* to the *biswedars*. They demanded abolition of the *biswedari* system, meaning thereby that the status of these occupancy-tenants must be raised to the level of proprietors. It was reliably reported that the state had promised to crush the tenants and all those who supported them.[69]

The political force of feudalism originated from land and the exploitation of the poor peasants who tilled the land. In fact, land was the main source of income of the state government,[70] and agriculture was the occupation of most of the Indian people because India was and still is a predominantly an agricultural country.

The East Punjab states of the Punjab were no exception to the prevailing conditions in other states of India. Almost 64% people in these states depended on agriculture for their livelihood.[71] There were no set rules for collecting land revenue. The mode of revenue collection was unscientific and largely depended upon the discretion of the state officials. The states'

---

68. *AISPC-Papers,* File No. 139, Part-I, 1937-42, Folio, 295-303.
69. *Patiala State Records,* Fole No. 6133, PSA : Patiala.
70. Somerset Playne, *The State of Patiala : A Biography Historical and Administrative Survey* (London, 1921), p. 22.
71. *Cenus Report of Patiala State* (1911).

officials had their own way. The states' records show that the land revenue differed from *pargana* to *pargana*. The state share in the land revenue was generally one-third but the system of charging one-fourth and two-fifth share in the crops was also in vogue. The state also charged extra dues known as *abwab*.[72] The land revenue comprised *batai* system and *kankut* system. The Government under the *batai* system got its share by actually dividing the produce, and under *kankut* system its share was determined on the basis of standing *kharif* crops. The *batai* share was realized generally from the *rabi* crops. If the crops were not easily divisible, the Government charged *zabti*, a cash rate per *bigha*.[73] *Batawa* officials were those who charged *batai*, and *kachhhu* officials were responsible for charging *kankut*.[74]

---

72. Popham Young, *Settlement Report of 1904*; Vaid, Chhajju Mal *Pepsu Muzarian De Ghol Ten* Communist Party (An article in Panjabi), published in a *Souvenir*, issued by the CPI on January 26, 1976, 73.
73. *Punjab State Gazetteers, Vol. XVII, A, Phulkian States Patiala Nabha and Jind* (Lahore : Punjab Government Press, 1909), p. 150; *Popham Young, Settlement Report of 1904*; Vaid Chhajju Mal *Pepsu Muzarian De Ghol Ten* Communist Party (An article in Panjabi), published in a *Souvenir*, issued by the CPI in January 26, 1976, 73 (For the detail of *abiana* see case No. 485/13 of 1929, PSA : Patiala).
74. *Ibid.*, As regards the administration of, the state, the Maharaja was the supreme head of the entire administrative edifice including the land revenue. He was virtually both the proprietor as well as the sovereign of the land and the share of the produce that was collected. All appointments of revenue officials were made in his name. He himself selected the higher officials. All revenue reforms had to receive his sanction. He could grant relief and even remit land revenue and other cesses. *Patiala State Records*, P.M.'s Office File No. 655; Young Popham, Settlement Report of 1904; Basta No. 50, File No. 565/C (Confidential weekly report) PSA : Patiala.

Excepting the Narnaul district,[75] the revenue was charged in cash or in kind *i.e., batai* and *kankut* depending on the nature of the land and crops. The state extracted one-fifth share from the inferior soil, or course, depending on rainfall one third from the superior lands and sometimes two-fifth of the total produce from the lands irrigated by means of wells. This revenue system prevailed upto 1861. After 1861 certain changes were introduced in the technique of revenue-collection. In 1861 itself the first contract was settled on cash basis in the district of the Patiala State. An average of the last twenty one year's revenue actually realized was assessed as the revenue for the next one year.[76] In 1862, 1868 and 1890, there were resettlement in the *jangal tehsils* of Bhatinda, Bhikhi and Barnala in the Ahmadgarh district. In 1864, 1868 and 1890 resettlements took place in the Narnaul district and in 1861, 1865, 1875 and 1887, there were resettlements in the remaining tehsils excluding the Pinjore *tehsil*.[77]

Of course, there were no uniform norms for collection of revenue and the fixed rules in the land revenue administration were conspiciously absent. In case of bumper crops the *diwan* of the state set aside the terms of agreement, and he extracted more revenue in kind. This corrupt and unfair policy of the feudal elite discouraged the agriculturists and they did not bother about bringing waste land under cultivation.[78] Without

75. In the Narnaul district a summary settlement had been effected by British Officers in the year 1857-58 and Patiala took over the cash assessments then imposed, when this tract was presented to the State as a reward in lieu of its active support to suppress the revolt of 1857. For details, see major Popham Young, *Report on the Settlement of the Patiala State*, (Ajmer : Scottish Mission, Industries Co. Ltd.,), p. 26.
76. Major F., Popham Young, *Report on the Settlement of the Patiala State : 1900-1908* (Ajmer : Scottish Mission, Industries Co. Ltd.).
77. *Ibid.*
78. *Punjab States Gazetteers, op. cit.,* p. 149. To add the miseries of the peasants, a large area of *birs* had been reserved for purposes

(Contd....)

making any improvement and innovations in the land revenue administration the government officials were always busy in increasing the revenue by corrupt means. The whole society felt demoralized by the tyrannical and dishonest practices of the revenue administration. The revenue assessment in cash went against the interests of the cultivators because they were generally deficient in money. The land revenue administration exploited and tortured the cultivators for about a century since its inception.[79] The cultivators were no longer an autonomous body. A *tehsil* or *pargana* was a unit in matters of revenue units. In each such unit a *tehsildar* was incharge of revenue collection. But the tehsildar and his subordinates did not discharge their duties honestly. Corruption reigned supreme. While assessing revenue in kind the cultivators were unnecessarily harassed for underweight assessment. They were compelled to make up for the shortage. The contractors squeezed the peasants as much as they could. The helpless peasants had no alternative but to surrender to the cunning and cruel whims and capacity of the revenue collectors. After all these extortions, the poor farmers cold hardly make both ends meet with whatever little was left with them.

From administrative point of view, the Patiala State was divided into four *nizamats* which were sub-divided into *tehsils* which further were bifurcated into *kanongo* circles, which again were split up into patwars.[80] The role of *lambardars* and *zaildars* who collected revenue directiy from the peasants was well-defined.[81] Two *batawas* and *kachhus* and two *maharrirs* called *likharies* were appointed for each circle, a sub-division of a *pargana* at the harvest time by the tehsildar. A superior *kachhus*

(78 Contd....)

of hunting. These reserves had proved to be a source of very great ruin to the cultivators in the neighbourhood. Wild beasts roam about destroying the crops of the agriculturists but they could not kill them or shoot them.

79. *Ibid.*, p. 150.
80. *Administration Report of Patiala State for 1929-30.*
81. *Ibid.*

got rupees sixty and the inferior one got rupees fifty for the season. But the *batawas* got simple rupees thirty for the season. The pairs of *kachhus, batwas* ad *muharrirs* (likharis) were servants of the state. However, one out of each pair of *kachhus* or *batwas* or *likharies* was nominated by the tehsildar and the other one called *sarkari* was appointed by the *diwan*. Both were servants of the state but were appointed in two different ways; the idea being that their mutual jealousies, rivalry and dependence on two different superior would be a check on their dishonesty.[82] All the revenue officials except the *tehsildar* were temporarily appointed for the harvest season. These temporary officials generally adopted corrupt methods to maximize their income.[83] A watchman appointed in a village in order to look after the grain and the crops got one *anna* and a half per day-half an *anna* being paid by the state government and one *anna* by the peasants.[84]

The land revenue system in this region of the Punjab suffered from many defects due to the negligence and dishonesty on the part of the *batawas* and they shirked hard work. As a result the land revenue system was not effective. The delay in effecting the *batai* often caused a great damage to the grain. In the *rabi* harvest, if the produce was small or the quality of grain had deteriorated in any way, then the state's portion was forced back on the cultivators and the government realized its full share of harvest, at a rate fixed by the *diwan* at each harvest with reference to the market current rate. Consequently, the poor peasants had to bear the burden of deficient crop on account of general mismanagement and corruption of the mercenary revenue officials. Though they even paid bribes to the corrupt officials, heavy fine and punishments were inflicted upon them by the *Malbakhana*.[85]

82. *Punjab States Gazetteers, op. cit.*, p.150.
83. *Ibid.*, p.152.
84. *Ibdi.*, p. 150.
85. *Malbakhana* was a kind of office of control started during the reign of Maharaja Karam Singh to enquire into and punish the wrong doing of the revenue establishment and *zamindars* who tried to profit by bribing them at the time of collection.

In order to do away with corruption and inefficiency, in the revenue administration, and to make it more effective, Maharaja Narinder Singh brought about certain changes in the revenue department. He contemplated fixing a cash assessment in place of *kham*.[86] The Diwan and some other officials did not approve of this idea. As a result, an officer with curtailed powers called *munsarim diwan* was appointed in place of the *diwan* whose services were dispensed with.[87]

Four officers called *mansarim-i-hadbast* were incharge of four divisions into which the state was divided. These officers conducted boundary survey and summarily settled the revenue for one year on the basis of the average *kham* collections of the last 22 years.[88] The average of twenty two years was nearly 23 lacs and a new assessment amounted to rupees 30,87,000. When this term lapsed, another similar settlement was performed for three years by which the revenue was reduced to rupees 29,39,000. The people accepted this settlement on the assurance that the demand would not be changed during the term of the settlement.[89] This settlement was made for three years by Maharaja Narinder Singh and there was a provision of revision after every ten year. Afterwards Major F. Popham Young fixed the land revenue for thirty years by effecting a regular settlement.[90]

Because of the special concessions which the *biswedars* received at the hands of the state authority, they were like feudal lords of the mediaeval European countries. They had plenty of lands at their disposal and were not to bother about the cultivation of the land. Moreover, the *biswedars* dominated both in the village affairs as well as in the state administration.

86. Collection in kind.
87. *Punjab State Gazetteers, op. cit.*, p. 151.
88. The name of this officer was after sometime changed to *mohtiman bandobast* and afterwards into *nazim*.
89. *Punjab State Gazetteers, op. cit.*, p. 152.
90. *Census Report of Patiala State* (1931); *Civil and Military Gazette Ltd.*, (The Mall), Lahore, p.13.

They could manipulate the laws of the state to suit their own ends. There were also no well defined rules of ownership or the rate of revenue to be paid.[91] Such an arbitrary system governing the *biswedar* tenant relationship was about to contain germs of future trouble.

The villages were divided into different pattis[92] according to the tenant's shares as proprietors. This system continued to prevail till 1929. On the basis of evidence furnished by a report of the committee which went into the enquiry of Rajomajra, we learn that after 1882, partition was made not only of the land but it was also made tenant-wise. Whatever dignity the tenant's ancestors had enjoyed in the early days ended with the forfeiture of their *jagirs* in 1882 in the village Rajomajra. The land now remained free-holding of one who was in possession of it, and it was with a view to ascertaining the area and the name of the owner of the land that charts were prepared by the Patiala state first in 1890-91,[93] styled as *Pamaish arazi kachh batai* and then in 1916,[94] under the appellation of *hissa-kashi*. The relations between the *biswedars* and the tenants in the structure continued becoming strained and bitter because of the rising tide of consciousness among the peasantry of their being exploited. The people thought that the Settlement Committee appointed to go into their difficulties and redress their grievances would greatly help.[95] But according to Popham Young, the Settlement Commissioner of the State, "the effect of the Settlement has been to create causes for disputes where none existed before and to aggravate ill-feeling where they did exist.[96]

The cause of these strained relations was the conversion of proprietary into tenancy rights; the pre-settlement proprietary rights received recognition both from the state and

91. *Punjab State Records*, Prime Minister's Office File No. 135 of 1931.
92. *Rajomajra Enquiry Committee Report*, PSA : Patiala.
93. *Ibid.*
94. *Ibid.*
95. *Ibid.*
96. *Ibid.* Popham Young, *Settlement Report of 1904.*

public opinion. But there was no clear understanding either as to how their rights were acquired or what they amounted to. In many cases, the proprietary title had been in dispute between the main body of the cultivators resident in a village on the one hand and on the other some individuals who claimed the entire biswedari right on the basis of inheritance from the founder. Sometime the latter alleged that their admitted rights as *mafidars* covered the proprietary title also. In such cases, the court of law would often allot to the main body of cultivators the status of occupancy. The tenancy was for the small proprietors, who happened to be shareholders in a village in which some one connected with the official class was an assignee of the revenue or the owner of a predominant interest therein, to become occupancy tenant and for old tenants in a biswedar estate to sink to the level of more tenants-at-will.[97]

Moreover, the influence of the landlord class led to the issuance of the hidayat in 1873 from the state authorities making it incumbent upon all occupancy tenants to make payments in kind.[98] However, the first step to ameliorate the conditions of tenants was the introduction of the 'Tenancy Law' in the state.[99] But it is to be noted that the principal objective of the tenancy reform was to appease the disgruntled tenants and to avert the agrarian unrest, which could harm the interests of the Rajas and *biswedars* to a large extent. However, the Punjab Act XVI was, very useful, though certain modifications were, of course, necessary and these were embodied in a Patiala supplement to that Act.

The tenants as a class were very happy when they learnt that their claims were being sympathetically considered by the state officials who now supposedly regarded landlords and the tenants with equal impartiality. The tenants jumped to the conclusion that their turn had come. At the time of the rent

97. Punjab State Records, Prime Minister's Office File No. 756, PSA : Patiala.
98. File No. R-11-2003/P.24, PSA : Patiala.
99. *Ibid.*, Popham Young, *Settlement Report of 1900-08.*

attestation, the whole tenant body affirmed that they had never paid rent which was customary for generations. On the other hand, it was found that the landlords were asserting that their tenants had always paid to them rack-rents, made up largely of a number of impositions known as cesses quite regardless of the actual facts. But to ascertain the fact, when there was no reliable record to refer to, was exceedingly difficult. A brief period of anarchy set in. Landlords refused to receive rents which did not include every sort of imposition which had been forced upon the weakest tenants by the strongest landlords in the neighbourhood and the tenants declined to pay rent at all, unless the landlords accepted the lowest share of the province,[100] which the most privileged tenants paid to the most considerate landlord. Though, the action was justified, very serious crisis took place which threatened to develop in the direction of murder and arson; but agrarian outrages were averted. The conflicts between the landlords and the tenants took another form. Now the *biswedars* took recourse to criminal courts in order to put pressure upon the tenants with whom they had dispute of a civil nature.[101]

Eventually on 15th July, 1894 the *batai* system was abolished but a cash rent of six *annas* per rupee as the land revenue was fixed. The tenants did not accept it and decided to carry on the struggle and thereafter even this rent was abolished and the tenants were accepted to be the full owners.[102] But the *biswedars* did not accept this settlement proposed by the state authorities. Thus, the struggle continued between them and the tenants.

To put an end to the tenants; struggle, the council of Regency ordered in 1903 a Regular Settlement and as a

100. *Settlement Report,* 1904 by Mr. Popham Young, Settlement Commissioner, Patiala State
101. *Ibid.*, Mr. Popham Young wanted to check them from doing so and also he wanted to protect the *biswedars* against exploitation by their tenants.
102. *Patiala State Records,* File No. 6157/6-2155, PSA: Patiala.

consequence divided the tenants into different categories, such as tenants-at-will and different standards of rent were fixed for different categories of tenants.[103] A reign of terror was let loose by the *biswedars* for the realization of rent in kind. The tenants then approached the civil courts for redress against the decision of these settlements but to no avail, as there too they had to cope with the *biswedars* who held authority.[104]

Being disappointed by the courts of law the tenants again resorted to the non-payment of rent. The state openly came out to the help of the *biswedars*. As a result, a group of tenants approached the Resident for the Punjab states at Lahore in order to appraise him of the situation. A commission, of course, was appointed to enquire into the condition of the peasantry. The commission submitted its report, which being in favour of the tenants, never saw the light of the day, despite persistent demands for its publication. Thus the position of the tenants remained the same. The main grievances of the agriculturists, which were responsible for the peasants' struggle in this region, are detailed below :

(i) The agriculturists were groaning under crushing land revenue rates which were double, in some cases triple or even higher than those prevalent in the adjacent British districts.

(ii) The land cesses mounted to Rs. 21/15/4 in contrast to Rs. 17/8/4 per Rs. 100/-of land revenue in the adjacent British territory—the former including Rs. 3/10 of *abwabi khidmat guzari* which was a disguised name for *begar* cess.

(iii) Though *begar* (forced labour) had been declared illegal, yet it continued.

(iv) As in British India, Punjab peasantry were involved in huge accumulated debts from which there was no hope of escape. As has been shown no relief was offered either

103. Mr. Popham Young, *Settlement Report of 1904.*
104. *Patiala State Records,* File No.50, Case No. 1560, 5; PSA : Patiala.

through Government agencies or Co-operative Societies.

(v) Most of the officials were not only unsympathetic but positively hostile to the interests of the agriculturists propaganda, and the woes of the *zamindars'* community owed, in no small measure, to their apathy and machinations.

The *muzaras* committees of the various states, had been publishing posters in *Gurmukhi,* from time to time, containing alleged grievances of the *muzaras* which were stuck on the walls of the houses in the villages to incite the tenants against the *biswedars* and the mal-administration of the maharajas of these states. The tenants gradually began to attend their meetings enthusiastically and participated in deliberations actively.

We shall now turn to certain movements in the East Punjab states-like the *Praja Mandal,* the Akali movement, the *kisan sabhas,* etc. which had influenced the peasants/tenants.[105] Besides, we know that the peasants unrest, depression and discontent in the agrarian field had been brewing for a long time which was intelligently exploited by various agitations launched by different political organisations.

In 1921, the non-co-operation movement, launched against the British Government by the Indian National Congress (hereafter INC), was at its height. At the same time the Sikhs started a religious struggle for the *Gurdwara* reforms known as the Akali Movement. After a constant struggle for five years against the *mahants* as well as the British Government, the Akalis succeeded in their mission for freedom in governing *Gurdwaras* by its own elected and responsible body by the passing of '*Gurdwara* Act of 1925'. Now came a split in the Akalis and they were divided into two groups. The leaders of the first cause while the other group which consisted of

105. Quarterly Register, April 1924; *Patiala State Records,* Prime Minister's Office File No. 747; File No. 737; file No. 750, PSA : Patiala; Personal meeting with S. Jagir Joga and Master Hari Singh on November 25, 1975 and December 19, 1978 respectively.

progressive Sikh leaders like Gopal Singh Qaumi, Master Tara Singh, Sewa Singh Thikriwala, Jathedar Teja Singh and many others, associated the leaders of the Sikhs Community with the leaders of the National Movement Struggling for independences.[106] The Akali *morchas* at *Jaito* and the Akali jathas, often passing through Patiala territory, sent a wave of enthusiasm which permeated the Sikh peasantry at the time.[107]

In the twenties of this century, the struggle for independence launched against the British imperialism by the INC was at its apex in British India. At that time, as has already been discussed, the condition of the native states was even worse than that of the subjects of the British India. The people were not free to launch struggle for freedom in the states openly.[108] In patiala State, it was even more trouble-some to launch such a campaign because the Maharaja was one of the favourite stooges of the British. But the brave men of the states, inspired by the INC. Indian States' People Conference, the Akali Movement and offer forces, felt that it was necessary to form some organization which could bring consciousness in the states people whose spirit had been paralyzed under long slavery and to redress their political and economic grievances. The outcome was the formation of the *Praja Mandal*.

Possessing a *sanad* of recognition of his sovereign rights or a treaty of alliance with the British power, every prince considered his big or small state at par with any other independent state of the world. But the British treated them as feudatory or subordinate states and did not accord to any Indian State, not even Hyderabad, the same political status or rank with diplomatic usage guaranteed to the smallest state in

---

106. Singh, Jagjit Aulakh, *IKK Jiwan-IKK Itihas*, (Panjabi, n.d.) 55 (The Akali leaders and the people of the states were determined to win *swaraj* and put the *Maharajas* and *nawabs* right and said that they would not rest until they turned the British out of India *Vide.*, Basta No.18, Case No. 224 of 1928-PSA : Patiala, 96.
107. *Ibid.*, 95 (Letter No. 110), Singh, Gandha, *Some Confidential papers of the Akali Movement*, 190.
108. Singh, Jagjit Aulakh, IKK Jiwan-IKK Itihas, (Panjabi, n.d.) 67.

Europe.[109] If at all sovereignty of the ruler had any meaning, it was in relation to his own subjects. He could approach his counterpart, the ruling prince of another state, but only through the officer of the political department of the Government of India. According to Gandhi, one of the princely rulers confessed that they were no better than *khansamas* of British rulers.[110]

Undoubtedly, the rulers of the native states were doing great service to the British power. They were maintaining well-equipped armies, generally British trained and often British officered, ready for use by the paramount power against political unrest and seditious anti-British propaganda.[111] Time and again the princes were referred to as helpers and colleagues in the great task of imperial rule[112] and were characterized as "a possible counterpoise to Congress aims."[113]

Under British protection, the princes enjoyed security not only against warring chieftains but also against their own subjects. They had full control over their life and property. The guarantee of British protection against revolt, the only way the subject of a despot can put an end to his oppression, had made the position really worse.[114] Jawahar Lal Nehru described the majority of these states as "sinks of reaction and incompetences.[115] The complete lack of civil liberties and the

109. Majumdar, R.C. (*ed.*), *British Paramountcy and Indian Rennaisance,* Bombay : Bhartiya Vidya Bhawan, 1963, 258.
110. Gandhi, M.K., *The Indian States Problem,* Ahmedabad : Navjeevan Press, 1941, 3.
111. *Report of the Indian States Committee,* 12; Dutt, R.P., *India Today,* (He has also quoted the view of Prof. Rushbrook William), 359-60; Dr. Walia, Ramesh, *A Study of the Praja Mandal Movement in the East Punjab States.* Patiala : 1974.
112. Diwan, Jarmani Dass, *Maharaja,* 296.
113. *Ibid.,* 297.
114. Dunber, Sir George, *India and the Passing of Empire,* London Nichalson and Watson, 1951, 150; *Report of the Indian States* Committee, 12; Sir Karnanith, Fitz also notes down this point very sharply in the book, *Twilight of the Marathas,* 175-76.
115. Nehru, Jawahar Lal, Presidential address to the Sixth Session of the All India States People's Conference, Ludhiana, 1939 (For more details also see, Sir Kernanith, Fitz. *Twilight of the Marathas,* 28).

ruthless suppression of individuals and confiscation of property had reduced these states to nothing better than prison houses.[116]

The States' people were bound to raise their voice of protest against such conditions and demanded a change. They could not remain unaffected by the dynamic changes that were taking place in the political and constitutional life of British India.[117] Warnings to this effect had been sounded quite early by some early British Statesmen, and the princes were asked to introduce constitutional and administrative reforms, but they turned a deaf ear to them. The states remained socially and politically backward, but still they were bound to accept influences from British Punjab, as there was a close identity or religious faiths among them and they cherished memories of a common past.[118]

Despite all this, the process of politicalisation in the stages was delayed because of the backwardness prevailing there. Their industrial backwardness negated any active participation of the working class. So it was left to the peasantry to assume the responsibility for unleashing a political movement. With the mass of the Indian people getting drawn into the freedom movement and larger section of the peasantry undergoing a radical transformation, the people in the states also experienced their first political awakening in the twenties. The Montague Chelmsford Mission in 1918, the establishment of the Chamber of Princes' in 1921 and the growing expectations regarding constitutional reforms were some of the causes that aroused an

---

116. Johan S. Hoyland, *India Crisis-The Background,* London : George Allen and Unwin, 1943, 92.
117. Chudgar, P,L., *Indian Princes under British Protection,* London William and Norgate Limited, 1929; (Author of the Montague Chelmsford Report in Para 157 said, Hopes and Aspirations may overlap Frontier Lines like sparks across a street. Similar was the warning of Lord Curzon), Lord Irwin speech delivered to the Chamber of Princes in 1931 also contains such piece of advice.
118. *The Tribune,* dated 2nd September, 1945, see Pattabhai Sitaramayya's article '*Problems of the* States'.

intelligent and keen interest among the people in the affairs of the Indian States.[119]

All India States People's organization had been organized earlier in 1922 but it could assume a concrete shape only in 1927. The principal cause of this delay was the Congress policy of Gandhi. The Gandhi—Irwin Pact, the failure of the second Round Table Conference and the withdrawal of the non-cooperation movement created a climate of despondency and despair. The left wingers in the Congress were unhappy and considered Gandhian leadership thoroughly ineffective and regressive.[120] However, as compared to Gandhi's attitude, there was Nehru's that clearly displayed his interest in the Akali agitation of 1921-24.[121] Gradually in all provinces, Congress Committees started lending a helping hand especially after the All India States' Peoples' Conference was born. But generally the Congress extended only moral support leaving practically everything to the people in the states where civil liberties were non-existent and rule of law quite unknown. To this may be added the words of Lala Duni Chand Ambalvi,[122] who observed : "I have always felt that the Indian National Congress failed in its earlier years in its obvious duty of voicing forth the grievances and taking up the cause of the people of Indian States and tackling the problems affecting them. I have never been convinced of the wisdom of the letting alone policy of earlier years of the Congress regarding the Indian States".

---

119. *Report of the Bombay Session of the Indian States People's Conference*, published by Prof. Abhyankar, G.R. and Manishankar S. Trivedi, 1928, Reference Section of the Central State library, Patiala.
120. Pattabhai, Sitaramayya, *History of the Indian National Congress*, Vol. II, 79; *Indian National Congress*, Report of the 51st Annual Session, 203-04.
121. Mitra, *ed., Indian Annual Register*, 1924, Vol.II, 187; Nehru, *An Autobiography*, 183-84.
122. *Patiala State Records*, Prime Minister's Officer File No. 655, PSA : Patiala; Sharma, Jagdish, *Indian Struggle for Freedom*, (Selected documents and Sources), New Delhi, S. Chand and Co., 1965, 598-605.

Though opposed strongly by the princes,[123] the States 'Peoples' Movement in about 20 years' time succeeded in focusing the attention of the people in British India on the problems of the state subjects. It withdrew the movement soon after the establishment of the *Praja mandal* movement at the national level which would have otherwise remained a local affair. The setting up of the *Praja mandal* in this region of the Punjab attained a special significance as it would successfully involve the peasantry in he freedom struggle.[124] that had started in the Punjab States.

In order to grasp fully the genesis of the state's people's movement, attention must be paid to the various socio-religious movements which went a long way in imparting political consciousness to the people of both British India and Indian States. K.P. Karunakaran has rightly written that, "social and religious reforms movements were often precursor to the political awakening in the country.[125] Pattabhi Sitaramayya regarded the socio-religious movements as, "so many threads in the strand of Indian Nationalism."[126] In the Punjab , there were three, not two religious communities : Hindus, Muslim and Sikh. The political scene here, therefore, always remained a little more complex than in other parts of the country. The Sikhs had their own specific socio-religious movements running parallel to the *Arya Samaj* and the Aligarh movement. Not every movement was, however, relevant for the native states of the Punjab. The princes being jealous of all sorts of extra-

---

123. Iyer, C.S. Ranga, *India Peace or War,* 156; (Documents and Resolution of the All India States' People's Conference available in original in the Reference Section of the Central State Library, Patiala, also quoted by Sharma, Jagdish, *India's Struggle for Freedom*; Handa, R.L., *History of Freedom Struggle in Princely States,* Delhi, n.d., 70-75.
124. *Chamber of Princes Records,* File No. CAS/L-9, PSA : Patiala.
125. K.P. Karunakaran, *Religion and Political Awakening in India,* Meerut : 1965, 22.
126. Pattabhai Sitaramayya, *History of Indian National Congress,* Vol. I, 14.

territorial loyalties and affinities, always took care to seal their frontiers against potentially dangerous idea. But some of these influences did percolate and affect their subjects. The *Arya Samaj* with all its aggressiveness and militancy in the initial stages attracted many Sikhs to its fold, but disenchantment soon set in when the *Samaj* believing in militant Hinduism started attacking the Sikh religion.[127] Despite all this, for a long time, the *Arya Samajists* dominated the Congress Movement in the Punjab. This single factor was enough to drive Sikhs and Muslims away from it. But Hindus, being quite advanced in the fields of trade and education, were drawn into the freedom movement quite early. These factors were not very operative in the states. Educationally the East Punjab states were backward. So Hindus could not take the lead in the political field there. It were the religious reform movements among the Sikhs which really created stir among the States' people. The *Kookas (Namdhari)* movement which was born about a decade later gave a big jolt to the Sikh masses. The latter is particularly important because it did the spade work for the more significant movement for the reform of Sikh shrines which gripped Punjab in 1924-25.[128]

All castes of Hindus, Sikhs and even Muslims could become *Kookas* but generally it were the Sikh peasants and artisans who were drawn towards the movement. It spread rapidly in Ludhiana and Ferozepur districts of the Punjab and the

---

127. Singh, Khushwant, *A History of the Sikhs,* Vol. II, Princeton New Jersey : Princeton University Press, 1966, (Dayanand, the founder of arya smaj, was contemptuous of Sikh theologions because of their importance of Sanskrit, his favourite for any one who did not measure upto him was Maha Murakh ('Great Fool') Nanak he denounced as a Dambhi (Hypocrite). Dayanand set the tone, his zealous admirers followed suit), 166; Dr. Ganda Singh, (*ed.*), *The Punjab Past and present,* Department of Punjab Historical Studies, Panjabi University Patiala, Vol. VII, Part-I, April, 1973.
128. Bajwa, Fauja, Singh, *Kooka Movement,* Delhi : Motilal Banarsidas, Delhi; 1965, 108.

Phulkian states of Patiala, *Nabha* and Jind. The British were alarmed by this new movement because its activities soon posed a grave law and order problem for the Government, as the *Kookas* started attacking Muslim butchers, either to gain popularity among the Hindus and the Sikh masses or out of fanaticism.[129] In due course of time, the British had received countless reports about the political design of the *Kookas*. Their independent *dak* (post) system, their whispering campaign about the divine powers of the *Satguru* who would banish all *Firangis* and would himself become the ruler, their effective boycott of everything foreign—all this was enough for the Government to take action but they were waiting for a convincing argument and this they could get when the *Kookas* attacked Malerkotla, and a pitched battle was fought between them and the troops of Malerkotla. Baba Ram Singh, their leader, was arrested and finally transported to Burma. Now the ruler of Patiala and the chief of other states ordered the arrest of all the *Kookas* in their states.[130] Consequently, temporarily this movement was blasted out of existence on the grounds of Malerkotla episode.[131] The movement, however, left a deep impact on the consciousness of the people of the states. The repression of the *Kookas* generated great bitterness against the prices and the *Kookas* later became the standard-bearers of all progressive movements. They assisted the Congress and the *Praja mandal* movement in these states.[132]

All activities of the *Singh Sabha* movement remained mainly confined to the British Punjab. Its leaders paid little

---

129. Ahuluwalia, M.L., *Kookas : The Freedom Fighters of the Punjab* Bombay : Allied Publishers Private Limited, 1965, 55-56; Dr. Bhagat Singh, 'The Kooka Movement', *The Punjab Past and* Present, vol. VII, Part-I, April 1973, 152.
130. Bajwa, Fauja Singh, *Kooka Movement*, Delhi : Motilal Banarsidar, 1965, 109.
131. Singh, Khushwant, *A History of the Sikhs*, Vol. II, 136.
132. Dr. Walia, Ramesh, *A Study of the Praja Mandal Movement in the East Punjab States, Patiala* : 1974, 95.

attention to the people of the states. If at all it reached the people of the states, it always remained in the loyalist hands. In brief, if the *Singh Sabha* movement in Punjab created a thunder, the people in the states felt its mild vibration. For example a splinter group of the Chief *Khalsa Dewan* named the Punjab *Khalsa Dewan* started functioning from village Bhasaur in Patiala State in 1906 under Babu Teja Singh's leadership. But it would not make much headway; the atmosphere in the states was not so congenial as in Punjab where there was at least some progress in education and cultural field.[133] Hence, its impact in the states was only indirect and very weak.[134]

The *Kamagatamaru* episode followed by the '*Budge Budge ghat* massacre does not require detailed statement, as the readers of the Punjab history are well aware of it. However, a few lines in connection with the impact of this event may be called for. The harsh and callous treatment meted out to those Sikh emigrants by the British rulers dealt a deadly blow to the prestige of the British empire among the Sikhs who had served the crown so loyally. Out of desperation and anger, hundreds of *Panjabis* living in U.S.A. and Canada, joined the *Ghadr* party of Indian emigrants. They were naturally receptive to revolutionary ideas and the policy of the *Ghadr* Party which advocated the forcible over-throw of the British rule in India. In 1914, many *Ghadrites* came to India to stir up rebellion against the British. They also tried to establish contacts with terrorist groups in others parts of the country and spread their activities in the whole Punjab. However, the impact of the

---

133. Singh Sabha, Bhasaur, Gurmate Ate Faisle, Bhasaur : 1904, 1-4; (For more detail see *Khalsa Samachar*, Amritsar from 1901 to 1905); Gurdarshan Singh, 'Origin and Development of Singh Sabha Movement; Constitutional Aspects' the Punjab Past and Present, Vol. VII, Part-I, 1973, 58; Memorandum submitted by a Sikh deputation to Lord Chelmsford in 1917, quoted in Sahani's Ruchiram, *Struggle for Reforms* in Sikh Shirnes, Amritsar : Sikh Itihas Research Board, S.G.P.C., 47-48.
134. Singh, Harbans, *The Heritage of the Sikhs*, Bombay; Asai Publishing House, 1964, 147.

Ghadr movement on the states was negligible. The *Ghadrites* could set up only one centre for arms manufacture at Lohat Badi in the Nabha state. Harnam Singh Chamak of this village later became active in the Akali movement. Dala Singh of Jaladiwar in the Patiala State and Karam Singh of Kapurthala state joined the Ghadr party abroad. They went to the university for the Tailers of the East in the U.S.S.R. and on their return, took active part in organising the first Communist groups in the states of Nabha, Kapurthala and Patiala.[135] After Sometime, Sewa Singh of Thikriwala village in the Patiala State founded *Praja Mandal* organization. There were reports that S.Gurdit Singh of *Kamagatamaru* fame had stayed in this area for some months and had occasional meetings with Sewa Singh Thinkriwala.[136] The latter might have received inspiration from Gurdit Singh and this led him to organize the peasant's movement in the states.

The *Babbar Akali* agitation rose in the form of terrorist groups functioning in the *Doab* region. Some of the *Babbar Akalis* belonged to the Kapurthala State. After its suppression, however, some of them degenerated and started playing in the hands of Maharaja of Patiala who utilized them for his own purposes.[137] Besides, the Akali Dal became quite active after the passage of *Gurdwara* Act in 1925 and this Dal launched the Gurdwara reform movement vigorously. In fact, this movement was born out of the *Singh Sabha* and the *Ghadr* movements.

---

135. *Ibid.*

136. Personal interview with Sardar Ujjagar Singh Bawa, a close associate of S. Sewa Singh. He tells, "I was quite young at that time and accompanied Sewa Singh to a number of such meetings. Sardar Gurdit Singh was present at the Lahore session of the *Punjab Riyasti Praja Mandal* which elected Sewa Singh as its President".

137. The case of Bijla Singh and his companion who worked against the Maharaja of Nabha Ripudaman Singh in Nabha Patiala dispute. References to their services are available in State files as also in *Some Confiderntial Papers of the Akali Movement,* edited by Dr. Ganda Singh, published by S.G.P.C., Amritsar, 182.

The former proved so powerful that even the British Government bowed before it, when the keys of *Nankana Sabhi Gurdwara* were given to S.Kharak Singh. He first decisive battle, in the words of Gandhi ji, was thus won.[138] After this, the *Akalis* held *morchas* at various places such as, jaito for the liberation of *Gurdwaras*. In brief, the *Gurdwara* reform movement left a great impact on the politics of the Punjab,[139] as it imported to the Sikh community great political and communal consciousness. The sweep of the movement was so great that its anti-imperialist and anti-feudal character led to the dissemination of militant nationalist and democratic idea, and brought the people of the states in contact with political currents existing in British India. In exploded the loyalist policies which the Sikhs had been pursuing uptil then and drew them straight into the stream of national politics.

The changes in India, no doubt, influenced the attitude of the people in the East Punjab States, but these were only indirect influences. However, all political activities in the British territories found a direct echo in the East Punjab State. It was only in the twenties that the political scene warmed up to an extent that the people in the states also became politically conscious. But this awakening was, in a large measure, due to the *Gurdwara* reform movement. The freedom movement in India did not inspire the people of these states, it only helped it. The shape, character and the dimensions of the tenants' movement were determined directly by the *Akali* movement.

In November, 1917, the October Revolution was successful in Russia. A big dent was made in the armour of imperialism which could never again be mended. Imperialism had already raised a signal of alarm. On 12th December, 1917, *'The Statesman'*, the Chief organ of the British Capitalism in India

138. File No. 914-II-1922, Home Political (National Archieves of India, New Delhi); *The Tribune* (Lahore), January 26, 1922; Sahni, Ruchi Ram, *Struggle for Freedom in Sikh Shrines,* Amritsar Sikh *Itihas* Research Boared, S.G.P.C., 160-162.

139. File No. 565/C of 1939, Prime Minister's Office Files, PSA : Patiala.

had declared, "In substance, the activities of the revolutionary leadership in India are but a most powerful ever been launched against a historical state".[140] After a few months the Montague Chelmsford Report clearly felt that "The Bolshevik revolution in Russia had given inspiration to political consciousness in India".[141] No wonder, the Chairman of the Reception Committee of a Communist *Kisan* Conference held in 1943, after extending the 'Red Salute', asked his audience—"Is there any reason that Patiala and other states must remain in the 12th century? Why can these not become like Russia or California"?[142] (The Comrade quoted here, had in the same breath asked for the setting up of factories). Russia was highly developed and so too was California.[143] So where was the anamoly? In fact, the Conference wished that every peasant must own and cultivate one's own plot of land; and this was already an article of faith with the Punjab Communists, with their roots in the self-cultivating peasant proprietors of Central Punjab. The Russian experience, too, had been seen through the eyes of the peasants with small holdings-early Bolshevik slogans (such as 'land to the tillers') and policies, especially those of the N.E.P. period.[144]

---

140. File No. 41/C PSA : Patiala.
141. C.Rajeshwara Rao, 'The decade after the Split : The Party's Policy and Programme proved right', Souvenir, issued by the Communist Party, January 26, 1976.
142. Poster announcing a *Kisan* Conference at Village Chaumar Mayscim October, 1943. It contains the address of the Chairman of the reception, October 14-15, 1943, Poster attached in *Patiala State Records*-Prime Minister's Office File No. 2193.
143. California occupied an important place in the hearts and lives of *Kirti* group of the Punjab Communists who had come to communism *via Ghadr* Party with its headquarter at California and who still maintained close links with the *Ghadr* organization in the united states and jealously guarded their organizational and financial autonomy *vis-a-vis* the CPI Communists.
144. For details see Joh, Bhagwan, *Communist Movement in Punjab*, Delhi : 1979, 96-99.

Hence, this revolution also inspired the people in the Punjab. The following note which was reported to the higher authorities in 1920, gives an insight into the kind of sensitivity displayed by the CID to, check the Bolshevik influence in the Punjab, because of its geographical proximity to Soviet Russia. 'A Durrani Pathan was recently found at Amritsar station talking Bolshevism and praising the Bolsheviks' representing that if they came to India, all wealth would be divided and there would be no more poor. He gave his name as Gulam Haider Khan and told that he was a horse dealer and going to Bareilly. It appears that there was a man of this name, resident of Kohat; enquiries are in progress.[145]

Above all the visit of Jawahar Lal Nehru to Russia and the views of Rabindernath Tagore had a significant effect on Punjab States. The *Kirti Kisan Sabha*, the Communist group and the *Ghadr* party whipped up agitation in these states for the upliftment of the poor and the exploited as was done in Russia. The *Hijrat* and the *Khilafat* movements made Muslims of Malerkotla dissatisfied with the British imperialists. The intelligentsia which went to Russia and the *Muhajir* immigrants inspired vision of a new political system on Russian style. A number of Communist cells grew up in the whole of the country. Ghulam Hussain in Lahore founded Communist Party and started an *Urdu* paper *'Inqlab'* for propagating Marxist ideology which greatly affected the peasants and workers of the areas under review. He received financial aid from Russia. However, the Communist party was held illegal and remained weak. The *Ghadrites* made efforts to stir up rebellion in the armed forces. Most of the army personnels who retired form the army and belonged to the agriculturist classes joined the *Gurdwara* reform movement and the peasants' and Workers' Party. The latter merged into the Communist Party in 1927-28. Hence, the Peasant's movement was caused, to a great extent,

---

145. Roy, Subodh, *Communism in India 1919-1924,* unpublished documents, 1971, 135 (For more detail, see G.Adhikari, *Documents of the History of the Communist Party of India,* Vol. I & II).

by the impact of external factors, though in the very beginning this impact was not very potent. But as time passed and political movement in India gained momentum, the people of these states also started agitation under the banner of the *Praja Mandal* movement and had an active support of the Punjab *Kisan Sabha*, which will be discussed at length in the following two chapters.

4 INVOLVEMENT OF POLITICAL PARTIES

This chapter has two main objectives, firstly, to present the facts about the activities of the major political groups and the interest they displayed in connection with agrarian problems, and secondly to measure the strength of each political group in this region of the Punjab. The chapter is divided into two sections—section one deals with the formation of the *Praja Mandal Organization* and its links with the peasants' struggle; while section two covers the development of party-politics and the involvement of the major political parties in this region. Attempt has also been made to highlight the impact of party-politics on the ruralites in particular.

Unlike many other native states, *Praja Mandals* in the East Punjab States were not formed by enlightened state subjects living in the British Indian cities directly under inspiration from the Congress movement. Instead, these were the handiwork of Akali workers[1] who themselves were the product of the *Gurdwara* Reform Movement. The *Praja Mandal* organization was first formed in the Patiala State; its office bearers were elected in a meeting held at village Saikha (Barnala *tehsil*), in February, 1928. The meeting was conducted under the

---

1. Dr. Joginder Dayal, Struggle of the States People and the Communists' (An article in Panjabee), published in *Souvenir* issued by the CPI on 26th January, 1976; Personal meeting with Shri Brish Bhan, Chandigarh (The akalis gave this movement a well determined and separate carder); Bawa Ujjagar Singh, *Amar Shaheed Sewa Singh Thikriwala (Punjabee),* 4; (For details regarding the factors led to its formation see Aulakh, Jagjit Singh, *Ikk Jiwan-Ikk Itihas* (Panjabi), 67; Bose, Nemi Sadhan, *The Indian National Movement* (An Ouline 76).

presidentship of Sardar Bakhshish Singh Kattu.[2] A little later, similar *Praja Mandals* were formed in other states.[3] With this it was felt absolutely essential by the founders of the States' *Praja Mandals* to set up a central body of this organization for the smooth development and planning of a united struggle in a common cause in the various states of the Punjab.[4]

Thus was formed the Punjab *Riyasti Praja Mandal* on July 17,1928 at village Mansa, with the avowed objectives of fighting for establishment of a representative government and safeguarding the people's rights and liberties.[5] The *Praja Mandal,* as it has already been stated, was formed to work in tune with the ideals of the Indian National Congress (hereafter INC) and the Akalis, who were struggling for independence. However, in view of the nature of this organization, it was not possible to set up these *mandals* (groups) of the Punjab States in the vicinity of the state territories. This is why the headquarters of the central organization were set up at a far off place like Amritsar and later on at Lahore in 1930, from where the Working Committee could guide more easily the activities of the *Praja Mandalas* of

2. to launch a struggle against the autocratic rule of states which was the root cause of their miseries and troubles; the unwarranted arrest of the beloved leader of the Sikh community-Sardar Sewa Singh Thikriwala, which agitated the minds of the people of the states and the advise of Shri Amrit Lal Seth, the then General Secretary of the All India States People Association etc. kindled the fire towards the formation of the *Praja Mandals* in the States, Bawa Ujjagar Singh, *Amar Shaheed Sewa Singh Thikriwala* (Panjabi), 4.
3. Giani, Nahar Singh, *History of the Freedom Movement in India,* 219; Chudgar, P.L., *Indian Princes Under British protection,* London, Willian and Norgate Ltd., 1929, 92-93.
4. For more detail about its formation see Report of Inspector General of Police dated 15.8.1928, given in File No. 224, PSA; Patiala; *The Jagriti* (Panjabi Monthly), August, 1965, 24; Aulakh Jagjit Singh, Ikk-Jivan-Ikk Itihas, 68.
5. Bawa, Ujjagar Singh, *Amar Shaheed Sewa Singh Thikriwala* (Panjabi) 181.

the states.[6] The Punjab *Riyasti Praja Mandal* had adopted its own constitution on August 10, 1928. In this constitution, it was provided that its organization would be extended to eighteen states.[7] But its activities practically remained confined to eleven states only.[8]

At the very outset, it is noteworthy to state that each State *Praja Mandal* had different objectives but the following were the common objectives of all of the states' *Praja Mandals*, under the control of the central body :[9]

1. *Rajas/Nawabs* should be given fixed salary/ allowances out of which they should manage their house and personal expenses;
2. Establishment of Councils for law making and District Boards;
3. To improve the working of the Law Courts by lessening influence of the *Rajas/Nawabs*;
4. To agitate for removing the grievances of the peasants in particular;
5. To obtain freedom of speech and expression;
6. To attain constitutional form of governments in the states to work for the welfare of the state;
7. *Nazoal* system prevailing in the states should be done away with. It was the system under which the land of

---

6. Bawa, Ujjagar Singh, *Amar Shaheed Sewa Singh Thikriwala (Panjabi)*, 181.
7. *Ibid.*
8. *Ibid, Punjab State Records*, Prime Minister's File No. 595, PSA : Patiala; Presidential address of Chhatar Singh Maur, Printed at the Mitter Press, Amritsar.
9. Dr. Joginder Dayal, *'Riyasti Lokan Da Ghol Ten'* Communists (Panjabi), *Souvenir*, issued by the CPI on January 26, 1976, Bawa, Ujjagar Singh, *Amar Shaheed Sewa Singh Thikriwala* (Panjabi), 181; *Patiala State Records*, Prime Ministers' File No. 746 PSA : Patiala.

the owner was attached to the state if the former did not leave behind a heir for five generations to inherit;

8. *Begar* (forced labour) system should be done away with in the states;
9. Loans taken from the State's subjects on the even of the first world war should be returned to them immediately;
10. Due justice should be done to the tenants/peasants;
11. Adequate scheme should be drawn up for the development of education;
12. *Birs* (forests) preserved by the states for hunting should not be maintained as the animals caused damage to the crops; and
13. The confiscated properties, titles and pensions, etc., should be restored to the Akalis and other political prisoners of these states.[10]

In fact, the *Praja Mandals* in different states had objectives specific to each state. But it is to be remembered that in the initial stages the *Praja Mandal* movement was primarily the movement of the Sikh peasants and it voiced the grievances of the farmers in its very first Conference", which was held at Mansa.[11] The activities of this organization have been briefly discussed here.

---

10. *Ibid;* Kapurthala State Records File A/5-1-45, PSA : Patiala.
11. Personal interview with Gujjar Singh of Dhanetha (Jind State), "Ex-soldier and former Akali Praja Mandal Worker". He stated "we were then in Egypt and the news from Punjab 'were disturbing all of us". (The agitation against the Rowllat Act, non-co-operation movement, the episode of *Jallianwala* massacre, forcible realization of war funds from the peasantry and brutal and barabarous British policy). Our officers were very much concerned over the signs of unrest among us. They held out meetings and told us that there was nothing to worry about. (In connection with the wide spread Punjab disturbances, see Sinha, Sardhar, *(Indian Independence in perspective,* Bombay, Asia Publishing Hosue : 1964, 56).

As already stated, the first sign of unrest among the people (particularly the peasants) of the states of East Punjab appeared in the twenties. The soldiers from the states, who were on active duty abroad became carriers of enlightened political ideas in the country-side after securing release from ideas in the country-side after securing release from the army.[12] The peasants in the states got their first lesson from these soldiers and came into clash with the British power in the Punjab. Hundreds of the simple minded, go fearing peasants and agricultural labourers participated in the *Gurdwara* Reform movement, courted arrest and faced *lathi* blows in the *Guru-ka-bagh* and other *morchas.*[13] Though the *Gurwdwara* Reform Movement ended with the passage of the *Gurdwara* Act in 1925, but the peasants were now ready to make any sacrifice at the bidding of their leaders.[14] For the first time, the princes' monopoly of leadership was being effectively challenged. If injustice in religious affairs was intolerable, so was economic, social and political high-handedness.

At the heels of the wave of mass politicalisation came the world economic crisis of 1928-29 which had a deep impact on the agrarian economy of the country in general and of the states in particular. Thus, the storm had been gathering for along in form of peasants' unrest, and the movement for reform of Sikh shrines had accentuated the situation. It is to be noted that the *Maharaja* of Patiala was not in the state when the agitation was launched by the Punjab *Riyasti Praja Mandal* and the Akalis, so was the *Maharaja* of Kapurthala. When/the *Maharaja* of Patiala came back in January, 1929, he was determined not to

---

12. Dr. Ganda Singh (*ed.*), *Some Confidenital Papers,* XXVI—of the introduction, also 138, 141, 142; *Quarterly Register,* April, 1924, Dr. Joginder Dayal, *'Riyasti Lokan Da Ghol Ten'* Communists (Panjabi), *Souvenir,* issued by the CPI January 26, 1976.
13. Dr. Ganda Singh (*ed.*), *Some Confidential Papers,* XXVI—of the introduction, also 138-142; Master Tara Singh *Meri Yad* (Panjabi), Amritisar : Sikh Religious Book Society, 1945, 92.
14. Maharajas' (Patiala) interview with Associated Press Representative dated February 6, 1929; *Patiala State Records,* Prime Minister's Office File No. 547 and 548, PSA : Patiala.

give free hand to the agitators. But he did not follow the policy of isolating the deputationists.[15] The movement was gathering power day by day. The state authorities mobilized all their resources to counteract the agitation.[16] It, therefore, became easy for the agitators to impress upon the ordinary villagers the tyrannical nature of the princely rule and the need for a struggle for civil rights. The leaders were no demanding the release of all political workers[17] and for this a petition was submitted to the district authorities on July 15, 1929. But it was rejected, now, the *Praja Mandal* movement made a bold start in the East Punjab States. The leadership and cadre were provided by the Akalis. The main aim as stated earlier, was to win political rights for the states' peasantry and to get their grievances redressed.[18]

In the Malerkotla State, the movement was being organised by Giani Kehar Singh of Chak village. Sardar Sewa Singh of village Bapla and Talib Hussain of Sherwanikot.[19] The main demands of the Malerkotla peasantry were to end corruption and illegal extraction of money by the nawab, the safeguarding of their rights in land and the bringing down of land revenue to the level of Ludhiana district in the Punjab.[20] These demands

15. Prime Minister's Office File No. 547 and 548 and 548, PSA : Patiala. (These files contain a detailed account of the steps taken by the State authorities to meet the situation).
16. (Some of the political workers were—Bhawan Singh, Hazura Singh and Harnam Singh of village Katran, Sham Singh of village Kanjala and Gian Singh of village Chhangli) *vide*; Prime Minister's Office File No. 578, PSA : Patiala.
17. Patiala State Records, Prime Minister's Office File No. 578 PSA : Patiala; Vaid Chhajju Mal, 'Pepsu Muzarian De Ghol Ten' *op. cit.*
18. *Communist Party :* (An Article in Panjabi) published in *Souvenir* issued by the CPI, on January 26, 1976.
19. *Patiala State Records,* Prime Minister's Office File No. 595 PSA : Patiala; Dr. Joginder Dayal, *'Riyasti Lokan Da Ghol Ten Communists',* published in *Souvenir,* issued by the CPI on January 26, 1976.
20. Talib Hussain rose to an important position in the Punjab *Riyasti Praja Mandal.* He edited the official organ of the Punjab *Riyasti Praja Mandal, "Riyasti Duniya".*

were published in the form of a poster termed "Malerkotla Indictment" by the state *Praja Mandal.* The people were asked to supply their grievances to the workers of the *Praja Mandal* faction. A demand was also made of the paramount power to hold an enquiry into the state administration and remove the nawab in case the charges were proved. The annual observance of the *Kothala* day in memory of the persons who had fallen to police bullets in 1927, became a rallying point for the state peasantry. The responsibility for the observance of the day was now taken over by the Punjab *Riyasti Praja Mandal* and workers from neighbouring states took part in the Malerkotla State. The annual fair of Chappar in Ludhiana district provided another occasion for the *Praja Mandal* workers to meet and chalk out their programme.[21]

In the Kapurthala State, the villages in the Bhunga pocket surrounded on all sides by the Hoshiarpur district, became a centre of *Praja Mandal* activities. The 'Dhut Group' of political workers, as it was called by the Kapurthala administration after the name of their village, was actively associated with the Punjab *Riyasti Praja Mandal* since its very inception. The group was led by Master Hari Singh. Here also the main demand centred round the reduction of land revenue, abolition of regressive and repressive taxes, end to corruption, more roads and hospitals in the rural areas and a responsible Government.[22]

In the Jind state the *Praja Mandal* launched a *morcha* against the state administration. The Sikh peasants in Jind State had their grievances against the state administration which went unheeded at the hands of Dr. Bihari Lal Dhingra, the Prime Minister. Their grievances related mainly to the revenue and

---

21. Giani Kehar Singh, *Dard Kahani* (Punjabee, n.d.).
22. This fair was held in July-August at *Chhapar* which was near Ahmedgarh railway station Ludhiana-Hissar railway line. Thousands of peasants from states also attended it. Political parties held groups on the occasion to propagate their programme and policies. *Vide.,* File No. 1/5-1-45, Kapurthala State Records, PSA : Patiala.

judicial administration of the state. The land revenue had been enhanced and corruption prevailed all round.[23] It was alleged by the *Praja Mandal* that choicest land in two Sikh dominated villages had been gifted to Dr. Dhingra by the *Maharaja* and cultivating owners were being dispossessed by him. Then there were grievances concerning the *begar* system and forcible supplies of fodder and other provisions for the guests of the *Maharaja* and his hunting parties. The Maharaja of Jind had little time for state affairs. He had left every thing to the care of his Prime Minister who was brought from British India. The Sikhs, though in minority in the state, were not ready to accept Dr. Dhingra as Prime Minister as they considered Jind to be a Sikh state.[24] Again, it was the Sikh peasantry that became the mainstay of the *Praja Mandal* in Jind state.

The character of the movement in smaller states was not in any way different from that in the Patiala State. Akalis formed the hard-core of the *Praja Mandal* workers everywhere and their main demands were concerned with the redressal of peasants' grievances. The only difference was that in smaller states the movement always remained on a low level. It neither attained the sweep it did in Patiala State nor could it attract the attention of the All India States' Peoples Conference.

---

23. Personal meeting with Master Hari Singh, Communist Office, Chandigarh; (Master Hari Singh was an elected member of the Kapurthala State Assembly. He always took active part in the proceedings and put searching questions on grievances of rural people. He remained an office bearer of the Punjab *Riyasti Praja Mandal* for a number of years. Another leading light of the *Dhut* group Baba Karam Singh was Chairman of the Reception Committee of the Ludhiana Session of the All India States' People's Conference held in 1939 under the Presidentship of Pt. Nehru) *Vide., Kapurthala State Records* File A/5-1-45, Punjab State Archieves, Patiala.
24. Longawalia, Bhagwan Singh, 'Mal-administration in Jind State', *Patiala State Records,* Prime Minster's Office File No. 595, PSA : Patiala.

In the East Punjab States, the five months preceding the Lahore session of the Indian National Congress witnessed a tremendous growth of the *Praja Mandal* movement. Its local units were set up in smaller states.[25] Now the anti-Bhupinder Singh campaign was stepped up. Sewa Singh Thikriwala undertook an intensive tour of the Patiala State excepting the Hindi speaking and the Hill areas. The territories of Patiala, Nabha, Jind and Malerkotla were contiguous to one another and the message which Sewa Singh carried reached not only the Patiala state but the rural folk in the adjoining states also.[26] Besides, on their return from Lahore, the *Praja Mandal* workers started making preparation for observance of the first Independence day. On 23rd January, 1930, Sewa Singh Thikriwala led a Procession of *kisans* from his village to Barnala, where a public meeting was held. The importance of the day was explained and a pledge was taken to liberate the people living in the states from the double slavery of the British and the princes. Processions and public meetings were also organized at Sunam and Mansa, two other strong holds of the movement. The success of the various public meetings and processions gave new fillip to the peasants' movement under the banner of the *Praja Mandal* Organisation.[27] The people's discontent was so wide-spread and so intense that the government had to take note of it. In 1937-38, the Prime Minister was reported to have drawn the attention of subordinate officials and asked them to tour villages and redress the general grievances of the peasantry.[28]

It was after the death of Sewa Singh Thikriwala, that dissensions in the Punjab *Riyasti Praja Mandal* leadership came to the surface. Soon two clear cut factions took shape. One was

---

25. *Ibid.*; Quarterly Register, April, 1924.
26. Bose, Nema Sadhan, *The Indian National Movement—An Ouline*, 76.
27. *Patiala State Records*, Prime Minister's Office File No. 555 PSA : Patiala.
28. *Patiala State Records*, Prime Minister's Office File No. 613, PSA : Patiala.

led by Harchand Singh Jeji[29] while the second faction was led by Bhagwan Singh Longowalia and Jagir Singh Joga. The members of the latter group came under the influence of Marxist ideology, although many of them might not have been enrolled as regular members of the Communist Party.[30] From 1936 onwards, Punjab Socialist and Communist leaders were to be seen addressing *Praja Mandal* conferences in and outside the Punjab States.[31] At these conferences peasants were asked to enroll themselves as members of *kisan* Committees in response to the call of the All India *kisan sabhas.*[32] In fact, the communists were them working in the Congress and in the Punjab *Riyasti Praja Mandal* and they were mainly responsible for organizing *kisan* Committees and encouraging new peasant's struggle. The *Praja Mandal* workers who belonged to the peasant class gradually turned more and more to the Communists for help and guidance.[33] It has been held that the impact of the Communist ideology on the national movement expressed itself

29. *Patiala State Records,* Prime Minister's Office File No. 750, PSA : Patiala. (For more detail regarding the peoples discontent see File Nos. 700, 710 and 730, Patiala State Records, Prime Minister's Office, PSA : Patiala.
30. Harchand Singh Jeji never occupied any office in the Punjab *Riyasti Praja Mandal* but his behind the scene activities made no less contribution to the movement. When we talk of his being the leader of one group, it only means that he had the de-facto leader of the faction.
31. Personal meeting with Sardar Jagir Singh Joga and Sardar Isher Singh Majhail, Arjun Nagar, Patiala.
32. Confidential Report (Weekly) from I.G.P. Patiala, dated 13.8.87, *Patiala State Records,* Prime Minister's Office File 1546, 1937; Copy of Report dated 20.4.39 (August 1936) from Inspector CID, Patiala, on the proceedings of a *Praja Mandal* meeting held at Khanna on 2.8.1936 under the presidency of Sohan Singh Josh; B.P.L. Bedi, Arjan Singh Gargaj, Karam Singh Mann and Baba Rur Singh were the most prominent leaders invited to speak.
33. *Confidential Report (Weekly)* from I.G.P. Patiala dated 13.8.37 21.10.37, 1.1.1938*etc. Patiala dated 13.8.37, (*15.1.1938) Prime Minster's Office File 1546 and 1547; also see Walia, Ramesh, *A Study of the Praja Mandal Movement in the East Punjab States,* Patiala : 1974, 131-32.

on three fronts :[34] *(a)* Complete independence as opposed to dominion status; *(b)* Complete abolition of feudalism; *(c)* An organization of peasants, workers and the youth into their distinct class organisation.

This latter impact had a particular significance for the states. Well known Communist workers from the Punjab frequently toured the states and lectured at public meetings organized by the *Praja Mandal* there. Sohan Singh Josh, Arjun Singh Gargaj, Karam Singh Mann and Baba Rur Singh were some of the prominent leaders who were often invited to address of the *Praja Mandal* Conferences in and outside the Punjab States.[35] The presidential address of the Praja Mandal Conference held at Mehlan (Jind State) is a fine specimen of the secular and radical approach of the organization in this period as compared to the early emphasis on religious issues under Akali influence. The address discussed the political situation in the country in 1937 and exhorted people to organize *Kisan Sabhas* and seek affiliation with the Congress Socialist party; fight for reduction in land revenue and abolition of excessive taxation and demand more roads, schools and hospitals.[36] Another representative document of this period was *Praja Mandal Amli* Programme (*Praja Mandal* Programme of action)

34. Walia, Ramesh, *A Study of the Praja Mandal Movement in the East Punjab States,* Patiala : 1974, 79; For more details see Balabshevish, V.V., and others (*ed.*) *Contemporary History of India,* New Delhi : People Publishing House, 1963, 153-54.
35. *Ibid.*
36. Report of a Public Meeting at Khanna held on August 2, 1936, *Vide., Patiala State Records,* Prime Minister's Office File No. 747; The Poster (in Panjabi) of Longowal Conference scheduled for 7th & 8th November, 1936, *Patiala State Records,* Prime Minsiter's Office File No. 737, PSA : Patiala. (For details also see *Patiala State Records,* Prime Minster's Office File 1544 and 1546 and 1937. The I.G. Politics Patiala issued a circular order to all *nizams* and S.Ps to submit regular weekly reports in view of the recent activities of the *Praja Mandal* their . . . identification with communist and socialist tendencies, and plans to form *kisan* Committees and *Praja Mandal* branches, circular No. 15 dated 28.8.1937, *Ibid.,* File No. 1546).

which could be termed as the Communist manifesto for the East Punjab States.[37] Its language was clearly Communist oriented, showing no influence of religion. It was prescribed by the Patiala State Government vide their *Gazette notification* dated 9th June, 1937. That the Communists were dominating the organization became clear at Anandpur Sahib where a *Praja Mandal* conference was held on 25th and 26th March, 1937.[38]

The conference had originally been announced by the Jeji faction of the *Praja Mandal* and Bhagwan Singh Longowalia and Jagir Singh Joga had not been invited to lecture. But the stage was captured by the supporters of the latter group on the very first day and the Red *Kirti* flag hoisted in the *pandal*.[39] During the course of their speeches, the speakers demanded true rule of the peasants and workers in the states, jobs for the unemployed, proprietary rights for peasants and establishment of representative government. The most significant aspect of the conference was that the slogan of long live Revolution was frequently raised and a frontal attack was launched against Jeji and his group.[40] According to Jagir Singh Joga, his *Praja Mandal* was a party of the poor and that of Jeji a friend of capitalists and feudal lords.[41] Giani Kehar Singh of Malerkotla openly declared that, "we have now come under the *kirti* flag which symbolizes freedom".[42] On the second day two separate *dewans*

37. Presidential address of Sri Chhatar Singh Maur, Printed at the Mittar Press, Amritsar.
38. *Patiala State Records,* Prime Minister's Office File No. 744, (Programme published by Jagir Singh Joga), PSA : Patiala.
39. *Patiala State Records,* Prime Minster's Office File No. 747, Proceedings of the Conference, PSA : Patiala.
40. Personal interview of S. Jagir Singh Joga; *Ibid.*
41. Proceedings of the Conference, *Patiala State Records,* Prime Minister's Office File No. 747, PSA : Patiala; Dr. Joginder Dayal, *Riyasti Lokan De Ghol Ten* Communists, *Souvenir,* January 26, 1976.
42. *Patiala State Records,* Prime Minster's Office File No. 747, PSA : Patiala (Proceedings of the Conference). Also confirmed from personal meeting with Master Hari Singh who was present in the Conference.

were held. While the Communist leaders' speeches continued in the Longowalia and Joga Conference, whose ideological shift towards the left and their working hold over *Praja Mandal* workers was no doubt influenced by their disillusionment with the Akali current and Master Tara Singh's pact with the Maharaja;[43] the second Conference was addressed by S. Kartar Singh Nagal, Rulia Singh of Faridkot and Ujjagar Singh Bhaura who concentrated merely on personal issues and side tracked the basic economic, social and political issues. In brief, it was under the banner of the Punjab *Riyasti Praja Mandal* that the peasants had held conferences, organized demonstrations, led deputations and submitted memoranda.

While these changes were taking place in the Punjab *Riyasti Praja Mandal*, the movement in other parts of the country was taking rapid strides. Pandit Nehru Called 1938 the year of "mighty awakening among the people of the states".[44] As a result of the general elections held in 1937, in nine provinces of the British India, Congress ministries were formed under the Government of India act of 1935. These ministries were not taking any action against the *Praja Mandal* workers operating from their area. They were instead rendering assistance to them in their work. The prices were much disturbed over these new developments. The Chamber of Princes held protracted discussions on the question of subversive movements from across the borders of the states and consulted legal luminaries whether the crown representative should be pressed to take action against the state people's movement being directed from basis in British Provinces.[45] However, their nervousness subsided only with the declaration of war in 1939 when the Congress ministries resigned. Under Rule 26 of the Defence of India Rules, all allegations and propaganda against the rulers and their administration was prohibited. The amendment to

43. Presidential address of Pandit Jawahar Lal Nehru to the Ludhiana Session of the All India States' People's Conference, PSA : Patiala.
44. *Chamber of Princes Records*, File No. CRS/3/45-PSA : Patiala.
45. *Ibid.*; Proceedings of the Standing Committee meeting dated January 16, 1941.

rule 26 was carried out in the light of the opinion given by Shri B.L. Mitter and the Chamber of Princes Standing Committee expressed its satisfaction over this. [46]

Condition in the Punjab, however, was quite different. The Unionist Ministry here under Sir Sikander Hyat Khan had adopted a totally hostile attitude towards the Congress and the states' people's movement.[47] This hostile attitude of the Unionist Ministry figured in the address of Baba Karam Singh Dhut at Ludhiana session of the All India States people's Conference who severally condemned the Ministry's policy of persecuting the workers of the *Praja Mandal* movement in the Punjab.[48] Had there been a Congress Government at the helm of affairs in the Punjab, the story would have been different. This was proved in the post war period when the Congress Government in Punjab rendered all assistance to the *Praja Mandal* in the states of Jind, Faridkot and Nabha and the movement there touched new heights.

Another factor that affected the movement was the death of *Maharaja* Bhupinder Singh in 1938. The death of this controversial figure resulted in significant changes in the *Praja Mandal* movement in Patiala and other neighbouring states. The young *Maharaja* Yadvindra Singh wedded the daughter of Harchand Singh Jeji, the arch-enemy of his father, and thus won a section of the Praja Mandal cadre to his side.[49] The withdrawal of Jeji and his group from the *Praja Mandal* left the field clear for the Communists who soon captured the organization.[50] This section of the *Praja Mandal* leadership included Jagir Singh Joga and Harnam Singh Chamak, Sardara

46. Sir Sikandar's address at the Patna Session of the Muslim League vide the Bombay Chronical dated 28th December, 1938 and the Bombay Sentinal dated 27th December, 1938.
47. *Patiala State Records,* Prime Minster's Office File No. 369, Baba Karam Singh Dhut's address, PSA : Patiala.
48. *Ibid.;* Personal interview with Sardar Jagir Singh Joga.
49. *Patiala State Records,* Prime Ministers' Office File No. 369, PSA : Patiala.
50. *Ibid.,* Personal Interview with Sardar Jagir Singh Joga.

Singh Yuthup and Hardit Singh Bhattal, all from the Nabha state, Kaur Singh Maur, Jaswant Singh and Gujjar Singh Dhanetha from the Jind State, Master Hari Singh, Basawa Singh and Chanan Singh from Kapurthala State, Sewa Singh Bapla and Giani Kehar Singh from the Malerkotla State and Sunder Singh, Atma Singh and Shamsher Singh from the Kalsia state. They supplied the Communist Party in the East Punjab States with its first cadre.[51]

Under the guidance of this radical wing of the Punjab *Riyasti Praja Mandal,* the political scene warmed up further. In addition to the sharpening of the tenant movement, unrest among the peasant proprietors of Patiala, Faridkot, Jind, Malerkotla and Kapurthala continued. It rapidly mounted in the tiny state of Kalsia which witnessed a regular peasant's revolt in 1938. However, the *Praja Mandal* in *Kalsia* was set up in February, 1940. It was a direct result of the Charik *Morcha*[52] which is discussed at length in the next chapter. The *Kisan* Committee and the *Praja Mandal* had common office bearers.[53]

An official report about Patiala State listed Dhuri and Suman as the two places where the Hindus were becoming Congress minded.[54] But the draconian state laws prevented people from participating in these activities. The *hidayat-88* in the East Punjab States and the Society Registration Act in the Faridkot state directly attacked people's right for association and free expression. The *Praja Mandal* organised a *satyagraha* at Sunam in 1938 demanding the repeal of the *hidayat.* The *satyagraha* with its head-quarters at Ludhiana, continued for some days and some arrests were offered. It was suspended on Gandhi's advice and on the reported assurance of the *Maharaja* of Patiala that the *hidayat* would be withdrawn in due course of time. The *Praja Mandal* leaders later alleged that the *Maharaja*

---

51. *Kalsia State Record,* File No. 164 (Dewan's letter dated November 20, 1938) PSA : Patiala.
52. *Kalsia State Record,* File No. 132, PSA : Patiala.
53. *Patiala State Records,* Prime Minister's Office File No. 756, PSA : Patiala.
54. Gandhi, MK, *Indian States' Problem,* 368.

had gone back on his assurances. They also complained that the Maharaja had used threatening language against a *Praja Mandal* deputation.[55] In the Faridkot state, the ruler was administering similar warnings to political workers against their seditious activities. Organizers of an Akali Conference held at Kotakpura, Giani Zail Singh, Gurbax Singh, Janga Singh and Sandhura Singh were called by the ruler and told bluntly to desist from holding political conferences in the grab of religious *dewans*. Therefore, all efforts were made that no *dewan* of this kind should be held at all efforts were made that no *dewan* of this kind should be held at all in the states.[56] But the events were moving fast. A *Zamindara Sabha* was set up on 24th July, 1938, and all the above named workers were associated with it. Through posters and pamphlets the Committee put forward the most progressive demands ever made by the *Praja Mandal* in the states of East Punjab.[57] The emphasis, however, was chiefly on peasants' demands, such as the auctioning of *Shamlat* lands should be stopped and the peasants should be allowed to sell their crops in any market town they liked and not necessarily inside the state.

With the passage of time, two demands came to the forefront, namely repeal of the Registration of Societies Act and full proprietary rights for the *kisans* through the abolition of the *ala malik* system.[58] Public meetings were organised by the *Praja Mandal* in favour of these demands during 1938-39. However, the state authorities employed all possible means to

55. Faridkot State Records, File No. 336, PSA : Patiala (The conference was an Akali Religious Conference but the demands voiced were all concerned with grievances of the peasantry).
56. Poster published in October 1938, Janga Singh's Pamphlet *"Dukhee Janta Ke Dili Ubal"*, Ferozepur city, Amrit Electric Press, 1939.
57. According to this system the name of the *Raja* was entered in the revenue records as upper owner of all agricultural lands in the state.
58. Avtar Singh, Din Dihare Rattan (Punjab), published by the author; *Faridkot State Records*, File No. 357, PSA : Patiala.

disturb the meetings.[59] *Praja Mandal* activities, therefore, remained restricted.

In the Kapurthala state, too, the *Praja Mandal* movement was very active. The Praja Mandal workers captured the stage at a public meeting held in the city under the auspices of National League,[60] and delivered speeches alleging Police complicity in the death of one Shanker Singh in suspicious circumstances and demanded a judicial enquiry into the affair. A demonstration was later staged in the city.[61] In the Nabha state, the *Praja Mandal* workers were being arrested in 1938 for hoisting the Congress flag and indulging in anti-state activities.[62] In May 1939, Kala Singh of Palasaur, President of the *Praja Mandal,* was challenged under provisions of the *hidayat-88.* Similar was the fate of *kisan* conference held at Chhapar fair in September, 1938.[63] Hardit Singh Bhattal who was to preside over the conference, was arrested from his Presidential procession and people were dispensed by force by the police of Malerkotla state. Sangat Singh, who presided over the Conference, in the absence of Bhattal, was also taken into custody. Some days later, all leading *Praja Mandal* workers of Malerkotla state, including Sahib Singh Salana from the Nabha state, were arrested and a case of murderous assault under section 307, Indian Penal Code was launched against them.[64]

As the above noted account shows the *Kisan* workers of the Punjab *Riyasti Praja Mandal* were everywhere actively carrying on their agitational work and some of them were coming under Communist influence. The state of Faridkot,

---

59. The National League was a local organization formed by some liberal minded citizens, but it was favouring the state Government as against the *Praja Mandal.*
60. Kapurthala State Recrods, File No. M/3-14-39, PSA : Patiala.
61. The Tribune (Lahore, August 24, 1938).
62. Salana, Sahib, *Aap Biti* (Panjabi), 134.
63. *Ibid.*
64. Personal interviews with Sunder Lal, Harbans Lal, Des Raj, Brish Bhan and Tirath Singh.

however, was an exception. Here a group of workers under Giani Zail Singh and Sundura Singh were nearer to the Congress ideology and still maintained their links with the Akali leadership in Punjab. Along with these activities of the *kisan* cadre of the *Praja Mandal,* work was also being undertaken in Urban areas of the East Punjab States by groups of Hindu workers under inspiration from the Indian national Congress in general and Pandit Nehru in Particular. This gave a new dimension to the movement and also created new problems for the *Praja Mandal* organization, giving birth to the urban-rural question.

All the rural leaders who started their political work in this period did not adopt an identical line of activities. Each one was pursing his own independent line without any co-ordination with others.[65] The sixth session of the All India States' People's Conference was held at Ludhiana in February, 1939 under the presidentship of Pandit Nehru in an atmosphere of peasants' struggle and agitation for the repeal of repressive laws. It was for the first time that the session was being held in Punjab. The important thing that is to be noticed was that the All India States' People's conference and the Indian National Congress both were attached to the movement in this part of the country. Pandit Nehru's participation drew thousands of peasants as well as other ruralisties; among whom large numbers were from the states. "I went to Ludhiana mainly because of Pandit Nehru but my participation in the session proved to be a turning point in my political career. From there I started working in the *Praja Mandal*".[66] This is what a prominent leader of the movement told me. Pandit Nehru was then at the zenith of his political career and was considered to be the most out-spoken champion of the States People's Cause.

The Punjab *Riyasti Praja Mandal,* which was playing host to the Ludhiana session, was now effectively under the control

65. Personal interview with Sunder Lal Advocate.
66. *Patiala State Records,* Prime Minister's Office File No. 756, PSA : Patiala.

of the Communists. The Conference *pandal* was named Sewa Singh Nagar and the Conference was attended by delegates from nearly all the East Punjab States including Patiala, Kapurthala, Kalsia Malerkotla, Faridkot and Nabha. Thousands of states people thronged to see and hear Pandit Nehru. The rulers already expected this and they therefore, tried their best to thwart the preparations of the Conference and counter the intensive propaganda being carried on by peasant workers in the countryside. The Malerkotla administration was particularly concerned as this state was very close to Ludhiana. According to an official report, the near famine condition prevailing in Patiala State and the shortage of canal water furnished good grounds to the *Praja Mandal* agitators for their work. Instructions were issued by the Inspector General of Police to all district officials to devotee their whole-hearted attention to anti-conference work.[67]

The issue of civil liberties in the states was naturally discussed at the Ludhiana session. Pandit Nehru, in his Presidential address, treated this as the focal point of the *activities.* It was, according to him, the immediate objective of the *Praja Mandal* while its ultimate aim was responsible government.[68] The Conference adopted two resolutions; one on responsible Government and the other demanding an end to repressive policies of the states and restoration of civil liberties. Baba Karam Singh Dut demanded the repeal of the oppressive policies of the states and made a special mention of the Faridkot Act , which he termed as '*kala kanun*[69] or Black Act.

---

67. Pandit Nehru's Presidential Address *Faridkot State Records.* File No. 369, PSA : Patiala.
68. His address in Urdu, *Vide., Faridkot State Records,* File No. 359, PSA : Patiala.
69. Sahib Singh Salana started his political career with the Ahmedgarh Train Dacoity case in 1929, as already seen. He was occupying important position in the District Ludhiana Congress Committee, was Secretary of the Ludhiana District Communist Party and was President of the Punjab *Riyasti Praja Mandal.*

The Punjab *Riyasti Praja Mandal* was now a purely political organization leading a movement for economic and political reforms and was firmly aligned with the All India States' People's Conference. But the movement had a new set back with the starting of the second world war in September, 1939. Most of the front ranking leaders and workers including Baba Karam Singh Dhut, President of the Punjab *Riyasti Praja Mandal,* Master Hari Singh, M.L.A., Harnam Singh Chamak, Hardit Singh Bhattal, Seth Ram Nath, Brish Bhan, Harbans Lal and others were arrested. In July 1940, Sahib Singh Salana[70] took over Presidentship of the *mandal* but against him also arrest warrants were pending. He toured some of the states and tried to activist local *Praja Mandal* but was soon arrested on 20th January, 1941, while attending a meeting of the *Praja Mandal* workers of Ahmedgarh (Malerkotla State) so the war years proved to be a period of slackness so far as the agitational activity of the *Praja Mandal* organization was concerned.

During the war period, the Communists and the Congressmen remained in jail or were interned in their villages. The *Praja* Mandal movement remained a leaderless movement functioning in a vacuum. The only exception could be made in the case of the tenants' struggle in Patiala state which continued unabated through out the war period. In early 1939, a *kisan muzara* committee had been formed with Narain Singh Bhadaur as President, Chand Singh as Secretary and Dharam Singh Dalelsingwala as Joint Secretary.[71] Tenants had long been nursing grievances against the Akalis and the Congress leadership that their case was not being adequately attended to.[72] The new Committee gave a new direction to their movement and at a largely attended tenants' conference at Jetheka held a few months later, a call was given for total stoppage of payment of *batai* (Landlord's share of the produce).

70. Report of the Inspector General of Police, Patiala State dated 7th February, 1939, Vide., *Patiala State Records,* Prime Minister's Office File No. 756, PSA : Patiala.
71. Personal interview with Dharam Singh Fakker.
72. *Ibid.*

Tenants removed total crops to their homes. The state Government taking it as a challenge to its authority let loose police repression but the movement continued spreading to village after village. About four hundred tenants' villages were affected by the new movement. Clashes took place between the landlords and their men and the police on one hand and tenants, their men and women on the other. The protest against the wave of repression, a deputation of 101 persons was taken to Simla. The repression subsided to some extent but tension survived throughout the war years.[73] In 1945, a new twenty one member *muzara* war council was set up. Under its leadership, armed guards were mobilised to defend gains of the movement. The gravity of the situation was recognized by the *Maharaja* of Patiala in one of his communications to the *Maharaja* of Jind, dated the 10th August, 1945.[74]

As already noted, some of the urban leaders of the *Praja Mandal* movement had been quite sympathetic to the tenants' movement and lent it their support. But very soon a rupture took place between the Congress minded cadre and the *Praja Mandal* and the peasant cadre owing allegiance to the Communist Party. Trouble had been brewing since 1942. Whereas Congressmen had been busy creating disturbances,

---

73. A copy of the letter was sent to the Nabha Government also, *Nabha State Records*, Prime Minister's Office File No. 82-83, PSA : Patiala.
74. *Linlithgow Papers,* MSS Eur F 125/88 (IOL)-See enclosure to the letter from H.D. Craik—Governor of Punjab to the Viceroy-Lord Linlithgow, dated January 3, 1939. NAI, New Delhi. (For further details relating to the Congress activities within the boundaries of Indian States also see a note of G.Ahmed of the Punjab CID who once remarked . . . . , prominent Congressmen, working under the cloak of one political organisation or another, are trying all they can to stir up unrest among the Indian States' subject . . . on the whole, it is apt that with the passage of time, it will more and more come out into the open and show its interest more clearly. At the present moment the Congress is not prepared to carry on a fight against 'British Imperialism' and Indian Autocracy' at the same time).

the Communists had been aiding the war efforts. More details in relation with the participation of various political parties and their mutual relations are discussed at length keeping in view the peasant's struggle in the states, in the second section of this chapter.

At the very outset, it is notable that the Indian National Congress (hereafter INC) had practically no say in the affairs of the East Punjab States, nor had this political organization adopted any policy of intervention.[75] But there was a marked change in the policy of the INC towards the rulers of these states when it came under the influence of Pandit Nehru and some other such persons who had started inclining towards socialist and leftist ideology.[76] With the rapid increase in the hopes and efforts to win freedom, the problems of the princely states attracted more and more attention of almost all the political parties. The All India States' People Conference (hereafter AISPC) was formed in 1927, after great efforts and perseverance. Soon, this organization not only established its relations with the INC but the two also grew close to each other. Consequenlty, Pandit Nehru was elected the President of AISPC held at Ludhiana in 1929. At this time, other political parties were the Akali Party, the Communist Party, the Socialist Party and the Praja Mandal organization which like Congress party not only kept themselves abreast of the policies of the States and the problems of the people (especially the peasantry) but also participated in the politics of the Punjab State owing to which on one hand, there appeared discontent among the peasants and the masses; and on the other, a new awakening overwhelmed the people in the princely states of Punjab.

All the people in general and the Sikh peasantry in particular felt the political impact in the States as a result of which they took part in the on-going movement. The Akali movement started in the beginning of 1920 itself and the post 1920 period was the era of reform movement. Agitations were

75. Walia Ramesh, *Praja Mandal Movement in the East Punjab States, Patiala* : 1972, 10-12.
76. *Ibid.*, 5 and 51.

launched against the rulers of the states, their polices and the mode of administration of their governments because the rulers and their governments were loyal to the British imperialists.[77] The form of the Akali movement which had been launched to fight imperialism and feudalism (*zamindari* system), gave birth to the nationalist and democratic ideas. During the Akali agitation, the people of the princely states not only came to know of the political activities in the neighbouring British Punjab but they were also deeply influenced by them.[78] As stated above, the Punjab States' *Praja Mandal* was formed in 1928 with a view to launch a drive to safeguard the rights and liberty of the common people and to supplant the dictatorial regime in the states with the Government formed by the elected representatives of the people.[79]

With the formation of Punjab States' *Praja Mandal* organization, the warmth of the political activities going on in the British Punjab, soon began to be felt by the people living in the princely states of the East Punjab and these activities proved immensely helpful in carrying the reverberations of freedom to the masses. The *Praja Mandal* organization organized the masses, particularly the peasants and the *muzaras* (tenants) on a large scale in the civil disobedience movement launched by the INC. Under the leadership of this very organization, January 26, 1930 was observed as the 'Independence Day' where people showed a new zeal and vigour. If one hand, the National flag was hoisted; one the other, the leaders denounced in their speeches the tyranny and cruelty unlashed on the innocent masses by the administration of the Punjab States. Moreover, they called upon the people, peasants and *muzaras* in particular to fight against the rulers of the princely states unitedly.[80] Thus,

77. *Ibid.*, 27.
78. *Ibid.*, 53-57 (The official report noted that the Akalis were trying to give a scular character to their movement).
79. *Ibid.*, 56-57.
80. Confidential note by Prime Minister of Patiala, IOR L/P&S/13/885 (IOL)-Quoted by Mirdulla Mukherjee in her article published in Studies in History Vol.1, No. 2, July-December, 1979.

a new environment was created to organize the peasant's stir and some new ideas to organize them came into existence. Now, the peasants' meets started being held on large scale in villages. It invigorated the political milieu and the peasants' movement began to succeed in becoming stronger and spreading itself.

During the period 1929-30 to 1934-35,[81] there was a remarkable increase in the number of the peasants' rallies. In this era, the Communists and the Socialists began to endorse these rallies under the stewardship of the INC.[82] In this way, apart from the Communists and the Socialists, the Congress also gained ground in the rural areas whereas it had exclusively been an urban party till now. On the other hand, the State *Praja Mandal,* which had been trying to represent the Congress, could not keep itself aloof from the new ideologies and its members were deeply affected by the contemporary political developments.[83] There was a large number of political activities holding radical ideas in this party who had borrowed many ideas from the Socialists; they had been constantly trying to convey these ideas to the masses.[84] While the leaders of the *Praja Mandal* started trying to give a practical shape to their ideas

81. Walia, Ramesh, *A Study of the Praja Mandal Movement in the East Punjab States,* Patiala, 1974, 115-120; Josh, Bhagwan, *Communist Movement in the Punjab* : 1926-47, Delhi : 1980. (Nabha and Jind States issued a common decree-known as Hidayat-88 because it was signed on 5th *Poh* 1988 *Bikrami,* Patiala promulgated it in its territory through a special *firman-i-Shahi* of January 14, 1931 which remained in operation till 1946 when it was finally withdrawn).
82. Walia, Ramesh, *A Study of the Praja Mandal Movement in the East Punjab States,* Patiala, 1974, 117 (The Punjab *Kisan* Committee was formed in march 1937. It was affiliated to the All India Kisan Organisation).
83. Confidential Note by the Prime Minister of Patiala, *op.cit.*
84. Josh, Bhagwan, Communist Movement in the Punjab, Delhi, 1979; *Linlithgow Papers,* MSS Eur F125/88(IOL)-see note by the Punjab CID on the development of Congress activities within the boundaries of Indian States dated December 30, 1938. Also see enclosure to the letter from H.D. Craik-Punjab Governor to the Viceroy, Linlitghow, dated January 3, 1939.

and programmes, the Communists and the Socialists paid their full attention to organizing the peasants and wanted to launch the peasants' stir vigorously for the acceptance of their demands. Many other political parties too played a role in carrying on the peasants' movement strongly.

The leaders of numerous political parties publicised the peasants' demands through posters, bills and public rallies and conferences. They acquainted the people with these demands whenever they went to the villages to organise rallies or to enroll members for *Praja Mandal* organization and the peasants' Committee.[85] Discussing the peasants' demands, like reduction of land revenue and *abiana*, relief from indebtedness, abolition of *begar*, right to shamlat or village common land, right of *shiguar*, amendment of *nazoal* laws, etc., before the people, they made them conscious of their problems. Actually, political workers were always on look out for an opportunity to exploit the injured feelings of the peasants/tenants to ensure the active participation of the peasants in this movement. We shall see that the peasants' movement was not conducted in an organized manner. It was launched in the form of non-payment of taxes, formidable processions or *morchas*. The method of conducting the movement in an organized manner won great popularity, and the Akalis adopted this method very carefully.[86] Other political organisations also adopted this very method and participated in this movement zealously.

However, when Master Tara Singh forged a settlement with Maharaja Bhupinder Singh in 1935,[87] it led to cataclysmic changes not only in the ranks of the Akali *dal* but also in the

85. PSR, PM's Office File Nos. 1546, 1547, 1550, 1553, 1554, 1555, 1559, 1561, 1563, 1573, 1574, 1650. (In fact, References to these activities are scattered all over the Punjab States Records), PSA: Patiala.

86. Nevertheless this movement did succeed in putting pressure on the states to introduce some reforms—such as enactment of some debt relief, Legislation on the lines of the Punjab Restitution of Mortgages Act, etc.

87. Walia, Ramesh, *A Study of the Praja Mandal Movement in the East Punjab States*, Patiala, 1974, 123-29.

politics of the states. Tara Singh had struck this deal to enlist the support of the Maharaja against the rivals of Akalis in the *Shiromani* Akali *Dal*; and *Maharaja* Bhupinder Singh also wanted to get rid of the agitation by the Punjab State *Praja Mandal* in which the Akalis had predominent influence.[88] The pact was, however, strongly criticized by all shades of opinions with in the *Praja Mandal* including the group led by Harchand Singh Jeji—a close associate of Master Tara Singh.[89] Consequently, a drive was launched to arrest the leaders and workers of *Praja Mandal* in large numbers; Bhagwan Singh Longowalia was among them. Now, the leaders of the *Praja Mandal* wanted to avenge the death of Sewa Singh Thikriwala. They, therefore, started struggle against the *Maharaja* with the objective of forcing him to accept all their demands without coming to terms.[90]

At this time, an important development that took place the political field was the Communists' own ideological shift towards the left and their growing hold over the *Praja Mandal* workers which was no doubt influenced by their disillusionment with the Akali current and Master Tara Singh's pact with the Maharaja.[91] From 1936 onwards, these Communists leaders were also under the influence of the leaders

---

88. *Ibid.*, 128.
89. *Ibid.*, 126-28.
90. *Ibid.*, 125-28.
91. PSR, PM's Office File Nos. 1544, 1546, and 1937 (I.G. Police of Patiala issued a circular order to all the *nazims* and SPs to submit regular weekly reports in view of the current *Praja Mandalists* activities, their identifications with the Communists and Socialists tendencies and plans to form *kisan* Committees and branches of their own organisation. It is circular order No. 15 of August 28, 1937) Vide., File No. 1546, PSA : Patiala; also see weekly Report (confidential) from I.G. Police, Patiala of June 30, 1937-This report is on the 5th Annual Conference of the *Riyastri Praja Mandal* held on June 8-10, 1937, at Amritsar. It notes the intermingling of people attending it and also the PPSSP's Conferences and the meetings of the Civil Liberties union being held on June 6-7, 1937, *Vide.*, File No. 1546-PSR, PM's Office Record.

of the *Praja Mandal* such as Bhagwan Singh Longowalia and Jagir Singh Joga who considered themselves to be Communists and has started laying emphasis upon the organization of peasants' unions and had ideological leanings towards the Communists. Their influence over the workers of the *Praja Mandal* organization had been continuously increasing because the Akalis had lost the confidence of the *Praja Mandalists* and after the agreement between Master Tara Singh and *Maharaja,* the Akalis had completely lost their hold over the *Praja Mandalists.* All of the *Praja Mandalists'* Conferences in the states and outside the states after 1936, were often addressed by the Communists and the socialists; they laid greater stress upon the problems and grievances of the peasants and with it they emphasized that the peasants should become the members of the peasants' Committees.[92] Undoubtedly, all these leaders were under the influence of the All India *Kisan Sabha.*[93]

As already stated in the first section, the differences among the Praja Mandalists had cropped up soon after the agreement between Master Tara Singh and Maharaja Bhupinder Singh and this organization split up into two factions.[94] But this very year

92. PSR, PM's Office File No. 1546, 1937 (see Report dated August 1936 from Inspector-CID, Patiala on proceeding of the *Praja Mandal* meeting held at Khanna on August 2, 1936, under the presidency of Sohan Singh Josh; also see file No. 740; Walia Ramesh, *A Study of the Praja Mandal Movement in the East Punjab States,* Patiala : 1974, 134-135 (Sohan Singh Josh, BPL Bedi, Arjun Singh Gargaj, Karam Singh Mann, Baba Rur Singh are mentioned as the more important Communists who had been invited to speak in this Conference).
93. PSR, PM's File Nos. 1546, 1547 (See in them Confidential Weekly Reports from I.G. Police, Patiala, particularly of August 13, 1937, October 21, 1937 and January 1, 1938). PSA : Patiala; Walia, Ramesh, *A Study of the Praja Mandal Movement in the East Punjab States,* Patiala, 1974, 134.
94. PSR, PM's Office File No. 1547 (See CWR from I.G. Police of August 10, 1938 and September 28, 1938); Walia, Ramesh, *A Study of the Praja Mandal Movement in the East Punjab States,* Patiala, 1974, 134.

in February, *Maharaja* of Patiala died and young *Maharaja* Yadvindra Singh was enthroned, who, a little later, married the daughter of Harchand Singh Jeji. With this, one faction of the *Praja Mandal* drifted apart from the main body under Harchand Singh Jeji's stewartship. This faction renounced the method of agitation and conformed to the constitutional methods. Besides, it became quite easy for the members of the other faction of the *Praja Mandal* who had socialist leanings to take measures to get the demands of the peasants accepted and to hold sway over the peasants' movement in a successful manner. They had been on a look-out for such an opportunity for quite some time so that they might be able to convert it into an armed or extremist movement. As the demands of the peasants had not been conceded as yet, the feeling of resentment had picked up among them. The extremist faction of the *Praja Mandal* taking full advantage of the situation, on one hand, established relations with the peasants and on the other started strenuous efforts to constitute the peasants' Committees and Congress Committees in the *biswedari* villages.[95] The results of these efforts manifested themselves very soon and the efforts were soon visible.

It was reported that some tenants had been there to see the Kapurthala *kisan* leader Hari Singh and S.Gopal Singh, MLA to ask them for their help in their struggle.[96] Several posters and pamphlets were published about the incidents of the village Qilla Hakim and Rajomajra in which the peasants/ tenants of these villages were asked to seek the help of the Punjab *Kisans* Committee Amritsar. Moreover, the workers of this group instructed the muzaras to attend the peasants'

95. PSR, PM's File No. 1547 *(Praja Mandal, Kisan* Organisation and Congress Committees were all the same. This probably reflects the increasing influence of Socialists and Communists-details in this connection we can have in the CWR from I.G. Police, Patiala of January 1, February 28, August 8 and 22, October 10 and November 27 of 1938), PSA : Patiala.
96. PSR, PM's Office File No. 1547 (CWR from I.G. Police of February 28, 1938), PSA : Patiala.

conferences as well as *dewans* outside the states.[97] Asking them to participate in several other political conferences also the workers pleaded that the peasants/tenants must maintain their contact with the outside peasants' Committees and peasants' organizations in the British Punjab and other provinces also. A *muzara* Committee was constituted in December 1938 to guide the *muzara* movement, steer it and to maintain mutual understanding. Its significance was that then the time was ripe for launching the peasants and *muzara* stir; and the rapid progress made by this movement during 1938-39 was evidence of it.[98]

We are aware of the fact that the *Praja Mandal* was closely related to the peasants' struggle and their organization. The fact is that the Punjab State *Praja Mandal* played a significant role in sterring this movement. The leaders of this organization made fiery speeches at the conferences held at Ludhiana and Gharancho in February, 1939 and called upon the peasants' Committees.[99] Consequently they began to join these committees overwhelmingly. At this stage, it was also learnt that the central peasants' organization at Amritsar had been

97. PSR, PM's Office File No. 1547 (meanwhile the tenants of Qilla kakim continued to refuse *batai* and the crops were harvested by the forced labour of neighbouring village servants. A *diwan* was held where protest against this forcible harvesting of crops was voiced. The *muzaras* also went to Patiala to register their protest-see for all this CWR from I.G. Police, Patiala of February 28, July 17, 1838 and March 1, 1939), PSA : Patiala.
98. PSR, PM's Office File No. 1547 (CWR from I.G. Police dated March 1, 1939), PSA : Patiala.
99. PSR, PM's File No. 2077 (It contains correspondence regarding anti-*Biswedari* movement in Patiala State—see in it a letter, No. 6742-x-c, June 30, 1939 from Inspector General of Police Talia Muhammad Khan to the foreign Minister of Patiala); File No. 1547 (Posters were brought out by Satpal Azad—General Secretary, Patiala State Congress Committee on the Qilla Hakim episode were distributed at the Ludhiana conference); also see CID Secret Abstract of Intelligence dated March 3, 1939 in the same file, PSA : Patiala.

taking abiding interest to intensify the *muzara* agitation. Meanwhile the *Praja Mandal* appointed an enquiry Committee to look into the grievances, problems and demands of the peasants and also make efforts of acquainting the masses with their problems and grievances.[100] Secondly, under the impact of *Praja Mandal* oranisation only this movement clearly developed close relation with the Congress and the peasants' committees; and with it the Congress gained a strong social base in the states of Punjab which had been coveted by it for quite some time.

Further, as the peasants' movement became stronger, the political parties and their workers and leaders were attracted towards this struggle. Many workers moved about the villages and encouraged the peasants and the *muzaras* whom they found fearing the administrations and governments of the Punjab States.[101] On the other had, the political ideologies of the leaders of this movement gradually underwent a change. The I.G. (Police) observed than that as the movement gained strength it could become uncontroblable for the government. This observation had weight[102] for the appeal of Ujjagar Singh Bhaura to the *muzaras* on behalf of the Akali *jathas* to adopt constitutional means fell or dealf ears. The peasants of these states were organized afresh and the peasant leaders of more and more progressive ideas came in the forefront in a bid to take the change of the movement in their own hands. Harnam

100. PSR, PM's Office File No. 1547 (CWR from I.G. Police, Patiala of March 29, 1939); File No. 1554 (CID Secret Abstract of Intelligence of June 9, 1939); *The Tribune* (Lahore), May 3, 1939. (The Chief and more strong wire pulling has been emanating from the Kisans, the Socialists and the Congress Organisation in the neighbouring territory of the Ludhiana district—For details see CWR from I.G. Police, Patiala of June 10, 1939, in File No.1554) PSA : Patiala.
101. PSR, PM's File No. 1555—see in it CWR of I.G. Patiala of July 28 and September 19, 1939, PSA : Patiala.
102. PSR, PM's Office File No. 1547—see in it CWR from I.G. Patiala of March 1, 1939; also see CID Secret Abstract of Intelligence of June 10, 1939 in File No. 1553, PSA : Patiala.

Singh Dharamgarh, Jagir Singh Longowalia, Jai Singh Daftriwala, Pritam Singh Gujran and many such other leaders were trying to make an impression upon the movement.[103] The I.G.(Police) also pointed out another aspect of this change that it had become dangerously explicit that the Praja Mandal organization, the Congress and the peasant workers were gradually forging a union though outwardly these politicalparties were supposed to retain their separate identity.[104] A new name *Kisan Muzara* Committee was given to the Committee of the *muzaras*.[105]

In June, 1940, when a large number of Socialists and Communists expressed their opposition to plunging into the molestorn of the second world war they were arrested in large numbers and imprisoned. Consequently, the *muzaras'* movement lost momentum for a while because now they stopped getting the support of the Communists.[106] In the beginning of 1941, an effort to launch this struggle afresh was made chiefly through those people who had affiliation with the Akalis of Master Tara Singh's group;[107] these people included Ujjagar Singh Bhaura, Narain Singh Bhadaur, etc.

---

103. PSR, PM's Office File No. 1553 (see proceedings of the meeting of the Working Committee of the Akali *Jatha* of Patiala State held at Dhuri on October 1, 1939. For this see CID Secret Abstract Intelligence, dated June 10, 1939), PSA : Patiala.
104. PSR, PM's Office File Nos. 1553, 1554 (see in these files Secret Abstracts of Intelligence of June 23 and 30, 1939, September 8 and 9, 1939 and also see CWR from I.G. Patiala of September 19, 1939 in file No. 1553), PSA : Patiala.
105. The inclusion of the word '*Kisan*' in the name of the organization was a sure indication of Communist influence. This is precisely what happened in British Punjab in then early thirties went under Communist and *Kirti* influence *Zamindar Sabha* changed its name to *Kisan Sabha*. Vide., PSR, PM's Office File No. 1553—in it see CWR from I.G. Police, Patiala of October 10, 1939, PSA : Patiala.
106. PSR, PM's Office File No. 1559 (see CID Secret Abstract of Intelligence of July 5, 1940), PSA : Patiala.
107. PSR, PM's Office File No. 1560 (See CID Secret Abstracts of Intelligence of January 3 and February 14, 1941), PSA : Patiala.

Taking advantage of the absence of the Socialists and the Communists, the Akalis of this group made earnest efforts to strengthen their hold among the peasant's—the position which they had forfeited owing to their extremist policies. They did get success to some extent because now this group of Akalis wanted to adopt the constitutional means, especially since by that time the Patiala ruler had appointed an enquiry Commission.[108]

Owing to their new policy and efficiency, Ujjagar Singh and his supporters felt attracted towards them. On the other hand, most of the armed Akalis such as Jagir Singh Phaguwalia and Wazir Singh Dafitwala-who were at the helm during the *muzara* agitation—wanted to come closer to that group of *Praja Mandal* when the influence of the socialists increased extraordinarily—particularly closer to that group of *Praja Mandal* which was led by Baz Singh Joga and also to Patiala Peasants' Committee which was headed by Harnam Singh Dharamgarh.[109] The efforts made by the armed Akalis were reflected in forming a separate and independent Akali *Dal* after isolating themselves from the loyalists. Pritam Singh Gujran and Wazir Singh Daftriwala of this group joined the loyalist group of Akalis in the middle of 1941.[110] This fresh change that was releced by the Akalis in the Punjab politics was a corollary of some unprecedented developments.

This polarization had taken place as a consequence also of the new position taken by the Akali *dal* in national politics on the British side in supporting the war efforts-a position born out of the increasingly communal and therefore compromising tendency of the *Shiromani Akali Dal.*[111]

---

108. This point we have already discussed above.
109. PSR, PM's Office File No. 1560 (see CID Abstract of Intelligence of July 12, 1940); File No. 1553 & 1555—in these files see Secret Abstracts of Intelligence of June 23 and 30, 1939, September 8 and 29, 1939, PSA : Patiala.
110. *Ibid.*
111. *Ibid.*, PSR, PM's Office File No. 1574 (see note dated May 7, 1941, PSA : Patiala).

In the wake of these developments, the Congress, the *Praja Mandal* and the Communists converged on one common platform and the socialists and other leftist elements such as Akalis, the Muslim League and the Unionists on the other. Soon there appeared a rift between the two.[112] For the first time, the Akali workers and leaders were forced to take a different stand from that of the *Praja Mandal* or from those who had full faith in secularism *i.e.* from those who had the socialist, nationalist and communist views.[113] Because of the peculiar situation in Patiala and other states too, it was not easy to carry out any political activity openly; so the objectives of the *Praja Mandal* and *Kisans* Committees were highlighted to the masses through religious *dewans*. For even the state government found itself helpless in imposing a ban upon the religious *dewans*. In this connection the files of Patiala State Prime Ministers' Office inform that the masses were convinced that the Akalis were opposed to the Socialists and were at logger-heads with the Communists. It had also become evident that the oppression could be countered more effectively through the *Praja Mandal* and also through the armed Akalis who defied the authority of the *Shiromani Gurdwara Prabandak Committee*.[114] So when the time was ripe for solving the problems Master Tara Singh succeeded in enlisting the support of even those Akali who were once opposed to his policies. But even now they had

---

112. Walia, Ramesh, *A Study of Praja Mandal Movement in the East Punjab States,* Patiala : 1974, 155 (S. Baldev Singh joined the Unionist Party's ministry in Punjab and also a Sikh Defence League was organized) *Vide., Ibid.*
113. An ordinary *Parja Mandalist* never had the occasion to differentiate between the Congress and the Akali Party. Now, Master Tara Singh's new policy was forcing him to make a choice. Vide., Walia, Ramesh, *A Study of Praja Mandal Movement* in the East Punjab States, Patiala : 1974; PSR, PM's Office file No. 1559 (CID Secret Abstract of Intelligence of April 26, 1940 and also CWR from I.G. Police, Patiala of June 19, 1940), PSA : Patiala.
114. For several the *Akali Dal* was a concrete historical reality, whereas the *Praja Mandal* was merely an abstruction. Vide., Walia, Ramesh, *A Study of Praja Mandal in the East Punjab* States, Patiala : 1974, 156.

sympathy for the demands of Akalis.[115] By now it had been clearly realized that the interests of the Sikhs were different. More jobs were demanded for the Sikhs. It was also vehemently demanded that their position in the army be kept in tact. To be brief, a separate Sikh state was demanded, and in the case of the princely states, identification of Sikh interests with the interests of Sikh rulers. It is within this larger context of the polarization (born out of the logic of communal politics) between Akalis on one side and *Praja Mandalists* including Congressmen and Socialists on the other that the next important stage in the *muzaras'* movement can best be understood. Thus the form or nature of this movement can thoroughly be judged or realized.

During the months-January to June, 1941, Ujjagar Singh and Narain Singh Bhadaur convened several meetings of the peasants in the British region in which resentment was expressed against the excuses given by the administration and governments of these states and the delaying tactics adopted by the rulers; their polices were denounced and a demand was made to expedite the publication of the report of the enquiry Commission and to quickly intimate its recommendation to the government.[116] Though the oppression and highhandedness of the *biswedars* towards the peasants were denounced in strong words in these meetings, no call was given for non payment of *batai* and the administration continued to enforme *batai* payment successfully. Even then it is to be noticed that the leaders of different political parties were successfully carving out a place for themselves in *muzaras'* politics. As a result, the government decided to adopt an aggressive policy in order to weaken them. In the region of British Punjab many leaders including Narain Singh Bhadaur and Ujjagar Singh Bhaura were thrown into jails.[117]

115. *Ibid.*

116. PSR, PM's Office File Nos. 1560 and 1574 (CID Secret Abstract of Intelligence of February 14 and 28, 1941, March 28 and 30, 1941, PSA : Patiala.

117. PSR, PM's Office File No. 1563, CID Secret Abstract of Intelligence of June 13, 1941); File Nos. 1560 and 1574, PSA : Patiala.

When the Socialist and the Communist leaders workers were released in 1942, they immediately resumed their political activities. Every political party tried to regain its strength and to have social base especially in the rural areas. The activities of the Communists seemed to be in full agreement with the new trends in the national politics which led the Akalis to join hands with them in large number. This alliance gave rise to a fresh and serious fear as the *muzaras'* movement could get the support of two political parties at the same time by virtue of which it could pose a challenge to the rulers of the states which possibly could not be faced. In fact, a large number of Akalis about whom it was thought that they were steadfast fighters to fight oppression, could give a new appearance to the *muzaras'* movement by allying themselves with the socialists and the Communists. The Socialists and the Communists were capable of straining themselves to acquaint the people with the problems of the peasants and to disseminate the secular ideologies through heir strong organizations and could fight as well; now when the Akalis joined them it became very difficult for the Governments in the states to crush the *muzaras'* movement easily and soon. This struggle assumed a new form. Meanwhile the Akalis captured the leadership of this struggle owing to the policies, activities and stimulating support of Master Tara Singh. This support came in various forms. For instance, the Akalis considered the resignation of the Hindu Prime Minister from his office to be their victory; they congratulated the *Maharaja* for having appointed a Sikh Prime Minister.[118] They now appealed to the *Maharaja* to appoint more and more Sikhs in the administration. The Akalis wanted the *Maharaja* to include only Sikhs in his cabinet. The Akalis wanted this so that the atmosphere of Sikhs' thinking could be maintained by their living in the proximity of the *Maharaja*.[119] It was also conveyed to the *Maharaja* that he should not marry

---

118. *Ibid.*, PSR, PM's Office File No. 1559 (CWR from I.G. Police, Patiala of April 27, 1940, PSA : Patiala).
119. PSR, PM's Office File No. 1573 (CID Secret Abstract of Intelligence of July 3, 1942, PSA : Patiala.

his sister into a non-Sikh family against the Sikhs' sentiments. Besides, the *Maharaja* should issue a decree that no one would smoke in the vicinity of the royal palace; it was also demanded that *Panjabi* should be made the official language.[120] Another demand was to reserve 60% jobs for the Sikhs in all the fields. The government was happy to concede a few such demands which proved immensely helpful to it to maintain friendly relations with Master Tara Singh.

Though it is true that the influence of the Akalis and Master Tara Singh was constantly increasing in the states, yet it does not mean that they were not being opposed; rather a rival group of the Akalis was organized under *Baba* Kharak Singh which started making vigorous efforts to expose before the people Master Tara Singh and the Akalis led by him. This group of the Akalis tried their best to expose Master Tara Singh's character by giving instances that his relations with the Sikh *Panth* were false and bogus;[121] and he was not sincere to the cause of the Sikhs in general and the muzaras in particular. However, it is to be remembered that the Akalis led by Kharak Singh confined their business only to defamation of Tara Singh. This group of Akalis neither extends any kind of help to the muzaras' movement nor did it seriously participate in the peasants' struggle. If at all, the workers of this group did try to prove their worth or to show their mettle, their efforts were confined only to prove themselves true and powerful leaders of the Sikh *panth* and to project themselves as severe enemies of the *Akali Dal* led by Master Tara Singh.[122] On the other hand, it was very difficult for Master Tara Singh and other members of the Dal to tolerate all this. So as far as possible, they demanded more and more concessions and rights for the Sikhs from the state government.

120. *Ibid.*, Also see file No. 1559, PSA : Patiala.
121. PSR, PM's Office File No. 1573 (CID Secret Abstract of Intelligence of July 17, 1942), PSA : Patiala.
122. It was openly declared that it was Master Tara Singh who had allowed the Sikhs to use Caps and attend religious *dewans* waring shoes. Vide., *Ibid.*

Master Tara Singh's group also made efforts not to alienate the *muzaras*. So whenever and wherever they got an opportunity they passed resolutions favouring their demands.[123] Because of the retention of Pritam Singh Gojran and Wazir Singh Daftriwala as the *muzaras'* leaders in Master Tara Singh *dal*, *muzaras* continued to cherish the hope that they would enlist the support of the Akalis in their struggle; at least it was in the air for some time that Master Tara Singh who had won the favour of the *Maharaja* of Patiala in particular and the rulers of other states as well, could prove to be of immense help to the *muzaras* as Master Tara Singh could win certain concessions and rights for the *muzaras* from the rulers of these states for their benefit.[124] The Akalis were very well aware that their condition and existence depended more on the will of the *Maharajas* and their officials and they could not find favour with them unless they rendered some service and help to the states. It was possible if the Akalis were isolated from the extremists.

It became clear from a report of the intelligence department that the state administration wanted to permit the Akalis to participate in the activities of the *muzaras* but keeping in view their previous records. The Master group could not be doubted of conspiring against the state. As far as the *muzaras'* movement was concerned, its objective was to keep the Akalis aloof from the Communists who were released from the jails recently and were engaged in winning the support of the masses. With a view to keeping the *muzaras* away from the communists, *Akali Dal* launched an *armrit prachar* movement. Therefore, even if

123. Akali *dewan* was held on June 27, 1942 where forty odd resolutions were passed and one of these stated that concession be given to the *muzaras* and the dispute be settled amicably. Let it be noted that this *dewan* was organized by the Master group. Vide., *Ibid.* (See CID Secret Abstract of Intelligence of July 3, 1942).

124. *Ibid.*, (An Akali Conference was held at Mansa which was attended by several *muzaras*, particularly from Ishangarh as well as other villages. Here, a resolution was passed in their favour (See CID Secret Abstract of Intelligence of July 24, 1942).

the Akalis contact with *muzaras* was an evil, it was definitely a lesser evil.[125] That the Akalis were fully aware of this and jealously guarded their position as the major allies of the rulers of Patiala in particular, becomes clear from their very reaction to the attempts of the landlords Association to reactivise itself towards the and of 1942.

By the end of 1942, the zamindara Association made efforts to make itself powerful once again and in no time this organization appeared as the close friend of the rulers in the states. The stalwarts of this organization knew that if they wanted to keep it strong in the political arena, they must have a powerful ally capable of backing the *zamindars* for a long time. They also realized that the existence and position of their orgnaisation was fully dependent on the existence and position of the *Maharajas*. The *zamindars'* organization was following in the foot steps of those Akalis whose objective was to use the states' power as a springboard for strongly entrenching themselves in the Punjab politics.[126] The Akalis had a somewhat reluctant hope that the zamindars would extend them some special help. Meanwhile, an agitation started against the *biswedars* though its pace was very slow but they were going slow in order to make their ground solid.

However, it should not be derived from it that their leaders had lost interest in the peasants' movement and they had lost their hope. Meanwhile the members of Master Tara Singh's Group held a *dewan* at Mansa and a large number of peasants reached there to participate in it. Even the common people participated in the dewan overshelimingly. They also gave wheat and other things as a token of their help because they were confident that the Akalis would also help them in their affairs.[127] But all their hard work was in vain as the Akalis passed

125. *Ibid.*, PSR, PM's Office File No. 770 (See Abstract of July 24, 1942 which is likely to have been prepared by either I.G. Police, Patiala or the Maharaja himself), PSA : Patiala.
126. *Ibid.*
127. PSR, PM's File No. 1573 (CID Secret Abstract of Intelligence of July 24, 1942), PSA : Patiala.

one resolution at this *dewan* for the welfare of the peasants which was not of much value.[128] We come to know from the police records of the states that the dispute and tension between the *biswedars* and the peasants had reached its climax in 1942. Though the *muzaras'* orgnaisation was not very strong, yet since their number was fairly large, every political party was making efforts from the very beginning to draw them towards it and to enroll them so that that party might attain a strong social base in the states.[129] But there was no such party which could have claimed the full support of the *muzaras* and have succeeded in gaining a social base. The report submitted by the S.P., CID of Patiala discloses that though the peasants' and workers' movement was palatable to the Communists, yet this movement lost its strength after the arrest of the Communist leaders and this struggle could not be strengthened for a long time to come.

After some time when the Punjab Government released eight Communist leaders, Sohan Singh and others, they started reorganizing the peasants and workers' movement. Their main objective behind it was to intensify the stir of the peasants. It was easy for the *muzaras* of the states to join this freshly launched movement in an organised manner. When the police officials toured Amritsar, Lahore, Taran Taran and other towns, they found that the Communists were constantly gaining ground[130] and they also reported that that time there were two Chief organized and powerful parties in the Punjab-one was *Akali Dal* and another was the Communist party. The Communists out-numbered the Akalis even so the Punjab Government had already interned a large number of prominent and frontline Communist leaders. The *Akali Dal* was constantly trying to check the growing influence of the Communists movement. But on the contrary, the Communists continued to

128. *Ibid.*
129. *Ibid.*, (See CID Secret Abstract of Intelligence of June 19, 1942 Entitled '*Muzara* Movement').
130. PSR, PM's Office File No. 1573 (Extract from CID Secret Abstract of Intelligence of June 19, 1942), PSA : Patiala.

forge good relations with the government. The imprisoned Communist leaders had also been released by which their party became stronger and with it the Communist movement continued to move from strength to strength. It is equally noteworthy to state that the Communist leaders had started making their organisation stronger and better organised.

Meetings began to be held on a very large scale. These measures of the Communists acted as a shot in the arm of the peasants' and workers' movement. The *muzaras'* movement got all the more help with the strengthening of the Communists hands and this struggle became fiercer and fiercer. Now, the States governments' would have to function carefully in the wake of this movement and would have to frame their policies after a lot of thinking because they considered it their duty to help the *muzaras.*

Thus, we can safely conclude that though other political parties had always been helping the *muzaras'* movement and had sympathy with this movement even now;[131] but truly speaking, the peasants and workers' movement banked upon the help of the Communists and it also managed to win popularity among the Communists.[132] Master Tara Singh's group, by entering into an agreement with the Maharaja of Patiala and by providing to this movement the aid of the State Government weakened it in Patiala state especially due to which the political prospects of Akali *Dal* were at once bedimmed.[133] When Master Tara Singh declared that the struggle against the *Maharaj* would serve no purpose as he was keen to give a hearing to the problems of the peasants as well as the other people and also to solve them, the *Akali Dal* led by him was exposed and it came as a shot in the arm of the Communists. Now, the Akalis turned to the cities to make them the centre of heir political activities. When the Akalis put the demands of reservation in the jobs, etc., the educated classes

131. *Ibid.*
132. *Ibid.*
133. Walia, Ramesh, *A Study of the Praja Mandal Movement in the East Punjab States,* Patiala, 1574, 156.

joined them.[134] The Akalis wanted to win the support of the ruralities on the basis of religious appeal and not on the plea to struggle for the acceptance of extremist demands of the peasants. In fact, the demands of the peasants were incongruent with the Akali policy of remaining loyal to the state. The situation became all the more complicated. Many political parties, particiaularly the Communists had started making efforts to draw the *muzaras* into their fold while the *biswedars* had not been making any efforts to hold the *muzaras* under their sway.

The success of the efforts of the Communists is reflected in the participation of a batch of forty peasants in a conference that was held in Bhakna village of Lahore district from April 12 to 14, 1939.[135] The sufficient funds raised by the members of this batch from the peasants indicated the enthusiasm shown by the tenants at that time. It was also found out that Harnam Singh Dharamkot was getting some posters (which condemned the attitude of the police and *biswedars*) distributed through such Akalis as were sympathetic to the cause of the peasants and also having leftist leanings.[136] At this stage, we come to know of the pledge which was taken under the Communist influence. From this fact also we come to know that side by side they tried to struggle against the sycophant Sikhs who, were led by Master Tara Singh. In this effort, they co-operated with the Akali group which had earlier formed the States' *Dal* (and was consolidated under the name of the rival Akali *jatha*, Patiala State) and which was unhappy under Master Tara Singh's collusion with the Patiala *Maharaja* and over the communal character of his politics. The Communists participated in and were prominent in the *dharmick dewans* held by this group to condemn Master Tara Singh's anti-national

134. *Ibid.*, 158 (Master Tara Singh was not a *Jat* but an *Arora* Sikh and his own base was in the towns of Punjab and not in the rural areas).
135. PSR, PM's Office File No. 1573 (CID Secret Abstract of Intelligence of April 9, 1943), PSA : Patiala.
136. *Ibid.*, October 3, 1942.

and communal politics. Expressing strong resentment over the communal aspect of Tara Singh's politics, they denounced him and his group.[137]

Jagir Singh Joga, a Communist of Patiala State made it apt that though they were assisting the Government of India, in the time of need, they would make it difficult for the Government to work whenever the time was ripe for such an action.[138] They would stand by the peasants and *muzaras* against the rulers and their governments. He also remarked that only time would tell whether it were they who were the true leftists or it was Master Tara Singh and his Akali comrades who had misled and betrayed the *panth*.[139] This projection of the Communists as the militant upholders of the Akali traditions of relentless struggle against oppression-of therefore being 'better Akalis'—was valuable ideologically in mobilizaing the *muzaras*. The Communists enjoyed a great advantage from the psychological view point in organising the *muzaras* since they started holding meetings against the Akalis. Whenever a meeting was convened by the party of Master Tara Singh. The Communists disrupted the meetings of the Akalis and finally they compelled the Akalis, who had already become weak from writhing, to yield.[140]

During 1943-44, the Communists kept up their hectic propaganda campaign among the *muzaras* and remained busy in organisaing them. Many *sabhas* were held under the banner of the Patiala *kisans* Communities and besides it, was started a vigorous campaign to enroll more and more peasants to the membership of Committee. The leaders and workers of the *Kisan* Committee started touring the areas of various districts

137. PSR, PM's Office case No. 565/C of 2000 (1943-44) (CID Secret Abstracts of Intelligence of March 13, 1943 and July 2, 1943), PSA : Patiala.
138. *Ibid.*, April 24, 1943 (Expediency here naturally refers to the side of the allies once the Soviet Union was attacked by Hitler).
139. PSR, PM's Office case No. 565/C of 2000 (1943-44) (CID Secret Abstract of Intelligence of June 4, 1943), PSA : Patiala.
140. *Ibid.*, June 4, and July 9 and 23, 1943.

and further more launched a vigorous campaign to induce the peasants to join the *Kisan* Committee and thus enable them to intensify the struggle for their rights. The propaganda campaign was carried on through religious dewans,[141] and it became clear that the Communists would come into power. We can have a detailed account of all the meetings of the Communists in the administrative reports which underlines the fact that the influence of the Communists had constantly been mounting among the villagers, particularly among the tenants and peasants.[142] With a view to get the grievances of the tenants redressed, a deputation of the *Kisan* Committee called upon the Prime Minister, I.G. Police and many other high officials of the Patiala State and very strongly advocated the need of solving the problems of the *muzaras*. By July 1944, not only Patiala Government had become gravely worried but the Governments of other states also seemed perplexed in the face of constant mounting Communist influence.

The rulers and their officers noticed that the bad plight of education in the princely states was also highlighted in the conferences, held by the *Kisan* Committees or Communists; and the Akali *Dal* led by Master Tara Singh was denounced. It was alleged that this group was hand in glove with the Maharaja and had been toeing the officials line. As a result, the states' authorities had permitted these Akalis to hold the Conference while restrictions were put on the *kisan sabhas*.[143] However, this biased policy of the rulers was denounced. A Communist

---

141. PSR, PM's Office Case No. 565/C of 2000 (1943-44) (CID Secret Abstract of Intelligence of June 2 and 4, July 9, 23 and 28, August 20, September 24, October 29, November 26, December 10, 1943; January 14, July 7, June 9, August 11, 18 and 25, September 1, 1944; also see case No. CB-1-2 of 2001 (1944-45). PSA : Patiala.
142. This term became increasingly common when reference was made to *muzaras'* activities or other Communists organised activities from about mid 1943; PSR, PM's Office case No. CB-1-2 of 2000 (1943-44) (CID Secret Abstract of Intelligence of June 2, 1944), PSA : Patiala.
143. *Ibid.*, also of September 15 and October 6, 1944.

leader expressed his party's attitude to the Akalis in these words : "We wish that the Akalis should subsist but they should be like Akali Phula Singh who was bold enough to have punished *Maharaja* Ranjit Singh, and not like the present day Akalis who are the Johlichuks (henchmen) of the *Maharajas* and their *ahalkars*". From the contemporary accounts he cited the example of Sewa Singh Thikriwala who sacrificed his life by fasting himself to death in the jail. They did not want the Akalis like Master Tara Singh who had sold himself into the hands of the Patiala *Maharaja*.[144]

The self-confidence of the Patiala Communists was expressed at Tungwali in the demand for the recognition of *Kisans* and Communists' organizations and student's Unions. This confidence grew out of the support that they had received from the *muzaras* who fully backed the Communists.[145] This fact is testified by the presence of a large number of peasants and *muzaras* at the *bhog* ceremony of Bhagwan Singh Longowalia at Longwoal village on October 5, 1944, and also by the large scale of contribution of money and grain by the muzaras at various Conferences.[146] All the important leaders and others who attended the ceremony presented red salute to the departed soul as a mark of homage. Speaking on the occasion, Achhar Singh Chhina and Jagir Singh Joga threw light on the mission of Bhagwan Singh besides expressing their views about the Akalis, the Congress, the *Praja Mandalists*, and the *Kisans Sabhas* as well as the Kisans Committees.[147]

From the reports of the overwhelming participation in the above states conferences and unfurling the red flag there, it can be deduced that the Communists had become not only bold, their influence among the peasants and tenants was also growing constantly and they had started working among the

---

144. *Ibid.*
145. *Ibid.*, (CID Secret Abstract of September 15, October 27, 1944 and January 26, 1945).
146. *Ibid.*, (also see of October 6, 1944, 16 and 23 March, 1945).
147. *Ibid.*, (also see Abstract of July 16, 1945).

peasants and other agriculturists fearlessly. In many villages they illegally held meetings and processions. In these meetings they made speeches which according to the authorities were provocative and highly objectionable.[148] If on one hand, they highlighted the demands of the muzaras, on the other they criticized the Akalis. The widening gulf between the Akalis and the Communists was clearly visible at this time as were the skin-saving tactics of the Akalis. Moreover, the signs of the weakening of the state regime were conspicuous, thus the communists went on gaining strength.[149] However, with a view to counter the growing influence of the Communists, the Akalis sent a special *jatha*, know as *dhadi jatha* to tour Patiala, Nabha and Jind states. It was to campaign in favour of the Akalis and against the Communists.[150] But by this time the people had been so much influenced by the Communists that the Akali *jathas* which had been sent to Jind state wrote to Amritsar *Akali Dal* that they could not nullify this influence unless they had an excellent speaker who could counter the Communists very effectively.[151]

Actually their fear was not unfounded since this *jatha* was not allowed to attend the peasants' conference at Moran. Its members were very much frustrated to find that the Communists held complete sway over the hearts of ruralites

148. *Ibid.*, (also see Abstract of October 27, 1944, January 26, 1945) PSR, PM's Office Case No. CB-1-2 of 2002 (1945-46) Reports sent in by *biswedars* to Government on February 22, 1946, February 1, 1947 (File on Landlords' Association, Patiala), PSR : Patiala.
149. PSR, PM's Office Files—case No. CB-1-2 of 2001 (1944-45), CID Secret Abstracts of March 16 and 23, 1945), PSA : Patiala.
150. *Ibid., The Tribune,* January 8, 1948 (A joint statement issued by *Riyasti Akali Dal,* Patiala State, The Akali *Jatha* and Patiala State *Praja Mandal*) *Vide., The Tribune,* January 10, 1948.
151. PSR, PM's Office, Case No. CB-1-2 of 2002 (1945-46), (CID Secret Abstract of July 16, 1945; *AISPC-Papers,* File No. 133, Part-I, 1948 (Patiala State) NMML, New Delhi (A letter from the President Patiala State *Praja Mandal* to the Prime Minister, Patiala. Its copies were also sent to the Ministry of other States, the AISPC, etc.).

so immense was their influence that neither did the people pay argument of the members of the *jatha* nor did they bother to listen to their propaganda songs; and their propaganda compaign against the Communists made little impact. Instead the miseries of the *jatha* multiplied when the Communists decided to follow them close on their heels. They not only pursued the *jatha* through many villages of the Phulkian States but also very strongly countered the propaganda campaign launched by them. Very strongly condemning their propaganda, the Communists told the villagers that the Akalis had sold themslves out to the state Govenments.[152]

Now onwards the leftists had constantly been spearheading the peasants' agitation. They had been holding meetings and Conferences in several villages where they propagated their ideology. They continued to tour different villages in order to enroll members for their organisation and to raise funds. A *muzara* war council was set up in 1945 which initially had 21 members and most of tem followed the leftist ideology. With a view to intensfy the *muzaras'* movement especially armed soldiers were recruited so that protection could be provided to the movement.[153]

Under the auspices of the *Praja Mandal,* a concerence was convened at Patiala on October 5-6, 1945, in which the stalwarts expressed their sympathy with the agriculturists of all classes and the Communists and their problems. A resolution passed at this conference demanded the abolition of *biswedari* system and the transfer of ownership rights to the muzaras. The demands included in this resolution indeed strengthened the peasants since these demands were supported not only by the *Praja Mandal* organization but enjoyed the full support of the

152. PSR, PM's Office files case No. CB-1-2 of 2002 (1945-46), PSA : Patiala; The Tribune, March 1,17,21,28,1948, June 2, 1948; also see File No. 509/6-5-Nabha State Records, PSA : Patiala; Walia Ramesh, *A Study of Praja Mandal Movement in the East Punjab States,* Patiala : 1974, 189-191.

153. *Ibid.*

Indian National Congress and the Communists.[154] When the country got freedom on August 15, 1947, the *Praja Mandal* became all the more enterprising and spirited and it demanded the formation of a responsible governments in the states immediately. The Akalis had sometime ago declared patiala a Sikh state where the Sikh culture and character would have been preserved, but after they joined the Congress Ministry in the Punjab there was a radical change in the situation and the Praja Mandal succeeded in enlisting support for its demand for the establishment of a responsible government.[155] The plea for the formation of constitutional government given by the *Maharaja* of Patiala in January, 1948 was rejected by both these parties. As a result, though stopped by the Akalis, the *Maharaja* in a desperate move threw his weight on the side of the *biswedars* and thus delivered a blow to the *muzaras'* struggle.

In May 1948, the President of the Patiala *Praja Mandal* issued an appeal to the ministers of the states which recounted the tale of heart-rending polices atrocities. This appeal was made on the basis of a report received from the *Praja Mandal* and contained a request to the states' rulers to intervene. Prior to it, the *Praja Mandal* Organisation also had submitted a memorandum to the Ministerial Council of state and the Prime Minister of India demanding the postponement of the distribution of land as well as the collection of arrears of batai atleast till the formation of responsible Governments in the states. It was also bemoaned that the rulers were more worried

154. Sardar Patel arrived in Patiala to inaugurate Pepsu and he was greeted with cries of '*Sat Sri Akal*' and 'Sardar Patel *Zindabad*', Vide., *The Tribune,* July 15-16, 1948; Memon, V.P., *The Story of Integration of the Indian* States, 1956, 249-59; Walia, Ramesh, *A study of the Praja Mandal Movement in the East Punjab States,* Patiala, 1974,191.

155. *The Tribune,* July 21, 1947 (See Statement issued by the Patiala State Akali *Jatha*); *The Tribune,* January 8 and 10, 1948 (See Statement issued jointly by the *Riyasti Akali Dal,* Patiala State, the *Akali Jatha* and Patiala State *Praja Mandal*); Walia, Ramesh, *A Study of Praja Mandal Movement in the East Punjab States,* Patiala, 1974, 170.

about their future and they had been siding with the sycophants and Communalists with all their hearts. Or they had been inclined to those *biswedars* and the Sikhs who had been supporting them under the leadership of Master Tara Singh.[156]

The agreement between the Praja Mandal and the Akalis was an unfortunate development and as was obvious from the memorandum, the Akalis had lost no time in crossing over to the *Maharajas'* side; and the *Praja Mandal* sized this opportunity to demand the merger of the East Punjab States into Punjab. This demand cropped up because the *Praja Mandalists* had been absolutely disappointed with the rulers for the latter had given concessions very reluctantly.[157] The demand put forward by them was made all the more pressing by the Akalis when they threatened to go ahead with their various political demands. Actually the Sikhs regarded the princely states as their personal property so they were not in favour of any such arrangements that might have increased the number of Hindus or catapulated the Hindu into a majority. With amazing swiftness they put forward another demand for the organisation of the Punjab states into a separate confederation so that the Sikhs might remain in majority. Surprisingly enough, the Congress Government at the Centre decided under Sardar Patel's leadership to concede this demand, the motive behind which was not to totally alienate the Akalis from the state administration.[158]

On July 15, 1948, the Union of East Punjab State named *Pepsu* was inaugurated by Sardar Patel. It was given the name

---

156. *AISPC-Papers,* File No. 133, Part I, 1948 (Patiala State), NMML, New Delhi; *The Tribune,* January 15, 1948; Josh Bhagwan, *Communist Movement in Punjab,* Delhi, 1979, 198; Walia, Ramesh, *A Study of the Praja Mandal Movement in the East Punjab States,* 1974, 193.
157. *The Tribune,* February 28, March 1, 2, 9, 24, 29—1948; Walia, Ramesh, *A Study of the Praja Mandal Movement in the East Punjab States,* Patiala, 1974, 182, 188-89.
158. *The Tribune,* March 1, 17, 21, 28, 1948, June 2, 1948; *Nabha State Records,* File No. 509/6-5, PSA : Patiala.

of 'Sikh Home Land' my him.[159] The formation of this union was accomplished under the supervision of the Patiala ruler and no ministry of any sort was constituted to assist him. Currently the Akali *dal*, the *Praja Mandal Sangathan* and the *Lok Sewa Dal* were jealous of each other and no agreement could be effected among the three dispite all efforts. Now, the *Praja Mandal Sangathan* entered the garb of *Pepsu Pardesh* Congress while the *Lok Seva Dal* was a political party patronised by the Maharaja. After the lapse of six months in such an indecisive situation finally the ministry was formed.[160] At the instance of Sardar Patel, the *Praja Mandal* Orgnaisation was split. Just as the Government leadership refused to join the Ministry headed by Gian Singh Rarewala, similarly the Akali also turned down the offer to join it.[161] The formation of this ministry disappointed the radical leadership of the *Praja Mandal*. As a result, no solution could be found out to the problems of the peasants and the *muzaras*. In fact, they were kept out of this ministry since they had supported the *muzaras'* movement which enjoyed the patronage of the Communists. Secondly, they were not known for their reformatory policy. Its clear cut evidence was their success in electing Jagir Singh Joga as the Chairman of the Patiala State *Praja Mandal*, who was a staunch *Praja Mandalists* with Communist leanings.[162] Some new developments were being expected in the Communists Movement at that time.

In 1948, Teja Singh Swatantra who had for long been associated with the workers' group of the Communists, left the official group of CPI and took upon himself the responsibility of constituting the red communists party. He included in his party many members of the Communists group led by Jagir

159. *The Tribune*, July 15, 1948; Walia, Ramesh, *A Study of the Praja Mandal Movement in the East Punjab States*, Patiala, 1974, 191.
160. The Tribune, July 16, 1948; Menon, V.P., *The Study of the Integration of the Indian States*, 1956, 248-250.
161. Walia, Ramesh, *A Study of the Praja Mandal Movement in the East Punjab States*, Patiala, 1974, 191-192.
162. *Ibid.*, 193.

Singh Joga.[163] Now, under the leadership of this party, the peasants and the *muzaras'* movement continued in the Punjab States even after the independence of the country despite these new developments, the grievances of the peasants/tenants were intimated to the masses in different forms and by means of meetings and their demands were stressed. However, the Communists had been expelled from the Congress and so the leftists in the states also put an end to the conflicting loyalty. At the same time, a rupture took place between the Congress minded cadre and the *Praja Mandal* and the cadre owing allegiance to the Communists' Party. Trouble had been brewing since 1942.

Consequently, the All India States' People's Conference set up a Regional Council for the Punjab States. Brish Bhan and Harbans Lal were elected as the president and secretary of this council respectively. At the end of war, therefore, there were three distinct political groups working in the East Punjab States : Akalis under the leadership of Master Tara Singh with Pritam Singh Gojran and Jagir Singh Phaguwalia as their local leaders; the Congress led *Praja Mandal* under Brish Bhan and Harbans Lal; and the Communists with their *kisans* organisations under the leadership of Jagir Singh Joga, Master Hari Singh, Harnam Singh Chamak, etc. As a result of these new developments, the character of each political group had completely changed.

The peasants/tenants movements led by various political parties in the east Punjab States, are discussed at length in the following chapters; of course, there too references are made to the activities of these political parties.

163. *Ibid.*

5 THE PEASANT'S STRUGGLE : 1900-1937

The first sign of agrarian unrest among the people in the states of the East Punjab appeared in the twenties of the twentieth century. However, stray cases of politically active individuals were noticed in some of the states[1] earlier also but prompt action by the authorities forestalled any organized movement.[2] The cause for the absence of any notable activity in the Punjab States in the post war period was absence of any numerically significant middle class intelligentia such as the one leading the movement in he Punjab cities, such as, Lahore, Amritsar, Ludhiana and Hoshiarpur. It was from these centres that the politics travelled to the countryside. But in the Punjab states the position was absolutely different. There it was the peasantry which was getting impoverished and that provided the nucleus. The semi-feudal rule was oppressive and the burden of rural debts excessive.

The peasant movement in the Patiala state under Maharaja Bhupinder Singh in particular and other states in general (during 1900-1937) was spontaneous. It was not well oriented and properly organised. At first it did not have its separate identity. The Punjab *Riyasti Praja Mandal* founded in 1928 had sympathy for the peasant cause because its leadership and cadres mainly came from among the peasants. Now, the peasant proprietors and the tenants adopted the agitational course. However, it is to be noticed that during the spontaneous phase of the peasant movement, which was characterized by sporadic

1. Patiala, Faridkot, Kapurthala and Malerkotla were the main states.
2. *Faridkot State Records,* File Nos. 23 and 37 (Confidential Diaries of District Magistrate No. 2920-21), PSA : Patiala.

peasant rising, the demands and leadership of the movement as distinct from the *Praja Mandal,* had not clearly emerged. Whatever type of leadership the movement had, their demands fused and general in nature as well as their ideological standing was hazy.

The earliest examples of agrarian unrest as well as the tenants agitation as witnessed in the Punjab were in the midst of the first decade of the present century. It was the peasantry that took up the initiative in raising voice against the oppressive and ruthlessly exploitive system of the British imperialism.[3] The agrarian unrest in the Punjab was caused by increase in land revenue, *abiana* (water tax) and official efforts to bring about a law restricting the ownership rights of the cultivators in the canal colonies.[4] Sardar Ajit Singh and Lala Lajpat Rai came into prominence during this agitation. Both of them were deported. The other agitators were also treated cruelly by the British bureaucracy. At the same time, the authorities thought it expedient to pacify the peasantry. The viceroy blocked the bill on the Canal Colony legislation.[5] Certain concessions were also given to the peasantry. Thus, their policy of pacification and appeasement checked the major Panjabi agitation against the imperialists. During this agrarian unrest and agitation, the peasantry of the states were too isolated to get involved. Moreover, the settlement operation going on in Paitala State during 1900-1908 kept the peasants busy.

Political awakeing in the states was hidden under the debries of mass illiteracy and poor industrialization—the

3. Chaudhary Sukhbir, *Peasants and workers Movement in India 1905-1929,* New Delhi : 1971, 10.
4. Rai, Satya M., *Punjabi Heroic Tradition : 1900-1947,* Patiala : 1978, 12-13; Syed Razi Wasti, *Lord Minto And Indian Nationalist* Movement, Oxford : 1967, 98-105; Sharma, Sri Ram, 'Punjab in Ferment in the Beginning of the 20th century', *Punjab Past and Present,* Vol, XIV-1, April, 1980, Patiala, 132-133.
5. Chaudhary, Sukhbir, *Peasants and Workers Movement in India : 1900-1929,* Delhi : 1971, 14; Rai, Satya M., *Panjabi Heroic Tradition : 1900-1947,* Patiala : 1978, 23.

conditions which were not conducive to emergence of proper leadership[6]. Besides, a technique of peaceful organization and protest which was developed in the British Indian provinces fell flat when followed in the region of Indian States.[7] Under the circumstances, though belatedly (in comparison with British governed provinces) the enlightened among the peasantry assumed the responsibility of unleasing a political movement, and also taking up the cause of their downtrodden brethren, within the Princely States.[8]

Feudal repression coupled with the fast deteriorating condition of the Punjab peasantry under the world economic depression stirred the peasantry in this region to action.[9] Number of peasant organizations like the *zamindar sabhas, Zamindara League* and the *Kirti Kisan* party sprang up throughout the province. There was unrest among the lower peasants because tenurial conditions were not satisfactory.[10] From the time of the first Summary Settlement in 1861-62 they had been restive. In the 20th century the States' rulers kept on imposing *biswedars* on peasants villages ignoring the rights of the cultivators.[11] On the appointment of revenue expert Popham Young in 1900, there was a fresh wave of violent peasants' agitation, but was curbed, of course, with great difficulty. Young underlined the fact that this was not the first instance of such

6. *Ibid.*
7. Mukherjee Mirdula, 'Peasants Movement in a Princely State in Patiala : 1937-48,' in *Proceedings of Punjab History* Conference, 18th Session, 1981, 311.
8. Walia Ramesh, *Praja Mandal Movement in East Punjab States,* Patiala : 1972, 10.
9. Of all sections of Society the economic depression effected the agrarian classes the most; thus giving a handle to professional agitators. Vide., *Punjab Administration Report for 1930-31,* 10-11.
10. For a detailed account of the origin of insecurity and dissatisfaction, see Chapter II.
11. For instance, in 1912, S. Arjun Singh *Rais* of Sagarian was granted a village worth income of Rs. 1000/-. *Vide., Patiala Gazettee* (Patiala), April 13, 1912,2.

violence as the *biswedars* and the *muzaras* of States had seldom been at peace in their mutual relations and dealings. The gravity of the situation can well be estimated from the fact that a great majority of the seventeen thousand disputes settled by the Settlement Courts pertained to tenancy rights. At the time of submitting his report Mr. Young was himself apprehensive[12] that it might not be the right solution to the tenurial problem-a statement which turned out to be prophetic. Though it was noticed that the new settlement was working well, the court notices concerning the land disputes issued in the Patiala Gazettee, show that the agrarian peace and harmony was never restored in the States.[13] Consequently, sudden random peasants' risings continued; and a *biswedar-muzara* clash rocked the Patiala State in the *rabi* season of 1911. The *biswedars* of village Qasaiwara informed the *tehsildar* that the *muzara* had not only refused to pay *batai* but they had also been uncivial in their behaviour. Now, the State Government appointed one *naib tehsildar* Puran Chand as Collector who was to be assisted by two *zaildars,* one *sufedopsh,* one *lambardar* and two *chaprasis.* The Collector along with his aids reached the said village on April 30, 1911. They appealed to both the parties to settle their claims amicably. However, the *muzaras* remained adament against sharing till May 4, 1911. The *chaprasi* proceeded to pacify the *muzaras,* who were in mood to, fight, was slapped. When the *tehsildar* intervened he too was dragged down from his horse. He as well as the *biswedars* were roughed up and lathis were freely used, leaving whole of the Collector's party and the *biswedars* injured.[14] We get many other instances of this type recorded in the Gazettee and reports.

As early as 1920, the *murzaras* of village Kishangarh refused to pay *batai* to the *biswedars.* After three years *i.e.,* in 1923, the *murzaras* of village Rajomajra stopped paying *batai*

---

12. Mr. Popham Young, *Report on Settlement of Patiala State,* 26-27.
13. *Punjab Administration Report for 1913-14,* 2; Patiala Gazettee, 1913.
14. PSR, PM's Office File No. 5804 (See letter of I.G.P. to H.H. dated 8.4.1939), PSR, Patiala.

to *biswedar*. From this time onwards *batai* was collected from the *muzaras* on gun point by the officials aided by the police.[15] Let it be noticed that at this time, there was discontent among peasants not only in the Patiala State but also in other princely states of the Malwa region. Typical of such peasants' unrest was the one witnessed in the Muslim state of Malerkotla. At Kothala village in this state a convention of the peasants was held on January 10, 1927. The tenants raised their voice against the *khwamim* (Muslim Landlords) and also formed a *Zamindar* Association.[16] They decided to send a deputation to the Viceroy at Simla, to highlight their genuine grievances. It was to present a charter of demands also. But the state authorities dealt most severely with the agitators. The state police opened fire on their *dewan* on 17 July, 1927. In this firing 14 men, women and children were killed and many were injured. Even false cases were framed against their leaders who had just returned from Simla. At this time, on the advice of Patiala Maharaja, the *nawab* of Malerkotla too stern action against the muzaras. The *kothala* episode symbolizes the general peasant unrest in this region and proved fore-runner of a mighty movement for the defence of peasant interests. It took hardly two years for the *muzaras'* agitation to raise its head in Patiala state in particular and in other states[17] in general.

In 1928 Baba Kharak Singh, a prominent Akali leader, toured the Patiala State to highlight the grievances of the tenants and highhandedness and repressive rule of Maharaja Bhupinder Singh. He also pleaded for the release of Sewa Singh Thikriwala.[18] During his tour he addressed number of public meetings at various places and attracted peasants in large number. In these meetings he preached the message of unity

---

15. PSR, *Ijlas-i-khas*, File No. 1264, PSA : Patiala.
16. The word *zamindar* has wide connotations—here it implies the peasants more specifically the tenants who were *adna-malik*.
17. *Khalsa Te Khalsa Advocate* (Amritsar), 9 February, 1928,1; *Khalsa Samachar* (Amritsar), 7 February, 1929, 1; *Babar Sher* (Amritsar), 23 February, 1929, 3.
18. For further details see PSR, P.M. Office File No. 542, PSA : Patiala.

and exhorted his audiences to associate themselves actively with the struggle launched by the Akalis. From the various resolutions passed and the speeches made by him during his visit it is clear that the main objectives of the Akali agitation were to attack the autocracy, to speak up for democratic rights of the masses and to seek redressal of their economic grievances. Even the formation of the Punjab *Riyasti Praja Mandal* on July 17, 1928 was announced during his tour.[19] It was an important landmark in the history of the peasant movement in this region of Punjab.

Undoubtedly, the formation of the said *Mandal* was a significant landmark in the history of the peasants' movement in these states. From its very inception, it espoused the cause of the peasants. Their major demands were as follows : [20]

(a) *Nazool* law should be changed in such a way that a property would lapse to the state only in those cases, where no one from the kith or kin had claim to a title;

(b) Ban on *shikar* for ordinary citizens should be ended;

(c) *Khush hasiyat* and *abiana* should be at par with similar taxes in the neighbouring British region;

(d) *Begar* system should be done away with;

(e) Repayment of water loan with interest was demanded;

(f) Schools should be opened;

(g) The milestones on roads should be inscribed in Punjabee;[21]

---

19. Home Political, 1926-31, Serial No. 390, File No. 1/1928, NAI, New Delhi; Gurcharn Singh, *op. cit.*, 61, Statement of Wazir Singh Daftriwala, Oral History Cell File No. 41, Deptt. of Punjab Historical Studies, Panjabi University, Patiala.
20. *Khalsa Te Khalsa Advocate* (Amritsar) 16 February, 1929, 1; *Kirpan Bahadur* (Amritsar), 11 June, 1931, 6.
21. These demands clearly show that character of the *Praja Mandal* organization *i.e.* It was a pro-peasants' organization.

(h) *Zaildaris, nambardaris* and *jagirs*, which had been confiscated during the Akali agitation and one which fines had been paid, be returned to the owners.

(i) Repression of police on *kamins* should be put to an end;

(j) Punitive police posts and *thikripahera* be removed from the villages;

(k) Parliamentary democracy should be established;

(l) The Maharaja should reduce and fix his personal expenditure;

(m) Restrictions on newspapers, meetings and processions be removed;

(n) Special class in jail be created for political and religious detainees;

(o) Full compensation be paid to owners whose land had come under roads and canals; and

(p) A suitable solution to the *biswedar-muzara* problem be devised and *batai* system be put to an end without payment of compensation to the *biswedars*.

The *muzaras* joining the *Praja Mandal* in large number frightened both the *biswedars* and the Maharaja. The latter under the circumstances thought it essential to win over the support of the *biswedars*. Its need and urgency was more pronounced in view of the fact that the *Maharaja* had reason to feel insecure as the All India States Peoples Conference was conducting an enquiry against him. The *biswedars* were equally prepared to make a common cause with him against the peasants. Finally, the Maharaja convened a meeting in 1929 of those *biswedars* whose lands were usually inundated. It were those *biswedars* who were not paid any compensation for the seasonal flooding of their lands. Surprisingly enough, they were supposed to continue paying land revenue at older rates. Besides, they feared the growing peasant truculence against which they greatly needed the state help; so they adopted a resolution to their own detriment that the Bhupindra Sagar lake or the Maharaja's *shikar* campaigns caused no inconvenience to them.[22]

Thus, by the start of 1930, the Maharaja and the *biswedars* were alarmed at the strength of the Praja Mandal. Consequently, a pro-rulers organization known as the Punjab *Riyasti Zamindar Praja Mandal* was formed to counter the propaganda of the Punjab *Riyasti Praja Mandal.*[23] It gave a call to all people of the East Punjab States to join this new organization as it genuinely stood for the peasant cause. The pro-government newspapers asked the people to remain vigilant of the moves of the conspirators and seek the redressal of their sufferings and grievances by praying directly to the rulers of these States.[24]

Besides, the *Praja Mandalists,* during this phase of their movement, received spontaneous support from the Akalis of the British Punjab. As the *Praja Mandal* leader Sewa Singh Thikriwala was not released, the Akalis decided to send to Patiala their emissaries *Baba* Kharak Singh and Master Tara Singh to launch an agitation against the highhandedness of the State ruler.[25] Now, the Maharaja took the suppression of the Akali stir into his own hands.[26] The itinerary of the Akalis' leaders was chalked out before hand; and the Maharaja

22. Daftriwala, *op. cit.,* 19.
23. *Sher Khalsa* (Lahore), 11 January, 1930, 2.
24. *Sher Khalsa* (Lahore), 12 August, 1929, 3.
25. We can have several references to this tour of the Akalis' leaders in various files. For a comprehensive study see PSR, PM's Office File Nos. 541, 542, 546-49 and 573, PSA; also see Home Political, 1926-31, Serial Nos. 565, 566, 570; File No. 17/1929; Foreign Department Progs., 1929, File No. 40-p (Secret); File No. 220-P (Secret), Foreign Department Progs., 1930, File No. 115-P (Secret) NAI, New Delhi.
26. The officials gave a long rope to the protestors because of two factors-one, the Maharaja was away to Europe and two, in a dilemma because of lack of instruction from the highest level and being their first experience with a major political agitation in this region. However, in his telegraphic instructions from Europe the Maharaja scolded the state officials for being too liberal towards the agitators.

succeeded in isolating the leaders from the mass of agitators. The States' authorities instructed the ruralities not to entertain the agitators.[27] The properties of those participating in the agitation were to be confiscated and attached. A strict but constant vigilwas kept on the activities of the agitators. A group of Akali preachers loyal to the Maharaja led by one Kartar Singh Diwana was also organized.[28] Consequently, the second time also the Akali agitation failed to achieve its purpose. But this agitation left deep impact on the vernacular press as it was divided into two factions-one supporting and other opposing the Maharaja. The farmer faction felt that as the Maharaja was a Sikh, he should not be harassed while the latter opposed him alleged that the papers favouring him had been bribed to play to his tune.[29]

Though the second Akali movement failed, the Maharaja released Sewa Singh Thikriwala on 24 August, 1929, because of the following factors : *(a)* This movement was able to mount a considerably pressure on the Maharaja; *(b)* he was convinced that the shape of things to come could be serious and worse; *(c)* to prop up his sagging image, as in the forthcoming First Round Table Conference where he was to represent the Indian Princes and *(d)* the appeal of moderate *panthic* leaders had left deep imprint on his mind.[30]

The release of Sewa Singh Thikriwala accelerated the intensity of the peasant movement. The *Praja Mandalists*

---

27. Gurcharan Singh, *op. cit.,* 36-39.
28. PSR, PM's Office File No. 544, PSA (IGP's letter to H.H. in which he conveys that Diwana was to head a counter Akali organization known as *Amrit Prachar.*
29. *Khalsa-Te-Khalsa* Advocate (Amritsar) and *Khalsa Samachar* (Amritsar) did not write against the Maharaja, while *Kirpan Bahadur Te Sangat* (Amritsar); *Kirpan Bahadur,* (Amritsar) *Babbar Sher* (Amritsar); were opposed to him. *Sher Khalsa* (Lahore) was often branded as the *"Patiala Akhbar".*
30. Home Political, 1926-1931, Serial No. 572, File No. 17/1929; Foreign Department Progs., 1929, File No. 264-P (Secret), NAI, New Delhi.

organized *dewans* in his honour. With this a new chapter was opened in the history of the peasant movement in the East Punjab States. Soon after the *Praja Mandalists* organized five *dewans* at different places.[31] At all these *dewans* Wazir Singh Daftriwala was invariably the stage secretary. At all these *dewans* the speakers raised their voice for abolition of the oppressive *biswedari* system in the states.[32] At the *Dewan* in Ubha, the first resolution passed pertained to the abolition of the *biswedari* system. The British Resident in the Phulkian States in his monthly report to the Government of India stated :[33] "Reports have been received from Patiala that an extensive propaganda is being carried on by Akali agitators and other malcontents against Patiala administration and that attempts are being made to corrupt the peasantry by urging them not to pay rent and taxes to landlords".

At the dewan in Ubha the first resolution that was passed pertained to the abolition of the *biswedari* system. Except *biswedar* Lachhman Singh of Barnala *tehsil,* all voted for the resolution. A few more resolutions pertained to the redressal of grievances were passed.[34] After this *dewan* there was much excitement among the peasants in the countryside. They felt satisfied with fact that at last there was an organisation which had taken up their cause with utmost sincerity.[35]

Around this time in 1929, a *muzara* Committee was set up, at village Sekha, by the prompting of Harnam Singh Dharamgarh and Wazir Singh Daftriwala. It was to safeguard the interests of the tenants and to maintain liaison with the Punjab *Riyasti Praja Mandal.* But this Committee remained

31. The First *Dewan* was held at Village Gharuan, the second at Bhadaur, the third at Mansa, the fourth at Ubha and the fifth at Dhuri. *Vide.,* Daftriwala, *op. cit.,* 31-32.
32. *Ibid.*
33. Home Political, 1930, File No. 19/5/1930, NAI, New Delhi.
34. *Ibid.*
35. Daftriwala, *op. cit.,* 32.

subservient to the *Praja Mandal*,[36] and did not achieve anything in its independent capacity. Thus, this wave of the peasant movement culminated in the holding of the Dhuri *dewan* in July 1931. At this *dewan* familiar resolutions were passed and the *biswedars* were the targets of attack in the speeches made by the leaders there.[37] Here, nearly all the prominent peasant leaders were arrested for making inflamatory speeches against the state.[38] These leaders were kept in Mohindergarh jail which was known to be a "Virtual hell". After some time the nefarious activities going on in this jail were reported in the vernacular press, becoming quite a scandal and a source of much embarrassment to the State.[39] These leaders were released only in 1933 when the sate felt secure enough from the action of these rebels when the *hidayat* of 1988 *Bikrami* had been instituted.[40]

In the village Rajomajra, which was an estate of Gurnam Singh, father-in-law of Maharaja Bhupinder Singh, the discontent of the tenants appeared in the form of an organized revolt. Encouraged by the *Praja Mandalists* they refused to pay *batai*.[41] The tenants had felt that Mr. Popham Young had not done justice with them by ignoring their proprietary rights.[42]

36. Walia, Ramesh, *op.cit.,* 95. When asked about the Committee Jagir Singh Joga recalled that there was such a Committee which came into existence but failed to recollect its exact function.
37. Foreign Department Progs., 1931, File No. 312-p (Secret)., NAI, New Delhi.
38. Among those arrested, the names of Wazir Singh Daftriwala, Hazoor Singh Matran, Harnam Singh Dharamgarh, Bhagat Singh Dhotogal and Atma Singh Rangia are worthy of mention. *Vide.,* Daftriwala, *op. cit.,* 34.
39. *Desh Dardi* (Amritsar), 13 March, 1933, 13; 15 May, 1933, 14; *Nawan Jug* (Lahore), 13 March, 1933, 10 and 14; 26 June 1933, 3; Oral History Cell, File No. 41 (In his interview Daftriwala has referred to this); Jagir Singh Joga also highlights this fact in his personal interview.
40. Home Department, Political-A, 1931, File No. 1348-18/12, NAI, New Delhi; *Nawan Jug* (Lahore), 31 July, 1933, p. 3.
41. PSR, *Ijlas-i-khas,* File No. 1264, PSA : Patiala.
42. *Ibid.*

The Kartar Singh–Gian Singh Rarewala Commission[43] found that there was some truth in their claims,[44] as is clear from an extract of the Reports[45] We have no hesitation in finding that the *jagir* was not absolute, and was merely a temporary arrangement for the purposes of land revenue collection through a middle man, having been elevated as jagirdar.

On April 23, 1930, the *muzaras* of Rajomajra waited on the Maharaja. But they were rebuked for their refusal to pay *batai* and the following *Ijlas-i-khas* order was passed :[46] "That the *biswedars* have proprietary rights over the land and are entitled to *batai.* We confirm on principle the order passed by the Cabinet of this case and have warned the tenants that they should comply with the orders of the Cabinet."

Disappointed with the attitude of the Patiala rulers, the tenants proceeded to present a memorandum to the agent of the Viceroy in Simla. Ninety tenants were detacted by the State police at Kalka on their way to Simla in June 1930.[47] They were arrested but later released. The Punjab *Riyasti Praja Mandal* at its Ludhiana session endorsed the case of the Rajomajra tenants and resolved to back them in their struggle against the highhandedness of the State authorities as well as the *biswedars.* By July 1931, Harnam Singh, a *biswedar* of Bhadaur submitted a petition before the *Ijlas-i-khas* complaining that the *muzaras* had refused to pay him *batai* for three successive crops. He held that they had been so provoked at a meeting of the Punjab *Riyasti Praja Mandal* held at Budhlada and some *muzaras* on their return proclaimed to others by beat of drum not to pay *batai* warning that those paying *batai* would be boycotted.[48]

43. This Commission was constituted in 1945.
44. The gross injustice meted out to the *muzaras* of Village Rajomajra can well be seen because the adverse verdict given by the Commission must have been the lightest possible for General Gurnam Singh—a *biswedar* of the village then (1945) was the maternal-grand-father of the reigning ruler.
45. PSR, Ijlas-i-khas, File No. 1264, PSA, Patiala.
46. *Ibid.*
47. PSR, PM's Office File No. 639 (See Telegram dated 11 June, 1930 from IGP to Home Minister), PSA, Patiala.
48. PSR, PM's Office File No. 5582, PSA, Patiala.

The State revenue minister took a serious note of the situation and sought advice of his high ups on the matter,[49] saying" : "I am afraid if no proper remedy is sought the situation may become difficult to be handled in the near future and the neighbouring villages may be affected".

In their struggle against the Maharaja, the *biswedars* and the British imperialists, the *Praja Mandalists* got some support and direction from the Indian National Congress. The first Regular Session of the Punjab *Riyasti Praja Mandal* was held in Lahore in 1929 at Lahore and coincided with the famous Congress Session. Besides eliciting suppot from the Congress, the leaders of the States' movement discussed their problems with the Congress leaders. They were advised to take up popular causes with a sense of National service in view and also to strengthen their own organizational base. There was a special reference to the Patiala *biswedari-muzara* problem.[50] At this time the Punjab *Riyasti Praja Mandal* presented a memorandum to the Viceroy, levelling serious allegations against Maharaja Bhupinder Singh of Patiala as well as the other rulers of Punjab States. Its Copy was also submitted to the annual session of the All India States People's Conference at Bombay in May 1939. As a result, a Committee headed by C.Y. Chintamani was formed. It found the Maharaja and the States' authorities guilty on at least twelve charges.[51] Though this

49. PSR, PM's Office File No. 639, PSA, Patiala.
50. Personal interview with Chhajju Mal Vaid., Jagir Singh Joga also agreed that at whatever opportunities they got, they used to discuss their regional problems with the congress leaders.
51. C.Y. Chintamani Committee was "... glad to announce to the public that has certainly been able to gather a good deal of material which when examined... eastablished a strong *prima-facie* case against the Maharaja". See *Indictment of Patiala,* Bombay, 1930 (Its first edition was sold like hot cakes. The State Government was apprehensive of the second edition which was to be published from London. On State Government's request the British Indian Government prohibited the import of the book to India) *Vide.,* Home Department Political-A, 1931, File No. 29/10, NAI, New Delhi; *Khalsa Samachar* (Amritsar), 5 June, 1930, 2.

Committee did not have any official standing but its shocking findings greatly lowered the prestige of the Maharaja. When its findings reached the official circles, they were highly upset. However, Maharaja Bhupinder Singh was a great manupulator. He approached the Viceroy to appoint an official Committee to go into the charges levelled against him. Finally, he got appointed Fitz patric, the then Resident for the Punjab States at Lahore and his personal friend[52] to Chair the official committee. It after its one sided hearings in Dalhousie totally exonerated the Maharaja.[53]

However, during this phase of the peasant struggle and Praja Mandal activities, the Maharaja had a reason to feel insecure. Now, the Patiala authorities or-ganised special Conferences to project the loyality of the subjects to the Maharaja. One such conference was organized on June 26, 1930 at Patiala. In this conference the representatives of various sections of the society expressed their spontaneous loyality (sic) to him. It is to be noticed that the representatives of Akalis, the Sikh community, *biswedars,* Hindus, Muslims, Christians, members of the bar and the mercantile community were present there. Their speeches were published in form of a booklet which was widely circulated.[54]

It is worth mentioning that the results of the official Inquiry Committee had encouraged the Maharaja who then made it mission of his life to crush his subjects in all possible manners.

52. Even before Fitz Patric completed his Inquiry, the Maharaja allegedly boasted that he could never go against him. On his retirement there was inquiry against Fitz Patric and he was reprimanded for staying in London in a rent free house provided by the Maharaja of Patiala. *Vide.,* Foreign Department Progs., 1935, File No. F 366-P (S); home Department, Political A, 1931, File No. 100/31, NAI, New Delhi.
53. Gurcharan Singh, *op.cit.,* 65-66;. Sarton, *op. cit.,* 134; Rosita Forbes, *India of Princes,* London : 1939, 51-52.
54. Spontaneous Expression of Loyality to His Highness Shri 108 Maharaja Dhiraj by his subjects and others (Patiala : 1930), PSA, Patiala.

As a result, great repression was practised on the people on the occasion of a dewan at Dhuri; public property and *Gurdwaras* were being confiscated and declared as state properties; an institution of capitalists and *biswedars* had been inaugurated with was to work for the gain of the Maharaja and as a reward for their services the *biswedars* were given possession of land; and the regours of the *begar* system had increased considerably to carry out the operation of constructing Bhupindra Sagar, Ladha *kothi* and dog show houses.[55] Hence, the Maharaja was bent on crushing the *Praja Mandal* and peasant agitation. The Chiefs of the three Phulkian States issued a common decree banning all political activities in the three states. The decree later became known as the *hidayat* 88' because it was singed on 5th *poh* 1988 *Bikrami.* Patiala State promulgated it in its territory through a special *farman-i-shahi* of January 14, 1932. According to this decree no society, association or organisation could be formed without a certificate of recognition from the State Government. A separate Committee was set up for receiving and deciding applications for such recognition.[56] Now all registered societies were required to submit annual lists of members with full addresses. If any society was noticed indulging in any undesirable activity the Committee could order withdrawawal of recognition and declare the society unlawful. The Committee could order confiscation of incriminating literature and place restriction on printing presses. It could order prosecution of persons and confiscation of property.[57] This, in fact, was a black law of the state, but it gave legitimacy to draconian powers which had been vested in the Maharaja. The decree was an indirect accxptance of the fact that the people's unrest in the Phulkian States was mounting.

---

55. PSR, PM's Office File No. 642, PSA : Patiala.
56. The Prime Minister , The Minister of Law and Justice and the Inspector General of Police were the members of this Committee. This displays the character and fairness of the Committee.
57. PSR, PM's Office File No. H-97B, M99B, H-102B, H-104B, PSA; Patiala.

The offices of the *Praja Mandal* were opened at places near to but outside the State. These offices were located at Chauke, Budhlada, Khadial, Gidderbaha, Jethuke, Potne,[58] etc. The Praja Mandal had already been holding its annual sessions and meetings outside the State. The shrewd Maharaja thought of another plan to weaken the peasants' struggle. He won over the most influential and outspoken leader of the Akalis namely Master Tara Singh to his side.[59] Besides, Sardar Sewa Singh Thikriwala was re-arrested under the *hidayat* of 1988 *Bikrami* and this hero of the poor *muzaras* died in the Patiala prison on January 20, 1935.[60] Now, five leaders of the Patiala *Praja Mandal* decided to go on a fast unto-death protesting against the conciliatory attitude of the Akali *Dal* towards the Maharaja and also demanded an inquiry into the circumstances leading to Thikriwala's death. But their fast did not seem to have achieved any thing substantial.[61]

---

58. Home Political, 1933, File No. 18/7/1933, NAI, New Delhi.
59. Especially the moderate Sikh leaders were strongly of the view that the Akali *Dal* should make up with the Maharaja if it desired to have unity in the Sikh *panth*. For some time the fight was considered Sikh panth. For some time the fight was considered as the : Soon after making an agreement with the Maharaja, Master ji observed that it had been done in consultation with the important *Praja Mandal* leaders including Harchand Singh Jeji. Punjab District *jathas* had also been taken into confidence. Tara Singh blamed the Patiala leaders for having backed out of the agreement, later. According to this agreement the Akali *Dal* was not to associate itself in the feature political activities of the *Praja Mandal* for which it had to face the consequences itself. In return, the State was not to victimize all those *Praja Mandal* activists who had participated in the Akali *Morcha*. Vide., *Khalsa-Te-Khalsa Advocate* (Amritsar), 16 February, 1929, 1-2-; *Khalsa Samachar* (Amritsar), 13 February, 1929, 1; *Sher Khalsa* (Lahore), 7 December, 1929, 1; *Akali Patrika* (Lahore), 26 January, 1936, 8-10; *Akali* (Lahore) , 13 January, 1937, 4, 22; Patiala Gazettee (Patiala) 7 May, 1936, 41-42.
60. Regarding Sewa Singh Thikriwala's activities after his release and his subsequent arrest-see Gurcharan Singh, *op.cit.,* 57-113.
61. *Daily Akali Patrika* (Lahore), 22 January, 1931, p.1.

Thus, for some time the muzara movement had reached low ebb, but inwardly the movement continued to gather strength, as large number of activists withdrew to the villages, where they began to educate the people, especially the peasants.[62] Even outside the state the leadership and workers of the *Praja Mandal* continued their activities, attacking the *biswedari* or *zamindari* system and the States' rulers by their propaganda.

In brief the *muzara* movement could not be totally and permanently crushed. There was a public meeting at Budhlada in October 1934; which had been attended largely by the Patiala peasants. In this meeting reduction in water rates, land revenue, and tax relief was demanded. The peasants also demanded the right to sell their produce in the Punjab *mandis,* as the prices of agricultural produce in the Punjab was higher. To substantiate it, let us note that the price of cotton was Rs. 4 and 6 *annas* in Breta *mandi* in the Patiala State while it was Rs. 5 and 4 annas at Budhlada; and the distance between the two *mandis* was only about 6 miles.[63]

In 1934, in the sub-*tehsil* of Ghanaur and Ghaggar, the peasants severely attacked the rise in *abiana* rates. They demanded parity of rates with British Punjab. They stated that in the Patiala State the *abiana* rate was one rupee and eight *annas* whereas in the Punjab it was only fourteen *annas.* Thus, it was ten *annas* higher than that prevailing in the Punjab. Particularly the *muzaras* of Atwana, Chamaru, Nadana, Kapoori, Khalaspur, Mahru, Majholi, Mandi, Pur, Rampur, Sarala and Souta were reported to be in a fighting mood. When the local officials such as the *tehsildar* and *nazim* did not listen to the genuine and rational demands of the *muzaras,* they sent number of petitions highlighting their grievances to the Viceroy at Delhi, but his response to the petition was lukewarm : [64]

62. See Oral History Cell File of S. Jagir Singh Joga; also personal interview with Jagir Singh. He realised that all the above mentioned factors did not kill the spirit of *muzara* movement.
63. PSR, PM's Office File No. 710, PSA : Patiala.
64. PSR, PM's Office File No. 700, PSA : Patiala.

A political conference was held at Chhappar from September 11 to 13, 1935. The high irrigation rates and land revenue once again agitated the tempers of the *muzaras*. One Bhagat Singh Dhatogal presented facts and figures about these rates. There, the tenants demanded immediate relief.[65] And, petitions of village after village kept pouring in, which made the Government to take note of their grievances. Finally the Finance Minister of State, Sir Fredrick Gauntlet ordered an enquiry into the questions of high *abiana* rates. The Government took five years to grant relief of three *annas* and that too only for fodder crop to the peasants. The state administration and the Prime Minister of the State were alarmed at the increasing discontent among the peasantry. He directed his subordinates to tour the villages ad remove peasants' genuine grievances.[66] However, the activities of the *muzaras*, in some form or the other continued even after the promulagation of the *hidayat* of 1988 *Bikrami* in the state. To substantiate, it will be most appropriate to reproduce here an event reflecting diffusion of the *muzaras'* awakening with its diverse ramifications. One Lal Singh[67] of village Chamaru organized a peasants' association known as *Jatha Dhukee Zamindar*. Its meeting was held at village Seel, nearly 6 miles from Patiala. This meeting attracted peasants from the neighbouring villages. There, a free vent was given to the peasants' grievances. Later a poster was distributed by Lal Singh at Bahadurgarh *tanga* stand to the incoming and outgoing passangers who were mostly muzaras;[68] this poster contained the following demands :[69]

(a) State should have a legislative assembly;

(b) More schools and Hospitals should be opened in rural areas;

65. PSR, PM's Office File No. 730, *Patiala. *PSA :
66. PSR, PM's Office File No. 750, PSA, Patiala.
67. He was a Clerk in The Patiala Court *Vide.*, PSR, PM's Office File No. 746, PSA : Patiala.
68. Later Lal Singh was terminated from service for such a daring act of insubordination. Vide. *Ibid.*
69. *Ibid.*

(c) There should be a parity of Land Revenue rates with the British territories;

(d) Nazool system should be abolished; and

(e) Step should be taken to curb rural indebtedness.

Hence, activities of the tenants in some form or the other continued even after the implementation of the *hidayat* of 1988 *Bikrami* in this region of the Punjab. The *Praja Mandal* was divided into the moderates and the radical soon after the death of Sewa Singh Thikriwala. One group was led by Harchand Singh Jeji—a rebellions feudal *biswedar* of Patiala. He desired that the principal objective of the *Praja Mandal* should be the removal of the Maharaja. The second faction, comprising of Bhagwan Singh Longowalia, Jagir Singh Joga, Wazir Singh Daftriwala and Pritam Singh Gojran, wanted that the *Praja Mandal* should only take up common issues and it should not act as a forum for members to seek redressal of their personal grievances, instead it should take up common causes.[70] At the Anandpur Sahib Conference of the *Praja Mandal* held on 25-26 March, 1937, the schism became very evident. The stage was set up by the moderates, but was captured by radicals who delivered fiercy speeches against the feudal order particularly in Patiala State.[71] In fact, the radicals had come under leftist influence after 1932 when they had gone out of the States to evade arrest under the hidayat of 1988 *Bikrami*. In brief, this schism and finally the split was a stepping stone towards polarisantion on ideological lines. The feudal elements were by and large isolated or they went into the Akali fold. It was after this that the focus of political action was shifted to the peasantry.

---

70. Harchand Singh Jeji remained a leader of one *Praja Mandal* group from behind the scene. See File No. 10, Oral History Cell, Punjab Historical Studies Department, Punjabi University, Patiala.
71. Jeji had personal enemity with Bhupinder Singh who had expelled him from the State and confiscated his property. File No.41, Oral History Cell, *op.cit.*

All India *Kisan Sabha* was founded in 1936 and it inspired the *Praja Mandal* to give a call to *kisans* to form their own committees; to get affliliation with *tehsil kisan* Committee which would enable them to join the all India *Kisan* movement.[72] As a result, the peasants' struggle in the states once again accelerated activities. A *kisan* Conference was to be held on 7-8 November, 1936; but the State authorities made it unsuccessful by its pre-emptive action. Delegates from distance places came on the appointed day but they had to return disappointed.[73]

It will not be out of place to state here that there were two groups of the communists in the Punjab-one group was led by Sohan Singh Josh while the other group, known as the *Kirti* party, was led by Teja Singh Swatantar. The latter faction of the leftists made inroads into the states and organized the *Kisan* Committees. Now, the *Kisan* leaders began to turn towards the communists and socialists for guidance as well as help because they found in them steadfast champions of peasants'/ *muzaras'* demands. Secondly they often felt frustrated in the *Praja Mandal* as it represented larger interests of general nature rather than the specific interests of the peasantry / *muzaras*.[74]

Fresh signs of peasants' activity were visible during the *rabi* season of 1937. Many peasant leaders such as Pritam Singh Gojran, Master Hari Singh, Sahib Singh Salana and Jagir Singh Phaguwalia were imprisoned. They were charged with inciting the peasants against the new *bandobast*.[75]

The peasants' struggle in the states assumed militant and radical colour on November 25, 1937. On that day the police

72. Walia, Ramesh, *op.cit.*, 132.
73. PSR, PM's Office File No. 737, PSA, Patiala.
74. Right from 1929 the Punjab CID found some links between the Lahore revolutionary group—the extremist Akalis, the *Kirti* group and the *Praja Mandal*. Vide., Home Department Political-A, File No. 575 of 1929, NAI, New Delhi; Walia, Ramesh, *op. cit.*, 134.
75. *Akali Patrika* (Lahore), 14 April, 1937, 4; 21 April, 1937, 8. (*Dewan* was held on the Baisakhi day at *Gurdwara* Damdama Sahib where the peasants were incited by fiercy speeches).

opened fire in order to avert a clash between the tenants and *biswedars* of Qilla Hakiman at the time of *batai*. In this firing two *muzaras* were killed and nine wounded seriously. The *muzaras* held that they were completely non-violent. An official committee appointed to conduct an inquiry upheld the official version that the police opened fire in self-defence.[76] But the non-official inquiry Committee[77] held the tenants 'non-guilty', and felt that the firing was unjustifiable, unnecessary, excessive and uncontrolled.[78] The growing leftist influence instilled militancy into the peasants' movement. The high-handed action and one sided inquiry by the state made the tenants realize miserable and helpless lot and also served as a symbol for the awakening of the peasantry. More and more villages were getting agitated.[79]

To sum up, there some casual and sporadic peasants' out bursts during the period 1920-1928. But during 1928 to 1938, the peasants' struggle was inspired by the *Praja Mandal* and to some extent by the communists and radical socialists. However, it is to be noted that the early leadership of the *Praja Mandal* leaders came under the complete influence of leftist ideology, they really championed the cause of the peasantry in the States. Another significant point worth mentioning is that this movement had two strands—one of middle peasants and second of lower peasants or the *muzaras*. While the agitation of the peasant proprietors never assumed the tempo of its counterpart in the Punjab, the tenants who had long standing grievances kept up their whimper, in this part of the Punjab.

---

76. PSR, PM's Office File No. 6157, PSA : Patiala.
77. This Committee was comprised of Wazir Singh Daftriwala and Lala Achint Ram of Servants of People Society. Vide., *op. cit.*
78. Walia, Ramesh, *op. cit.,* 133.
79. We can have references ot the revolting villages such as Rajomajra, Bhadur, Kishangarh Pherwahi and Kishangarh Sadha Singhwala, etc. in number of files of PSR, *Ijlas-i-khas* File Nos. 652, 1261, 1263, 1938, 1946-47, 2077 and PM's Office File Nos. 5804, 5982, PSA : Patiala.

Thus, the peasants' struggle which began in 1928, culminated at the Dhuri *dewan* towards the end of 1931 and this may be considered its first period. The second period was a slightly quiscant period which started from 1932, with the implementation of the *hidayat* of 1988 *Bikrami* when attempts were made to suppress all political activities and this period ended in 1936. By 1939, many *Praja Mandal* leaders were inspired by the socialistic philosophy and with this the peasants' struggle gathered momentum. At this time, there was a rising wave of *Kisan* activity in the neighbouring British Punjab as a result of the formation of the All India *Kisan Sabha*. Consequenlty, in the states also, the movement once again began to pulsate with life. Now, there was a violent *muzaras-biswedars* clashes at Qilla Hakiman. Under the circumstances the Maharaja of Patiala was forced to institute a Constitutional Reforms Commission[80] in January, 1938. But it proved to be an exercise in futility as the Maharaja passed away soon after constituting the said Commission. Consequently the tenants movement continued.

80. For further details see correspondence between N.V. Gadgil and Balwantray Mehta from April 23, 1938 to July 24, 1938 in *AISPC-Papers*, File No. 178, NMML, New Delhi.

6 THE PEASANT'S STRUGGLE : 1938-1948

Except for some intermittent spans of low activity, the peasants' movement in the East Punjab States during this period was in full swing. This period may be termed as 'the organized phase of the peasants' struggle in this region. It is no less important to state that the polarisation of the movement, leaders and activists on ideological lines also emerged during this period and the leftist influence added an element of militancy to the movement. It is equally significant to note that the peasants' struggle was dominated by the tenants, while the middle peasants and the peasant proprietors played just a secondary role in it, and at times practically an insignificant role.

Maharaja Yadvindra Singh's predecessor and father Maharaja Bhupinder Singh had tried to crush the movement ruthlessly; even then the *Praja Mandal* and its byproduct, the peasants' movement became a formidable force by the middle of 1933. Before his death, Maharaja Bhupinder Singh, however, appointed constitutional Reforms Commission. It had revived the peasants' hope of getting justice from the new Maharaja Yadvindra Singh whose clean image along with puritanical announcements aroused great expectations.[1] But soon all hopes

1. An excerpt of Yadvindra Singh's inauguration speech is reproduced verbatim as follows :
I realize that circumstances are fast changing in India and that the time when the states and the rulers lived and worked in isolation, imparting the conditions around them, are rapidly disappearing. No barriers can be erected against ideas and I recognize that the time has come when traditional policy of the States may require modification and adjustment in light of what is happening in the rest of this great country.
Vide., Administration Report of Patiala State for the Year 1938-39, 9-11.

were belied, because no reforms were forthcoming. Instead in a subtle move Yadvindra Singh brought about a split in the Akali Praja Mandal ranks by conciliating Harchand Singh Jeji,[2] in fact winning him over by marrying his daughter, Mohinder Kaur.

Master Tara Singh being loyal to the Maharaja of Patiala, some Akali leaders like Wazir Singh Daftriwala, Pritam Singh Gojran and Jagir Singh Phaguwalia joined radical group of the *Praja Mandal.* In fact, this radical group was formed by some of the Akali workers, such as Bhagwan Singh Longowalia and Jagir Singh Joga, who were annoyed with the loyalist attitude and activity of Master Tara Singh. The *valto face* of Harchand Singh Jeji was the final signal for such feudal elements who, out of expediency rather any philosophy or mission, had associated themselves with the progressive programme of the *Praja Mandal,* to part ways with the organization.

In these days it was difficult to distinguish between an Akali, a communist or a *Praja Mandalist.* 'For many the Akali *Dal* was a concrete historical reality, whereas the *Praja Mandal* was merely an abstraction.'[3] In reality, the *Praja Mandal* was a mixture of Akalis and Communists. The *Praja Mandal* then was a conglomerate of politicians who believed in diverse ideologies. Political activity being legally banned, the religious Congregations (*dewans*) were well suited to propagate political views. The Akali *Praja Mandal* was now fully dominated by the Communists, the moderate and feudal elements being completely isolated from it, the peasants' movement now adopted a violent and radical line of action.[4]

---

2. Harchand Singh Jeji remained a leader of *Praja Mandal* faction from behind the scene. He had a personal enemity with Bhupinder Singh who expelled him from the State and confiscated his property. See for further details-Oral History Cell File No. 10 and 41, Historical Department, Panjabi University, Patiala.
3. Walia, Ramesh, *Praja Mandal Movement in East Punjab States* (Patiala : 1972), 156.
4. PSR, PM's Office File No. 737, PSA : Patiala; Walia, Ramesh, *op. cit.,* 132.

Some prominent *Praja Mandal* leaders[5] from the Patiala State attended the Sixth All India States People's Conference held at Ludhiana from 15-17 February, 1939. It was presided over by Jawaharlal Nehru. But the Reception Committee was headed by Karam Singh Dhut, the then General Secretary of the All India States' People's Conference, Mr. Rangil Dass Kapadia observed in his report : [6] "Ludhiana has brought the problem of the States much nearer to the Congress than hitherto. It used to be the complaint of the State people that the Congress has not taken sufficient interest but since Haripura this old-standing complaint has been wholly obviated and the trains hitherto coursing along different lines are approximating to a point of convergence at the Tripura junction through the level crossing at Ludhiana".[7]

It was at this conference that the slogan of '*batai nahi deni*' (*No batai*) for the Patiala *muzaras* was coined. By this time there was a spate of litigation against the *muzaras* and several were being ejected from the lands that they had occupied for long durations.[8] Thus, the *muzaras'* movement in the States got intensified in the wake of the Ludhiana Conference. In the very beginning of 1939, *muzaras'* committee was set up under the presidentship of Narain Singh Bhadaur. Chand Singh was appointed its General Secretary, while Dharam Singh Fakkar and Gurdev Singh Josh were appointed its joint Secretary and propaganda secretary respectively.[9] The offices of this committee were also set up at Budhlada (Hissar District), Buchcho *mandi* (Ferozepur District) and Shena (Ludhiana District). Hence, the committee and its members mostly

---

5. Bhagwan Singh Longowalia, Harnam Singh Dharamgarh, Jagir Singh Joga, and Master Hari Singh were the leading figures.
6. For further details see *AISPC-Papers,* File No. 187 NMML, New Delhi.
7. Personal interview of Chhajju Mal Vaid, and Master Hari Singh.
8. Vaid, Chhajju Mal, *Comrade Dharam Singh 'Fakkar'–Ik Jeevan-Ik Prerna* (Bhatinda : 1980), 9.
9. PSR, PM's Office File Nos. 756, 5982; *Ijlas-i-khas* File No. 2226, 2077 and H. 134, PSA : Patiala.

functioned from outside the Patiala State, but these places were conveniently situated to conduct propaganda work in Patiala villages.[10] The agitation was kept up by posters, pamphlets and communications to the Press.[11] Its principal objectives were as follows : *(a)* To help organize local committees and to send workers to *biswedari* villages to educate the *muzaras* on the lines of the manifesto of the committee; *(b)* To collect funds for the activities of the State Committee; *(c)* To organize *muzaras'* meetings; *(d)* To defend *muzaras* in their legal battles against *biswedars*; *(e)* To send deputations (*jathas*) of the *muzaras* to the higher official of the states and British Indian Government and highlight the grievances of the *muzaras*; and *(f)* To print and distribute propaganda material.[12]

Thus, the propagandists travelled from village to village and carried out their activities vigorously. Special *muzaras* committees were set up in those villages which had been intensively effected. For instance, one such committee headed by Sarwan Singh was set up in Kosaiwara village of Bhatinda *tehsil*. Its main functions were to collect contribution for the State *muzara* committee and send weekly information to the committee. It was to prevent *muzaras* from paying *batai* and responding to court summons. The state administration tried to apprehend its members but in vain. Instructions were also issued to the S.H.O. of Mansa Police Station to keep an eye on their activities and procure evidence to frame changes against them.[13]

Soon after the setting up of the *muzara* committee, a meeting of the *muzaras* was called, at Plahra village, to chalk

10. PSR, *Ijlas-i-khas*, File No. 2077 (Confidential Note of IGP., dated 30.5.1939), PSA : Patiala.
11. *Ibid.*, (I.G.P.'s Note to the Prime Minister, dated 30.6.1939).
12. The material regarding various functions of the committee have been collected from different files of *Muzaras'* Movement. See particularly PSR, *Ijlas-i-khas* File Nos. 2077, 2226; PM's Office File No. 756 and 5982, PSA : Patiala.
13. PSR, PM's Office File No. 5982 (See I.G.P.'s letter to Prime Minister), PSA : Patiala.

out a plan of action. In response to the call, the *muzaras* reached in large numbers. However, the venue of the meeting had to be shifted to Pakho, a village in the Nabha State because section 144 was enforced in Plahra village. '*No batai*' campaign under the leadership of Gurbaksh Singh Chakerian and Dharam Singh Fakker, was decided to be launched at this meeting.[14] However, it was left to be approved by a larger gathering of State *muzaras*. Soon after another meeting of the *muzaras* was called at Dadra where the decision on 'no *batai*' campaign was postponed due to thin attendance. Now, the *muzara* committee deputed a delegation headed by Dharam Singh Fakker to contact the leaders of the All India *Kisan* Sabha.[15] They met *baba* Rur Singh Churchak, President of the Punjab *Kisan Sabha*. Since then the *muzara* Committee of the Patiala State came to be known as the *muzara-kisan* Committee.[16] After this there was no separate *kisan* committee of the middle peasants in the East Punjab States. A state level conference of the *muzaras* was convened at Jethuke in the Ludhiana district on 23-24 April, 1930. The slogan which gained currency at the conference was—'the cry

---

14. Vaid, Chhajju Mal, *op. cit.,* 8.
15. Fore more details see Josh, Bhagwan, *The communist in the Punjab : 1920-1945* (Delhi : 1979), 117-18, 121, 129, 135, 138, 184; Dutt, R.C., *India Today* (Bombay : 1947), 276-280, (The leaders with socialistic leanings within the Congress always had their sympathies for the peasants. The communists then affiliated with the Congress were instrumental in founding the all India *Kisan Sabha* in 1936. The branches soon sprang up throughout the nation and it pressed for the agrarian legislation. The first session was held in December, 1936 concurrently with the Faizpur session of the Indian national Congress. At Faizpur the Congress also adopted the agrarian programme (For further details see AICC files of this year).
16. A special file on the communist movement in Patiala state was kept by the *Ijlas-i-khas*. From which two references are of special note-the first one is above and the second one says—"It appears that the *kisan* and the *muzara* committees are now working under instructions of the Punjab Communist Party. *Vide., Ijlas-i-khas,* File No. 2226, PSA : Patiala.

of tenants is to take possession of lands from which they have been ejected and stop paying the *batai*. No fewer than six resolutions were passed concerning the peasants' problems at this conference. These resolutions are as follows : [17]

(a) The committee submits that for about last one century, their forefathers have been declaring themselves to be landlords, but they fail to understand as to why they have been deprived of their legitimate rights by giving *biswedari* rights to others, and pray that the settlement of the land revenue be left to them.

(b) The committee conveys its sympathies to the families of those who were shot dead at Qilla Hakiman and Dhuri. They also condemn feverish activities on the part of the state officials.

(c) The committee unanimously resolves that His Highness may be requested to cancel *hidayat* of 1988 Bikrami and release the prisoners unconditionally.

(d) The committee submits that the tenants of 784 villages are not prepared to accept the constitution of the contemplated Assembly unless the system of universal franchise is brought into, force.

(e) The committee condemns the action taken by the police at Barnala in particular and Patiala state in general in arresting innocent people.

The Jethuke conference, falling just in the midst of the *rabi* season of 1939, gave a call to the *muzaras* to refuse to pay *batai*. As a result, anti-*batai* campaign started from Bhadaur, home village of Narain Singh, President of the *muzara-kisan* committee. In several villages the *muzaras* began to take possession of lands from which they had been earlier ejected and the defiance of the *muzaras* in their refusal to pay *batai* reached its peak. The state police let loose a 'region of terror'.

---

17. A copy of these resolutions was sent to the State Officials by Chand Singh Bhadaur. See PSR File No. 2077, PSA : Patiala.

The *muzaras* were mercilessly beaten up, their houses destroyed and even their women were maltreated.[18] The *muzara* committee sent telegrams to the Maharaja informing him about the police atrocities on the muzaras.[19] The demands around which the *muzara kisan* committee was agitating were the following :[20]

I. *Kankut* system of appraisement be abolished and the *muzaras* in any case should not be forced to pay higher *batai* rates to the *biswedars* than the land revenue charged by the state;

II. The *muzaras* be given share in shamlat;

III. The *muzaras* be treated as absolute owners;

IV. *Nazool* be abolished and the *biswedar* in no case be permitted to succeed in preference to the rulers;

V. Those arrested for participating in the movement be released;

VI. The activists of the movement should not be victimized;

VII. The movable property of the *kisans* forcibly auctioned be returned to them, or also adequate compensation be paid;

VIII. The *kisans* be permitted to defend their cases from persons even outside the state.

IX. The *muzara-kisan* committee be recognized as a genuine representative body of the *kisans* of *biswedari* villages in the State; and

X. *Lambardars* should not be exclusively appointed from among the *biswedars* who are confined absentees.

---

18. A number of propaganda posters of *muzara* organisation have highlighted such maltreatment. *Vide.,* PSR, *Ijlas-i-khas* File No. 2077, PSA : Patiala.
19. The *muzara committee* sent its regular telegrams to the Maharaja at Chail (Simla Hills). *Vide., Ibid.*
20. *AISPC-Papers.* File No. 139, NMML, New Delhi.

The state authorities considered this agitation a part of 'Civil Disobedience Movement'. At least 1300 tenants were sent to prison and warrants were pending against the thousands.[21] The state authorities got nervous and the Secretary of the Prime Minister of the Patiala state in particular, in a letter to the I.G. Police, conveyed the massage of the Maharaja that the tenants movement must be stopped and strong action taken in consultations with the district authorities against the agitators.[22]

We shall now turn to that section of the agriculturists who were tenants and submitted to the exploitation by *biswedars* (refer to first Chapter). The relations of the tenants and the *biswedars* continued to deteriorate with the passage of time. It makes an interesting study as to when and why this movement started. The *biswedars* and the tenants were in conflict for preservation but the tenants united themselves against the *biswedars* only in the beginning of the twentieth century. The main reason was the growing consciousness among the peasantry of their rights. The peasants of the British territory, who were enjoying a free life and paid only a fixed revenue to the state established contacts with the peasantry of the Patiala State in particular and other *Phulkian* states in general. The peasants of Patiala state had begun to realise their rights. The rising tide of nationalism in the country and the movement connected with it were also destined to have their influence on

---

21. The villages that were most intensely involved in the *muzara* agitation were Nishangarh Pherwahi, Kishangarh Sedha Singhwala, Bir Khund, Chakerian, Bakshiwala in Mansa *tehsil*; Bhadaur, Kot Duna, Jangiana in Barnala tehsil; Ghatwali, Qasaiwara, Dhen Singh Khana, Dalel Singhwala in *tehsil* Bhatinda; Gobindgarh Jejian in *tehsil* Sunam and Nihalgarh in *tehsil* Bhawanigarh. Originally starting from Bhadaur in Barnala *tehsil*, the movement spread to the areas of Bhatinda, Mansa and sunam *tehsils*. *Vide.*, The references of disturbed villages are found in number of files of the PSR, *Ijals-i-khas* File No. 652, 1262, 1263, 1946-47, 1968, 3077, 5982 and 5804, PSR : Patiala.
22. I.G.P.'s confidential note to Prime Minister dated 30.6.1939, PSR : *Ijlas-i-khas*, File No. 2077 (Also see letter of the Secretary to the P.M. and to I.G.P. dated 3.5.1939), PSA : Patiala.

the movement of the tenants, and the peasantry in the East Punjab States organized itself in the form of *Kisan Sabha*.[23]

In the Patiala State, the tenant movement started from a village near Dhuri, called Rajomajra.[24] Apart from Rajomajra, there were other places where the disputes of the *biswedars* and the tenants existed. The foundation of this dispute was laid by the system of *batai*, which was changed from cash to kind and it was to be 1/4th of the harvest and the *biswedars* were made the owners of the land while the tenants were declaring themselves as the owners of the land just like *biswedars*.[25]

Many *Kisan Sabhas* were held in different places to get the demands of the tenants accepted by the Government. *Kisan* Conferences were held where these parties also participated. A *Kisan Sabha* held at Chao in Ludhiana district, demanded the amelioration of the sufferings of the tenants, Similarly, another conference was held at Shehna village (District Ludhiana) under the presidentship of Rattan Singh Mangali on 7th and 8th July, 1938. About 300 persons attended it.[26] A procession was also taken through all the main streets of the villages of Shehna. The precisionists carried posters bearing the inscription.[27]

Be-dakhal hoiyan zamina vapis deo
Jagirdari dhakka band karo

---

23. Patiala State Records, Prime Ministers' Office File No. 101, PSA : Patiala; Rajomajra Enquiry Committee Report, PSA : Patiala.
24. Personal meeting with Shri Chhajju Mal Vaid., at Fazilka on Sept., 18,1979, and Master Hari Singh at Chandigarh, March 17, 1979.
25. Vaid., Chajju Mal, *'Pepsu Muzarian Da Ghol Ten-Communist Party'* (an article in Panjabi) published in Souvenir, issued by the CPI on Jan., 26, 1976. Patiala State Records, File No. 2077, PSA : Patiala.
26. *Ibid.*, Vaid., Chajju Mal, "*Pepsu Muzarian Da Ghol Ten-*Communist Party" (an article in Panjabi) published in *Souvenir*, issued by the CPI on January 26, 1976.
27. Patiala State Records, File No. 2077, 75; also Basta No. 13, Secret Abstracts of Intelligence, July 28th, 1944, PSA: Patiala.

Many political slogans were raised among which the slogan 'stop *batai* system' was enthusiastically repeated. Thereafter Jagir Singh Joga performed the flag hoisting and made a short speech wherein he pointed out that the red flag represented the poor labourers and peasants to whichever community and nationality they belonged. The labourers and *kisans* should, therefore, rally round the red flag.[28]

There was another conference attended by over seven hundred men, mostly tenants held in the village Gujarwal. The conference commenced with recitation of the following lines of a poem :[29]

Uth jag kisana sutia hoiya lal sawera hoy,
Uttar dakhin pachhim jhulian lal phurera hoy.

The *kisan* conference expressed its resentment against the organized looting of Patiala State *muzaras* by the State officials and the *biswedars.* It requested the *Maharaja* of Patiala to stop action against *muzaras* and also to abolish the *batai* system. It also requested the state authorities to publish the *Muzara* Commission Report which had duly been completed for sevenyears.[30] Finally, the conference assured *muzaras* that the *kisan* Committee would support them if they made any effort to secure their rights. It will not be out of place if some more *kisan* conferences during 1938-48 as also the issues discussed there by the leaders are cited here. For this purpose a table is prepared which is given below : [31]

28. *Patiala State Records,* File No. 2077, PSA : Patiala, 76.
29. *Patiala State Records,* Basta No. 13, A Secret abstract of intelligence, July 28th, 1944, PSA : Patiala.
30. Prime Minister's Office File no. 2077, PSA : Patiala, 79.
31. The above data is based on the *Phulkian States Records* Files-File Nos. 6157, G-2155, 541, 542, 547, 548, 549, 552, 553, 555, 556, 563, 564, 566, 567, 568, 569, 578, 608, 609, 613, 623, 624, 630, 639, 642, 644, 654, 655, 667, 669, 670, 672, 675, 689, 690, 692, 697, 700, 702, 703, 710, 713, 715, 724, 727, 729, 739, 733, 734, 737, 742, 744, 745, 746, 747, 750, 756, 772.

Date	*Place-Where The Kisan Conferences Held*
July, 1938	Ludhiana and Abdullapura (Jagadhari)
April, 1939	Jethuke
May, 1939	Panchhat (Jullundur)
June, 1939	Ludhiana and Takhatpura, P.S. Nihalsinghwala, Ferozepur
July, 1939	Garangan, P.S. Kharar (Ambala), Chak Bhai Ram Singh (Ferozepur), Budhalada (Disft. Hissar), Sangrur, Assarpur, P.S. Ghula (Karnal).
August, 1939	Budhalada (Hissar District)[32]
September, 1939	Kalan, P.S. Budhalada, Alampur Mandran, P.S. Boha, Narur (Jullundur)
October, 1939	Bhadeli, P.S. Sahena (Ludhiana), Khamonon-Kamli, P.S. Bassi
November, 1939	Jallianwala Bagh (Amritsar).
December, 1939	Gurdwara Khadial (Karnal)[33]
June, 1940	Mauli Bedwan (Ambala)

32. Conference was held on 14th, 15th and 16th August, 1939; *muzaras* of Sunam, Dhuri, Barnala, Bhatinda and Mansa participated in it. Similarly, almost all the *kisan* conferences were attended by the leaders of various political groups. The *kisans* and the *kisan* leaders went from their native places to participate in these conferences even after walking a distant of 10 to 15 miles. *Vide., Records of Patiala, Kalsia, Faridkot, Kapurthala and Jind States.*

33. Though the *dewan* was religious, it was held with political purposes and was not only by *muzaras* and their leaders but the leaders of other political parties also participated. It is to be noted that during this period under review, such *dewans* were political in nature.

February, 1941	Shehna (Ludhiana)
April, 1942	Jethuwal P.S. Shehna (Ludhiana)
April, 1943	Bhakna (Amritsar)
July, 1943	Rar (Tehsil Mansa) and Ambala
April, 1944	Barnala (Patiala)
August, 1944	Kuleri (Hissar District)
September, 1944	Bhugwali (Patiala) Tungwali (Ferozepur), Barnala (Patiala)
October, 1944	Bhadaur; Ugrajan, P.S. Sunam; Malerkotla; Sangrur (Jind State)
January, 1945	Bhadaur
March, 1945	Dhanaula (Nabha State); Mandauli Kalan, P.S. Morinda (Ambala); Gujjarwal (Ludhiana); Kakrala (Ludhiana); Maur (Jind State); Dialpur, Haryal, P.S. Lehra
December, 1945	Mehmudpur (Malerkotla); Kotakpura; Goriana, Jaito (Faridkot); Aaspur (Karnal); Dwali; Rampuraphool; Logowal; Phaphra, Juwaharke, Mathiasar; Anandpur; Amritsar and Lahore[34]

34. The *muzaras* Conference held in January, 1945 was attended by approximately 4000 *muzaras,* who came from villages—Kishangarh, Kartarsinghwala, Bhadaur, Damdamasahib, Dipgarh, Qasaiwala, Talwandisabo and many others. Similarly, all other conferences held in 1945 were attended by large number of *kisans.* The prominent leaders who organised and participated in these conferences can be gathered from the record files of these states. Let it be noted the above data is collected from the records files of different. Phulkian States, preserved in the PSA : Patiala.

In these conferences, the *kisan* leaders fired the zeal of the tenants against *biswedars*. To cite an example, the tenants-at-will of village Dhanoli Khurd, P.S. Dirbha were so aroused that they rioted and injured the police party under the D.M., Sunam, who had gone there to help the revenue officers to aid the *biswedars* in taking over possession from the tenants. Similarly, the occupancy-tenants of Bakshiwala, P.S. Sunam were reported to have taken possession even since bandobest.[35] The *kisan* leaders criticized the *batai* and the *kankoot* system and exhorted the *muzaras* to follow the example of Bardoli.[36] The state policy of *mamla abiana* and *hasiyat* tax was also condemned and the high-handedness of the states' authorities and the *biswedars* was attacked.[37] In each conference, a few resolutions were passed in which the *muzaras* were directed as follows :

(a) No *muzara* should have any sort of association with the *biswedars*. Even if a *muzara* was found calling '*taeh*' to a *biswedar* he would be fined Rs. 5/-;

(b) No *batai*, '*kankoot*' or '*girdawari*' be paid at all. A *biswedar* who accompanied the *girdawar* or kankoot' Officer, was to be resisted or attacked, if necessary;

(c) In case the state authority ordered the forcible payment of *batai*, the crops be laid waste before any officer visited them to effect the *batai*. Corn was not to be kept in the houses for the state employees may seize it;

(d) The *kamins* (menials) were asked not to continue their relations with the *biswedars*. A recalcitrant kamin would be compelled to leave the village.

(e) The orders issued by any court should not be complied with. If a *muzara* was sentenced to fine, he should not pay it but undergo imprisonment in default of payment of fine;

35. Basta No. 15, CBI-I-Z, Pol. CID, 1945-46, PSA : Patiala.
36. Basta No. 50, S. No. 1546, File No. 565/C-1939, PSA : Patiala.
37. *Ibid.*

(f) The *biswedars* be put to trouble by every means and they should be compelled to leave their villages;[38]

(g) The *muzaras* who had not received reply to their petition to the state authorities, were exhorted to conduct propaganda from village to village;

(h) Rupee one per head be raised from every *muzara* by way of subscription;

(i) The posters, which were published for the *muzaras* should be kept by themselves and not handed over to any *biswedar* or his employee. They should be distributed among the public in time.

(j) The tenants were urged to organize themselves to get their alleged grievances redressed.[39]

While tracing the genesis of the tenant movement, it will not be out of place to cite here the following main demands of the tenants which were placed before the state authorities :

I. The ejection of the *muzaras* from land should ceases;

II. The land which was lying useless for want of cultivation should be given to the *muzaras*;[40]

III. Sufficient water supply should be arranged in the canals and the canal tax should be at the same rates as it was in the British territory;

---

38. In every *biswedari* village here lived only one or two *biswedars* families and the remaining were *Muzaras*. It was, therefore, easy for them to tease the *biswedars*.
39. S. No. 1563, File No. 565/C-1939, PSA: Patiala.
40. Demanded from the state authority to give away the state *birs* (forests) to the state *kisans* in order to strengthen the grow more food campaign and to improve their economic condition, vide., *Patiala State Records* and the *Records of Malerkotla and Kapurthala States*, Basta No. 13,50, 85.

IV. *Batai, malba* and *nazool* systems and the *girdawari* should be abolished in all the states of East Punjab;[41]

V. *Begar* (forced labour) and *thikri pehra* (duty of a night watchman) should be abolished;

VI. Remission in or reduction of revenue be made and the increased taxation in Nabha and Malerkotla States be abolished;

VII. All the tenants of all the 784 Patiala villages, many of whom had paid *batai* since before the year 1918 and who had been declared *'ghair maroosi'* for unknown reasons be declared *'Maroosi'* and thus the discrimination between *'maroosi'* and *'ghair'* maroosi' be removed;

VIII. The land be restored to the *muzaras* from which they had been dispossess-ed and the revenue be assessed on the same scale on them as it was levied on the land of the general public or at the rates prevalent in the neighbouring areas of the Patiala state;

IX. The action against *muzaras* under section 424 I.P. and also the looting of *muzaras* by the state officials and *biswedars* be stopped;

X. The non-occupancy tenants be recognized as occupancy tenants and the system of assessment in cash be introduced also; the land revenue should be realized by *tehsil* authorities;

XI. The tenants (evidently occupancy tenants) in 784 villages of Patiala state declared themselves to be landlords and wanted the existing record land owners to be altogether eliminated and the settlement of the revenue to be made with them;

---

41. File No.M/3-22-40 (File contains various Pamphlets in Panjabi,) PSA : Patiala ; *AISPC-Papers,* File No. 138 (Part One), Private Papers Section, Nehru Memorial Musium and Library, New Delhi.

XII. The confiscated property be restored and the execution of decrees be stopped;

XIII. *Hidayat* of 1988 (*Bikrami*) should be annualled;

XIV. Responsible Government should be set up in the states; the right of franchise should be given to the tenants to elect the *zaildars* and *lambardars* for the terms of three years; freedom of speech and press was also demanded;

XV. The punitive police posts should be removed;

XVI. The price of grain should not be allowed to fall lower than in the British *illaga*; the Government agencies to buy grains in the market should be established.

XVII. Cases running against the anti-fascist comrades (Communists) should be withdrawn; the officers should be stopped from concocting false cases against the tenants;

XVIII. *Kisan Sabhas,* the student unions and the *Praja Mandals* should be acknowledged as lawful organizations.[42]

The demands of the *kisans* were thus voiced and the state was urged to stop their exploitation at the hands of the *biswedars.* A deputation of the *muzaras* met the Maharaja of Patiala to get their grievances redressed and when they were ignored, they started taking possession of the *biswedars'* lands forcibly. They also decided in a conference at Anandpur Sahib not to pay *batai.* Consequently, the *muzaras* of various villages (*e.g.* Bir Khurd, Jangiana, Karamgarh, Bassi, Dipgarh, Alamgarh, Madran, Satika, Mallsinghwala, Moolasinghwala, Khiwa, Shehzada Singhwala, Talwandi Sabo, Chinarthal, Teona, Pujarian, Jarkian, Bhadaur, Kot Duna, Jeonda, all the

---

42. Memorandum submitted by the members of the Patiala War-council, *Patiala State Records,* File No. 565/C-1939; *Kalsia State Records,* File No. 164, PSA : Patiala. (The various demands of the peasants can be gathered from various posters, pamphlets distributed in the villages and the memorandum submitted to the rulers. For this and has to see the records of all the states of East Punjab).

villages of Bhudhalada), refused to pay *batai.* At the same time a large number of posters both in *Panjabi* and *Urdu* were published and circulated among the rural masses. Through these posters the *kisan* Committees and other political organizations continued their war against the state authorities. It was made clear through these pamphlets that the *jathas* of *kisans* would go and attack the places of the Maharajas and *nawabs* and soon there would be the rule of the peasants in the Punjab.[43] Similarly, many *jathas* of *muzaras* were sent to Lahore to meet the British Resident and also to Simla to place their grievances and demands before the higher authorities of the British Government.[44]

There were, actually, four political parties active in the *kisan* front-the *kisan* Committee, the Communist, the Ridha Sigh party and Col. Raghbir Singh Akali Group-which were of the view that it was an imperialistic war.[45] At this time, the All India *Kisan Sabha* demanded the imposition of ceiling on land holding and distribution of surplus land to agricultural labourers and poor peasants. In their conference of 1945, it was stressed that question of taking concrete action to impose ceiling on land holdings had become a burning issue and its significance was all the more in view of the Government of India schemes for higher agricultural production and organization of agricultural economy.[46]

In brief, various bodies of the tenants demanded from time to time that the poor peasants who received land in distribution should be allowed to pay rent direct to the Government and in no case the rent be more than one sixth of the gross produce. If the existing rent was less than that, it should not be increased. The Government after deducting charges should pay the rent as compensation to the landlord. This compensation to the

43. *Kalsia State Records,* File No. 132, PSA : Patiala.
44. *Patiala State Records,* Prime Ministers' Office File No. 750, PSA : Patiala.
45. *Patiala State Records,* File No. 2077, PSA : Patiala; Basta No. 13, File No. 2001, PSA : Patiala.
46. *Patiala State Records,* File No. 2077, PSA : Patiala, 81

landlords was in no case to exceed a period of 10 years and after that the Government should collect only land revenue. The person receiving land should be made full owner immediately after the first year's rent was paid.

The peasants' unrest culminated in two violent incidents. The firing cases of Rajomajra and Qilla Hakim are the glaring examples of the ruthless persecution of the state Government.[47] A brief summary of these two cases would not be out of place here.

Raipur Quilla Hakim case provides an interesting study of the tenants' movement in the Patiala State. According to the judicial enquiry Commission, which investigated the happenings at Quilla Hakim in 1937 (on the 11th *Maghar,* 1944 Sambat),[48] an incident happened at Raipur Quilla Hakim, *tehsil* Dhuri, district Bassi, in which firing was reported to have been ordered. As a result of this firing, 11 persons received injuries and 2 out of them, subsequently died. The state issued orders on 29th of November, 1937 to the Commission to proceed immediately to hold a judicial enquiry into the incident.[49]

The Commission headed by the Judicial Magistrate reached Quilla Hakim on the morning of the 30th November, 1937. The village people were informed about it so that those who wanted to say something might appear before the Commission and give their statements. On that day the tenants of the village were reluctant to come and help the enquiry. However, the Magistrate explained to them the purpose of the enquiry and that there was nothing to be afraid of. Next morning regular enquiry began. Statements of over 49 witnesses were recorded. The statements of the tenants, *biswedars,* their agents, *lambardars, safedposhes* and *zaildars,* were all taken

47. Dr. Joginder Dayal, '*Riyasti Logan Ka Ghol Ten*-Communists' (an article in Panjabi), published in a *Sourvenir,* issued by the CPI on January 26, 1976, 91-95.
48. File No. 6175, Report of Judicial Enquiry into the happening at Raipur Quilla Hakim *Patiala State Records,* PSA : Patiala.
49. *Ibid.,* Copy of the poster preserved in *Patiala State Records* Prime Ministers' Office File No. 750, PSA : Patiala.

at the village. Instead of discussing the evidences recorded, it would be more appropriate to give a brief history of the case, given in the revenue records.

Raipur Quilla Hakim was a *biswedari* village and its tenants were given the status of occupancy-tenants under sections 5 and 8 of the tenancy Act, paying *batai* to the landlords. The landlords regularly received the share of the produce since the regular statement, with a few exceptions on some occasions when some tenants now and then refused to pay rent; and the tenants reportedly admitted the status of the landlords and acknowledged themselves to be tenants.

But gradually due to non-payment of rent the *biswedars* were obliged to institute suits for the recovery of the rent and apply for ejectment. Though the *biswedars* obtained decrees against the tenants, some remained unexecuted and this fact emboldened them to withhold the payment of *batai* altogether and they posed themselves as owners of the lands. The tenants under the circumstances expressed their inability to pay the land revenue to the landlords. This state of affairs continued till 1930 when the tenants again began to pay the land revenue. The landlords took proceedings against the tenants to the law courts and some of them were ejected. The tenants thereupon began to submit petition after petition to His Highness contesting the landlords. The *Maharaja* asked the Minister of Law and Justice to hold a thorough and exhaustive enquiry into the matter. Diwan Bahadur Pindi Dass Sabharwal submitted a detailed report on the 11th June, 1933. When the final orders on this report were still awaited, the *biswedars* submitted another petition. The case was finally decided by the *Ijlas-i-khas* committee that the tenants' claim to ownership was frivolous and so their claims were rejected and an order was passed that action be taken accordingly by the revenue authorities.

However, the tenants were not prepared to give *batai* to the *biswedars* inspite of the above orders. On this the *biswedars* applied to the revenue authorities for the division of the produce. The revenue authorities also favoured them. But the tenants were determined not to allow *batai* under any circumstances.[50] The *tehsildar* along with the *mukhtiars* of *biswedars* and some policemen went to collect *batai.* Some 120 villagers including male and female persons reached Chhaur and openly refused to obey and the *tehsildar* failed in his mission. Now the *nazim* accompanied by the Superintendent of Police, Sunam, 4 Head Constables and 11 constables out of whom 11 had guns went to the village. He had with him some licence-holders, *safedposhes* of the *Illaqa* and some *lambardars.*[51]

But the tenants did not listen to any advice and they refused to come to him. Rather, they gathered near the mosque and did not allow the *batai* even at the cost of their lives. 3 tenants were taken into custody. As soon as they were arrested, some 300 to 400 people came to the street in front of *Hattai.* The *nazim* seeing this attitude of the tenants, proceeded to the Chhaur of Bhanga Singh where the *batai* was stopped. Hence, the tenants succeed in their agitation.[52]

It was really one of the most important cases in the Patiala state and was destined to serve as a precedent to solve the disputes between the tenants and the *biswedars.* The case arose out of a century old dispute between the tenants and the *biswedars.* It not stood the span of more than a generation but also resisted the colossal labour and energy of several enquiry committees appointed off and on by the Patiala State. From the records of this case now preserved in the Punjab State Archives, Patiala we learn that the limitation was sent to the Commission on the 7th of September, 1945. the first open sitting of the Commission, however, came up on the 13th of September, 1945, in which both the parties were directed to appear before the Commission on September 23, 1945. They were also directed

50. *Patiala State Records,* Prime Ministers' Office File No. 6157/6-2155, Punjab State Archives, Patiala; Personal meeting with Chhajju Mal, who took an active part in almost all the *morchas* in the East Punjab States.
51. *Patiala State Records,* File No. 6157/6-2155, PSA : Patiala.
52. Prime Ministers' Office File No. 6157/6-2155, PSA : Patiala.

to file a list of the *biswedars* and tenants respectively. The second sitting was fixed for 9th October, 1945. On this date the representatives of the *biswedars* filed a list of all the *biswedars* but the representatives of the tenants pleaded their inability to cope with the work entrusted to them but submitted that the number of the tenants was about four hundred. Consequently, the enquiry was fixed for October 18, 1945, and on this day the statements of both the parties were recorded. The next sitting was fixed for 25th October, 1945, when the statement of the *daftar-qanungo,* Dhuri was recorded. This case was no adjourned to 14th November, 1945. The *Sadar-qanungo,* Bassi, was also summoned with all the relevant records previous to the statement of 1905.

The Commission was, however, not satisfied with the production of the old records and felt the necessity of making a searching enquiry into all relevant previous record besides the one that had already been brought before the previous Enquiry Committee of 1931. So, the Commission visited Bassi and ransacked the whole record pertaining to the dispute. Both the parties engaged counsels, who addressed the commission at a considerable length for 4 days. The *biswedars* explained that the village was founded by their ancestors, Kaula Singh, Balla Singh and Daula Singh and the defendant tenants had been cultivating the land and paying *batai.* A dispute, however, arose regarding the right to receive *batai* and some of the tenants submitted to the *batai* rights of the *biswedars* while others denied that claim to them. But generally the land remained with the tenants. This led the Commission to the conclusion that if the position of the *biswedar* was that of *"ala-malik"* or *'teluqdar',* which in the state terminology, was equal to *biswedar,* the tenants' ancestors were a sort of *'adna-maliks'* (inferior owners) and were entered in the old records as *'zamindars'.* In the Punjab, the one was termed as 'superior owner' or *'ala-malik'* and the other was described only as *'adna-malik'.* The rights of the inferior proprietors some times extended over the whole estate including the waste land and in other cases they were confined to their separate holdings and the waste land was at the disposal of the superior or *'ala-malik'* subject to certain rights of use enjoyed by the village community. In such cases the *'ala-malik'* continued to receive a share in some districts in kind and in other districts it was commuted into cash by the collectors a fixed percentage of the land revenue. The Financial Commissioner had declared that both-*'ala-malik'* and *'adna-malik'* would be liable for the land revenue, but he laid down no specifications. But in actual practice only inferior landlords who were actually in cultivation were held to be liable for the land revenue.

The occupancy tenants, holding on privileged rents were in possession of a part of proprietary rights but they differed from inferior owner in as much as their rents were, within certain limits and circumstances, liable to enhancement and their rights of transfer were subject to limitations based on the superior rights or another person who was recognized as landlord. Because of the circumstances it was felt that the occupancy tenancy could get nothing beyond the land revenue and it was to be deposited in the state treasury. The tenants, moreover, had not yet submitted to that position either on account of obduracy or as they alleged, on account of the justification of their case.

It would be interesting to point out here that in the course of this enquiry, the representative of the tenants asserted that in the preparation of this record of enquiry, they should not be referred to and recorded as tenants but only as a party. But the *biswedars* claimed that the defendants be declared as tenants and that rent would be equivalent to the land revenue. Apart from this consideration, the Commission was satisfied with the documentary evidence and by the analogy prevailing in other districts of the Punjab that the plaintiffs were *biswedars 'ala-malik'* and the defendants were *'adna-malik'*. The Commission recommended to the Patiala State Government that Revenue record be amended accordingly. The above findings brought the Commission to the other part of the issue as to what relief the parties were entitled to. In this respect, it goes without saying that in the cases of divided ownership of the proprietors profits were shared between the two classes and following the precedents of other districts of the Punjab as well as of the

United Provinces, it was thought advisable that the claims of the superior owner of a share in the *batai* over the inferior proprietor, be converted into a cash levy as a surcharge upon the land revenue calculated at a certain percentage or a fraction in a rupee without, of course, the imposition of cesses which was though to be an anachronism and no, case would be made out of it. This method as stated above, could be enforced either by framing a rule or by some special order of legislative measure by the State Government. In this arrangement the defendants were to have the status of a *malik-qabza' i.e.* that of an inferior proprietor with the right of letting, mortgaging, selling their lands as they pleased and having their own tenants if they so liked and the *biswedars* as superior proprietors were to get a certain share in the land revenue without coming in conflict with the defendants in any manner. The surcharge or the addition in the land revenue was termed as *haq-malikan.* In regard to the rate of this surcharge the pint was not free from difficulty.

However, the Commission submitted that the rate in other places varied with the locality and on the terms of mutual contract. In this controversy the Commission could see no scope or room for mutual agreement and if the parties were left to strike mutual agreements, there was a danger of the whole matter again being shelved and thrown into cold storage. The Commission took note of the fact that under the tenancy law, this surcharge could go to the extent of two *annas* in a rupee but the equities of the case in Rajomajra village demanded that it should not, in any way, exceed one *anna* in a rupee on the land revenue. It also pointed out that in case the defendants did not again submit on the point of surcharge on the land revenue, two ways were open to the Government. One was that of the enforcement of the rule of law and the other of conciliation. Finally, the Patiala State agreed that the land revenue in comparison with the rates prevailing outside the State, might no come down very much; the other via media would have been that the ascertained land revenue might be accepted by the Government including the surcharge rent payable to the *biswedars.* Under this system of fixed surcharge of a fraction with or without the land revenue, the *biswedars* were enabled to hold their former position and the right of superior proprietorship while the tenant class was to find itself to be in an elevated and privileged position by this division of ownership into superior and inferior one.

Thus, these two incidents showed that the tenant movement which started in 1928 had now reached a decisive stage. As will be shown later, it was an indication of the growing communist influence on the *kisans* struggle in general and the tenant movement in particular.[53] It also symbolizes the impatience leading to desperation which had overtaken the general peasant masses of the state. It was in these circumstances that Maharaja Bhupinder Singh announced the setting up of a Constitutional Reforms Committee which was wholly consisted of officials. The Committee was to recommend changes in the Constitution of the State "with a view to giving the subjects a definite voice and share in the making of law and the administration thereof in the State".[54] It was to submit proposals within six months. The Maharaja, however, died within a fortnight of the appointment of this Committee and so it went into cold-storage. But the appointment of the Committee provided a fit climax the to the ten year old *Praja Mandal* movement which had been guiding the *muzaras* movement in the State. Consequently, the tenant struggle against the states' authority continued more vigorously. Now

53. Well known Communists workers from Punjab were the most frequent speakers at Public meetings organised by the *Praja Mandal.* Sohan Singh Josh, Arjan Singh Gargaj, Karam Singh Mann and Baba Rur Singh were some of the prominent Communist leaders. *Vide.,* (Report of a public meeting at Khanna held on August 2, 1936), *Patiala State Records,* File No. 747; (The poster of Longowal Conference scheduled for 7th and 8th November, 1936), Patiala State Records, File No. 737, PSA : Patiala.
54. The Committee was consisted of *nawb* Liyakat Hiat Khan, Prime Minister of the Patiala State—as Chairman; Raja Hari Krishan Kaul, Revenue Minister; Major K.M. Panikar, Foreign Minister; Capt. H.M. Raina, Law Minister; Major S. Ajmer Singh, Accountant General. *Vide., The Tribune* (Lahore), January 23, 1938; *Ibid.*

the tenants' movement was assuming the shape of a mass movement.

A new environment was created to organize the peasants' stir. At the same time, some new ideas to organize the peasants came into existence. The peasant meets started being held on large scales in villages. It invigorated the political milieu and the peasants' struggle began to succeed in becoming stronger. It continued spreading itself. It is to be remembered that the peasants' conferences and peasants' movements were held mostly in the regions of the British Punjab; there was a remarkable increase in the number of the peasants' conferences; especially during the period from 1939 to 1945,[55] when a large number of peasants participated in them. Several memoranda and deputations were sent. With this, the peasants also stopped paying land revenue and abiana and began to occupy the lands of the *zamindars*. In fact, the peasants struggle soon took the form of showdown and many a time the peasants forced the rulers and their governments to yield to them.

During the first half of 1939, the *muzaras'* movement took rapid strides and swept all the states of the East Punjab. It had become a common thing in the villages of all the states, particularly *Patiala*, not to pay batai.[56] In other words the peasants had started opposing their immediate masters. The news of the violent incidents between the *biswedars* and *muzaras* continued to be received. At a few places the latter had started excerising the strength of their muscles for a forcible occupation of the land of the former from where they had earlier been ejected by the *biswedars*.[57] In some villages, the peasants

55. Josh, Bhagwan, *Communist Movement in the Punjab*, Delhi 1979, 93, 104-107.
56. PSR, PM's Office File No. 1547 (CWRS' From I.G. Police, Patiala of March 3, April 24, May 1, 18 and 31, June 2, 9 and 30, 1939) : File No. 1554 (CID Secret Abstract of Intelligence of may 19, 1939); also see file No. 1555, PSA : Patiala.
57. PSR, PM's Office File No. 1554 (CWR from I.G. Police, Patiala of May 31, 1939—Kishangarh and Qilla Hakim were especially noted for this), PSA : Patiala.

started ploughing the standing crops with a view to refusing payment of the *batai* and other taxes;[58] all these tactics were a part of their agitation. Now, a conference was held on May 19, 1939 at the village Shehna in Ludhiana district which was attended by a large number of peasants and tenants of different villages. It was decided here that a petition should be sent to demand the abolition of the *batai* system and a deputation should be sent to the Maharaja of Patiala to demand the collection of land revenue in cash.[59] The said deputation met several state officials including the *nazim* and the Superintendent of Police of their area in order to acquaint them with grievances and problems of the peasants. There were many such peasants who went to Chail to see the Maharaja of Patiala.[60] Finally, it was decided to send a deputation of 100 peasants to call upon the British Resident at Simla, it was to reach Simla on foot. Its members were supposed to acquaint the British resident with the problems and the atrocities committed by the states' administration. Several peasants/tenants from Bhadaur and its subordinate villages, with a springing of tenants from Tamkot, Rampura, Kot Duna, Joondan, Dalelsinghwala and Jalaldiwala had gathered at Takhatpura in Ferozepur district on 31st May, 1939. The *jatha* started from Takhatpura and it

58. PSR, PM's Office File No. 1554 (CWR from I.G. Police, Patiala, June 2 and 9, 1939); File No. 1555 (CWR from I.G. Police, Patiala). PSA : Patiala.
59. PSR, PM's Office File No. 1554 (CID Secret Abstract of Intelligence of May 19, 1939), PSA : Patiala.
60. 34 *muzaras* of village Kishangarh came to see the I.G. Police on April 29, 1939 to register protest against the imposition of a punitive police post and police highhandedness. *Muzaras* of Kharaksinghwala and Karangarh also came to express their inability to pay *batai*. 300 *muzaras* of Bhadaur also came to the I.G.P. on May 19, 1939 to register their protest. *Vide.,* PSR, PM's Office File No. 2077 (CWR from I.G. Police, Patiala 61. of May 19 and 31; also see confidential note on "the non payment of *batai* movement' by Hari Kishan Kaul, Revenue Minister, Patiala of June 2, 1939—Campfield Simla-E-File No Correspondence regarding '*anti-biswedari* movement in Patiala State) PSA : Patiala.

headed towards Ludhiana. On June 1, 1939 and had stopovers at many places enroute when the peasants' leaders threw light on the sufferings, grievances and problems of the peasants in their speeches.[61]

Raising the slogan '*muzara* Committee *zindabad*', the *jatha* kept on surging ahead. Slogans like '*biswedari* system *murdabad*' were also raised. The hand bills which contained the details of the atrocities being committed by the *biswedars* were distributed. These handbills also carried details of the problems of the peasants as well as their legitimate demands. When this *jatha* reached Ludhiana, it was advised by the Government officials to send a deputation of five peasant leaders to Simla to call upon the British Resident. These five leaders were Anokh Singh Joondan, Khunda Singh, Anupgarh, Bishan Singh Chinarthal, Chanan Singh Bhadaur and Muni Lal Kalia. The *jatha* accepted the advice but a problem arose when Pandit Muni Lal Kalia, MLA and President of Ludhiana Committee was included in the deputation. The deputation waited upon the Resident on June 10, but the British Resident refused to see them on the plea that Pandit Kalia was not an inhabitant or subject of Patiala State. On the other hand, members of the deputation refused to call upon the British Resident without Pandit Kalia.[62] However, later Muni Lal was replaced by Partap Singh and another member Bishan Singh of Chinarthal was dropped and replaced by Sunder Singh Kishangarh. Soon, public rallies were organised at Simla, under the banner of Himachal State *Praja Mandal*. The conduct and

---

61. PSR, PM's Office File No. 2077, (CID Secret Abstract of Intelligence of June 9, 1939), PSA : Patiala.
62. *Ibid.*, (See in this file posters in Panjabi entitled-'*Mirdai biswedaran de zulam da Shikar ho ke ujre hoe mazlooman di ravanqi*' and *zalim ate nirdai biswedaran di nadrshahi* : Fortnightly Report for Punjab for the first half of June, 1939, Home Political File 18/6/1939, NAI, New Delhi; *The Tribune* (Lahore), June 13, 1939; PSR, PM's Office File No. 1554 (CID Secret Abstract of Intelligence of June 9, 1939); File No. 1555 (CID Secret Abstract of Intelligence of June 16, 1939), PSA : Patiala.

the attitude of the British Resident was strongly condemned in these rallies and also dilated upon the peasants' demands.[63]

Thus, we get a fairly good idea of the attitude of the British Government towards the peasants'/tenants in particular and other people in general. Soon this deputation came back without seeing the British Resident. But soon after another *jatha* of a hundred peasants left for Simla. As it was proceeding towards Simla, the Local Congress Committees, at various places, extended their full support to it and accorded a warm welcome. Many Congress as well as the peasants' leaders made speeches in which the peasants' problems were highlighted and their demands justified. They infused a fresh vigour in them (peasants, tenants and agricultural labour) and called upon them to join the *kisan* Committees. The members of this *jatha* were also directed to constitute such committees in all the Punjab states.[64]

After a few days when the *jatha* was proceeding via Ludhiana and Ambala districts, the police prevented it from marching further. Now, a five member deputation (to represent this *jatha*) was escorted by the police to Simla. The other members of the *jatha* were sent to the village Shehna in Ludhiana district.[65] The deputation had a long meeting with the British Resident on 21 June. The members put their grievances and legitimate demands before the Resident and also acquainted him with the atrocities perpetrated by the states' rulers and their officials. They also vented their fears before the Resident that they would be tortured by their rulers the moment they returned to their states.[66] We can infer from this

---

63. *The Tribune* (Lahore), June 14, 1939; PSR, PM's Office File No. 1555(CID Secret Abstract of Intelligence of June 16, 1939), PSA : Patiala.
64. *Ibid.*, (This appeal was made by Master Gajjan Singh, President *Kisan* Committee, Ludhiana District.).
65. *The Tribune* (Lahore), June 25, 1939; PSR, PM's Office File No. 1555 (CWR from I.G. Police, Patiala of June 27, 1939), PSA : Patiala.
66. *Ibid.*

as to what an extent the peasants were afraid of the administrations and how oppressive the Governments in the States were. At this time, the Revenue Minister of Patiala State was also at Simla. He also had a meeting with the deputation. He assured them that they would not be harassed after their return and the solution to their problems would be found out soon.[67]

Following this, the deputation returned to Ludhiana where they discussed with the local leaders the outcome of the meeting they had with the British Resident; subsequently all the five members reached the village Shehna where the remaining members of the *jatha*, other peasants, *muzaras* and the common people had been waiting for them. After having briefed them about the meeting with the Resident, all the five deputationists returned to their respective places. The meeting between this deputation and the Resident had some important effects :[68]

(a) Under its impact, the *muzaras* movement embraced the common people of all the states of the Punjab;

(b) Under its impact only the movement clearly developed close relations with the Congress and the Kisan Committees. With this, the Congress gained a strong

---

67. PSR, PM's Office File No. 1555 (CWR from I.G. Police, Patiala of June 27, 1939), PSA : Patiala.

68. The Commission was to enquire into the causes of disputes between the *biswedars* and occupancy tenants generally in all the villages of the state; with special reference to those of village—Kishangarh, Raipur Qilla Hakiman, Sedhasinghwala, Rajomajra, Bhadaur, Karamgarh, Rampura, Dhansinghwala, Kot Duna, Khewa Shahzadsinghwala, Pherwahi, etc. *Vide.,* PSR, PM's Office File No. 2077 (See Order No. 23 of *Ijlas-i-khas,* Patiala of July 17, 1939-File is on correspondence regarding anti-*biswedari* movement). Let it also be noted that Capt. S. Madanmohan Nath Raina (Minister of Law was the Chairman of this Commission and other members were S.D.K. Sen (Foreign and Education Minister), Major S. Harbans Singh (Revenue Commissioner and S. Fazi-i-Hamid (Assistant Secretary), *Ibid.,* PSA : Patiala.

social base in the East Punjab States which had been coveted by it for quite some time;

(c) While proceeding towards Simla, these *jathas* acquainted the masses of the villages enroute with the grievances, problems and demands of the peasants;

(d) Presurised by the British Resident, the *Maharaja* of Patiala appointed a Commission in July 1939 to investigate the Problems of the *muzaras*.

Denouncing this Commission, the Punjab State *Praja Mandal* started that it was only an eyewash as it was consisted only of the Government officials. But undoubtedly, it was a great victory for the downtrodden *muzaras* and peasants, for the Maharaja of Patiala had paid his attention to their lot for the first time. The example was soon followed by the rulers of other states as well.[69] Besides, it also became evident that whenever there was an agitation, it did lead to certain results. At least, the *muzaras* flatly refused to pay *batai* until the reports of the Enquiry Commission was submitted. So, more and more villages joined this struggle for non-payment of *batai*.

During the second half of 1939, the muzaras were carrying out their activities more vigorously. It was reported by the Superintendent of Police Barnala that the muzaras who had mortgaged their lands as security for loans, were very well determined to get back to their lands. About 90 *muzaras* had forcibly occupied their lands, having snatched them from moneylenders. It was also reported that the *muzara* movement was constantly gaining ground.[70] A new received from Qilla Hakim pointed out that many *muzaras* had occupied the land from where they had been ejected by the *biswedars*, having forcibly relieved the *biswedars* of it and started ploughing it. Though we come across from the weekly reports that the *batai* had been realized in some villages, but in general, the peasants'

69. PSR, PM's Office File No. 1555 (CWR from I.G. Police, Patiala of August 12, 1939), PSA : Patiala.
70. *Ibid.*, (CID Secret Abstract of Intelligence of June 30, 1939).

attitude towards payment of *batai* was not favourable and mostly they were bent upon non-payment of *batai.* At this time members of the deputation that had returned from Simla had spread the word among the *muzaras* that their problems would not be solved easily, nor was there any possibility of an early settlement of their disputes with the biswedars.[71] Consequently, the movement for non-payment of *batai* was becoming stronger. To substantiate, a change in the attitude of those peasants who had already paid a part of *batai* and were in favour of paying more was noticed; now they were also making up their mind not to pay any *batai.*[72] Though in most of the *biswedari* villages *batai* had to be realized by the use of force, the peasants bluntly refused to pay money for punitive police stations; at every such occasion some unpleasant situation was created which infused a new life in the *muzara* movement.

The demands of the muzaras were repeated time and again at the *kisans* conferences where the speeches made grew more and more acrimonious. An impressive and inspiring conference was held at Budhlada from August 14 to 16, 1939. Nearly 200 peasants attended it. The resolution passed here stated that the *batai* would not be paid on the forthcoming *kharif* harvest at any cost; the peasants would not depose before the Enquiry Commission and a propaganda committee would be set up in each *tehsil* whose chief function would be to propagate the non-payment of batai.[73]

Another conference was held at this very place on 26th September, 1939, in which it was decided that strict measures would be taken for the non-payment of *batai.* It was resolved neither to pay any *batai,* nor to have any relations with the *biswedars.* It was decided that if the police exercised force or complelled the peasants to pay *batai,* the crops would be destroyed. It was also decided not to pay any fine and to

71. *Ibid.,* (CID Secret Abstracts of July 14 and 16, 1939) and also see CWR from I.G. Police, Patiala of July 16, 1939.
72. This observation is related to village Bhadaur, *Vide., Ibid.*
73. PSR, PM's Office File No. 1555 (CID Secret Abstract of Intelligence of August 25, 1939), PSA : Patiala.

persuade the tillers and the farm labourers not to do any work for the biswedars. If they were found doing any work for them they could have been turned out of the village.[74]

Thus, the attitude of the peasants went on hardening. It was reported that the batai of the *kharif* harvest was not paid in general. We came to know this fact from the police reports covering the period from August to November, 1939. So, the situation had been worsening and there was every possibility of the situation getting aggravated in most of the villages; peasants were not paying *batai* and some newly founded villages; had also strongly refused to pay the batai. Now, it was being presumed that peasants in more and more villages would also refused to pay *batai*.[75] At the same time, it was reported that it was difficult for the *biswedars* to be secure in the villages for long. At almost all the places, the *batai* was being collected with the police help and suppression.[76] The peasants of village Kishangarh, who had not paid *batai* earlier also, again refused to pay any kind of additional amount of money for keeping the punitive police stations in their villages. On the other hand, the forcibly occupied lands of many *biswedars*. In the meantime, when the henchmen of some *biswedars* carried away the harvest from the disputed land at Qilla Haḳim, it resulted in another clash between the peasants and the biswedars.[77]

On the other hand, the peasants again tried to bring their problems and grievances into the notice of the administration as well as the British Resident. A large number of peasants from

---

74. PSR, PM's Office File No. 1553 (CID Secret Abstract of Intelligence of October 6, 1939; CWR from I.G. Police, Patiala of October 10, 1939), PSA : Patiala.
75. *Ibid.*, (CWR from I.G. Police, Patiala of November 15, 1939).
76. *Ibid.*, (Secret Abstract of Intelligence of November, 17, 1939), Dharamgarh, Bir Khurd and Pharwahi were the villages which had been included in the resolution.
77. Fortnightly report for Punjab for the first half of December, 1939-Home Political, File No. 18/12/1939; *The Tribune* (Lahore) November 29 and 30, 1939, NAI, New Delhi.

Bhadaur and several other adjoining villages submitted a memorandum to the Prime Minister of Patiala State. A huge procession in Lahore was planned to be taken out under the leadership of Harnam Singh Dharamgarh—Chairman, Patiala Peasants' Committee and Ajmer Singh Tamkot and many other peasant leaders. A batch of 30 *muzaras* was sent from Hissar district to Bhatinda. Bhatinda had become an important centre of the *muzaras'* movement by now.

Pandit Muni Lal Kalia, the Congress leader of Ludhiana, who had accompanied a deputation to Simla, went to Bhatinda and from there he sent a number of *muzaras* to Amritsar. In fact, it was a *jatha* of 30 peasants which reached Ferozepur from Bhatinda by train. Then, after having walked on foot for three days, it reached Amritsar on November, 9, 1939, but by this time the strength of the *Jatha* had risen to 70. This *jatha* organised a *muzara* conference at Jallianwala Bagh (Which had become a sacred sport for the patriots and pilgrims) under the chairmanship of Ajmer Singh Tamkot. Many important leaders like Harnam Singh Dharamgarh, Wazir Singh Daftriwala, Jagir Singh Phaguwalia and Pritam Singh Gujjran attended the conference.[78] Many resolutions were passed in which the *Maharaja* was appealed to publish the report of the Enquiry Commission at the earliest and to get the conduct of the officers of the State Government, who were oppressing the *muzaras* at the instance of the *biswedars*, investigated. Rehabilitation of these peasants and *muzaras* was also demanded who had been compelled to run away from their villages to other places because of the oppression let loose by the pdice,[79] the Government officials and the *biswedars*. The *jatha* was

78. PSR, PM's Office File No. 1553 (CWR from I.G. Police, Patiala of December 16, 1939; CID Secret Abstract of Intelligence of November 17, 1939), PSA : Patiala; Fortnightly Report for Punjab for the first half of December, 1939—Home Political File No. 18/12/1939, NAI, New Delhi.

79. PSR, PM's Office File No. 1553 (CID Secret Abstracts of Intelligence of December 1 and 22, 1939; CWR from I.G. Police Patiala of December 22, 1939), PSA : Patiala; *AIPSC-Papers* File No. 139-Part I. 1939-42, Folio 295-303, NMML, New Delhi.

supposed to call upon the Resident but he was not in the city at that time; so after waiting for some time, when all of their efforts to see him were frustrated, it had to leave for Lahore.

Now, this *jatha* started making efforts to forge relations with the Congress. Efforts were also made to establish similar relations with the leaders of many other opposition political parties but it appears that this jatha could not arrest the attention of people even in Lahore and as a result it had to leave Lahore also.[80] Besides, the *muzaras* who had gathered at Patiala at this time to see the Prime Minister, called more peasants from the adjoining villages and it was decided that instead of meeting the Prime Minister, they would directly call upon the *Maharaja*. Efforts were also made to translate this resolution into action. They made their intention clear that they would not leave the place until they were able to see the Maharaja. Despite the threat of the *muzaras* to call their families to Patiala, the *Maharaja* was not ready to see them. Some *muzaras* made an abortive attempt to win an audience with the *Maharaja* by lying before his car when he was on his way to a public rally.[81]

The General Secretary of the *muzara* committee appealed to the people not to enlist themselves in the army until *batai* was officially abolished in the states. The appeal also called upon the people to ostracise those peasants and the *muzaras* who paid *batai*. It was also urged that no respect be paid to officials of the Revenue Department in particular and other Government officials in general. The imprisoned peasants were also ask to revolt.[82]

---

80. PSR, PM's Office File No. 1663 (CID Secret Abstracts of January 5 and 19, 1940; CWR from I.G. Police, Patiala of January 26, 1940), PSA: Patiala.
81. PSR, PM's Office File No. 1564 (CID Secret Abstract of Intelligence of March 1, 1940); also See File No. 1559 (CWR from I.G. Police, Patiala of April 20, 1940) PSA : Patiala.
82. PSR, PM's Office File No. 1559 (CID Secret Abstracts of Intelligence of May 3 and 24, 1949); File No. 1564 (CWR from I.G. Police, Patiala of March 25, May 5 and 21, June 8, 1940) PSA : Patiala.

Another meeting of the *Muzara* Committee was held which was attended by about 40 to 50 peasants including many famous peasant leaders like Harnam Singh Dharamgarh, Ajmer Singh Tamkot, Pritam Singh Gujjran, etc. The meeting decided to send the problems, grievances and demands of the peasants in writing to the Maharaja and the British Resident because despite the repeated promises, the Enquiry Commission had done little till then. The meetings held at Hissar and Karnal districts demanded an abolition of *batai*, fair treatment to the women arrested from the village Dhansingkhana as well as to the arrested peasants, and expediency in submission of the Enquiry Commission report.[83]

Another meeting held at Budhlada decided that kankut would not be accepted until the Enquiry Commission submitted its report. A conference of the peasants and tenants was held at Anandpur also on the occasion of '*Hola Mela*'. The office bearers of the Amritsar Peasants Committee showed sympathy for the peasants on this occasion. Besides, they strongly condemned the policies of the state governments, their attitude towards the peasants and their relations with the *biswedars*. The Secretary of the *muzaras'* Committee, Narain Singh Bhadaur appealed very strongly to the state governments through a poster to concede the *muzaras'* demands, solving their problems quickly.[84]

The peasants of Kishangarh village went to Patiala where they submitted a memorandum to the Prime Minister and the Revenue Minister of that state complaining against the punitive police stations and also demanded to take immediate decision on the report submitted by the Enquiry Commission. But all these demands fell on deaf ears. It was a matter of surprise that a long striggle notwithstanding, the collection of *batai* on 1940

83. PSR, PM's Office File No. 1553 (CID Secret Abstract of Intelligence of December 1 and 22, 1939), PSA : Patiala *AISPC-Papers* File No. 139, Part I, 1937-42, Folio No. 295-303, NMML, New Delhi.
84. PSR, PM's Office File No. 1553 (CID Secret Abstract of Intelligence of December 22, 1939, January 1 & 19, 1940; also CWR from I.G. Police, Patiala of January 26, 1940), PSA : Patiala.

kharif crops was easily made in the months of April-May,[85] but the help of the additional police and the officials of the Revenue Department had to be sought for making the collection. But in some villages, as per government records, practically no collection of *batai* was made and it was left to the courts to decide the case; in other words, it was decided to realize *batai* from the defaulters through prosecution. Thus, various factors were jointly responsible for the weakening as well as fizzling out of the *muzara* agitation; as a result of which at about all the places, the capacity to oppose or to fight was stamped out as suddenly as it had risen.[86]

On the other hand, the *muzara* movement reached its pinnacle for some time owing to the success of the deputation which had gone to Simla and the non-payment of *batai.* The Maharaja now appointed an Enquiry Commission. In the wake of these developments, the courage of the peasants rose so much that despite the government policy of strict interference and repression, they became capable of fighting for their rights with greater vigour and strength.

Thus, there was no hope of an early settlement if the states' governments adopted the policy of keeping the peasants aloof from the villages plagued with political unrest and checking the political leaders from reaching these villages. The enquiry Commission also started its proceedings. All these steps were taken to stall an early solution to the peasants' problems. Thus, the hope of their success were dashed. However, even the failure of the Lahore deputation carried on the people's movement for quite some time. At the movement was fully dependent

85. PSR PM's Office File No. 1564 (CID Secret Abstract of Intelligence of March 1 & 3, 1940); File No. 1559 (CWR from I.G. Police, Patiala of April 20, 1940), PSA: Patiala.
86. PSR, PM's Office File No. 1564 (CID Secret Abstract of Intelligence of April 26, 1940 and CWR from I.G. Police Patiala of June 19, 1940); also see File No. 1559, PSA : Patiala. (For several the *Akali Dal* was a concrete historical reality, whereas the *Praja Mandal* was merely an abstruction) Vide., Walia, Ramesh, *A Study of the* Praja *Mandal Movement in the East Punjab State,* Patiala. 1974, 156.

upon the peasants and due to their limited resources there was very little hope of its success. Secondly, the organized power of the *biswedars*, the continuous help of the State's government to them and their policy of repression continued to keep this movement weak. Political instability also weakened the movement.[87]

Consequently, the *muzaras'* movement lost momentum for a while because now they stopped getting the committed support. Actually they lost the source of their help. Harnam Singh Dharamgarh—an important member of Patiala Peasants' Committee-along with some of his associates was arrested by the Patiala State police when they were touring the state secretly to get stock of the situation. With their arrest the *muzara* workers who were trying to wind up or abandon the movement every where were no in a difficult situation. The fact that when the leaders of the *muzaras* were released they were neither welcomed by any one nor were they taken out in a procession. This was done so that this movement might get an opportunity to receive fresh fillip. It was a sufficient evidence of the dropping spirit of the *muzaras*. No body paid much attention to the discontent and resentment expressed at Bhadaur by the *muzaras* and their leaders, recently released from the jails.[88] When these leaders expressed their desire to march from Bhadaur to Patiala, they got only a limited support, but practically such programme could not materialize.[89] The *batai* for the *kharif* crops of the year 1940 was collected very easily. So much so that in some of the villages there did not remain even a single peasant worker who had not paid *batai*. Only the

87. PSR, PM's Office File No. 1563 (CID Secret Abstract of Intelligence of June 13, 1940); File No. 1559 (CWR from I.G. Police Patiala of April 20, May 5, and 21, June 8, 1940), PSA : Patiala.
88. Ibid., (CWR from I.G. Police, Patiala of December 5 and 19, 1941), File No. 763 (CID Secret Abstracts of Intelligence of January 2, 10 and 24, 1942), PSA : Patiala.
89. PSR, PM's Office File No. 1573 (CID Secret Abstracts of Intelligence of April 17 and 24, 1942); File No. 770—for further details, PSA : Patiala.

persons who were facing prosecution in the law-courts did not pay any *batai.*

Consequently, the Government kept on collecting *batai* successfully. Despite the efforts made by them, the peasant leaders could not disseminate the decision not to pay any batai,[90] but this matter was to serious to be forgotten easily. The fear generated by the pace with which the *muzara* movement was being conducted, goaded on the contemporary leaders to carry it forward, and they prepared those leaders who had become powerful to try their strength against Patiala State, and convinced them that they could use their strength against the State Government.

Though this activity did not lead to wide-spread non-payment of batai, yet it was considered to serious to be ignored. The danger of the movement, pushed forward by its own momentum, getting out of the relatively safe hands of the present leaders or the leaders becoming so powerful that they could use their strength against the state itself, thus destroying their usefulness to the administration which was based on their being popular as well as loyal was recognized as early as in 1939. Thus, when it was noticed that these leaders were successfully carving out a place for themselves in *muzaras* politics, the Government decided to adopt an aggressive policy in order to weaken them. Many peasant leaders including Narain Singh Bhadaur and Ujjagar Singh Bhaura were arrested and thrown into jail.[91]

However, by the end of 1942, again an agitation started against the *biswedars.* Of course, the pace of this agitation was

---

90. PSR, PM's Office File No. 2226/100—File on correspondence regarding Communist Movement in the Patiala State (see note of September 12, 1943 on Communist Movement in this region of the Punjab submitted by the S.P. Incharge CID, Patiala); File No. 1560 (CID Secret Abstract of Intelligence of January 3, 1941), PSA : Patiala.
91. *Ibid.,* (CID Secret Abstract of Intelligence of June 19, 1942); File No. 1563 (CID Secret Abstract of Intelligence of January 13, 1941), PSA : Patiala.

slow, but it was going slow because its leaders wanted to make their ground solid. Though we gather from the police reports that the policy of non-payment of *batai* had weakened but for some time; the *muzaras* and the *biswedars* continued to oppose each other. Ujjagar Singh Bhaura and Narain Singh Bhadaur had helped keep the issue alive politically. The isolated but tough and continued resistance offered by some villages, especially Kishangarh,[92] also kept the banner flying. When there was no hope of submission and publication of the report of the Enquiry Commission, the peasants/tenants lost their patience. In spite of this another *jatha* of five *muzaras* from Budhlada visited Lahore and got an assurance from the Secretary to the British Resident that a decision would be taken soon and efforts would be made for the speedy solution of their problems and redressel of their grievances. Soon after a report was received in Kishangarh some time in January, 1942 that if the police chowkis (posts) were dissolved there was every possibility of the exercise of force by the peasants to occupy the land of the *biswedars.* The *muzaras* refused to pay *batai* in some other villages also and it was reported by the S.P. (Barnala) that the *muzaras* were having illicit arms in some village.[93] Soon, orders were issued to seize their arms. However, this step of the Government could not calm the *muzaras.*

After a brief interval, another *jatha* of five *muzaras* from Takhatpura village of Ferozepur district went to Lahore to call upon the Resident. Its members were told that the Resident was reaching Patiala on February 7, 1942 to decide their cases.[94] Subsequently, fifty *muzaras* met at Patiala on February 6, 1942 to see the Resident but he returned to Lahore without having a

---

92. *Ibid.,* (CID Secret Abstract of Intelligence of August 28, 1942) PSR, PM's Office File no. 1559 (CID Secret Abstract of Intelligence of August 2, 1940); File No. 1263, PSA : Patiala.
93. PSR, PM's Office Case No. CB-1-2 of 2000 (*Bikrami*) (S.P.'s note on the Secret Abstract of Intelligence of July, 7, 1944; CID Secret Abstract of Intelligence of September 8, 1944); File No. 763 (CID Secret Abstract of Intelligence of January 2, 1942), PSA : Patiala.
94. *Ibid.,* (CID Secret Abstracts of Intelligence of January 24 and February 3, 1942.

word with them. When some peasants again went to Lahore to see him, they were informed that the Resident had asked the foreign Minister of Patiala to look into their grievances and the Problems.[95] In the meantime, the rumours were rampant that the *biswedari* system had been abolished in 27 villages. Consequently, a *jatha* of 5 rebel *muzaras* which was on tour, reported that it had gained a remarkable success in raising the funds and getting the local help for revising the *muzaras'* movement in the Branala and Sunam regions. Dharam Singh Fakkar of dalelsinghwala—a well known Communist and peasant worker also accompanied this *jatha*.

In March 1942, about 12 *muzaras* tried to call upon the Maharaja of Patiala but without any success. Now, they tried to stop the Maharaja's car when he was going to address a public meeting. The police again foiled all their efforts. Despite this despair and restlessness, the *muzara* movement committee convened a meeting at Jethuwal in Ludhiana district where they were to take a decision on raising their efficiency in the time to come. It decided to set up the office of the *muzaras* Committee at Ludhiana in order to develop an understanding within the organization and it was also decided to get the accounts of the committee audited. It was also resolved that in order to intensify the stir, the weekly-'Phulkari' published from Lahore, would be made use of. Besides, it was decided to send a deputation to call upon the Prime Minister of Patiala, but actually no such deputation was sent. Only a handful of *muzaras* did not pay *batai*. No one paid due attention to the appeal of Narain Singh Bhadaur that the peasants should carry their crops home.[96]

As stated earlier, the *muzaras'* movement got weakened for some time after 1939 and then the *biswedars* felt secure. But after a very brief span, laxity, idleness and indifference of the *biswedars* again contributed a lot to the revival of the

95. *Ibid.*,(CID Secret Abstract of Intelligence of February 15 and 18, 1942).
96. *Ibid.*, (CID Secret Abstract of Intelligence of February 9, 1945), PSR : PM's Office File No. 770 and 1973 (CID Secret Abstracts of April 17 and 24, 1942), PSA : Patiala.

muzaras struggle. In June 1942, the S.P. reported that as far as the checking, scuttling or repressing the *muzaras* movement was concerned, the State Government were not getting any sort of help from the *biswedars.* The *biswedars* had disorganised to such an extent that they could not even attend to their domestic affairs efficiently. They proved lax in the performance of their duties also because they, in reality, had been officially deprived of the right to collect *batai.* However, they were not at all surprised, "because, in fact, they don't possess so much sense" that they could have used this "God send opportunity . . . to stand upon their own legs". The reasons for this were that "a majority of them are illiterate addicted to drinks and loose morals. They have not been imparted such a training as may enable them to keep their *muzaras* under control". Apart from being incapable to handling the situation "the *biswedars* do not take the muzaras as human beings and are out to exercise their full sway over them, legitimately or illegitimately and that, too, mostly through their inefficient mukhtiars". Thus, when the system of carrying out *batai* operations through the police was withdrawn, they could enjoy no position. The situation was further complicated by the fact that on the one hand, political bodies and communists in particular were trying to win over the *muzaras* and on the other, the *biswedars* were not making any efforts at keeping the *muzaras* under control.

In the meantime, the *muzaras* movement again gathered momentum and now the leftists strongly entrenchd themselves in the movement. A conference of the *muzaras* held in district Sunam voiced its opposition to the Fascist ideology. But the police with the help of the *biswedars* succeeded in getting it in writing from the villagers that the Conference should not be allowed to be held there. Its organisers were asked not to hold the Conference there; they were warned if they held the Conference there, action would be taken against them under the Defence of India act.[97] Now the leaders and organizers of

97. *Ibid.*, (CID Secret Abstract of Intelligence of March 2, 1945); PSR, PM's Office File No. 2226/100 (CID Secret Abstracts of Intelligence of August 28 and October 3, 1942). File No. 1573, PSA : Patiala.

the Conference brought out pamphlets in Punjabee condemning the attitude of the police and the *biswedars*. Many other pamphlets and posters carrying their appeals to the rulers, their ministers, officials and political agents against the atrocities being perpetrated by the *biswedars* were also brought out under the supervision of the leaders like Dharam Singh Fakkar of Dalelsinghwala-Secretary *Kisan* Committee. Patiala, Ishar Singh Tamkot-Deputy Secretary *Kisan* Committee, Patiala,[98] etc.

It was obvious to all that the problem could be solved only after the settlement of the dispute between the *biswedars* and the *muzaras*. Despite the fact that numerous obstacles were posed in the way of the *muzaras* and holding of the *Kisan Sabhas* by the peasants, this agitation continued to move from strength to strength and reached its pinnacle when the Patiala *Kisans* Committee convened its 4th Conference at Tungwali in Ferozepur district.[99] Harnam Singh Dharamgarh presided over this conference and several others like Achhar Singh Chhina-President, Punjab *Kisans* Committee, the Communist leader Jagir Singh Joga, Ajmer Singh Tamkot, Ishar Singh Tamkot, Chand Singh Bhadaur and many more Communist and peasant leaders attended it. Demands of the *muzaras* were highlighted. Chhina said in his address that the Patiala authorities and its Prime Minister had assured them that they would be allowed to hold conference and meetings within the jurisdiction of Patiala State but now they had gone back on their assurance, and political meetings had been totally banned. He also remarked that he was in favour of abolishing the rights of the *biswedars, jagirdars,* and government servants not merely in Patiala State but in other states as well. Moreover, he wanted to free the states from the imperialist influence. He called upon the peasants to organize themselves and also predicted that the time was imminent when the *jathas* of the *muzaras* would

98. *Ibid.,* (CID Secret Abstract of Intelligence of March 2 and 6, 1945).
99. *Ibid.,* (CID Secret Abstract of Intelligence of March 2, 1945), PSR, PM's Office Case No. CB-1-2 of 2001 (1944-45) and of 2002 (1945-46), (CID Secret Abstract of Intelligence of February 2, 16; March 9, 16, 12; May 25; June 29, 1945, July 7 and September 9), PSA : Patiala.

have to come out of the villages and occupy *Moti Mahal* (Royal Palace). A government of peasants and workers would be formed.[100] Other speakers also condemned the repressive policies of the rulers of these states.

On the other hand, the *biswedars* were very much worried and perplexed in wake of the contemporary developments. They feared lest the state Government should give verdict in favour of the muzaras.[101] The failure of the state government in stemming the rising tide of the *muzaras* movement suggested that the fear of the *biswedars* was fully justified and natural since the *muzaras* and their representatives faced little difficulty in meeting the top ranking officers. The *biswedars* also feared that any verdict in favour of the *muzaras* would not only ruin them but also prove to be detrimental to the interests of the state governments, at least in the time to come-since the *muzaras* movement had become a part of the peasants' movement plaguing the British Punjab and of the *Kisan* party, the complexion of which was on all counts leftist or communist. Another argument offered, in fact a thinly veiled threat, was that such a decision during the war would hamper the efficient prosecution of the war efforts.[102] To finally clinch the issue, they gave the example of British Punjab where the same Tenancy Law was in operation and no concessions were being given to tenants, and wondered why Patiala wanted to take the lead in this matter. The *biswedears* also feared that the success of the peasants/*muzaras* struggle might generate fear and effect change in the hearts of a section of small *biswedars* inducing them to join the *muzaras* in making trouble and creating such a situation as might culminate in a massive Communist movement in the princely states, leading to dangerous results for the *biswedars* as well as for the state administration.[103]

100. PSR, PM's Office Case No. CB-1-2 of 2002 (CID Secret Abstract of Intelligence of June 15, 1945), PSA : Patiala.
101. *Ibid.*, (also see CID Secret Abstracts of Intelligence of May 18 and June 8,1945).
102. *Ibid.*
103. *Ibid.*, (also see CID Secret Abstract of Intelligence of March 2 and 9, June 29, 1945).

Meanwhile the muzaras, under the direction of the *Kisans* and Communists' organization, stepped up their agitation. The Patiala Kisan Committee called on the tenants to remain firm in their resolve for they would very soon be able to do away with *biswedari* system. The *nazim* and other concerned revenue officials had started dispatching complaints that the muzaras had been withholding *batai* and had also started forcibly occupying the lands of the *biswedars*.[104] Later on, more news about the forcible occupation of lands of the *biswedars* by the *muzaras* in different parts of the state, dropped in. Many meetings were held, posters and pamphlets were distributed as well as pasted on walls of houses in villages.[105]

Influenced by the ideologies of the leftists, *Malwa* state Akali *Dal* had also started functioning effectively and was quite active. A religious *dewan* was held at *Nabha* in which more than 7000 peasants and tenants took part. B.P.L. Bedi—a socialist leader of Punjab, Harnam Singh Dharamgarh, Jagir Singh Joga and several other leaders attended this *dewan*. The demands of the *muzaras* were highlighted and the tenants were told that the signs of the weakening of the state regime were conspicuous. By June 1945, the reports of the realization of *batai* on a none too large scale, had started trickling in—and this was the result of the untiring efforts of the peasants and workers.[106]

Now, the deterioration of the situation had been well defined due to which the Maharaja of Patiala decided to hold his court at Bhadaur despite its being the worst region from law and order point of view. The court was held on June 23, 1945 and attracted a large number of people. Both the *muzaras* and *biswedars* were heard very patiently and finally were

---

104. *Ibid.*
105. PSR, PM's Office File No. 2077—Correspodence regarding anti-*biswedari* movement (see Confidential Report about proceedings of the *Kisan* Conference held at village Shehna in Ludhiana district on July 7 and 8, 1945, CID Abstract of Intelligence of March 2 and 9, 1945), PSA : Patiala.
106. *Ibid.*, (also see CID Secret Abstract of Intelligence of July 13, 1945).

advised to work for a mutual settlement of the dispute between them. Thus, the problem failed to be solved even by holding the *darbar.* Now, the movement picked up vigour and took the shape of a conflict between the Police and the *muzaras.* In Kot Duna village, almost all the peasants refused to pay *batai.* The *biswedars* and the *muzaras* walked out of the meeting convened by the district authorities despite all the efforts of the *tehsildar* and the police to persuade them. A batch of 50 *muzaras* left for Patiala to lodge a complaint against the officials of Patiala State. They also tried to see the Inspector General of Police and to apprise the state administration of the police atrocities. When the peasants began to occupy the lands forcibly, the police resorted to repressive measures. As a result, many peasants left the village but soon they got reports of harassment of their women folk and children.[107] When a violent clash took pace between the *biswedars* and the *muzaras* at Bhadaur also, some *muzaras* set out to meet the Maharaja of Patiala to complaint against them. When they failed to get any satisfactory answer, they marched to Simla.[108]

In Dharamgarh village, the tenants began to take possession of land forcibly. To escape retaliation by the police many of them fled the village but their women and children were reported to be harassed by the police. Two more villages, Gurbazpura and Dasaudisinghwala were also declared the disturbed and troubled areas. At Gurbaxpura, some *muzaras* attacked the police guard to secure the release of some *muzaras* who had been arrested in connection with a case. A group of peasants from Dharamgarh village left for village Ugarahan under Harnam Singh's leadership. Almost all its members were carrying red lags in their hands. They were accorded a warm welcome and they spent the night there also. Actually this *jatha*

107. *Ibid.,* (Fortnightly Report of I.G. Police, Patiala of July 15, 1945).
108. *Ibid.,* (See CID Secret Abstract of Intelligence of July 27, 1945 and also fortnightly Report of I.G. Police, Patiala of August 17, 1945).

was bound for Moran Village in Jind state where it was to participate in a conference.[109]

Commenting on the contemporary conditions at the end of June, a sub-inspector of the Criminal Investigation Department who was attached to the political wing disclosed that the relations between the *biswedars* and the *muzaras* had been deteriorating with every passing day. The *muzaras* by now had organized themselves well in order to clam their rights. They were also raising funds for it now. They had started threatening the *biswedars,* the police and even the state authorities that they would either kill or get killed but would not pay *batai.*[110]

The following observation was made about the recent clash between the *muzaras* and the police—'It can be inferred from this clash that the *muzaras* were organizing and preparing themselves against the police, the had collected the arms and if such propaganda was allowed to reach the *muzaras* in the villages, it was feared that the situation would get out of control. The *biswedars* had also taken a serious note of such an agitation. The meeting held on June 28, 1945 decided to make an appeal to the Maharaja of Patiala to take stringent measures against the *muzaras* and to exhort the state administration to come down with a heavy hand on the *muzaras* who were withholding *batai.* The offending *muzaras* must be evicted from the land which should be restored to the *biswedars*. It was also submitted that *batai* should be collected by the state authorities; the cases against the *muzaras* should not be withdrawn and

109. *Ibid.*, (CID Secret Abstract of Intelligence of August 17, 1945); PSR, PM's Office Case No. 238/SPC dated Delhi, September 16, 1945, PSA: Patiala.
110. PSR, PM's Office case No. CB-1-2 of 2002 (1945-46) (CID Secret Abstracts of Intelligence of June 8, July 13 and Of August 17, 1945), PSA : Patiala; PSR, PM's Office case No. T-1 of 2001 (1944-45)—File Non 'Landlords Association', Patiala (see Reports sent in by *biswedars* to the Government on June 1, July 17 and 28, December 3 and 22, 1945 *August 8, November 1, 6 and 22, December 16, 1946) PSA : Patiala. * February, 22, 1946.

the *biswedars* should be protected against the assaults and highhandedness of the *muzaras*. Actually they acquainted the state with their problems and grievances in a resolution which was submitted to the state through a deputation. A meeting was convened by the *biswedars* in which it was stated that the state authorities had forsaken the *biswedars* and now they were at the mercy of the *muzaras*.[111]

In the end of June itself, a massive peasants conference was held at Moran, a village in Jind State. There the *muzaras* were instigated against the *biswedars*. The peasants activities gave a great set back to the honour of the Maharaja and the state administration. The Government continued to lose its esteem in the eyes of people. Another impact of the conference was the likelihood of the suspension of the Akali agitation in the states, because while addressing the rallies of the *muzaras*, their leaders had alleged that the Akalis were the hired agents of the rulers and their governments. The state authorities had imported them in order to make themselves powerful, actually the peasant workers were their well-wishers. These developments were gradually making an impact upon the people's hearts.[112]

Another peasants conference was held on a large scale at Shahena village of Ludhiana district on July 7-8, 1945 in which the key slogan raised the abolition of *batai* system. About 700 peasants ad tenants pledged to assist the peasants committee. Here also, the red flags appeared in large number which stood testimony to the fact that the leftist ideology had deeply influenced the peasants. In this conference, the *muzaras* were exhorted to keep themselves aloof from the *biswedari* system in the manner of Russian peasants during the October Revolution of 1917. The plundering of the *muzaras* by the State

---

111. *Ibid.*, PSR, PM's Office Case No. CB-1-2 of 2002 (1946-46) (CID Secret Abstract of Intelligence of February 8, 1946), PSA : Patiala.
112. *AISPC-Papers,* File No. 133A (1945-46-48)—note on Tenants problem in Patiala State submitted by All India States' People Conference, Patiala State), NMML, New Delhi.

governments and the *biswedars* was severely criticized. At Bhadaur, Achhar Singh Chhina rejected the Maharaja's claim that he had been sent by God and was his spokesman. He added that God had decreed the *muzaras* not to pay *batai*.[113]

Now, the *muzaras* become all the more formidable and violent. On July 7, 1945 when an effort was made to restore the land to the *biswedars* as per the order of the District Magistrate, there took place a murderous assault in Dhandali Khurd village in Sunam district. A number of *muzaras* reached there to protest against it and attacked both the police and the revenue officials. The police fired in retaliation killing two *muzaras*.[114] Meanwhile, the peasants started forcibly occupying the lands of the *biswedars* in Badshiwala village.[115] About sixty peasants set out to call upon the Maharaja in order to submit a petition against the highhandedness and atrocities of the *biswedars*. These peasants came from various villages of Patiala. It is believed that the Maharaja gave them a patient hearing and also gave them an assurance of decent treatment and fair deal.[116] The *biswedars* of village Dasaundasinghwala wrote to the Secretary of the *zamindara Sabha* that the *muzaras* had assaulted them with clubs and sticks, destroyed their standing crops and forced hem to leave the village. But the Inspector General of Police contended in one of his reports that the *muzaras* were sell-determined not to pay *batai* to the *biswedars*.[117]

However, the most important thing here is to find out the view point of the *biswedars*. On August 14, a meeting was held at Patiala, which was attended by almost all the *biswedars* who

113. People's Age Vol. 5, No. 33, February 16, 1947, Archives of Contemporary History, J.N.U., New Delhi.
114. *Ibid.*
115. *Ibid.*, PSR, PM's Office Case No. T-1 of 2001 (1945)—File on Landlords' Association, Patiala—see letter dated January 13, 1947 : PSA : Patiala.
116. This Account is based on *Pepple's Age*, Vol. V, No 33, February 16, 1947, ACH, JNU, New Delhi.
117. *Ibid.*

came from almost all the states, especially from the regions affected most. The contents of the speeches made at the meeting reflected a growing disappointment among the *biswedars* because of the unsympathetic attitude of the Government. As the meeting opened, the Chairman took a birds' eye view of the *biswedars* position. It was also mentioned that there were dacoities in villages on every passing day and it seemed as if there had been a meeting in the villages. The Chairman also disclosed that he along with some other *biswedars* had talked to the Maharaja and had also offered to, part with his land in return for an adequate compensation. But despite their righteous conduct, the Maharaja did not co-operate with them. Another *biswedar* who was present in the meeting observed that the *muzaras* could meet the Maharaja at will-recently about 200 *muzaras* from various villages had left to call upon him while the petitions made by the *biswedars* were spurned. He resumed, "You will always be at the receiving end if you continue to remain peaceful and passive. If our just demands are not met sympathetically, we shall go to Simla, meet the President, see the Viceroy, here, you can get nothing but humiliation".

The *biswedars* were of the opinion that the Prime Minister Hardit Singh Malik had been instigating the *muzaras* against them. They also felt that the Court held by the *Maharaja* at Bhadaur was not the product of a wise counsel, rather it had adversely affected the prestige of the Maharaja of Patiala. Actually the *biswedars* had lost their nerve and had been disillusioned with the Government to such an extent that a desperate course was suggested to them. Nirpal Singh of Bhadaur, the Secretary of the meeting, suggested that all the members of the *Zamindara Sabha* should see to it that each of them recruited 15 youths in a *jatha* and it was to be named *Darauli Jatha*. He also contended that each member of this *jatha* must be trained in handling the stick and always be at the back and call of the *zamindara Sabha*. He observed that these youths could be recruited from any section of the society, even from among the untouchables. The need of the hour was the strong youngmen. The names of the *jatha* members were to be kept secret and they were to be on their toes round the clock. The motive behind the formation of such *jathas* was very simple. As the *muzaras* attacked the *biswedars* in an organized manner, the *biswedars* wanted to pay them back in the same coin.[118]

Soon this agitation assumed the form of a conflict between the *muzaras* and the *biswedars,* with the states intervening mainly to institute cases of non-payment of *batai* and criminal assault. There were arms attacks at various places; these attacks were made to collect the *batai* forcibly and suppress the *muzaras'* agitation. Captain Jaswant Singh Jeji—a *biswedar* fired at his *muzaras* in Gobindgarh village, killing one and wounding seven. He *biswedars* alleged in their petition that they and their families had been attacked by the *muzaras,* so they had to fire in self-defence. The *muzaras* even now refused to pay *batai* without making any bones and sent on occupying more and more land unceasingly.

Under the auspices of the *Praja Mandal,* a Conference was convened at Patiala on October 5-6, 1946, in which the stalwarts expressed their sympathy with the *muzaras* and the Communists as well as their problems. A resolution passed at this conference demanded the abolition of *biswedari* system and transfer of ownership rights to the *muzaras.*[119] The demands included in this resolution indeed strengthened the peasants' struggle.

On December 10, 1946, a meeting of the All India States' *muzaras* Committee was convened which was attended by nearly 20,000 *muzaras.* In the beginning of 1947, the *muzaras* of about 228 villages participated in the struggle for non-payment of *batai.*[120] It was reported that by now them *muzaras* had occupied 1,32,650 bighas of land. Sticks and stones acted as their weapons—they had enduring unity—they were standing like watchmen on the occupied land. The Secretary of

118. *Ibid,* No. 35, March 2, 1947, ACH, JNU, New Delhi.
119. People's Age, Vol. V, No. 45, May 11, 1947, ACH, JNU, New Delhi.
120. *Ibid.*

the *zamindara Sabha* had cautioned the Government that if the *muzaras* were given a long rope and allowed to create disturbances, the princely states of Punjab would have to pass through travails of revolution within six months-a revolution similar to the French Revolution[121] of 1789.

The incident that occurred in Naraingarh on 23rd January 1947 gave a new turn to the *muzaras* struggle. The local *biswedar* Devinder Singh, who was also the Deputy Commissioner of his district got some *muzaras* assaulted by the hired *goondas* (hooligans) which resulted in a flare-up and the villagers chased the *goondas* who took shelter in the houses of the biswedars. For some time the *muzaras* waited for them to come out and then returned to their places. In the meantime four police vans reached the *biswedars'* houses at night and as soon as the day broke they attacked the houses of the *muzaras.* The males were beaten and even women were humiliated. No sooner did this news spread than the tenants and peasants from neighbouring villages started reaching Naraingarh in an overwhelming number. Consequently, the police had to retreat to the *biswedars'* houses. About 100 rounds were fired in which 53 *muzaras* were injured, three of them very seriously.

Next day, a *jatha* of the *muzaras* left for Patiala state to seek justice from the authorities, but it was intercepted by the police; many *muzaras* were arrested but were let off at a considerable distance from the city from where it was not so easy to come back on foot. As in the past, the news of this incident also soon spread to all the states. A *jatha* carrying red flags in hands and singing a revolutionary song headed for Naraingarh enroute many other villages. The *Kisan Sabha,* the *Praja Mandal,* the Communists and several other political organizations rendered full help to this *jatha* which acted as a shot in the arm for the peasants' movement. The movement gained a momentum in almost all the states of the Punjab. Now, the Revenue Minister's bid to conduct investigation in the whole affair and to revert the *muzaras* of Naraingarh against *Praja*

121. *Ibid.,* AISPC—papers, File No. 133A, 1945-46, NMML, New Delhi.

Mandal and the Communists also failed when about a dozen *jathas* converged there from the neighbouring villages. Now, the Revenue Minister packed up from Naraingarh. Soon after his departure, about 500 volunteers from the adjoining villages reached Naraingarh and took out a huge procession there which helped in ejecting into the minds of the *muzaras* a firm determination of conducting the *muzaras'* movement all the more dedicatedly.[122]

The incident of Naraingarh had at least proved that a new phase had dawned in the peasants' movement since this incident had strengthened the base of the *muzaras* movement in other states also. Prior to it, such unity and enthusiasm had never been seen among the peasants and common people of any village despite the innumerable atrocities unleashed upon them by the Government. But after this event, it became evident that the *muzaras* had started thinking on the lines of fighting against the Government repression unitedly. Now, they started their struggle regarding it as a part of the greater started their struggle regarding it as a part of the greater struggle for independence and every effort was made to transmit the news of Naraingarh incident and its importance to the *muzaras* and the people living in other states.

In the meanwhile, the clashes between the *biswedars* and the *muzaras* continued as before. Five *muzaras* were shot dead in Kalvanjara village in cold blood by the *biswedars*. The peasants who had forcibly occupied the lands belonging to the *biswedars* were fired at about seventy times. The *biswedars* had already made up their mind to teach a lesson to those *muzaras*. The women in Khariwala village were belaboured and the standings crops of the peasants who were away to Patiala in connection with a court case were burnt to ashes by the *biswedars*. Another *muzara* was killed in village Changaliwala and a number of *muzaras* were evicted from their

122. B*iswedars* continued to complain of lack of assistance from officials and police. Most of the reports do not indicate any action beyond instituting of cases, etc. *Vide., Ibid.*

lands by the *biswedars* in Naiwala village. They were fired upon; two *muzaras* were killed and 59 wounded. [123]

Such incidents had become widespread in the whole state. In fact, the Government had been following the policy of non-intervention in regard to the conflicts between the biswedars and the *muzaras*.[124] Out-side Patiala there seemed a miraculous rise in such incidents and very soon they assumed such complexion that the state could not remain unaffected by them. When the country got freedom on August 15, 1947, the *Praja Mandal* became all the more enterprising and spirited, and it demanded the formation of a responsible Government in the states immediately.[125]

Let us now have a look at the *muzaras'* agitation in states other than Patiala. In the Malerkotla and Faridkot states, peasants did not have full proprietary rights on the land held by them. They were treated as occupancy tenants, and in the revenue record it was the prince or some landlord who was known as *'ala-malik'* or the super-lord. The peasants in the Malerkotla state never accepted this position as the situation there was worse than in Faridkot. The reason for such a situation was clear, the muslims were mainly the landlords, while the cultivators were mostly Sikhs. An enquiry had been conducted into their claims but its findings and recommendations were never seriously accepted by the *nawab* or his *biswedars*.[126] The

---

123. People's Age, Vol. V, No. 45, May 11, 1947 (ACH, JNU, New Delhi).
124. The biswedars continued to complain of lack of help from officials and police. Most of the Reports also do not indicate any action beyond institution of cases, etc.
125. PSR, PM's Office case No. T-1-2, 2001 (1945)—File on landlords' Association, see orders passed on requests from *biswedars* dated 15.12.1947, 10.5.1948 and 3.6.1948; AISPC-Papers, File No. 133, 1948(Patiala State), NMML, New Delhi, (See memorandum submitted by the Patiala State *Praja Mandal* to the Prime Minister and the State Ministry Government of India).
126. Giani Kehar Singh, *Praja Malerkotla Di Dard Kahani,* Printed and published by Jagir Singh Joga, Amritsar; Desh Dardi Press, Introduction, 1-2.

peasants had continued their struggle. One of these was the agitation launched by the peasant proprietors of Malerkotla state against encroachment on their rights by the *khawanin* (muslim landlords), who did not permit them to dispose of their land according to their will.

The *nawab* was accused of taking undue benefit of the *nazool* laws and taking possession of lands when there were legal heir alive and who had a legitimate claim.[127] Nothing else can make the peasant more agitated than a danger to his proprietary rights in land. The peasants, therefore, met in a convention at Khottala on 10th January, 1927 and decided to set up a *zamindara* Association for the safeguard of their rights. They also decided to lead a mass deputation to Simla that summer and present a petition to the Viceroy. The proposed move was widely publicized and people were asked to send their grievances to this newly formed body to be incorporated in the petition. This greatly irked the state authorities and made the *nawab* and *khawanin* quite panicky. A campaign of villification was let loose against the *Zamindara* Association and a puppet National Zamindara Association was set up with loyalist aims and objectives. But nothing could check the advance of the agitation. As the news of the proposed *morcha* to Simla spread, the anxiety of the *nawab* mounted. In utter desperation, a meeting of the association was attacked by the state police and the armed forces on 18th July, 1927, killing 14 men and children.[128] Hundreds of peasants were arrested including many on their return from Simla and a conspiracy case was launched. One of the office-bearers of the Association, Talib Hussain, turned approver and the accused were sentenced to long term of imprisonment. Talib Hussain later retraced his steps and publicly apologised for his misconduct and became a leading advocate of the tenants movement in the state.[129]

---

127. *Ibid.*, 39, 42 and 49.
128. Giani Kehar Singh, *Praja Malerkotla Di Dard Kahani,* Printed and published by Jagir Singh Joga, Amritsar, Desh Dardi Press, 67.
129. Walia, Ramesh, *A study of the Praja Mandal Movement in he East Punjab States,* Patiala : 1947, 82-83.

Khottala episode symbolized the general peasant unrest in the state and it was also the beginning of the powerful movement for defence of the peasants' interests. It took hardly two years for the tenant agitation to raise its head in other states. This episode would have remained an isolated affair, had it not taken place at a time when the general tide of freedom movement in the country was rising high.

In the thirties and forties, in Malerkotla state, the movement was being organised by Giani Kehar Singh of the village of Chak, Sewa Sigh of village Bapla and Talib Hussain of Sharwanikot.[130] The main demands of the Malerkotla peasantry were to end corruption and illegal extraction of money by the *nawab*, the safeguarding of their rights in land and the bringing down of land revenue to the level of Ludhiana district in the Punjab.[131] These demands were published in the form of a poster termed 'Malerkotla Indictment' the state *Praja Mandal* and people were asked to supply their grievances to the *kisan* leaders. A demand was also made of the paramount power to hold an enquiry into the state administration and remove the *nawab*, in case the charges were proved. The annual observance of the Khottala day in memory of the persons who had fallen to police bullets in 1927 became a rallying point for the state peasantry. The annual fair of Chhapar, district Ludhiana, provided an other occasion for the peasants to meet and chalk-out their programme for further agitation.[132]

In Jind State, the peasants launched a *morcha* against the state administration. The Sikh peasants in the Jind State had

---

130. Hussain Talib rose to an important position in the Punjab *Riyasti Praja Mandal.* He was a forceful writer and an effective speaker. He also edited "*Riyasti Duniya*" *Vide.,* File No. 578; File No. 595; PSA : Patiala.

131. Giani Kehar Singh, *Praja Malerkotla Di Dard Kahani,* Amritsar, 90-93.

132. Chhapar is near Ahmedgarh railway station on Ludhiana-Hissar Railway Line. Thousands of peasants from states also attended it. Political parties held conferences on the occasion to propagate their programme and policies.

their grievances against the state administration which went unheeded at the hands of state officials, particularly the Prime Minister, Dr. Bihari Lal Dhingra. These grievances were mainly related to the judicial and revenue administration of the state. Land revenue had been enhanced and corruption prevailed all round.[133] It was alleged by the *kisan* leaders that the choicest land in two Sikh dominated villages had been gifted to Dr. Dhingra by the *Maharaja* and the cultivating owners were being dispossessed by him. Then there were grievances concerning the *begar* system and forcible supplies of fodder and other provisions for the hunting parties of the *Maharaja* and his guests. Again it was the peasantry that become the mainstay of the agitation in the State.

The character of the tenant movement in the Jind State was not in any way different from that in the Patiala State. The Akalis formed the hard core of the peasant workers everywhere and their main demands were concerned with the redressal of the peasant grievances. The only difference was that here the movement always remained on a low level. It neither attained the sweep it did in Patiala nor could it attract the attention of the Indian States' People's Conference.

Unrest among the peasants rapidly mounted in the tiny State of Kalsia which witnessed a regular peasant revolt in 1928. This state was consisted of two chunks of territory; One, the main block of villages round Chhachhrauli, the capital town bordering the Ambala District, and the second, a small twenty square miles seven-village pocket of Charik in the Ferozepur District. The Charik pocket was more than a hundred miles away from the capital and was beyond any effective administrative control from the state headquarters.[134] The peasants movement in the Ferozepur district had made rapid

133. Longowalia, Bhagwan Singh, *'Mal Administration in Jind State'*, *Patiala State Record*, File No. 595; A personal interview with Gujjar Singh Dhanetha village also confirmed the material published in the booklet.
134. *Kalsia State Records*, File No. 25 of 1938, PSA : Patiala.

strides in the thirties and Baba Rur Singh had emerged as an influential leader having been elected to the Punjab Assembly in 1937.[135]

It was mainly under his inspiration that the Charik peasants set up their own *kisan* agitation in early 1938 and presented a charter of demands to the Kalsia ruler.[136] The charter contained 28 demands and some of the most important are as follows :[137]

(a) The land revenue of Rs. 2-8-9 per *ghumaon* was very high which the *kisan* could not afford in those days of comparative cheapness and it must be reduced and brought in level with the rates current in the adjoining British *illaqa* which was between 0.12.0 and Rs.1. per ghumaon in different places;

(b) Begar was too heavy and must be done away with altogether;

(c) Indebtedness Bill should be brought in force;

(d) Necessary arrangement for the timely and adequate supply of canal water should be made in agreement with the Canal Authorities and the revenue rates by reduced so as to be compatible with the current economic conditions;

(e) All the lands of *zamindars,* now held by the *shahukars* or other zamindars under twenty years agreement, should be restored to the *kisans* without any payment.

---

135. (Rur Singh was an able organiser leading the *kisan* Committee, a Communist controlled organisation of the peasants) *Vide.,* Shamsher Singh Gill, *The Woeful Tale,* published by the author as Secretary of the *Illaga Charik Kisan* Committee.

136. *Kalsia State Records,* File No. 25 of 1938, PSA : Patiala Gill, Shamsher Singh, *The Woeful Tale,* Published by the author.

137. Charter published in *The Tribune* (Lahore) dated 12th June, 1938; The copy of this Charter is also available in *Kalsia State Records,* File No. 25 of 1938; PSA : Patiala.

The people of the *illaqa* Charik were bent upon getting their grievances redressed and were fully prepared to undergo any amount of suffering for their just and lawful demands.[138] So, they launched an agitation in support of their demands, held public meetings and sent *jathas* to the state capital. They raised slogans like, "redress our grievances", "grant us our legitimate rights", "give us the desired protection of a good government and make friendship with us as ever". But all their appeals fell on deaf ears. Now the local peasants came out with a firm determination to demand their just rights and enrolled themselves in a committee entitled, "The *illaqa Charik Kisan* Committee". The Committee had held some open air meetings in the villages and had also affiliated itself with the provincial *kisan* Committee of Punjab.[139] The Committee had resolved to get the demands of the peasants fulfilled at any cost by all non-violent means.[140]

The Charik movement had full co-ordination with the agitation of the people of Chhachhrauli and the surrounding villages in support of similar demands. However, Moga was generally the centre of their activities but the tenants were reported to have held a meeting at Ludhiana, with a view to launching their movement in the state at mass scale. Now a *jatha* of the *Kisan* Committee held a big red flag demonstration in front of the *dewans'* residence and the police station on 29th July, 1938 but no arrest was made. Getting no response from the state administration, the committee decided to boycott the annual cattle fair at Charik which was to be held in the month of September 1938. All entrances to the site of the fair were blocked by women volunteers and prospective buyers and sellers were dissuaded from participating in the fair. There were reports of earthen ovens (*tandoors*) at the fair site having been snatched by the volunteers of the *kisan* Committee.[141] Nails

138. *Kalsia State Records,* File No. 25 of 1938, PSA : Patiala.
139. *Ibid.*
140. *Ibid.*
141. *The Tribune* (Lahore), September 17th, 1938 (Statement of the Dewan).

were spread on the roads to puncture the tyres of the vehicles. The boycott of the fair proved a big success.[142]

About the agitation, a police report said[143] that the agitation was increasing day by day. Open defiance was being preached, the prestige of the police was being lowered, bad and indecent speeches were being made in every part of the state and feelings of hatred against the ruler and the administration were being created. Repressive policy would have to be adopted. This might lead to further trouble but there was no other way out. However, the state authority lacked police force to curb this agitation.

The cumulative effect of this situation was that the agitation continued unabated. Conditions were getting worse as no *lambardar* cared for the *tehsildar* or any other state official. *Jathas* continued marching to the state capital throughout the months of October and November. State officials apprehended difficulties in the realization of land revenue in December 1938 because of the ruffled feelings of the *kisans* over the Charik morcha.[144] A *jatha* of 20 tried to force their entry into the fort on 12th November, 1938 but only five arrests were made. To the earlier demands of the *kisan* Committee, now was added another one for the release of the arrested workers. The Kalsia ruler was forced to come to terms with the agitators. A public *durbar* was held at Charik on 27th November, 1938 where the

142. (The total income to the state upto 19th September 1938, penutimate day of the fair was a paltry sun of rupees one thousand as compared to rupees eight thousand of the previous years. Total number of the cattle sold in the fair was 789 as against 4861 in 1937, their total value being rupees 28,488 and Rs. 2,07,625 in 1938 and 1937 respectively) *Vide.*, Report of the superintendent of Police dated 25th Sept., 1938, *Kalsia State Records,* File I & II, PSA : Patiala.
143. Report of the Superintendent of Police dated 30th August, 1938, PSA : Patiala.
144. *Kalsia State Records,* File No. 164, (Dewan's letter dated 20th November, 1938), PSA : Patiala.

ruler of Kalsia state promised to fulfil all the main demands of the peasants.

The Charik *morcha* was indicative of the new mood of the state's people. It brought into bold relief the total bankruptcy of the administration in the smaller states. The *morcha* also underlined the effective help which the movement at some places was receiving from the British territory. The formation of the *Praja Mandal* in Kalsia in February 1940, was a direct result of this *morcha.*[145]

In the Faridkot state, the ruler was administering similar warnings to political workers as well as the *muzara* leaders.[146] The *raja* called all the important workers to his palace and told bluntly to desist from holding political conference in the garb of a religious *dewan.*[147] But the events were moving very fast. A *Zamindar Sabha* was set up on 24th July, 1938. The state Government promulgated the Registration of Societies Act in 1938, on the lines of the *hidayat* 1988 (*Bikrami*) enacted six years earlier by the Phulkian rulers. However, the political parties put forward the most progressive demands.[148] The emphasis however, was chiefly on peasants' demands, like the one that the auctioning of *shamlat* lands should be stopped and the peasants should be allowed to sell their crops in any market they liked and not necessarily inside the state. They also demanded full proprietary rights for the *kisans* through the abolition of the *ala-malik* system.[149] Public meetings were organised by the *Praja Mandals* at Kotakpura in favour of these

145. *Kalsia State Records,* File No. 132, PSA : Patiala.
146. The main organisers of a political conference held at Kotakpura were Zail Singh, Gurbax Singh, Jang Singh and Sandhura Singh, Vide., *Faridkot State Records,* File No. 336, PSA : Patiala.
147. *Faridkot State Records,* File No. 336, PSA : Patiala.
148. Poster published in October 1938, and Janga Singh's Urdu-Pamphlet *'Dukhee Janta De Dili Ubal',* Ferozepur City, Amrit Electric Press, 1939. Preserved in PSA : Patiala.
149. *Faridkot State Records,* File No. 4, PSA : Patiala; Avtar Singh, *'Din Dihare Raatan'* (Panjabi)—a booklet-published by the author, *Faridkot State Records,* File No. 357, PSA : Patiala.

demands in 1938, but heavy brickbatting was done by loyalists and squads of drum and *cannister* beaters were employed by the administration to disturb the meetings.[150]

Another *Kisan* Conference was held at Wadanikalan, on October 10, 1938. The leaders who addressed the conference referred to the evils of the administration. Evils like *begar malba, chowkidara* were condemned and the *muzaras* and other people were asked to unite and fight against the *batai* system, corruption in the revenue department and highhandedness of the police and *biswedars.* They were exhorted to continue this struggle till the state authorities yielded.[151] Another big conference was held at Muktsar on October 30, 1938, under the presidentship of Sardar Lal Singh, an advocate of Ludhiana. The demands discussed above appeared in almost all the speeches delivered there.[152] In brief, this struggle continued till their demands were met.

The seed of the agrarian unrest and disturbance of peace had been sown in the Kapurthala state since the beginning of the thirties. Begowal, Talwandi, Chaudharian and some more were the villages where the unrest had its origin but the activities of the tenants' leaders had also inspired the tenants of the surrounding villages.[153] The fact that the cultivators of other places in the *tehsils* of *phagwara, Bhunga* and *Sultanpur* had not joined their fellow-cultivators in this agitation, establishes that their demand was ill-conceived. But this version given by the State officials does not appear true, because later on it was admitted by the state authorities that the party officers of the state such as *lambardars, zaildars, patwaris* and school teachers had a hand in strengthening and directing the agitation.[154] For instance, Sardar Abdul Haq, Revenue Minister

150. *Faridkot State Records,* File Nos 1 and II (Material given in Panjabi), PSA : Patiala; File No. 108, PSA : Patiala.
151. *Faridkot State Records,* File No. 3, PSA : Patiala; File No. 108, PSA : Patiala.
152. *Faridkot State Reocrds,* File No. 4; File No. 357, PSA : Patiala.
153. *Kapurthala State Records,* File No. 556/3/15-37.
154. *Ibid.*

of the State (and brother of the Chief Minister) took a prominent part in the agitation through the agency of his subordinates in the villages. Some of his subordinates who openly took part in spreading the disturbances were given undue promotions.[155]

It was the *Zamindara League* (non-communal and anti-communal) which made, from the very beginning, serious attempts to achieve its objects like *(i)* the amelioration of the economic condition of the agricultural classes and their social and political advancement; *(ii)* Constitutional reforms-like the welfare, prosperity and the Progress of the agriculturists in other directions. Let us first of all have a look on their grievances. The main grievances of the agriculturists are detailed below :[156]

(a) They were groaning under crushing land revenue rates which were double, in some cases triple of, or even higher than those prevalent in the adjacent British districts, while the measurement scale was smaller;

(b) The land Revenue amounted to Rs. 21/15/4 in contrast to Rs. 17/8/4 per Rs. 100/- of Land Revenue in the adjacent British districts, the former including Rs. 3/10 of *abwahi khidmatguzari* which was a gilded name for *begar* cess.

(c) Their economic condition was pitiable. They were involved in huge accumulated debts from which there was no hope of escape except through Government (State) help; etc.

During the course of their struggle the Zamindar League demanded that :[157]

---

155. *Ibid.*
156. *Kapurthala State Records,* File No. M/3-33-37, Part-B, No. 569, Re-Land Revenue (Many grievances of the agriculturists are given in this file), PSA : Patiala.
157. *Ibid.,* (Many more demands put forward by the Zamindara League are also cited in one of the pamphlets which are given in this file).

(i) The land revenue should be assessed on the principles and rates prevalent in the adjacent British districts and steps should be taken to place the land assessment on an equitable basis;

(ii) measures should be devised to emancipate the agriculturists from huge indebtedness and afford them economic relief otherwise beneficent activities should be extended to the rural areas on increasingly liberal scale;

(iii) *begar, malba, batai* and *nazool* systems should be immediately abolished; etc.

When the state government did not come for their just demands the agriculturists sped up their agitation. Now a big demonstration was staged in the city. With this, the Muslim tenants refused to pay the customary rent to the landlords.[158]

In 1938-39, there was a peasant agitation against *malba* tax which was being charged at the rate of six per cent of the land revenue.[159] The people refused to pay the tax and the *lambardars* expressed their inability to do anything in the matter. The situation became quite grave at village Narur which was described as a storm centre of the agitation. The state Government held the extremist political workers led by Master Hari Singh and Chanan Singh Dhut.[160] The agitation won a partial victory when the Maharaja granted relief to the tune of a total sum of rupees sixty five thousand.

The agrarian agitation in Nabha state was led by the Praja *Mandal* workers in 1938. Many of the workers of this organization were arrested because they were, according to the state authorities, indulging in anti-state activities. Notable among those arrested were Sahib Singh Salana, Hardit Singh Bhattal, Hira Singh Bhattal and Hardial Singh of Nabha. Even the state Government admitted that certain, "malcontents had

158. *Kapurthala State Records,* File No. 556-J/3/15/37, PSA : Patiala.
159. *Kapurthala State Records,* File No. M-3-14-39, PSA : Patiala.
160. *Ibid.*

been arrested for their defiance of some of the states' existing laws". Similar was the fate of the *Kisan* Conference held at Chhapar fair in September, 1938.[161] Hardit Singh Bhattal who was to have presided over the conference, was arrested from his presidential procession and the tenants were dispersed by force by the police of the Malerkotla State. Sangat Singh who presided over the conference, in the absence of Hardit Singh Bhattal, was taken into custody. Some days later, all leading workers of Nabha as well as of Malerkotla States, Including Sahib Singh Salana were arrested and a case of murderious assault under section 307 of the Indian Penal Code launched against them.[162]

It was under the leadership of the Punjab *kisan Sabha* that a *Kisan Sabha* was set up in Patiala. The tenants' movement went on during the second world war also. In 1946, a tenants' convention was held at the village Dalelsinghwala.[163] The convention formed a 'Tenants War Council' and it provided war leadership to the movement. In almost all the villages of the tenants, the payment of *'batai'* was topped. The stop-*batai* movement had to bear with limitless atrocities. Even the firing at Kishangarh could not suppress this movement. Many leaders attained martyrdom in this movement.[164]

Like Patiala, in Una *tehsil* also, the tenants had been fighting against the exploitation of the owners right since the first *bandobast*. In 1936-37, this movement acquired war

---

161. Salana, Sahib Singh, *Aap Biti*, 134.
162. *Ibid.*, 136; AISPC-Papers, File No. 138 (Part-I) 1933-48 (Private papers Section, Nehru memorial Musium and Library New Delhi), 911.
163. Personal interview with Master Hari Singh (Chandigarh). Master ji was at that time the General Secretary of the Punjab *Kisan* Sabha, also took part in the Convention. This is also supported by Vaid Chhajju Mal and Sardar Ishar Singh Majhail.
164. Master Hari Singh, *'Punjab Wich Kirsani Lahar'* (The Farmers' Movement in Punjab-Before and after Independence), in Punjabee, published in a Souvenir, issued by the CPI, on January 26, 1976.

proportions. The tenants refused to get the standing crops assessed. But in 1946, this movement gained still greater momentum. In 84 villages, the payment of *'batai'* was discontinued.[165]

The state continued sucking their very blood. Therefore, in 1948, they took an active part in the up-coming movement for ending royalty (Raja-shahi). As a result of the upsurge among the people of the states, in 1948, all the states of the Punjab merged and the Pepsu was formed.[166] As a consequence, the struggle of the peasants and *muzaras* in the state lasted till 1956, though, after the general elections, the Pepsu Assembly had passed an Act[167] for effecting land reforms. The last phase of this struggle had been traced in the next Chapter.

165. *Ibid.*
166. *Ibid.*, Vaid, Chhajju Mal, *'Pepsu Muzarian Da Ghol Ten* Communist Party' *Souvenir*, Issued by the CPI on January 26, 1976.
167. *Patiala State Records,* Prime Ministers' Office, case No. 565/C, of 1939, PSA : Patiala.

7 The Peasant's Struggle : 1948-1956

The period between 1948 and 16 may be considered as 'the organized phase' of the peasants' struggle in this region of the Punjab; the peasants' movement was in full swing during this period in the Patiala State, particularly in the regime of Maharaja Yadvindra Singh. He was considered an enlightened ruler. It is worth mentioning that the peasants' struggle during this period was dominated by the tenants while the middle class peasants and peasant proprietors played just a secondary role in it. If at all their role was noticed at times, practically it was an unimportant role. It is equally important to note that the polarization of the leaders of the peasants' struggle and activists on ideological lines also emerged during this crucial period of ten years. The Communist influence added an element of militancy to the movement.

Though, as we have noticed in the preceding chapter, Yadvindra's father the predecessor, Maharaja Bhupinder Singh had tried to crush the movement ruthlessly, even then the *Praja* Mandal and its byproduct, the peasants' movement became a formidable force by the middle of 1938. Before his death, he had, however, appointed constitutional Reforms Commission. It had revived the peasants' hopes of getting justice from the new Maharaja Yadvindra Singh. His clean image along with puritanical announcements aroused great expectations.[1] But

1. An excerpt of Maharja Yadvindra Singh's Inauguration speech is reproduced verbatim as below :
I realize that circumstances are fast changing in India and that the time when the state and the rulers lived and worked in

(Contd...)

soon their all hopes were belied, when Maharaja Yadvindra Singh brought about a split in the Akali-*Praja Mandal* ranks by conciliating Harchand Singh Jeji, in fact, winning him over by marrying his daughter Mohinder Kaur.[2]

Sardar Vallabhbhai Patel, who was then the Home Minister as well as Deputy Prime Minister of free India, was instrumental in integrating all the Indian princely states with the rest of India in 1947. At this time the Maharaja of Patiala held an important position among the Indian Princes. He headed the princely delegation which met Cripps Mission in 1942 and as also a member of the Negotiation Committee of the Princes instituted under the cabinet Mission. Plan to formulate the terms on which the states were to accede to the Indian Union, again Patiala was the first to accede to the Indian Union on March 13, 1947. After the resignation of the *nawab* of Bhopal, he became the Chancellor of Chamber of Princes. With this his position became more formidable. As a result, he could persuade the rulers of twenty two states even before the country was freed, to join the Indian Union.[3] The Maharaja of Patiala and Sardar Patel collaborated in persuading the rulers of other States to join the Indian Union. Over five hundred States were integrated into

---

(Contd...)

isolation, ignoring the conditions around them, is rapidly disappearing. No barriers can be erected against ideas and I recognize that the time has come when traditional policy of the states may require modification and adjustment in light of what is happening in the rest of this great country.

Vide., Administration Report of Patiala State for 1938-39, 9-11. CSL, Patiala.

2. For more details see File Nos. 10 and 41—Oral History Cell, Department of Punjab Historical Studies, Punjabi University, Patiala.
3. *All India States People's Conference Papers* File No. 134, NMML, New Delhi; Gur Rattan Pal Singh, *The Illustrated History of the Sikhs* : 1947-1978, Chandigarh : 1978, 92-98; *Ganda Singh, Patiala and East Punjab States Union : Historical Background,* (Published by Pepsu Archieves, 1951), 92-98.

eight Unions. One of these unions was Pepsu comprising of Patiala, Nabha, Jind, Malerkotla, Faridkot, Kapurthala, Nalagarh and Kalsia. It was inaugurated by Sardar Patel in Patiala on July 15, 1948.[4] The Akali leader Master Tara Singh welcomed its formation as Sardar Patel called it the 'Home Land of the Sikhs'. It was held that the Pepsu enjoyed financial and political viability. It had 2,721,935 Sikhs against 1,704,339 Hindus and 55,913 Muslims inhabiting it according to the census of 1951.[5] It is to be noted that, later the Akalis used in their favour the phrase—'Home Land of the Sikhs' and demanded the retention of the Pepsu as well as the merger of the Sikh majority areas of Punjab into Pepsu and the formation of the *Panjabi* Speaking State.[6] In the context of present circumstances, it is not a healthy term as the misguided as well as the Sikh fundamentalists wrongly interpret this phrase. However, it is to be noticed that Sardar Patel praised highly the Maharaja for his services and patriotic lead for the unity and integrity of India. Also, the Maharaja of Patiala was named as the Rajpramukh of Pepsu.

At the time of formation of Pepsu, there were three political groups or claimants for power—the Praja Mandal, the *Akali Dal* and The *Lok Sewak Sabha.*[7] As regards the formation of ministry, no agreement could reach among the three political parties. The Government of India proposed to install a coalition ministry of all the three parties. Finally, the Union was formed on August 20, 1948 with Maharaja of Patiala as *Rajpramukh.* On August 22,1948 a care taker Government headed by Gian

4. *Patiala and East Punjab States Union, op. cit.*, 9.
5. *Facts About Pepsu* (published by Patiala Directorate of Information and Public Relations, Pepsu, July 15, 1953).
6. *The Hindustan Times* (Delhi), June 2, 1948; For further details, *Patiala and East Punjab States Union Since Inauguration,* published by Directorate of Information and Public Relations, Pepsu (n.d.), 1.
7. This was a political group formed by Col. Raghubir Singh and later on this group was merged itself with the Congress on the eve of first general election in 1951.

Singh Rarewala[8] was formed. Though efforts were made to form a representative ministry, but for the resilence of the *Praja Mandal* and resistance of the *Akali Dal* to the Rarewala or Raghubir Singh's leadership could not be overcome. At last, on January 13, 1949, a ministry of *Lok Sewak Saba* and four rebel *Praja Mandalists* namely Giani Zail Singh, Ram Nath, Nihal Singh Takshar and Harcharand Singh, under Gian Singh Rarewala was sworn in.[9] But after 10 months *i.e.,* on November 18, 1949 this Interim Government was replaced by a Care-Taker Government comprising Gian Singh Rarewala and M.R. Bhide.[10] Col. Raghubir Singh formed his Congress Ministry on May 23, 1951, of course, after dissolving his *Lok Sewak Sabha* Party and had joined the Congress, with Brish Bhan as Deputy Chief Minister, along with three of his nominees as ministers and also two of his Harijan supporters as deputy ministers.[11] Hence, between July 1948 and May, 1951, four Interim Ministries, three of which were headed by Gian Singh Rarewala and one by Col. Raghubir Singh, were formed in the newly created Pepsu. Finally elections were held in Pepsu on January 7, 1952 to elect 60 members to the Pepsu State Assembly. These were completed on February 10, 1952 and the party-wise result were as follows :[12] The Congress could secure 26 while the Akalis 19, Jan Sangh 3, Communist 3, KMPP 1, S.C. Federation 1, and independent 1.

Thus as no political party got absolute majority to form the Government independently, Col. Raghubir Singh of the Congress majority party, was invited to form the Government. He formed the Government with the help of some independent

---

8. Gian Singh Rarewala was born in 1901 and died in 1979. He had witnessed all important events during the freedom Struggle.
9. Menon, V.P., *The Integration of the Indian States,* Bombay : 1956, Vol. I, 248-49; Walia, Ramesh, *op. cit.,* 192.
10. *Ministry of States Government of India,* File No. 3(85) P/49, NAI, New Delhi.
11. *Historical Background of Pepsu,* A State Government Publication, 1952.
12. Our Rattan Pal Singh, *op. cit.,* 23.

members. But on the very first day of the Assembly session his Government was defeated. As a result, Gian Singh Rarewala, the leader of the Akalis with the support of non-Congress MLAS formed the Government on April 22, 1952. However, soon nineteen ministers including Rarewala were unseated by the Court of Law. So within a year after its formation this ministry was dissolved by the centre. There was constant tension and bitterness between the centre. There was constant tension and bitterness between the centre, and the state due to the proposed Tenancy Legislation by the Rarewala Ministry. However, the principal reason for its dissolution was its misrule and lawlessness. The peasants' problem, of course, was vital for the survival of any ministry in the newly formed Pepsu. Thus, before discussing the problem of Tenancy Legislation, it is absolutely essential to write in detail the problems of the cultivators which this state had inherited.

The Pepsu state effected revenue settlement and formulated tenancy laws from time to time on the pattern of the Punjab province.[13] Nevertheless the Pattern of relationship was inevitably to be different because the states had conferred special rights on the *biswedars*; and secondly, in most states the land administration and the conditions of tenure were brought in line with the Punjab at later dates. But in the Patiala State the decennial cash assessment was made as early as 1862; however, regular settlement starting in 1901 was completed in 1909. Similarly, Faridkot State was not systematically settled until 1909-10. On the contrary, large portion of Jind State had summary settlement between 1857 and 1866 and its first regular settlement shorty afterwards. In Nabha the regular settlement of different parts of the State accomplished at intervals between 1873 and 1901. Also in Kapurthala the first settlement was affected as far back as 1865. Settlement operation in Malerkotla *Riyast* began in 1987. In Nalagarh, where conditions were altogether different, if compared with those in the plains, a

13. *Report on Agrarian Reforms in Pepsu, Government of India,* Ministry of States, 1952, 4.

portion of the state was settled towards the close of the 19th century, while another portion was settled just in 1924.[14]

Though the conditions were different in different states. On the whole the problem of the peasantry was uniformally of the same nature. It was limited to the claims put forward by *(a)* occupancy tenants; *(b)* groups of special tenants and *(c)* proportion of tenants-at-will who had been deprived of rights of occupancy or ownership which belonged to them.[15] In contrast to them was the landed aristocracy who asserted their rights on superior ownership.[16] Another side of the tenancy problem was related to the grant of greater rights to tenants-at-will, generally on the lines of legislation enacted in several states including the Punjab.[17]

The whole problem thus revolves around the fact that there was serious dispute between the *biswedars* and tenants in almost al the states of Pepsu. But this conflict was acute in the Patiala State. In the first decade of the 20th century when Major F. Popam Young's Settlement was in the process, the *biswedars*-tenants conflict existed. A very close examination of his final Settlement Report testifies to this thing. Although the right of occupancy appears to have been well settled and recognized, it was not known as to how these rights were acquired and what they were like. Referring to the *biswedars*-tenants conflict or relations existing at that time Mr. Young writes,[18] "In many cases in which the proprietary title had been in dispute between the main body of cultivating residents in the villages, on the one hand, and on the other, some individual claimed the entire *biswedari* right on the score of descendent from the founder, or alleging that his admitted right as *mafidar* covered the proprietary title also, the state courts would often allot to the former the unasked for status of occupancy tenants. In fact,

14. *Ibid.*, 4-5.
15. *Ibid.*, 5.
16. *Ibid.*
17. *Ibid.*
18. *Ibid.*, 8.

occupancy rights were generally awarded as a kind of compensation to the unsuccessful claimants of proprietary rights, and often, fear, as a sop to the conscience of officers who knew well that they were favouring men of their own class." Mr. Young further writes, "There was throughout the state a strong offensive and defensive alliance between *ahalkar* and *biswedars*. The *ahalkar* was not a biswedar generally contrived to become one, and the *biswedar* found that it was necessary to salvation to obtain a footing in the official camp. The tendency was for small proprietors, who happened to be shareholders in a village in which some one connected with the official class was an assignee of the revenue, or the owner of a predominant interest therein, to become occupancy tenants, and for old tenants in a *biswedari* estate to sink to the level of mere tenant-at-will. Moreover, the influence of the biswedars' class had to the issue of a *hidayat* in 1872 from the supreme authority in the state, making it incumbent upon all occupancy tenants to pay kind rents.[19]

His Report further records that during the Settlement Operation there had been : a campaign of highhandedness and aggression on the part of a number of the *biswedars'* class. This led to so many law suits and criminal prosecutions that during the Settlement operations an attempt was made to ascertain the positions, and define the right of the tenants throughout the State. The Punjab Revenue At was applied to Patiala with some modifications and, during the subsequent investigations as many as 34,394 occupancy tenancies were established, representing a total area of 305, 161 acres.[20]

Hence, from Mr. Young's Final Settlement report it may be assumed that many tenants with proprietary rights were recorded as occupancy tenants and others as the tenants-at-will. But according to Venkatachar Report, which was

19. Major F. Popham Yong, *Final Report of the Settlement of the Patiala State* (1900-1908 A.D.) (Ajmer Scottish Mission Industry Company Ltd., 1909), PSA, Patiala.
20. *Ibid.*

submitted after four years, there were tenants of long standing in *biswedari* estates and in many cases there had been continuous litigation. It was absolutely difficult for both the parties to furnish documentary evidence for the change in the record of right.[21]

But the situation as it prevailed in 1948, as well as the policy programme of the Congress favoured the peasants in granting them rights. The cultivators of the Faridkot and Nalagarh States were recorded inferior landowners whereas the rulers of these two states were recorded as superior landowners over the entire area of their respective State.[22] However, the cultivators could not be ejected as they had hereditary rights, of course, without having proprietary rights.

Now, there was a change in the attitude and the policy of the Government. Consequently, the Pepsu Government on August 20, 1948, conferred proprietary rights on inferior landowners, otherwise it would have been done on a later date.[23] This gave new hope to the tenants to secure their rights of ownership, even if necessary through struggle. The decision to institute an Agrarian Reforms Committee in May, 1950 to ponder over the Congress decision to abolish landlordism, gave further hope to the tenants. In fact, this became an important factor which gave them a hope of transforming a vision into reality because encouraged by these circumstances the peasantry of the Pepsu States entered into a new phase of its struggle.

The Peasants' problem became complicated and assumed varied dimensions for a number of reasons, after the formation of Pepsu. Firstly, there was sufficient shift in the balance of forces in favour of the tenants after the liberation. Before

21. *Report on Agrarian Reforms in Pepsu, op. cit.*, 9.
22. *Ibid.*, 20
23. Government of Patiala and East Punjab States Union, Patiala Revenue Department, Notification No. 14(7) B-51-14-13-date 7th June, 1951, and the *Pepsu Government Gazette* (Extra-ordinary) No. 4, dated 5th April, 1952, PSA, Patiala.

independence the peasants had to struggle against feudalism, imperialism and exploitation by the *biswedars*. Indeed, their struggle against *biswedari* failed because princes, feudallords and the British Government combined to push the peasants in a tight corner. However, after independence, and the formation of Pepsu, the position of the Princes and *biswedars* was comparatively and considerably weakened and as the peasants felt encouraged to strike at the root of feudalism as well as to make a final assault against feudal order and its supporters *i.e.,* imperialists. Secondly, again after partition, a large number of Muslim tenants migrated to Pakistan in 1947. As a result, the landlords occupied their lands and they too refused any settlement with the tenants who migrated from Pakistan to India.[24] Moreover, the landlords who had migrated from Pakistan and had been allotted land here, treated the tenants cruelly.[25] Thirdly, the landlords, after independence feared lest the Congress Government should pass legislation against them and in favour of the tenants. As a result's the biswedars tried to evict their *muzaras* forcibly on one pretext or the other.[26] But the tenants frustrated their attempts to do so. Fourthly, the tenants had pinned great hopes on the abolition of princely states and formation of National Government, as they were convinced that their fight against *biswedari* was interlinked with the princely order.[27] But all their hopes were dashed to the ground with the formation of Pepsu with Maharaja of Patiala as its *Rajpramukh.* So they had no other alternative but to wage a fresh struggle against the feudal lords and the newly formed Pepsu Government. Lastly, the system of *biswedar*—tenant

---

24. Address of Jagjit Singh Lyallpuri—President Reception Committee—12th Annual Session of All India *Kisan Sabha,* held in Moga on September 13-19, 1954 (Bharat Printing Press Moga), 6.
25. Bhag Singh Sajjan's Statement (recorded personally). He is member of Punjab State Committee CPM.
26. *The Tribune* (Ambala Cantt.), October 10, 1950.
27. *Patiala Tenants on the March*—issued by Muzara Committee Lahore (Progressive Publishers) (ND), 3.

relation was based on the acceptance of certain unwritten codes of conduct but under changed circumstances neither the *biswedars* nor the tenants for the protection of their interests were prepared to abide by these unwritten rules. As a result of cumulative impact of these factors the landlord—tenant dispute became all the more acute.

The *farman-i-shahi*, which had been implemented by the erstwhile Patiala State, was discontinued in the wake of partition and wholesale migration. Again, confronted with the new situation, the Pepsu Government tried to solve the *biswedar*-tenant problem by reviving the *farman-i-shahi*. Besides, the new Government in Pepsu had not formulated any policy with regard to peasantry. It adopted a policy of compromise but it was into accepted fully by the tenants as well as the *biswedars*. The forcible implementation of *farman-i-shahi* led to the clashes between the police and the tenants, especially at places such as Anupgarh, Mulewala, Dunakot, Gurthali and Kartarsingwala. The tenants frustrated the attempts of the *biswedars* and the State police to realize *batai* and make possession of land. This success of the peasants against the combined force of the *biswedars* and police enhanced the prestige of the peasants' movement; and it spread to new areas, including villages, belonging to tenants-at-will—like Dharamgarh, Dhandoli, Shafipur, Bakshisinghwala, and Dalelsinghwala, etc.[28]

As a consequence of the initial success, there was a tremendous upsurge among the peasants. Now, a large number of occupancy tenants, tenants-at-will, poor peasants and other oppressed and exploited sections of the rural society joined the movement making it truly peasants' struggle. Initially, the peasanats' movement began as a '*no batai*' agitation but very soon, it underwent a transformation; and the peasants began

28. *Muzarian-Kisana De Mittor Kaun*, published by Tenant Committee, Pepsu (Ludhaiana : Civil and Military Press, May, 1949), 40.

to demand abolition of *beswedari* system without compensation.[29]

It is to be noticed that after 30th May, 1950, the peasants movement became well organized and militant. The change in the character of the movement is evident from the slogans, the peasants had adopted during the period. It also displays the deepening of the contents of demands. The slogans adopted by the peasants present five fold dimensions of the movement. The tone and intensity of the above mentioned slogans indicates radicalism. It is quite evident that the peasantry was under the influence of the communist Party leadership and that is why the peasants' movement assimilated militant and radical tone and temper. To substantiate, let us discuss, at some length, the warlike conflict of the Kishangarh peasants, here.[30]

Kishangarh,[31] a village in Bhatinda district was one of the important centres of the peasants' struggle in this region. The study through out the period of our brave and heroic sturggle[32] of the peasants of this village has come down in the history of the Pepsu as a great event, a brilliant chapter because the peasants of this village fought against the power of the *biswedars* on the one hand and police and military on the other.

---

29. *Ibid.*, (See also Extract from the fortnightly report of Regional Commissioner, Pepsu for the period ending 30.5.50 Ministry of States File No. 3(39)-F/49, NAI, New Delhi, 47.
30. *(a)* Capture the land; *(b)* Resist eviction; *(c)* Confront *biswedars' goondas*; *(d)* Demoralise the bureaucracy; *(e)* Propagate Your achievements; *(f)* Win allius from among the peasant proprietors and genuine anti-feudal elements; *(g)* Avoid clashes with police; and (*h*) Spit whole fire on notorious *goondas* and anti-social elements.
31. Kishangarh is situated at a distance of 100 Kilometers from Patiala, the then Capital of the State and was the most significant nuclear of the peasants' movement in Pepsu.
32. Vaid, Chhajju Mal, "Tenant Movement in Pepsu", *op. cit.*, Master Hari Singh, *Peasant in Freedom Struggle*, Vol. II, New Delhi, 1984, 255.

They were led by the Comrades Dharam Singh Fakkar[33] and Jagir Singh Joga. Their objectives were—non-payment of *batai* and restoration of land to the tiller as early as 1946.[34] Now at the request of Bhagwan Singh and Syasat Singh,[35] the revenue staff was sent to the village to implement the *farman-i-shahi* (the royal order). But the staff on its way from Bareta to Kishangarh was greeted by the tenants of the village with cries of "nor a grain of batai", "not an inch of land." Consequently, the revenue staff retreated to Bareta.[36] Enraged at this the biswedars sent armed goondas to crush this peasants' resistance. Reaching Kishangarh, they set up their camps in the fields. Getting this information, Dharam Singh Fakkar and Chhajju Mal mobilized nearly 5000 peasants from neighbouring villages to reach Kishangarh. Reaching there, they surrounded them from three sides. No sooner the militant peasants moved towards the enemy camp, the hired *goondas* and the *biswedars* took to heels[37] to save their lives.

Biswedar Syasat Singh, dismayed at this defeat, got warrants of arrest against thirty five young peasants of Kishangarh, issued. On March 16, 1949, a contingent of 100 policemen went to this village to effect the arrest. A sub-

---

33. He was born in village Dalelsingwala of Bhatinda district. He was a very popular peasant leader who led the peasants' movement before and after independence. Fakkar won the Pepsu Vidhan election as Communist candidate in 1954. As a member of Vidhan Sabha he alongwith other Communist member fought on the floor for the cause of poor peasants. He remained the General Secretary of the *Pepsu Kisan Sabha* for may years.
34. *Kishangarh, The Peasant's Heroic Defence of His Land,* Published by *Pepsu Kisan Sabha,* Bhatinda (Sangrur, Mittal Printing Press (nd), 29.
35. Syasat Singh and Bhagwan Singh were the *biswedars* and were both superintendent of Police. The former being posted in his native district of Bhatinda. They too were very influential. We easily can understand the situation.
36. Vaid, Chhajju Mal, "Tenant Movement' in Master Hari Singh's *Punjab Peasants in Freedom Struggle, op. cit.,* 256.
37. *Ibid.*

inspector was killed in the clash between the tenants and the police. At this the Deputy Commissioner Bhatinda sent another contigent of 100 policeman to besiege the village. The village *panchayat* tried to explain the real situation, but was not listened to by the Deputy Commissioner who insisted on the surrender of underground peasants. The panchayat's efforts to satisfy the authorities and avoid confrontation failed. Finally, when the peasant leaders and activists did not surrender, army was called out by the state Government headed by Rarewala. The village Kishangarh was besieged by 400 troops, tanks and fire-armed cars. The martial law was promulgated.[38] In the early hours of March 18, 1949, the villagers were served an ultimatum to vacate their houses within 10 minutes and gather at the *biswedar's haveli* which was later on extended 5 minutes more. Enraged at the unwarranted use of the army, the villagers went on house tops and raised slogans—'*Inqlab Zindabad*', *Rarewala Wazarat Murdabad*', and '*Dharam Singh Fakkar Zindabad*'. On the expiry of the ultimatum period of 15 minutes to vacate the village military action was taken. Three persons were killed and twelve wounded. Dharam Singh Fakkar and Mohinder Singh were arrested. Twenty six tenants were accused of criminal offence.[39] However, all this oppression by the state Government could not kill the spirit of the peasants and also of their struggle. Thus, Kishangarh became a symbol of the peasants' movement and is quoted to this day as an instance of the heroic armed struggle of the *Lal* Party and the militancy of the *muzara* movement.[40]

Undoubtedly, the Kishangarh episode a was a turning point in the history of the peasants' movement. The Peasants

38. Kishangarh, The Peasants' Heroic Defence of His land, Published by *Pepsu Kisan Sabha*, Bhatinda (Sangnur, Mittal Printing Press) (nd), 36-40.
39. *Ibid.*, 40-42 (List of arrested Peasants) bearing their names are given.
40. *The Hindustan Times*, Delhi, February 12, 1950; Ministry of State File No. 3(39)-P/49, NAI, New Delhi; *The Tribune*, March 20 to 23, 1949 (Also this account is based on interviews with Chhajju Mal Vaid, Master Hari Singh and Jagir Singh Joga).

of this village were the pioneers of the struggle against feudalism and imperialism, because they imparted new horizons. They made the struggle more intensive as well as extensive. The police repression and also the resistance of the peasants converted the simple peasants as heroes in the eyes of the peasants of surrounding villages. During the course of peasants' struggle in Kishangarh village, the *jathas* of peasants of the neighbouring villages had also participated.

Politically it became more significant as the political parties wanted to capitalize the situation politically. So the Communist Party of India, the Congress and the Akali Party got involved in Kishangarh struggle. Now, it was apt that no Government could survive in Pepsu without solving the problem of the peasants.[41] Under the changed situation the Akali Party appointed an Enquiry Committee[42] to personally visit Kishangarh and to prepare a report based on the information the members could get from peasants outside the village by the police posted there. The Committee in its report made two important observations. Firstly, contrary to the police version, the Committee claimed that 24 persons were slain in the military-cum-police action. Second, the Committee demanded that the Central Government should make an enquiry into Kishangarh episode. Accordingly the Central Government sent its representatives to enquire into the episodes of village Kisangarh, Malerkotla and Nalagarh.

However, the *biswedars* met the representatives of the Central Government and they expressed their displeasure at

41. *The Daily Akali Patrika* (Jullundhur), March 24, 1949, 3.
42. This Committee was consisted of Kartar Singh Darves, the Secretary, Sarwan Singh, Jathedar Akali Jatha of District Barnala and Hari Singh, Jathedar of District Bhatinda. See *The Daily Akali Patrika*; Jullundhur, Report of Inquiry Committee. April 10, 1949 (The Pepsu Congress President Brish Bhan also wrote a letter to the President to Indian National Congress regarding the critical situation prevalent in the village Kishangarh and demanded immediate enquiry by the Congress. See *All India Congress Committee Papers*, File No. 13/1948-49, NMML, New Delhi.

the activities of the Communists and the declared policy of the Government to abolish *biswedari*.[43] The policy of the Government, of course, could not be reversed; but the constant pressure of the *biswedars* got to some extent the policies of the State Government amended. By order (*farman-i-shahi*) of the *Rajpramukh* the share of *biswedar* was reduced from one-third to one-fourth and the tenants were now free to purchase this partition at a price determined by the revenue authority.[44]

However, the peasants were not satisfied with this decision as the amendment fell short of the target fixed by them. Consequently, the Pepsu *Kisan Sabha* and the *muzara*. War Council decided to continue their struggle with renewed vigour. They also wanted creation of local leadership, mobilizing trained volunteers and education of masses through pamphlets. Teja Singh Swatantar wrote pamphlets entitled, "Tenant Struggle for land in Pepsu", "Attitude of Political Parties" and a "Time for Akali Dal to take decision."

The Government realized the gravity of the situation. It made adequate police arrangement to check the peasant upsurge and arrest peasant leaders and Communist workers. With this objective in mind, the State Government raised a big police force. Five punitive posts were set up—each consisting of 200 horsemen, in highly disturbed villages. The State authority was determined to eliminate the Communists.[45] But it is to be remembered that the Government was also keen about solving the peasants' problems. On August 20,1949[46], the Government issued an ordinance abolishing *biswedari*.

Revenue staff escorted by the police, *biswedars*, their *goondas* arrived there for settlement regarding the divisions of the land. But the peasants' gave tough resistance. The police

---

43. *The Daily Akali Patrika* (Jullundhur), July 11, 1949, 1.
44. *Report on Agrarian Reforms in Pepsu, op. cit.*, 10.
45. *Muzarian-Kisanan De Mittor Kaun,* Published by Tenant committee Pepsu (Ludhiana Civil and Military Press, May 1949), 40.
46. *The Tribune* (Ambala Cantt.), August 22, 1949.

did not succeed to arrest the warranted leaders of the peasants' movement.[47] It is to be kept in mind that the police action was not only confined to the villages mentioned in the foot note No. 47, but was extended to 50 more villages which were considered as the stronghold of the peasants' struggle. But they failed in their efforts to arrest the warranted leaders of the movement everywhere. Now, the peasants began to occupy the biswedars' land legally or illegally. Though the State Government warned against the illegal occupation of land, but could not stop them from doing so.[48] Instead, the occupation of land by the peasants gained momentum. Fearing danger to their lives, the *biswedars* left the villages and fled to the cities for shelter and safety.[49] A large number of *biswedars*, of course, willingly and unconditionally, surrendered their lands to the *Kisan Sabha*. Many others signed their lands in favour of the peasants. However, the police continued to harass the peasants as well as the communist workers. Many of them were implicated in false cases, making the peasants more determined against the Government which is vivid from their reaction.

A peasants' conference was held in the middle of 1951 at village Naiwala. While the Conference was in progress, the police arrested a prominent peasant leader Chanchal Singh Cabha, but the volunteers of the Conference saved him from

---

47. Vaid, Chhajju Mal, "Tenant Movement" in Master Hari Singh's *Punjab Peasant in Freedom Struggle*, New Delhi, 1934, 258 (According to S. Bachan Singh, in October, 1950, Bhagal Singh *Biswedar* of village Rakhara alongwith his thirty armed *goondas* attacked the village and looted the crops. Even the District *nazim* Raghbir Singh who being relative of the *biswedar* provided assistance against the tenants. So Bachan Singh was Ex-MLA of Pepsu and he told me this in person. (Village Naraingarh, Chanarthal, Birkhurd, Jassarwal, Moharsinghwala, Mullewala, Dhapai and Bakhara were the main villages where a tough resistance was given by the peasants).
48. *The Tribune* (Ambala Cantt.), October 27, 1950.
49. *Kishangarh a Peasant's Heroic Defence of His land,* Published by *Pepsu Kisan Sabha,* Bhatina (Sangrur, Mittal Printing Press) (nd), 49-50.

the clutches of the police. Thus, no amount of repression could crush a militant peasants' movement and pacify them.[50] At this time the Pepsu Congress Committee published its enquiry Committee report in connection with the police atrocities, especially in Kishangar, Najaura and Fategarh villages. This report sought the end of police repression at once or resignation of the Government.[51] Hence, the pressure of the political parties and the growing strength of the peasants' movement forced the Congress Government at the centre to appoint a Committee headed by C.S. Venkatachar[52] in May 1950 to examine the system of land tenure in Pepsu and to recommend such changes as might be essential to solve the peasants' problems.[53] Meanwhile, the Pepsu Tenancy (Temporary Provision) Act was promulgated in January 1952. This Act protected the tenants against expulsion from land.[54] Another Committee consisting of seven members of the Pepsu Assembly was appointed which was to submit its report within three months. It was headed by Dara Singh.[55] The findings of the two Agrarian Reforms Committees were in favour of the tenants. The local Congress leadership also favoured the cause of the peasants but the Government at the centre though committed to the abolition of *biswedari* system, was not prepared to harm its support base among the *biswedars* by accepting the recommendations of these committees. The central leadership was in favour of *Bhoodan* movement which urged the biswedars to voluntarily donate their land and avoid clashes with tenants. Inspired by this movement, Raja Harpal Singh of Bhadaur, one of the biggest and known *biswedar* of Pepsu, transferred the proprietary rights over his 5000 acres of land to his tenants without any

50. Vaid, Chhajju Mal, "Tenant Movement in Master Hari Singh's *Punjab Peasant in Freedom Struggle*, New Delhi, 1984, 260.
51. *The Daily Akali Patrika* (Jullundhur), November 10, 1951, 2.
52. C.S. Venkatachar was a ICS—Regional Commissioner and Advisor, Rajasthan in May, 1950.
53. *The Tribune*, May 12, 1950.
54. *The Hindustan Times* (New Delhi), January 3, 1952, 2.
55. *The Pepsu Legislative Assembly Debates* : Official Report, Vol. I, Sr. No. 4, May 8, 1952, 143.

compensation.[56] He also urged other *biswedars* to follow in his footsteps.

In the Kisan Sabha meeting held on May 23, 1952 at Mansa,[57] the State Revenue Minister Tara Singh exhorted the *biswedars* to transfer their lands to the occupancy tenants without any compensation. The appeal had a desired effect. *Biswedars* of different areas in Pepsu transferred about 85,200 *acres* of land to their tenants without compensation.[58] For instance, one *biswedar* of Talwandi Sabo-Shamsher Singh Sidhu transferred 26,000 *bighas* of land without any compensation. Also the *biswedars* of villages Kahangarh, Kishangarh Pharwahi and Mal Singhwala announced the transfer of their lands to tenants without any compensation. The *biswedars* of Talwandi Sabo, Khatriwala, Kharaksinghwala, Gobindpura, etc. also surrendered their claims on about 55,000 acres of land.[59]

After the ouster of the Congress Ministry headed by Col. Raghubir Singh, the Akali United Front Ministry headed by Gian Singh Rarewala, was set up. It had in the election manifesto, announced the twenty-four point programme.[60] Among them the following points relate to the tenants' problems : *(a)* abolition of *biswedari* and *jagirdari*; and transfer of land to the landless cultivators; *(b)* immediate solution of the tenancy problem and stopping of ejectment of the tenants; and *(c)* fixation of uniform rate of land revenue and *abiana* (water-rate).

---

56. *The Tribune*, March 24, 1952, 6.
57. This meeting was presided over by Jagir Singh Joga and a large number of biswedars had been invited so that they could be persuaded.
58. *Jagbani* (Jullundhur), July 17, 1984 (see an article by Sarwan Singh Bir.).
59. Gupta, C.L. 'Bhatinda the Storm Centre of People's Movement' in 21st National Conference, All India *Kisan Sabha*, Bhatinda, Souvenir, 1973, 35.
60. *The Tribune*, April 9, 1952.

But the Ministry did not bother about the implementation of these points. As a result, the situation continued to be explosive. There were news of clashes between the tenants and the *biswedars* is Sangrur and Bhatinda districts over the possession of land. Two *biswedars* were slain in a tenant—*biswedar* clash at Kanwala, a village near Sangrur. For *muzaras* of village Nanakpura were seriously injured. The Working Committee of the Pepsu Congress Party discussed the situation arising out of these clashes. The Committee through a resolution urged the Government to convene a special session of the Pepsu Assembly to discuss and review the "critical agrarian as well as law and order situation in the State.[61] Harbans Lal, the President of Pepsu State Congress moved a resolution, for the removal of police posts in forty villages, in the Pepsu State Assembly. He alleged that the United Front Government was helping the *biswedars* and had created terror and panic in the villages. He levelled a serious charge that the Government was deliberately curbing the strength of peasants to keep them out of power.[62] After a lengthy debate, it was decided to withdraw police posts but warning the peasants to desist from forcibly occupying *biswedars* lands. In case they did not desist, a firm action would be taken against them. The Government press note vividly displays vaccilation instead its determination to implement land reform. It was declared policy of the then Government to abolish *biswedari* and make the tiller of soil owner. Steps were being taken to implement this policy. Law had already been enacted to prevent the eviction of tenants who paid rent regularly.[63] The Agrarian Reform Committee, appointed in May 1952, submitted its report in June, 1952 recommending :[64]

(a) That the benefits of the biswedari abolition legislation should be extended to those occupancy tenants who

---

61. *The Statemsman* (New Delhi), July 1, 1952, 1.
62. *Pepsu Legislative Assembly Debates,* Vol. I, S. No. 3, May 6, 1952, 85.
63. *The Tribune,* June 4, 1952, 3.
64. *Report on Ag1arian Reforms in Pepsu, op. cit.,* 40.

held these on March 11,1940 and were dispossessed for non-payment of amounts decreed against them;

(b) that the legislation should provide for vesting of proprietary rights in occupancy tenants with a suitable procedure for the payment of compensation; and

(c) that the amount of compensation due to a *biswedar* should not include arrears of rent.

The Agrarian Reform Committee also pointed out that "Whatever may be the justification for large and well managed individual farms, a system in which a substantial proportion of the rural population is without land or subsists on very small and uneconomic holdings is no longer tenable.[65]

The Central Government had realised the gravity of the situation caused by the peasants' movement. It desired to establish peace in the Pepsu region. To control the peasants' movement and appease the peasants Dr. Kailsh Nath Katju, the Union Home Minister paid personal visit to the disturbed villages to asses the situation and to conduct an on the spot enquiry into the strained relations between the peasants and the *biswedars*.[66] The Home Minister's visit to villages Akharpura, Bijalpur, Land Benjara, Bakhera in Sangruru district and Kahangarh and Kishangarh in district Bhatinda, itself vividly displays the gravity of the situation caused by the peasants' struggle as well as the desire of the Central Government to maintain peace and order in the region. The dialogue between the Home Minister and the peasant leaders indicate that the Government's immediate aim was to persuade the peasants who had forcibly occupied the *biswedars'* land to pay the land revenue to the Government. The peasants agreed to pay the land revenue on the condition that the land for which they would pay revenue should be shown in their names in the official records. They also wanted the police posts set up in Kisangarh for the last 15 years to be removed. Addressing the

65. *Ibid.*, 31-39; *The Statesman*, June 30, 1952, 5.
66. *Report on Agrarian Reforms in Pepsu, op. cit*, 34.

peasants, Dr. Katju made the following statement which displays his regret and anguish over the response of the peasants to his proposal. This was a unique care in the whole of the country where land revenue was not being paid and so it was a great injustice to the country,[67] he observed.

As a result of the Home Minister's personal visit, the Agrarian Bills based on the recommendation of the two Agrarian Reform Committees, were introduced in the State Assembly in the summer session of 1952. For the first time, a tenancy legislation favourable to the peasants was under active consideration of the Ministry of which Communist party of India was a constituent. Thus, the effort of the Government brought about a change in the attitude of the peasants and consequently the movement began to be quite mild which, of course, was one of the causes leading to the dissolution of the Lal Communist Party led by Teja Singh Swatantar. Its members began to return to the parent Communist Party.[68] With this the violent phase of the peasants' struggle came to an end for the time being.

Going back to the question of peasants' struggle, we may observe that Kishangarh had become the symbol of the state—wide struggle between the tenants and *biswedars*. However, there were other centres of the peasants struggle. These villages[69] belonged to Sangrur, Barnala and Bhatinda districts. The nature and the tone of the peasant movements in these centres were similar to that of Kishangarh. It gives the impression that the peasant movements were highly organized

---

67. *The Tribune*, September 1, 1952, 8.
68. *The Tribune*, August 4, 1952, 3.
69. (Some of the important villages were—Qilla Hakiman, Rajomajra, Bhadaur, Kotduna, Rampur, Jaodan, Dalelsinghwala, Naiwala, Kahangarh, Qasaiwala, Talwandi Sabo, Khatriwala, Kharaksinghwala, Bakshiwala, Kanwala, Nanakpur, Bijalpur, Karamgarh, etc. etc.) For more details see PSR, P.M.'s office File Nos. 6157 and 10189—*Ijlas-i-khas*, File Nos. 1261 and 2077, PSA, Patiala.

and politically motivated; and the motivating force in these movements was the Lal Communist Party. In other words, this Party was playing an active role at the back of these movements.

The peasants' movement was in its infancy during the late 1930s but it had matured into an organized struggle with proper leadership following. The prospectus of its success can be gauzed from this previous results and the response which it got from the Government. Before making an estimate of its history and success from 1952 to 1956, let us analyse the demands of the peasants. Their demands can be divided into the following sections :

1. The peasants were original owners of land but they were deprived of their rights by the *biswedars*. So abolition of *biswedari* and *batai* system were the main demands of the tenants ever since the peasants' struggle came into being;

2. The demands of proprietary rights for occupancy tenants without compensation and occupancy rights for the tenants-at-will restoration o land from which tenants had been expelled and distribution of surplus land among the landless cultivators, were natural corollaries of demand for the abolition of the *biswedari* system; the *biswedars* had been misusing the *beers* (forests) and *banger* (waste-land) land for hunting at the cost of community interest. The peasants demanded the declaration of such land as *shamlat*.

3. Some demands were of punitive or curative nature. These included demands, such as preventing the *biswedars* from ejecting peasants from land, cancellation of arrears of rent claimed by fraudulent means, punishment of quality landlords and officials, realization of land revenue directly by the *tehsil* authorities, release of persons convicted in connection with the current peasants' movement and withdrawal of cases against them; and lastly, the removal of punitive police posts from Kishangarh and other villages.

It will not be out of place if we state the fact that from the very beginning of the peasants' movement to the year 1948, when Pepsu was formed a large number of demands of the peasants got accumulated. The references to these demands were made in pamphlets, memorandum, petitions and resolutions. Most of them we can have in the Punjab States records, Prime Minister's office files and *Ijlas-i-khas,* the *Kisan Sabha* publications and several newspapers.[70] Number of these demands e have cited above.

Instead of sympathising with the peasants for their genuine grievances and demands, the State Government considered the peasants struggle, as a law and order problem. The Congress Government at the centre was in favour of granting the rights of the peasants but it did not like the presence of the radical communists in the peasants' movement. So it desired to suppress the peasants' movement. It was intended to do so because the Congress Government was not prepared to show the signs of weakness in its stand and in the process live credit to the Communists. It may be believed, such a policy would have encouraged the Communists to launch such struggle in other regions. Unable to suppress the popular and powerful peasants' struggle by force,[71] Rarewala Ministry was dissolved and President's rule was imposed on the state in March 1953.[72]

---

70. PSR, PM's office File Nos. 10189 and 5304; *Ijlas-i-khas* File No. 2077—*Patiala De Muzarian De Ghol Ten Tuhada Farz,* published by Secretary Muzara Committee, Riyasat Patiala (Lahore : 1947), and Hindustan Times (New Delhi), November 15, 1952, 4.
71. During this period, there was a genuine problem of law and order which had been created by the free booters and adventurers who resorted to loot and day light plunder. From the press reports one can gather the idea that there were large number of such gangs of dacoits who had created insecurity of life and property in this region. Incidentaly these docoits were popular among the poor peasants and a large number of folk songs were sung in their praise which we can have even today.
72. *'Election Menifesto of the Pepsu Communist Party'* Awami Printing Press, Jullundhur, 1954, 6.

P.S. Rau, adviser to the *Rajpramukh,* was sent to crush the peasants' agitation ruthlessly. CRPF was called to help the revenue officials in realizing land revenue from the tenants. Now, the police helped the *biswedars* in expelling the tenants from land. Also, tenants leaders were arrested and were involved in false cases. Consequently, the non-cooperative and non-payment tendency of the defaulters, slowly declined and the standing arrears began to be cleared village by village.[73] It is estimated that during the first six month of the President rule approximately sixty five lakhs rupees were recovered.[74] Even the police punitive posts were set up at several places, at the cost of the villages[75] for the purpose of collection of land revenue but of no use. Out of Rs. 277 lacs the arrears of these posts due to tenants, the New Government realized the arrears of Rs. 1.24 lacs during this period.[76]

The adviser to the *Rajpramukh,* P.S. Rau paid a visit to Sangrur and Bhatinda districts and met the representatives of both the tenants and the *biswedars.* Here the peasants' problem was acute because the relations between the *biswedars* and the tenants had been strained. Tne adviser formed a three fold policy : *(i)* He wanted to do away with lawlessness in the state and he succeeded in it; *(ii)* He decided to recover the arrears despite the suggestion of the Rarewala Government to waive off the arrears of rent and that the opposition of some political parties had also sternly opposed; *(iii)* He decided and planned to introduce an agrarian reforms. Despite the fact that the Dara

73. *President Rule in Pepsu* (March 1953 to March 1954), published by the Pepsu Government, 33-35.
74. *What the President Has Done For Pepsu During the Six Months (March-August, 1953),* published by Pepsu Government, 1953, 10.
75. The Previous Governments had set up punitive Police Posts in villages—dipalpura, Mirza Goomti Kalan, Phoal, Ghanas, Pakha, Mehta, Daula, Rookekhurd, Rooke Kalan, Dirbha, Moonak, Bareta, Boha, Tamkat, Balian, Kumberwal, Naiwala, Katera, Karianwala, Bhunder, Chawke, Ritho, Ballo, Bheni, Jaseajulana and Safidon.
76. *What President Rule Has Done For Pepsu, op. cit.,* 11.

Singh Committee had suggested to waive of the arrears of rent and that almost all the opposition parties had very strongly opposed, the Government's adviser Mr. Rau insisted on the collection of rent arrears.[77]

It is worth noting that in this region, Sangrur and Bhatinda were the main districts where the problem was most serious as far decades the relations between the *biswedars* and *muzaras* had been strained.[78]

The peasantry had been crying for reforms. Despite all the fall talk and assurances from the Government, thousands of tenants' families were in danger of being expelled from land which they had been cultivating for generations. The problem assumed an alarming dimensions as the *biswedars* ejected the tenants-at-will from their land on the excuse of self-cultivation by mechanized farming. So was the fate of the occupancy tenants. Thousands of tenants were served with notice of ejectment. But in most of the tenancy villages, the occupancy tenants did not want to part with even a bigha of land or pay any share of the produce to *biswedars.*[79]

Besides, the issue of the peasants in Pepsu attracted the countrywide attention because of the imposition of the

77. *Hindustan Times* (New Delhi), June 15, 1953 (See Pepsu News letter in which the following social and political implications of collection of arrears of rent were mainly putword : *(a)* The tenants have not been saving this amount and the burden will fall on their earnings; *(b)* In the absence of savings, they will be forced to borrow. This will lead the tenants in the claches of the Sahukars (Money lenders); *(c)* Out of court Settlement of these decrees with the aid of pro-*biswedars* police and the revenue department is likely to encourage corruption in the field staff and will adversely affect the tennats; *(d)* Payment of arrears will imply exporting capital out of rural areas and impoverishment the agrarian economy; *(e)* He may lead to the growth of democratic forces and continuation of exploitation, instability and intrigue in the local politics; and *(f)* There is danger of the Reforms being.
78. *Hindustan Standard* (Delhi), April 14, 1953.
79. *Times of India* (Delhi), April 20, 1953.

President's rule. Three members of Parliament visited the Pepsu State. They criticized the adviser's regime for adopting wrong methods and alleged that the State was suppressing the peasants and helping the biswedars in ejecting tenants on a large scale. They urged that the legislation should be introduced in the state at once for the stoppage of eviction and abolition of *biswedari* system.[80] The tenants of village Kartarsinghwala near Bhatinda complained about police excesses in forcing them to pay batai to their *biswedars* and land revenue arrears for the last 7 years in one instalment only, which were not wholly due from them.[81] N.P. Rao, the General Secretary, All India *Kisan Sabha* equated the President rule in the state with the "Police Raj". He said, "The Pepsu tenants want only what is their due and nothing more."[82] He clarified that the tenants of Pepsu state had never refused to pay land revenue. They merely demanded the recognition of their proprietary rights in land. He also protested against the large scale of ejectments.

Meanwhile, three important acts were, however, passed and promulgated during the President's rule in the state in order to reform the existing tenancy laws in the State. The Pepsu Abolition of Ala Malkiat Rights Act, 1953 raised inferior proprietors to the status of full proprietors. The Pepsu Occupancy-Tenants (Vesting of proprietary rights) Act gave full proprietary rights to the Occupancy tenants. The third act *i.e.,* the Pepsu Tenancy and Agricultural Lands Act, 1953 raised the status of tenants-at-will to that of full proprietors. The permissible limit for personal cultivators was fixed at one-half of the area owned by the landlord subject to a maximum of thirty standard *acres* and a minimum of ten standard acres.[83] The Communists, however, were not happy at the new agrarian legislation. They did not want that the *biswedars* should be paid compensation for the land confiscated from them. But

80. *The Tribune,* May 22, 1953.
81. *The Statesman* (New Delhi), May 23, 1953.
82. *Hindustan Times* (New Delhi), June 10, 1953.
83. *President Rule in Pepsu, op. cit,* 4-5 (For more details regarding tenancy acts see next Chapter).

according to the constitution, compensation had to be included in the legislation,[84] observed the State Government.

The Communists instigated the peasants to resort to agitation. In view of the continued activities of the Communists, the President rule in Pepsu launched another full scale police offensive against the peasants' struggle. The police arrested some top *Kisan* leaders and issued warrants against many others. Police punitive posts were set up in many villages, such as Baroda, Ghamo, Jhaloor, Kalait, Bhartana, Shawlar Kalan, Nidana, Kalwa, Danauda Kalan and Nagra, the centre of tenants's movement. The Press reported cases of police high handedness and cruelty perpetrated on tenants in several villages.[85]

After one year of dissolution of the State Assembly and the President rule, the mid-term poll were constitutionally due in March, 1954, and actually were held at the same time. On the eve of these elections, the political situation in the state underwent a change as new political alignment began to emerge. The princes and the *biswedars* joined the Congress enblock leaving the Akalis in wilderness. Giani Kartar Singh, the Chief of the Akalis had declared his party's desire to compromise with all non-Congress parties to defeat the Congress. The leftist parties were no less bitter than the right wing Akalis. The Communists and the left-wing of the Akalis had an agreement with Haryana *Praja Mandal* and Forward Bloc formed a Democratic front.[86] The front drew most of its strength from the tenancy area. Divided as the opposition parties were they could not form a common front against the Congress. The Congress party, therefore, won the mid-term

---

84. *All India Kisan Sabha Bulletin*, Vol. I, Nos. 3 and 5, September and December, 1952 and Vol. II, Nos. 1 and 2, January and February, 1953; also Personal interview of Late Brish Bhan, in May 1980.
85. *Biltz*, News Magazine (Bombay), October 17, 1953.
86. *The Statesman* (New Delhi), January 15, 1954, 1.

elections with thumping majority in Pepsu State Assembly.[87] Led by Col. Raghubir Singh who was later succeeded by Brish Bhan after the former's death on January 7, 1955, the newly formed Government was influenced and dominated by the *biswedars.* So they continued to evict the peasants by virtue of one of the provisions of the Pepsu Tenancy and Agricultural Lands Act, 1953. It is to be remembered that the *biswedars* were able to blunt the edges of the agrarian legislation of 1953. They also insisted on the payment of compensation and arrears of rent. This Act was to be operative after June 2, 1954 giving adequate right to the *biswedars* to evict the *muzaras* and secure *benami* holdings. So a large number of tenants were evicted, and police repression was resorted to. The *biswedars* of Rajgarh, sub-*Tehsil* Samana was formed to have made entries in revenue records about the tenure of land under the tenants. This was detected by the Patiala Deputy Commissioner. To substantiate, in 16 cases the land under the tenants was shown, by the patwari in revenue records, as land under self-cultivation of biswedars.[88] It was reported by the press that a large scale *benami* transfers took place before the enactment of the Pepsu Tenancy and Agricultural Act of 1953. Though the President signed it on November 16, 1953, it was gazetted on December 3,1953. The 15 days delay was stated to have cleverly used by the *biswedars* to transfer their lands to their close relatives, thus multiplied many times the 30 *acres* permitted for self cultivation.[89]

The postponement of this Act for a year after June 2, 1954 led to more exploitation and ejectments of tenants on the plea of reservation of land for self-cultivation.[90] The State Government's policy of vaccilation led to the renewal of peasants' movement. About 700 peasants of the *Kisan Sabha* staged a demonstration of protest at Patiala. This demonstration was led by Harnam Singh Dharamgarhia. Their main slogans were 'release detainee M.L.As', 'stop ejectment of tenants, and

87. The Party position was—Congress : 37; Right Wing Akalis : 10; Left Wing Akalis : 2; Communists : 4; and Independent : 7.

88. *The Tribune,* June 3, 1954.

89. *Statesman* (New Delhi), June 4, 1954.

90. *Statesman* (New Delhi), August 21, 1954.

ldown with police repression.[91] The State *Kisan Sabha* in its annual conference condemned the postponement of agrarian reforms and reviewed the deteriorating agrarian situation resulting in large scale ejectment.[92] It is important to state that hundreds of delegates representing 30,000 peasants attended this conference. Moreover, as the All India *Kisan Sabha* was dominated by the Communists, Mr. N. Parshada Rao, the General Secretary of the Communist Party and member of Parliament very actively took part in the *Kisan Sabha* activities. Mr. Rao appealed to the State Government to immediately stop eviction of tenants under any pretext and to reduce the compensation amount to be paid by the tenants-at-will.[93]

As the opposition of the tenants to the continued eviction from land by the *biswedars*, the State Government thought of adopting a piecemeal measures to satisfy them. In fact, its principal motive was to postpone the land reforms, the Congress Government got the Pepsu Agricultural Tenants (Temporary Protection and Disability) Bill passed in the face of strong opposition. The Act, as we can see from its title, was a temporary measure which was meant to maintain status-quo. Thus giving time to the *biswedars* for making efforts to pressurise the Government at centre for the removal of terms concerning ceiling of land. The Land Reforms Act was postponed on the plea that the State Government did not have proper data to formulate the reforms. The opposition parties thought that the Government had delayed the Act intentionally on baseless grounds. They argued that Dara Singh Committee Report has supplied sufficient data to the Government to formulate the reforms. Moreover, passing of the Pepsu Agricultural Tenants (Temporary Protection and Disability) Bill amounted to preventing the tenants from acquiring proprietary rights in their holdings by paying compensation.[94] The Pepsu

91. *The Tribune*, June 13, 1954, 6.
92. *The Tribune*, August 29, 1954.
93. *The Tribune*, October 12, 1954.
94. *Pepsu Vidhan Sabha Debates*, Vol. V.S. No. 4, December 20, 1954, 354-371.

Tenancy and Agricultural Lands Act was at last passed by the State Legislative Assembly on March 1, 1955. Now, occupancy tenants could acquire ownership rights by paying twelve times the land revenue and tenants-at-will by paying ninety times the land revenue.[95] The clauses relating to ceiling of land was kept pending for one year to enable the *biswedars* to retrieve their position by organizing and press-uprising the Congress Government. It was no secret that the ruling Congress party in Pepsu state was dominated by the *biswedars* who wanted to protect their own interests and made every effort to achieve it. The *biswedars* organized themselves. They demonstrated against the land ceiling Bill of thirty *acres* of land. This Bill was lying pending before the Pepsu Assembly. On such demonstration of *biswedars,* led by Raja Maheshinder Singh Congress M.L.A. from Bhatinda was held against the Land Ceiling Bill. The *biswedars* also decided to send a deputation against this bill to Delhi to represent their case with the Prime Minister—Jawaharlal Nehru.[96]

The Pepsu Vidhan Sabha, at last, passed the Pepsu Tenancy and Agricultural Land Act, 1956. Accordingly land ceiling on individual holdings at thirty standard *acres* was imposed. Thus, Pepsu became the first State in India where ceiling was imposed.[97]

The peasants' struggle in Pepsu State aimed at abolishing of *biswedari* and grant of proprietary rights to the peasants. Though it acquired political orientation, especially, in the sphere of programme, action and strategy from the Communists party in its true nature and contents; but basically it was a movement with economic interests of peasants in mind. The struggle attracted and inspired different categories of tenants such as occupancy tenants, tenants-at-will, etc. The political parties such as, the Congress, the Akali and the Communists were not openly

95. *Pepsu Vidhan Sabha Debates,* Official Report, Vol. VI, S. No. 6, March 1, 1955.
96. *The Tribune,* September 22, 1956.
97. *The Tribune,* October 11, 1956.

hostile to the cause of the tenants. They all supported the movement. From 1948 to 1952, the peasants' movement was militant in its posture and action. When the Government declared the policy of abolishing *biswedari,* the movement became mild in its line of action. Despite this declared policy of the Government, it took more than three years for the State Government to adopt a definite policy of land reforms. The delay was caused by an unholy alliance between the Congress and the *biswedars.* They could not undo the policy of abolition of the *biswedari* and feudalism. But they modified the reforms because the tenants could not acquire land without compensation. Moreover, they shielded the *biswedars'* interests by clandestine and foul means like *benami.*

8 REFORMIST POLICY : TENANCY LEGISLATION

The tenancy relation in the East Punjab States were similar to those in the Punjab. In both the regions, most of the owners of land were also cultivators, popularly known as *khudkashtkar* (self cultivators). The revenue administration in both Pepsu and Punjab was prejudiced in favour of land-owners and also the *biswedars.* The owners of the land occupied about 67% of the total area of the East Punjab States. The occupancy tenants, tenants-at-will, lessees and mortgagees were the principal tenure holders.[1] The areas under these classes of cultivators are shown in the table given below : [2]

Table : Pattern of Land Relations in East Punjab States

Class of Tenure	*Total Area Acres*	*Percentage*	*Cultivated Area Acres*	*%age*
Owner including State	40,29,036	63	27,60,936	58
Occupancy tenants	6,37,331	10	6,21,501	12
Special Tenants	77,941	1	75,971	2
Tenants-at-will	10,06,532	17	10,11,393	20
Lessees	1,45,930	2	1,29,776	3
Mortgagees	4,09,869	7	3,84,901	8
Total	63,46,633	100	69,84,406	100

1. G.D. Patel, *The Indian Land Problem and Legislation,* Bombay; N.M. Tripathi, Ltd. Law Publishers, 1954, 322; *Report on Agrarian Reform in Pepsu,* Government of India, Ministry of State, 1952, 5 (for more details see statistical tables Appendix 8 to 11).
2. *Report on Agrarian Reforms in Pepsu, op. cit.*

The following conclusion may be drawn from the above table. 45% (22,23,470 *acres*) of the total area cultivated land was owned by the peasants having no proprietary rights in land. The largest amount of land *i.e.,* 10,11,333 *acres* was cultivated by the tenants-at-will while the occupancy tenants cultivated 6,21,501 *acres* of land. Both kinds of tenants cultivated one third of the total cultivable land. By 1952, 8% of the total cultivable land was under mortgages. From the total area of the tenure holders and the tenants-at-will, along with cultivators as lesses and mortgages, it may be deduced that the issue of tenancy rights was very confusing. Subsequently, it agitated the minds of the legislators as well as the cultivators.

The relations between the landlords and occupancy-tenants as reported by the Venkatachar Committee[3] were strained[4] because many cultivators who claimed to having proprietary rights in the past were under the *biswedari* system recorded as occupancy tenants or tenants-at-will in the records. In the interest of such tenants the Patiala state issued the *farman-i-shahi* (Royal Ordinances), according to which the land was to be divided between the *biswedars* (landlords) and occupancy tenants on the following terms :

(1) In case of the occupancy held under section 5 of the Punjab Tenancy Act of 1887[5], it was provided that one-third share would be granted to the landlords and two-third share to the tenants; (2) In case of the occupancy held under sections 6 and 7 it was provided that two-fifth share would be given to the landlords and three-fifth to the tenants;[6] and (3) The land so divided was to be held in full ownership by the landlords

---

3. The Venkatachar Committee was constituted in 1950 to investigate into the agrarian problems of the Pepsu; particularly problems related to the above mentioned category of tenants.
4. *Report of Agrarian Reforms in Pepsu, op. cit.*
5. For details see *The Punjab Tenancy Act of 1887,* Printed at the *Wazir-i-Hind* Gas Press, Amritsar, 1907, Third edition, PSA, Patiala.
6. For more details relating to sections 6 and 7, see *Ibid.*

and tenants with corresponding rights in *shamlat deh* (The common land of the village). The state regarded this *farman-i-shahi* in connection with the partition of land as "the most fair and just settlement" of the problem.[7] Some newspapers also believed that it would put on end to the dispute between the *biswedars* and occupancy tenants[8] But the tenants were not satisfied with this decision. The *farman-i-shahi* had some loopholes. It treated all occupancy holdings equal and did not take into consideration changes in rent. The tenants paying nominal rents were supposed to sacrifice one third of their holdings. The condition that tenants would have to pay all the arrears of *batai* and other dues to the landlords, fixation of one third of the produce of the *biswedar* and payment of all that was due to the landlord was not acceptable to the tenants. Moreover, this legislation ignored the problem of tenants-at-will, instead it stated that the status of the tenants-at-will bear no comparison to that of the occupancy tenants.[9] The award of March, 1947 did not find favour with the *biswedars* either. They did not want to part with any part of land over which they had proprietary rights by virtue of their being *biswedars*. Thus both the parties were not interested in getting the *farman-i-shahi* implemented.

After the formation of Pepsu in August, 1948, the attempt of the new state Government to solve the tenant problem by implementing the *farman-i-shahi* by force[10] led to clashes between the police and the tenants. The heroic and brave struggle of the tenants at village Kishangarh[11] had created its history. It made the government realize the strength and will

7. *The Tribune* (Lahore), March 23,1947.
8. *Ibid., Report on Agrarian Reforms in Pepsu, op. cit.*, 10.
9. *Ijlas-i-Khas* File No. 2077, PSR: *Report on Agrarian Reforms in Pepsu, op. cit.*, PSA, Patiala, 10.
10. Help of Police and Revenue officials was taken in the implementation of the Royal Ordinance. *Vide, Report on Agrarian Reforms in Pepsu, op. cit.*, PSA, Patiala, 11-12.
11. Village Kishangarh was in District Barnala. Kishangarh : *The Peasants Heroic Defence of His Land* (Bhatinda : By Pepsu *Kisan Sabha*, Mittal Printing Press), 14 (nd.)

of the peasants to secure their rights. Now the Government was convinced that their problem could not be solved by force and no legislation could be enforced against their wishes. The Government, therefore, decided to introduce such reforms in the existing tenancy laws which could meet their demands to a reasonable extent. Subsequently, the Government issued an ordinance No. XIII on 15th August, 1949 to amend the law regarding abolition of occupancy tenants ad *biswedars.*[12] Accordingly the share of the latter was reduced from one third to one fourth of the holding and the share of the former was fixed at[13] three-fourth. Now, the tenants also got the right to purchase the *biswedar's* share. But this ordinance too remained ineffective as there was no committee to regulate the partition operations. So, this ordinance was further amended in 1950.[14] The amended notification (issued on 25th April, 1950) empowered the Government to control and direct the operation of division of land. The limits of one third and three-fourth of the Land holdings in the case of *biswedars* and occupancy tenants respectively was subject to change. According to this amendment ordinance, the tenants who paid to the *biswedars* nothing more than land revenue and the rates and cases was entitle to the complete holding. The purchase price of the landowner's share was fixed at 100 times the land revenue.[15] The occupancy tenants who had been ejected from their and during the 7 years preceding the March 11, 1947, the date of the issuances of *farman-i-shahi,* were asked to deposit compensation for the *biswedar's* share and obtain proprietary

---

12. *Patiala and East Punjab States Union Government Gazette,* published by Authority, August 15,1949, 590-598. See also minority of States Government India, File No. 3(39) P/49, NAI, New Delhi (for further details see Appendix-VIII).
13. *The Pepsu Code of Laws,* Vol. II, Bhupindra State Press, Patiala, 1951, 305.
14. *Ibid.*
15. *Patiala and East Punjab State Union Government Gazette,* 1950, 171-174; *Report on Agrarian Reforms in Pepsu, op. cit.,* 10-11 (For further detail see Appendix-IX), PSA, Patiala.

rights over their holdings. The ordinance was implemented fully where the problem of occupancy tenants was not serious, but in the Bhatinda district the problem was acute.[16] Thus this new tenancy legislation also d'd not Satisfy the demands of the tenants. Conscious of their past strength as well as influenced by the progressive leadership, they rejected the legislation and opposed its implementation. Now they began to occupy the *biswedars'* lands forcibly. As a result, the Government threatened to take action against these intruders.[17]

The Union Government was alarmed at the increasing strength of the peasants' movement backed by the Communists. At the suggestion of the Pepsu Government, the Central Government decided to appoint a Committee constituting of 4 members,[18] with the following terms[19] of references :

(a) To examine the existing tenancy relationship (other than the rights of occupancy) in land in the Patiala and East Punjab State Union and to purpose such changes in the as may be necessary;

(b) To examine the existing system of land tenure in Patiala and East Punjab States Union; and

(c) To propose such changes as in it may be necessary, keeping in view the requirements of the agricultural economy and welfare of the different sections of the rural population.

---

16. *Patiala and East Punjab States Union Government Gazette,* 1950, 593.
17. *The Tribune* (Ambala Cantt.), October 17, 1950.
18. C.S. Venkatachar, I.C.S., Regional Commissioner and Advisor, Rajasthan (Chairman); Tarlok Singh, ICS, Deputy Secretary to Planning Commission (Member); J.N. Shrinagesh, ICS, (Commissioner Jullundhur (Member); and Rajbir Singh Kang (Secretary) were the members of the Committee.
19. *Government of India Ministry of States,* Letter No. 53 (39) 4/49, dated may 11,1950, published in *Patiala and East Punjab States Union Government Gazette,* July 23, 1950, 513; *Ministry of States,* Government of India, File No. 3(39)-P/49, NAI, New Delhi.

In 1952, Venkatachar Committee recommended that the provisions of the Punjab Occupancy Tenants (Vesting of Proprietary rights) Act, 1957 should be followed and those tenants should be made proprietors on payment of compensation to the *biswedars.*[20] The tenants of former Faridkot, Kapurthala and Malerkotla States paid rent in cash and were not liable to ejectment like the tenants-at-will. In Faridkot state there were five classes of tenants [21] and they paid rents at different rates. In the former Malerkotla State tenants described as *dakhilkara* had rights equal to those of occupancy rights. The *nawab* and the collaterals were entered in the records either as *khawanins* or as *biswedars.* Out of every hundred rupees received from the *dakhilkara* the *biswedar* got seventy six rupees and the balance was credited to the Government. In 9 villages, over an area of 2,483 acres, a class of tenants known as *muzarian maurusi* were shown under *dakhilkars* but rent was payable to the *dakhilkara* by muzarian maurusi. By Notification of April 28, 1951, the Pepsu Government announced that the holders of these tenancies should be deemed to be occupancy tenants under section 8 of the Punjab tenancy Act, 1887.[22] The Committee recommended that the proprietory rights should be conferred on such tenants without any payment of compensation.

The different categories of tenants[23] under special tenures in Kapurthala State were made occupancy tenants under the above Pepsu Government notification of April 28, 1951. However, the committee made no special recommendations for these tenants because government had already given

---

20. *Report on Agrarian Reforms in Pepsu, op. cit.,* 11.
21. *Muzarian-i-Shartiya, Muzarian Chakotedaran Khas, Muzarian Tabe Merzi Malik, Muzarian Bila Taivan, Chakote daran Nautor* were there (for meaning see glossary).
22. Government of Patiala and East Punjab States Union, Revenue Department Notification No. 8-B, dated Patiala, the 28th April, 1951 (For detail see Appendix-4).
23. *Muzarian-i-Darbandi, Muzarian-i-Bardashat Sabak, Muzarian-i-Jadid* and *Muzarian-i-Bashara* were the main kinds of tenants.

occupancy rights to them.[24] The former rulers of Faridkot and Nalagarh had special rights in their villages. The State Government conferred proprietary rights on the *adna-malik* (inferior landowners) of the these States by a Notification of June 7,1951. As regards the abolition of *ala mal-kiat* (superior rights) the Committee recommended its abolition as well as the *talukdar* Act of 1951 and subsequently the *adna-maliks* (interior owners) were to be made proprietors on payment of compensation equal to eight times the amount of rent or other dues to the *biswedars*.[25]

Obviously, the problem of the tenants-at-will was quite complex. Though out of the total area of 63,46,639 *acres*, 10,46,532 *acres* were held by them, the Pepsu Government like the Punjab Government, was late in enacting legislation for their protection. But now because of the enactment of the tenancy reforms in other states, the issue of the tenancy reforms had become most urgent. The quasi-permanent allotments of land to the displaced owners of land from the West Punjab was not less responsible for their urgency. Subsequently, in connection with tenancy reforms. Venkatachar Committee made the following suggestions :

(a) That the limit for personal cultivation should be fixed at hundred *acres* in accordance with the recent legislation in the Punjab;

(b) That action should be taken to ensure cultivation of land under the State fallow Lands Act or any appropriate legislations;

(c) That the term of tenants-at-will should be five years;

---

24. *Report on Agrarian Reforms in Pepsu, op. cit.,* 11 (For more details see also Appendix-X), PSA, Patiala.
25. Government of Patiala and East Punjab States Union, Revenue Department Notification No. 14 (17)-B/51-132, dated Patiala, the 7th June, 1951 (For further details see also Appendix-XI and XII), NAI, New Delhi.

(d) The tenants who had cultivated lands continuously under the same *biswedar* from a date prior to May 1,1940 should be declared protected tenants; and

(e) That the maximum rent payable by a tenant should not exceed one-third of the crop on the value thereof.

It is to be noticed that in making these recommendations. The committee was guided by the provisions of the Punjab and Bombay Tenancy legislation. However, the committee came to the conclusion that the recommended measures by themselves offered an adequate solution of the weaknesses of the rural economy.[26]

The Congress Government in Pepsu resigned one month after its formation on March 19, 1952.[27] Now, Giani Gian Singh Rarewala formed a United Front Ministry (with the Akalis, the *Praja Mandal* and the Communists), on April 22, 1952. This ministry appointed another Committee of 7 members in 1952, headed by Dara Singh, MLA.[28] This Committee was to submit its report within a period of three months. The terms of reference of Committee were as under :

(i) How to bring about a coincidence between the ownership of cultivation;

(ii) What should be maximum or minimum limits to the size of holdings and units of self cultivation;

(iii) What should be the solution of the financial implications of the proposals in the first term of reference; and

---

26. *Ibid.*, 29.
27. S.Raghbir Singh headed the Congress Government Vide., *The Tribune* March 5,1952.
28. The other members of this Committee were S. Gurdial Singh, S. Sunder Singh, S. Gurbhajnik Singh, S. Bachan Singh, S. Pritam Singh Sidhu, and S. Sampuran Singh Dhaula. The Secretary of the Committee was the Revenue Secretary. Vide., *The Pepsu Legislative Assembly Debates, Official Report,* Vols. No. 4, May 8, 1952, 143; See also a *Ministry of States,* File No. 17(10) PA/32, *op. cit.*

(iv) What type of protection should be provided to tenants-at will during the termination period.

What was the need of instituting this committee when the Venkatachar Committee was busy in preparing its report. It can be deduced that there was no major difference in the terms of reference of the two committees. True it is, this Committee was a Supplementary Committee and it differed from the Venkatachar Committee on the following points :

(a) The members of the former committee were from outside the State except the Secretary;

(b) They all were administrators, whereas the members of the former committee were political persons and having perhaps better knowledge of the problem;

(c) It may be persumed that the United Front Ministry perhaps had no confidence in the former Committee appointed by the Central Government;

(d) The Dara Singh Committee was instituted comprising persons elected by the peasants and having their confidence.

The Pepsu Legislative Assembly passed a non-official resolution sponsored by the Congress party urging the Government to immediately abolish *biswedari* system[29] in States. The Venkatachar Committee had submitted its report in June, 1952, with recommendation which have been mentioned above. The Dara Singh Committee also submitted its report within the stipulated period of 3 months with the following recommendations :

(a) That the land should belong to the tiller and not to the absentee *biswedar*;

(b) That the maximum and minimum Units of Land, which a tiller should possess, be fixed; and

29. *The Pepsu Legislative Assembly Debates,* May 8, 1952, 189, PSA, Patiala.

(c) That the compensation if any to be fixed for acquiring proprietary rights should be minimum possible so that abolition of *biswedari* system could be effected without delay.

The Dara Committee pointed out in its report that there were 2,60,600 *acres* as disputed area, spread over 500 villages. It recommend that the best solution of the problem was to give proprietary rights to the tenants and pay compensation to the *biswedars.* This committee also recommend to waive of the rent arrears due to the *biswedars* in order to seek cooperation of the tenants regarding the proposed agrarian reforms. However, the Government turned down this suggestion of the Dara Committee.[30] However, on the basis of the recommendations of both these committees, the United Front Government prepared the following three bills[31] and introduced them in the State Assembly :

(i) The Pepsu Tenancy (Temporary Power) Bill, 1952;

(ii) The Pepsu Occupancy Tenants (Vesting of ownership) Bill, 1952; and

(iii) The Pepsu Agricultural Lands (limitation of ownership) Bill, 1952.

The first Bill sought to minimize the possibilities of ejectment of tenants and to fix a limit of maximum rent payable by the tenants-at-will. The tenants ejected after May 1, 1947 were eligible to claim the lands from which they had been ejected. The other two bills sought to settle the age-old agrarian disputes, which had been the main cause of law and order problem at the harvest time. The Pepsu Occupancy tenants (vesting of proprietary Rights) Act, 1952 provided the abolition

---

30. *Dara Singh Committee Report,* quoted in 'Tenant Struggle in Pepsu and the Communist Party', Souvenir, issued by the CPI (Jullundhur) Printing Press, 1976, 75; The Hindustan Times (New Delhi), September 20,1952,8.
31. *The Pepsu Report of the Administration* from April 1,1952 to March 31,1953, Published by Pepsu Government, 67.

of occupancy tenures and the vesting of proprietary rights in the occupancy tenants on the payment of compensation to the *biswedars* over an area of 2,60,000 *acres.*

The sudden adjournment 'sine die' of the Assembly session at the time when the discussion on the abolition of *ala malkiat* Rights Bill was in progress, brought the session to an abrupt end on November 25, 1952. However, the adjourned session was summoned on December 22, 1952; and the Pepsu Tenancy (Temporary Provisions) Amendment Bill, 1952 was adopted by the Legislative Assembly. The Bill on the abolition of *ala malkiat* was also passed. But in the mean time the State was placed under the President's Rule. The proposed Bills were, therefore, referred to the Ministry of States, Government of India, for being enacted as President's Acts.[32]

Though P.S.Rau, advisor to the *Rajpramukh* and administrator, during the President's Rule from March 1953 to March 1954, was determined to find a definite solution, yet the Government had to face two major difficulties. Firstly, *biswedars* numbering 37 filed petitions challenging the validity of the *biswedari* ordinance for the abolition of *biswedari* system in the States. Out of these only twenty petitions were admitted.[33] Though the Pepsu High Court held the main provision of the ordinance as constitutional, a part of it was declared null and void.[34] Due to the increasing pressure of the mighty lobby of the *biswedars* the Government adopted a rigid posture as it was not prepared to concede the demands of the tenants. Now

32. *The Tribune,* November 26, 1952, 1; Pepsu Legislative Assembly Debates, Vol. II, S. No. 5, December 22,1952, 420-421; The Pepsu Report of Administration, *op. cit.,* 68.
33. (The previous attempts to solve it had failed because they always came too late; and now the Government was not prepared to compromise with any group of the people that defied the law of the land) Vide., *The Tribune,* April 13, 1953; see also *President's Rule in Pepsu*: March 1953 to March 1954, Published by the Pepsu Government, 4.
34. *The Tribune,* May 10,1953 (For more details see the amended Act No. IV of 2007 BK, published in the *Pepsu Code of Laws* Vol. II, 301-374).

a terrible repression was again let loose against the tenants during the President's Rule. All sorts of repressive measures were adopted to terrorise the tenants. Consequently, their resistence broke down and the standing arrears began to be cleared[35] village by village.

After the tenants were forced to be helpless, the Government took up three Tenancy Bills which had been prepared by the United Front Government and introduced in the Legislative Assembly, but had not been passed as the Assembly was dissolved. The Bills are as under :

(i) The Pepsu Abolition of *ala malkiat* Rights Bill, 1953;

(ii) The Pepsu Tenancy and Agricultural Lands Bill, 1953;

(iii) The Pepsu Occupancy Tenants (Vesting of Proprietary Rights) Bill, 1953.

After being approved by the various bodies and securing the assent of the President of India these Acts were promulgated-the first two on August 18, 1953 and the third on the 6th December, 1953.[36] Now, the Pepsu Abolition of *ala malkiat* Act, 1953 removed *ala malkiat* rights and raised inferior proprietors to the status of full proprietors in about thirty six thousand *acres*.[37] Compensation to the ex-*ala maliks* was fixed at five times of the annual rent. It was claimed that the Act was fully implemented and all kinds of brokers were eliminated. From the day of its implementation, the gazette notification extinguished all the superior rights of *ala-maliks* and vested full rights in adna-maliks.[38]

The institution of *ala-malik* had come into existence with the collision of princely politics on agricultural economy. The

35. *President Rule in Pepsu, op. cit.,* 4-5 and 34-35.
36. *President Rule in Pepsu,* op. cit., 4-5; The Tribune, June 6, 1953.
37. *The Tribune,* June 6, 1953.
38. (For further details see *The Pepsu Abolition of Ala Malkiat* Rights Act, 1953, *Pepsu Government Gazettee,* September 12, 1953, 252-254).

original peasant proprietors were described as *adna-malik* or inferior landowners and the wealthy or influencial persons of the state-the malguzaras and aristocracy were called as *ala malik* or superior landowner.[39] These two categories of owners existed mostly in Kapurthala and Barnala districts. There existed different terms and conditions of payment of land revenue.[40] The condition of *the adna-malik* was quite miserable as thev had no rights on the lands lying in the villages but the *ala-maliks* enjoyed the rights of fauti-farari.[41]

To overcome the difficulties of the *adna-maliks,* the Abolotion of the *ala-maliks* rights Bill was passed in 1952 which sought to abolish the superior ownership and vest full ownership in the *adna-maliks* immediately. The compensation would be five times the annual dues payable to the *ala-maliks* or superior owners. However, the United Front Government agreed to reduce the compensation to a nominal rate of one *pie* for every rupee of annual rent payable on the land. But this compensation proposed by the United Front Ministry was too little, the Government felt. Hence the rate of five times the rent was restored. At this rate the compensation payable per *acre* was 9 *annas.* Thus the total compensation payable for over 36,000 *acres* was estimatd at Rs. 21,000.[42]

The second Act—the Pepsu Occupancy Tenants (Vesting of proprietary rights) Act., 1953 was meant to give full

39. 'Land to the tillers' (Patiala Directorate of Information and Public Relations, Pepsu : 1953), 13.
40. (Besides paying land revenue in 36,023 *acres* of land, the *adna-maliks* also paid a cess of 1½% to 10% of the land revenue. Over an area of 4000 *acres* their dues took the form of fixed payment in cash. On 5454 *acres* of land no rent was fixed. In respect of 3298 acres rent exceeded one *anna* per rupee of the land revenue over an area of 21,397 *acres* the rent varied from 5 to 6 ½% of the land revenue) Vide., *'Land to the Tillers', op. cit.*
41. *Fauti Farari* means the land lying vacant on account of the death or desertion of the tenant. It was reported that *muzaras* occupied such land, they were liable to prosecution for criminal trespassing.
42. The Pepsu Abolition of *Ala Malkiat* Rights Act, 1953, *op. cit.,* 252 *Land to the Tillers, op. cit.,* 14.

proprietary rights to the occupancy tenants and settle the rate of compensation payable to the *biswedars*. Let it be noticed that this Act covered an area of 97,000 *acres* which involved an amount of compensation of Rs. 17.91 lacs.[43] A pertinent question arises *i.e.,* why it did not cover the whole state. According to P.S. Rau, advisor to *Rajpramukh*, it was not possible to enforce the ordinance in the entire area, as a major part of the State had already been covered by the provisions of the Act of 1950. The problem in about 3,76,898 *acres* out of total area of 6,37,331 *acres* (earlier held under occupancy tenures), mostly in Fatehgarh, Kandaghat and Mahendragarh districts, had been solved. For the area which this Act did not cover, P.S. Rau offers an argument, very weak of course. He States : "It was not possible to enforce the ordinance in the whole area because in 208 villages involving 8, 393 holdings and a total area of 143, 252 *acres*, the tenants' attitude was hardly helpful. And the attitude affected that of the tenants occupying another 117, 118 acres".[44] Holdings the previous governments responsible for not introducing tenancy legislation in the entire area of the Pepsu, Rau observed : [45] "Indeed every measure for the abolition of *biswedari* rights had so far been but a temporary polnative of restricted application. Implementation of the policy of abolition of landlords' rights had always suffered from not being pursued to its logical conclusion".

The Pepsu Occupancy Tenants (Vesting of proprietary rights) Act, 1953 was a significant step because it was framed to grant full proprietary rights to the occupancy tenants with almost immediate effect. The new Act abolished the proprietary rights of the *biswedars* and their right to collect the arrears of rent. However, the arrears of rent legally sanctioned were included for the purposes of compensation.[46] This Act offered

43. *Preisident's Rule in Pepsu, op. cit.,* 4.
44. *Land to the Tillers, op. cit., 8.*
45. *Ibid.*
46. *The Statesman* (New Delhi), September 7, 1953, 1 (The arrears of rent covered by certain decrees which could be executed and rent within the limitation *i.e.,* for the last three years was to be taken into account).

terms and conditions for determining of compensation. Since the most urgent problem of the tenancy occupancy was to decide about the amount of compensation payable to the *biswedars,* the Act offered the following procedure for determining of compensation : [47]

(i) Where the rent payable by the occupancy tenants is expressed in terms of the land revenue in respect of land, the amount of compensation shall be twelve times the annual rent thereof exclusive of land revenue rates and cesses;

(ii) Where the rent payable by occupancy tenant is not so expressed in terms of the land revenue in respect of the land, and :

(a) If the rent is payable in cash whether as a fixed amount or at a fixed rate with reference to the area of the land, the compensation amount shall be 12 times the annual rent, thereof exclusive of land revenue and rates and cesses or twelve times the land revenue including rates and cesses payable by the *biswedar* in respect of land, whichever amount is less; or

(b) If the rent is payable wholly or partly by a division or appraisement of the produce on the basis of *batai,* the amount of compensation shall be 12 times the land revenue including rates and cesses payable by the *biswedar* in respect of land.

(iii) Where no rent is payable by the occupancy tenants in respect of the land, the amount of compensation shall be an amount equal to the land revenue and rates and cesses payable by the *biswedar* in respect of the land.

It was also decided for the convenience of the occupancy tenants the amount of compensation was to be paid in twelve

47. *The Pepsu Occupancy Tenants* (Vesting of Proprietary Rights) Act, 1953, *Pepsu Government Gazettee,* September 12, 1953, 259-260.

half yearly installments provided that the total amount of compensation was more than two hundred and fifty rupees, in case of compensation being less than that amount, it was to be paid in one installment. As regards the *shamlat deh* the occupancy tenant could claim his share in it, in the proportion to his holding after becoming the owner of the land. The act also specified the kinds of occupancy tenants who could be benefited by it.[48]

(i) A person who recorded soon before the commencement of this Act, as an occupancy tenant in the latest annual record, or

(ii) A person who was recorded in the record of rights of any of the estates of the former Faridkot State as *(a) muzara-i-shartial, (b) chakotedar khas, (c) muzara table marzi malik, (d) muzara bila taivan* and *(e) chakotedar nautor* of any *biswedar* not being the Government; or

(iii) A person who is recorded in the latest annual records of any estate of the former Malerkotla State : *(a) dakhilkar* and *(b) maurusi*, or

(iv) A person was recorded as an occupancy tenant in the annual record on the 11th March, 1940 : *(a)* where right of occupancy in land has been extinguished but partition proceedings under the *farman-i-shahi,* No.6 dated the 11th March, 1947, or the Patiala and East Punjab States Union Abolition of *Biswedari* Ordinance, 2006 B.K. have not been finally completed, or *(b)* While who has been dispossessed or deprived of his rights to the occupation of the land at any time after the 11th March, 1940, but has not been granted any relief under the Patiala and East Punjab States Union Abolition of *biswedari* ordinance, 2006 B.K.

The Act incorporated clauses pertaining to compensation much higher than proposed by the United Front Government, but P.S. Rau justified this act on the superficial understanding

48. *The Pepsu Occupancy Tenants Act, op. cit.*, 257-258.

of utilitarian principle which to him appeared to be nothing or more than a compromise. Rau stated :[49] "All reforms, whether economic, social or religious are bound to touch the susceptibilities of one section of the people or the other. But the best measures are those which seek maximum good of the maximum number." Rau thought that it was the only way out for solving the agrarian question under the prevailing circumstances. He was convinced that the Government efforts would be appreciated by the *muzaras* and they must co-operate in the implementation of the Act. It appears that Rau was right, as far as the claims that the *muzaras'* exploitation by the *biswedars* would be soon ended but he appeared to be apprehensive of the *muzaras'* reaction to the clauses of compensation.

The third Act *i.e.,* the Pepsu Tenancy and Agricultural Lands Act, 1953 was by far the most significant link in the line of agrarian reforms in the East Punjab States as it raised the status of tenants-at-will to that of full proprietors. The landowners who had no tenants under them were not effected by it. It effected merely those and owners whose land was partially or wholly cultivated by the tenants-at-will. Its principal aim was to raise the status of maximum tenants-at-will to that of the peasant proprietors not subject to ejectment.[50] The limit allowed for personal cultivation was fixed at ½ of the area owned by the land owners subject to a maximum of 30 standard *acres.* So long as the tenant continued paying his rent, he could not be ejected. Moreover, the tenants could now by the land under their occupancy on payment of the compensation of two hundred rupees per *acre* or at 9 times the land revenue whichever was less. Even the tenants-at will was given the right to buy the house of the *biswedar* if constructed on the area covered this Act.[51]

---

49. *Land to the Tillers, op. cit.,* 11.
50. *President's Rule in Pepsu, op. cit.,* 5.
51. *The Pepsu Tenancy and Agricultural Land Act, 1953,* Pepsu Extra-ordinary Gazette, November 28, 1953, Chapter-II (Reservation of Land for personal cultivation), Sections-5 and 6, 416; The Tribune, November 25, 1953, 9.

Every land proprietor, owning an area about 30 standard *acres* had to intimate his reservation to the collector of the State within six months from the date of enforcement of the Act. The defaulter was liable to lose his right altogether. However, land in the hands of widows, minors, charitable institutions had been exempted from this Act. The significant feature of this Act was that the *malkiat* passed to the tenant the day he had paid the first installment; nor was any rent paid during the period the installment was due. Even on the balance of compensation no interest was payable.[52] Another noteable feature of this Act was that the *benami* transaction should not deprive him of the land and the land should remain with the tenants as the means of their livelihood.[53] This Act also offered some more facilities to the tenants and their interests were safeguarded. For instance, he could purchase the site of his dwelling house in the village and secondly a ceiling on rent at one-third of the produce or its equivalent was put and landowner charging more was liable to a penalty; in certain circumstances the tenant was given the right to carry out improvement even against the wishes of the *biswedar*; fourthly, the *muzara* was granted corresponding share in the *shamlat* land on payment of suitable compensation; and sixthly, the tenants-at-will were also allowed to enjoy all the benefits extended to the other tenants in evancuce areas; they enjoyed protection against eviction.[54]

The State Government was empowered to acquire *banger* lands and it was estimated that 3 to 4 *acres* of *banger* land could be easily acquired for the settlement of evicted tenants.[55] However, the State was to pay compensation at the rate of Rs.

52. *The Tribune,* November 25, 1953, 9; *New Tenancy Legislation in* Pepsu (Patiala Directorate of Information, Pepsu, Dec., 5,1953), 4.
53. *New Tenancy Legislatiion in Pepsu, op. cit.*
54. *The Pepsu Tenancy and Agricultural Lands Act, 1953, op. cit.,* 218-226 (For further details see also section 15 clauses, 1-8, Section 17, Clauses 1-2, Section 21, Section 23, Clauses 1 and 2).
55. *Ibid.,* 426-428, Chapter V, Section : 33-38.

100/- per *acre* or forty five times of the land revenue, whichever was less.[56]

As a result of the implementation of this Act, it was hoped that no tenancy would be left after the expiry of 5 years. The *muzara* would have by that time become permanent tenants or acquired proprietary rights, thus eliminating all intermediaries.[57] Hence the tenancy legislation earned the praise of the *muzaras*/peasants. Also, the author of the Acts was hailed not only as liquidator of dacoits and killers but also as a liberator of humanity in Pepsu form the clutches of the biswedars.[58]

Before the abolition of President's rule in the East Punjab States, the two Acts-the Abolition of *ala-malkiat*, 1953 and the Pepsu Occupancy Tenants (Vesting of Proprietary Rights) Act, 1953 were introduced and implemented while the third Act-the Pepsu Tenancy and Agricultural Act, 1953 was kept pending to give sufficient time to the *biswedars* to demarcate for self-cultivation. After the abolition of the President's rule, the Congress Ministry was formed in March, 1954 which continued in office till November 1956. The first two Acts were approved by the Assembly soon after the formation of the Congress Ministry under Col. Raghbir Singh. But the third Act *viz.*, the Pepsu Tenancy and Agricultural Act, 1953 involved a lot of controversy over which there was a serious clash of interest between the *muzaras* and the *biswedars*. The latter desired to retain maximum land with them beyond the ceiling of thirty standard *acres*. How seriously the *biswedars* were interested in these issues that they made representation to the Prime Minister. They, therefore, evicted a large number of cultivators, particularly the tenants-at-will by force and fraud in order to indulge *benami* transactions. The land was freely transferred to the relatives in order to increase the area of self-cultivation.

56. *New Tenancy Legislation, op. cit.,* 5.
57. Peasants sent a telegram to P.S. Rau, advisor to the Pepsu Government, The Tribune, January 15, 1954, 10.
58. *Ibid.*

After the passing and enforcement of these Acts, there were some complaints of change of entries in the revenue records. For example, there were large number of tenants-at-will who had been described as share-croppers in the revenue record, now.[59] Moreover, we have already noted that 37 petitions were filed of which 20 were admitted. One *biswedar* Mr. Hari Krishan Khosla challenged the Pepsu Tenancy and Agricultural Act, 1953 in the High Court pleading that section 3 of the Act fixed an arbitrary, inadequate limit for the ejectment of tenants-at-will and had wrongly banned the conversion limit to 60 ordinary *acres*. He further pleaded that the provision 26(1) of the Act regarding compensation was violative of Article 31(2) of the Indian Constitution.[60] The problem of assessing the rate of rent payable by the tenants-at-will also came in the way of the Act. The Planning Commission suggested that the land rent should be so fixed that a fair wage remains for the cultivator after meeting the expenses of cultivation and other risks. Therefore, according to it, a rate exceeding ¼ or 1/5 of the produce could well be regarded as justifiable.[61]

Now, the Legislative Assembly took up the Pepsu Tenancy and Agricultural Lands Act, 1953 at the request of some members to amend it. The Assembly at this time was dominated by the Landlords who wanted to safeguard the interests of the *biswedars* at all costs. Being in majority, it was possible for them to amend the Act, and secondly they could delay its implementation. These members pleaded with the house that the persons in the armed forces in the Punjab States could not exercise the right to reserve land for personal cultivation within the statutory period of 6 months. So, they wanted that there

59. 'Pepsu News Letters', *The Hindustan Times* (New Delhi), June 6, 1954, 10.
60. The article reads, "The when such law is passed, it must provide for payment of an amount to the owner, either by fixing the amount or by specifying the principle upon which it is to be determined and given". Also see *The Statesman* (New Delhi), June 6, 1954.
61. 'Pepsu News Letters', *The Hindustan Times* (New Delhi), June 6, 1954, 10.

should be a provision in the Act to give them suitable time. The Bill thus sought to extend this period. This amendment in the Bill was also supported by S. Jagir Singh Ohuguwalia—leader of the United Front Group. He also demanded that this benefit should be given to refugees, widows, minors convicts and undertrials. The other members of this group also backed this amendment but the Congress party opposed it at the movement and the proposal was lost by the majority of vote.[62]

However, the Agrarian Committee of the Planning Commission advised the States' Government to make any amendment in the Act. The meeting of the Reforms Committee was attended by three Central Ministers *i.e.,* Gulzari Lal Nanda, K.N. Katju and Rafi Ahmed Kidwai. The Committee wanted the Act to be worked in its original. In the meantime data regarding the consequences of the measures to be collected. On the advice of the Planning Commission, the Pepsu Government decided to postpone agrarian reforms for a year and it was done by issuing a notification.[63] To alley the fears of the *muzaras* the States' Government issued an ordinance providing for the temporary protection from ejectment and the imposition of certain disabilities on agricultural tenants.[64]

Now, a controversy cropped up between the Planning Commission and the Pepsu Government. The former's main proposals were meant to strengthen the position of the *biswedars* as well as of other landowners.[65] It was openly alleged that the one year of postponement would be fully utilized by the *biswedars* to evade the provisions of the act by following mechanized farming, by employing ejected tenants

62. *Pepsu Legislative Assembly Debates,* Vol. IV, S. No. 42, July 12, 1954, 187-188; Ministry of Home Affairs, Government of India, File No. 17/33-Judl. NAI, New Delhi.
63. *The Tribune,* June 2, 1954, 3; *The Statesman* (New Delhi), August 21, 1954.
64. *Patiala and East Punjab States Union Gazette,* published by authority, October 14, 1954, 551-552 (For further details see Appendix-XII).
65. *The Statesman* (New Delhi), August 21, 1954 (See—'Minutes of the Meeting').

as hired labourers. Thus, there was a fear of the proposed Gandhian economy of small peasant proprietors being turned into a capitalist economy of the *biswedars.*[66] In order to present its cause to the Planning Commission for modification regarding the Pepsu Tenancy and Agricultural Lands Act, 1953, the Pepsu Government directed the revenue authorities to collect necessary information. The following table is prepared[67] after acquiring information by the State Officials :

The table points to the gravity of the tenant problem. The ratio between the landowners and tenants was tentatively 3 : 1. The area under self-cultivation and under tenants indicates a bigger gap. To substantiate, the total area under self-cultivation was to the tune of 43,78,018 *acres* and the total area under tenants was 1,58,314 *acres.* The problem was serious in Kapurthala and Narnaul districts where the ratio was much less than other districts. Here nearly 36% of the total land was under tenants cultivation whereas in other districts the proportion was roughly 11%. Hence, in this region the number of self-cultivating landowners was very large in proportion to the tenants-at-will. Because of their strength and domination, *biswedars* were seriously interested in depriving the tenants of getting occupancy rights. Since the area under tenants cultivation was just less than 10% it can be concluded that there should have been no hesitation on the part of the *biswedars* to permit occupancy rights to the tenants. On the contrary, in this region the cases of tenants eviction were maximum. Secondly, where the cases of eviction were very few, such as in Kapurthala and Narnaul districts, there was seemingly a balance between the two. Hence, the biswedars in these two districts were not interested in opposing the grant of occupancy tenants to the *muzaras.*

Another aspect which needs to be analysed is that in Patiala, Sangrur and Bhatinda districts, they probably needed

66. *Ibid.*
67. For more details see *The Tribune* August 27, 1954, 5. For Table see *Pepsu Vidhan Sabha Debates Official Report,* Vol. V.S. No. 6, December 22, 1954.

Table : Showing the Land Owned by Different Kind of Owners

District	No. of Land Owners	Area under self-cultivation in acres	No. of Tenants	Area under tenants in standard acres	Private Land based out by Govt. in standard acres	Area belonging to religious or Charitable institutions in standard acres	Land alienated by landlords in favour of sons, grandsons, wives daughter etc. in acres
Patiala	1,22,266	11,60,768,	46,855	1,27,644	5,446	13,380	7,356
Sangrur	1,18,244	10,55,455	43,500	1,57,093	4,160	21,605	12,346
Bhatinda	1,59,361	13,99,872	30,972	1,72,517	51	1,295	19,196
Kapurthala	18,357	83,293	10,277	38,809	273	3,621	1,766
Narnaul	58,739	6,78,630	26,710	47,319	63	3,153	8,788

the services of the *muzaras* for the cultivation of the land, declared as self-cultivating area. Therefore, they might have *tried* to evict *muzaras* and consequently make the labour force readily available for the cultivation of their own land. It seems to be a plausible explanation because in Kapurthala and Narnaul districts, the ratio between the *biswedars* and *muzaras* is far less indicating the availability of the larger number of tenants-at-will. That is why, there was a strong reaction to the postponement of agrarian reforms in the region comprising Patiala, Sangrur and Bhatinda districts. In the village Kotduna about thirty thousand tenants/peasants assembled for the annual session of the State *kisan sabha* and they strongly condemned the ejectments and falling agricultural prices. As a consequence of these factors, they were determined to revive the anti-feudal tenants movement.[68]

On the other hand the Pepsu Legislative Assembly passed the Pepsu Agricultural Tenants (Temporary Protection and Disability) Bill 1954 on December 24, 1954. The Akalis-Communists collectively opposed it. Even it was opposed by two Congress members.[69] Their principal objection was that the government had favoured the *biswedars* and it prevented the *muzaras* for a year from acquiring proprietary rights in their holdings. But this bill disallowed ejectment of tenants from their holdings to vacate land for the landlords personal cultivation. The then Pepsu Congress Chief Giani Zail Singh assured the tenants on 4th February, 1955 that the State Congress would shortly appoint a committee to study agrarian reforms measures, especially the problems of tenants-at-will and landless labour.[70] He stressed that the East Punjab States must fall in line with the rest of the country in regard to agrarian

68. *The Statesman* (New Delhi), August 21,1954, 1.
69. *Pepsu Vidhan Sabha Debates,* Vol. V, S. No. 4, December 20, 1954, 354-375 (Dal Singh and Nihal Singh were the Congress Leaders).
70. (Giani Zail Singh, after the formation of the Pepsu in 1948, served as Minister of Revenue (1948-49) and Minister of Public Works Department and Agriculture 1951-52. He served as Pepsu Congress President and later became the member of *Rajya Sabha* from 1956-1962). Vide., *Ibid.*

reforms in the light of the resolutions passed by the avadi session of the Congress in 1955.[71]

At last the Pepsu Tenancy and Agricultural Lands Bill, 1955 which incorporated all the clauses of the Pepsu Tenancy and Agricultural Act, 1953, was introduced in the Pepsu *Vidhan Sabha* for its consideration on February 28, 1955.[72] The representatives of the United Front charged the Government with 'indecisiveness in formulating the interests of *biswedars*'. One Mr. Beant Singh of this group alleged that the Bill was intended to safeguard the interests of the *biswedars* and called it as "Landlord Protection Bill".[73] In fact, this bill had ignored the Venkatachar Committee's recommendations as also of Dara Singh Agrarian Reforms Committee's. It only protected the big *zamindars*.[74] As regards the Congress party, 15 of its members (all agriculturists) were opposed to the *biswedari* system. They pleaded with the Chief Minister to seek prior approval of the party which was favourable to the adoption of the Bill in its original form. However, majority of the Congress members in the Assembly were interested in delaying the adoption and implementation of the Bill.

After prolonged debates, finally the Bill was passed on March 1, 1955, but it was gazette dater the assent of the *Rajpramukh* on March 5, 1955.[75] The Act Sought to lay down the rights of the tenants-at-will and codify the relations between

71. *The Times of India* (Delhi) February 6, 1955, 07.
72. *Pepsu Vidhan Sabha Debates,* Vol. VI, S. No. 5, February 28, 1955, 246. (We have already mentioned that the Act was promulgated during the Presidential Rule but two of its clauses were suspended last year by the State Assembly during the Winter Session).
73. *Pepsu Vidhan Sabha Debates,* Vol. VI, S. No. 5, February 28, 1955. 275-276.
74. *Pepsu Vidhan Sabha Debates,* Vol. VI, S. No. 5, February 28, 1955, 281 (S. Bhagwan Singh, Secretary—Agrarian Reforms Committee constituted by the Congress, criticized the Bill describing it as "senseless, anarchic and chaotic").
75. *Patiala and East Punjab States union Gazette,* March 5, 1955, Part, III, Section I, 917-935.

the owners and the cultivators of the million *acres* of land. It tried to raise as many tenants-at-will to the status of full proprietors as possible. For each proprietor a permissible limit was fixed which was 10 standard *acres*. For other, the limit was half of the total ownership, subject to a minimum of 30 standard *acres* of 60 ordinary *acres* of land. Those owing upto 20 standard *acres* of land could take up the area for self-cultivation within the permissible limit at any time during the next 5 years. Those owing more than 20 *acres* were to reserve that area within a period of 6 months and the rate of compenasation was fixed 12 times of the land revenue for occupancy tenants and 90 times the lnad revenue for tenants-at-will. The Act also sought to protect cultivators form ejectment. It provided that tenants would not be ejected from such lands except on any of the following grounds :[76]

(i) That the land comprising the tenancy has been reserved by the landowner for his personal cultivation. No tenant shall be ejected after the completion of five years from the commencement of the President Act;[77]

(ii) That the tenant has failed to pay rent within six months after it falls due;

(iii) That the tenant not being a widow, a minor or a member of the armed forces of the Union, has, after the commencement of the President's Act, sub-let without the consent in writing of the landowner, the land comprising his tenancy or any part thereof;

(iv) The tenant has without sufficient cause failed to

76. *The Pepsu Tenancy and Agricultural Lands Act; 1955, Pepsu Government Gazettee,* March 5, 1955, Chapter-III, Section-7, 920-922.

77. The said period of 5 years shall commence—*(a)* in the case of a widow on the termination of the life interest of the widow; *(b)* in the case of a minor on the attainment of maturity and *(c)* in the case of a member of the Armed Forces of the Union, on his discharge or retirement from service, as the case may be. Vide., *Ibid.*

cultivate personally such land in the manner or to the extent customary in the locality in which the land is situated.

(v) That the tenant has used such land or any part thereof in a manner which is likely to render the land unfit for the purpose for which it was leased to him; and

(vi) That the tenant, on demand in writing by the landowner has refused to execute a *kabuliat* agreeing to pay rent in respect of his tenancy in accordance with the provisions of section 9 and 10.

However, most of the proposals of the Government of the East Punjab States to amend the Tenancy and Agricultural Land Act were rejected by the Planning Commission. It did not agree with the clause which gave the right to the *biswedars* to evict the tenants from their permissible self-cultivation area upto thirty *acres* and also other suggestion meant to give them better facilities concerning eviction.[78]

The State Government wanted to maintain status-quo for a period of another seven months. It, therefore, decided to extend the life of the most controversial piece of legislation which was to expire on December 31, 1955. Therefore, the Pepsu Tenancy and Agricultural Lands (Amendment) Bill, 1955 was placed before the *Vidhan Sabha* for consideration. After thorough discussion, the Bill was passed by majority votes.[79] The Pepsu *Vidhan Sabha* appointed a Select Committee on August 21, 1956 to consider; examine and submit report on the Tenancy and Agricultural Land (Second Amendment) Bill, 1956.[80]

78. *The Hindustan Times* (New Delhi), August 28, 1955.
79. *The Pepsu Vidhan Sabha Debates,* Vol. VIII, S. No. 61, December 9, 1956, 601-618; *The Tribune,* December 1, 1955.
80. The Select Committee was comprised of S. Harcharan Singh-Revenue Minister (Chairman), S Amir Singh Chaudhari, S Dharam Singh Fakkar, S. Gian Singh Rarewala, S. Gurbakhashish Singh, Harchand Singh, S. Jangir Singh, Thakur Singh Kala (Advocate General). Vide., *Ibid.*

A demonstration was organised on September, 1956 at Bhatinda against the 30 standard *acres* ceiling by the Pepsu landlords Bill. This demonstration was led by the uncle of the Rajpramukh, Maheshindra Singh. A resolution was passed against this proposed Bill. They also decided to send a deputation to Delhi to present their case before the Prime Minister, Jawahar Lal Nehru. This deputation went to Delhi on September 22, 1956.[81] As a result of it, a Select Committee was instituted. Its purpose was to introduce certain agrarian reforms especially with a view to protecting the tenants against eviction and fixing for allottees a higher limit for reservation of land for personal cultivation. The committee was headed by Harcharan Singh, the State Revenue Minister. The Selection Committee submitted its report on September 30, 1956, which was gazetted on October 4, 1956. The Committee recommended the following provisions to be incorporated in the Bill : [82]

(i) That the permissible limit in the case of allottees should be made from 30 standard *acres* to 40 standard *acres*. The Committee was of the view that the permissible limit of biswedar/landowner, whether allottees or others not to be expressed in terms of ordinary *acres*;

(ii) That no tenant shall be liable to ejectment from any part of the soil the permissible limit of a landowner if the area held by such tenant not exceed 5 standard acres or from an area of 5 standard *acres* the area held by him exceeds 5 standard acres, until alternative land allotted by the State Government to the tenants.

(iii) That no tenant holding land under a landowner for constantly 12 years or more within the permissible limit of a landowner is liable to ejectment for the area of land held by him if area does not exceed 15 standard *acres*.

(iv) That the right of a tenant to acquire proprietary rights in respect of land held by him under a landowner

81. *The Tribune*, September 22, 1956.

82. *Report of Select Committee, Pepsu Government Gazettee*, October 4, 1956, 327-333.

should extend to the tenant in such a manner that the land acquired by him does not exceed his permissible limit.

The Tenancy and Agricultural Land Bill was presented before the *Vidhan Sabha* on October 9, 1956 for consideration. After thorough discussion, the most controversial Bill—'The Pepsu and Agricultural Lands (Second Amendment) Lands Act, 1956, was unanimously passed by the *Vidhan Sabha* on October 10, 1956.Thus the passage of this Act fulfilled the cherished dream of the *Praja Mandalists* who had been fighting for the just rights of the tenants.[83] Moreover, Pepsu was the first State in India where a ceiling was imposed on individual holdings. To substantiate, let us state its provisions[84] here :

(a) No person was entitled to own or hold as landowner or tenant more than 30 standard *acres* under his personal cultivation;[85]

(b) In case of displaced persons they were allowed to retain 40 standard *acres* or 100 ordinary *acres* of land.[86]

(c) Ceiling of landholding was not to apply to Orchards, specialized forms engaged in cattle breeding, dairying or wool raising, sugarcane farms operating by sugar factories, efficiently managed farms and land belonging to registered co-operative farming societies provided the land owned by a member did not exceed the permissible landowners were allowed to retain 10 standard *acres* above permissible limit for planting Orchard within two years. Failing to do so, the land was liable to be confiscated;[87]

---

83. *Pepsu Vidhan Sabha Debates; Officials Report,* October 10, 1956; The Tribune, October 9, 1956.
84. *The Pepsu Tenancy and Agricultural Lands (Second Amendment) Act., 1956,* Pepsu Government Gazettee, October 30, 1956, 469-478.
85. *Ibid.,* Section-4, 470.
86. *Ibid.*
87. *Ibid.,* Section-32K (Exemption from ceiling on land), Clauses 1 and 2, 475-476.

(d) The landlords or the tenants were debarred from acquiring or possessing by transfer, exchange, agreement or settlement any land which with or without land already owned or hold by him in aggregate exceeded the permissible limit.[88]

(e) The provisions of ceiling were also extended to the future acquisition by inheritance. The provisions of the Act were not applied to the lands owned by or vested in the State Government, lands belonging to religious or charitable institutions but not to a *mahant, mohtamin* or manager thereof or the lands granted to any members of armed forces of the Union for gallantry.[89]

The Compensation of the surplus acquired land was paid to the owner on the following patterns : [90]

(a) "For the first 25 standard *acres* of Land, 12 times the fair rent;

(b) For the next 25 standard *acres* of land, 9 times the fair rent;

(c) For the remaining land, 90 times the land revenue (including rates and cesses) payable for such land or 200 rupees per acre, whichever is less; and

(d) Compensation in case of *banger* land, 45 times the land revenue payable or 100 rupees per acres whichever is less".

Hence, the Pepsu Land Commission decided and determined the amount of fair rent. To conclude in the perspective what followed after 1956, the above Legislative measures improved the lot of the tenants/peasants of the *Malwa* region or East Punjab States where their struggle was

---

88. *Ibid.,* Section-32L (Ceiling on future acquisition of Land), 476.
89. *Ibid.,* Section—32P (Exemption of certain lands), Clauses—a, b, c, and d, 477-478.
90. *Ibid.,* Section 32—G (Principles for payment of compensation), Clauses—a and b, 474.

the most intense. Most of them especially with Occupancy rights had been granted proprietary rights by the year 1953. This section of the peasants was very active in the peasants' struggle in this region. But they withdrew themselves from the scene the moment they achieved their target. From that time onward the peasants' movement in this region became mild and protracted. But the issue of the tenants-at-will whom occupancy rights were yet to be granted remained pending till 1956. With the decline of the peasants' struggle, the pressure of the tenants-at-will also declined. The Planning Commission and some of the Congress members, however, compelled the State Government to legislate in favour of the tenants-at-will/ peasants before the merger of the Pepsu with the Punjab in November, 1956.

Lastly, let it be noticed that during the course of Tenancy Legislation none of the major political group took keen interest in the issues relating to the well-being of the tenants; instead the powerful lobby of the *biswedars* exercised heavy pressure both on the State and Central Governments to ignore the just demands of the tenants which had considerably weakened the peasants' struggle.

9 LEADERSHIP OF THE PEASANTS' MOVEMENT

A movement without leadership is like a ship without a rudder. It plays a vital role in all the movements as it gives direction and purpose to the movement. Though the leaders were not the generators of the peasants' movement, but they had a definite role to play. They organized and framed programme and line of action of the movement. Suffering from the drawback of lack of cohesion due to the nature of peasants work and their isolation from one another, the role of leadership in the peasants' movement became important as the leaders in this struggle acted as mobilisers and articulators[1] of the peasants societies. They guided and inspired the peasants to achieve their objectives. They were the agents and link between the peasants and the state or political power. Within the peasants' community, they interacted with the members for building up cohesiveness and making available resources to the community.[2] However, the community leadership depended upon the type f structuring of the social relationship in a village. It was a kind of arrangement of the relation of the parts to the whole over the network of interpersonal relationship wherein a leader played the role of fulfilling the wants and needs of community.[3] No body could become a leader unless he was endowed with distinctive qualities of character and personality. A leader must possess all-round knowledge of the environment

1. Gunsfield, Joseph R., Functional *Areas of Leadership in Social Movements* in L.P. Vidyathi, Bombay : 1967, 22.
2. Cartwright, Drawin, Arvin Zander (Ed.), *Group Dynamics : Research and Theory Evenston,* Illineis, Row Paterson Co. 1956, 438.
3. Mehta, Shiv Rattan, *Emerging Pattern of Rural Leadership,* New Delhi : 1972, p. 2.

and conviction, for he was to act as an organizer, mobiliser and articulator of his community.[4] He must display will-power and conviction. Let us also not forget the fact that in a rural society socio-cultural factor was equally significant[5] because in such societies where in the social status of an individual was based on number of factors such as caste, age, physical strength, occupation and income.[6] The dominant caste played a vital role in rural areas in exercising more dominance, night be numerical, ritual, economic or political.

Let it be noticed that the peasants' movement in its early stages was led by persons from movements as the *Singh Sabha*, the *Kuka*, the *Gurdwara* Reform, *Ghadar*, Non-co-operation, Jallianwala Bagh Tragedy, *Babbar* Akali, Civil Disobedience, Boycott of Simon Commission and Quit India. Most of them took active part in these movements at one time or the other. It was a part of process of political socialization. But it does not suggest that the peasant leaders had no social status. They were, in fact, men of conviction devoted to the cause of peasantry. In fact, these leaders moderately educated belonging to the middle rung of the peasantry, displayed awareness of the problems confronted by the peasantry. They found it necessary to build bridges between the peasants of the East Punjab States and the national upsurge in order to lend support, strength and respectability to the movement against the feudal order.[7] This explains the reason why they sought inspiration from the national struggle for freedom and why the Punjab *Riyasti Praja Mandal*, the Akalis the Communists and the Congress supported the cause of the peasants/tenants. In 1928 some of

---

4. Lassawell, Harold D. and Kaplan Abraham, *Power and Society; A Framework for Political Inquiry*, New Haven Yole University Press, 1950, 9.
5. Lewis Oscar, *Village Life in Northern India*, New Forh Vintage Book, A Division of Random House, 1958, 127.
6. Loomis Charles, P. and Beagle Allan, *Rural Social System*, New York, 1959, 342.
7. Mathru, K.G., *Leadership in Rural India*, in L. P. Vidyarthi, *op. cit.*, 263.

the prominent peasant leaders were office-bearers of the *Riyasti Praja Mandal.* Sewa Singh Thikriwala was the elected President and Jaswant Singh Danewala its Secretary. Prominent *Praja Mandal* leaders connected with the peasants' movement in these states at that time were Jagir Singh Joga, Ajmer Singh Tamkot and Harnam Singh Dharamgarhia. Bhagwan Singh Longowalia and Master Hari Singh were other important office bearers.[8] The first regular conference of Punjab *Riyasti Praja Mandal,* held at Lahore from December 27 to 29, 1929, lent support to the cause of the tenants. A large number of tenants from Patiala and other states participated in this Conference. They took out a procession through the main *bazars* of the town drawing the attention of the people towards the excesses of the states' authorities.[9] Soon Lahore, Simla, Delhi and Amritsar became the centres of propaganda warfare against the rulers of the East Punjab States. The leadership of the *Praja Mandal* wanted to draw people's attention towards the lot of peasants and seek their support for their cause. Also, they wished to build up pressure against the Government in which they succeeded.[10]

The peasants as well as their leaders became conscious of their own problems and role they could play in ameliorating their lot by taking part in the activities of the Punjab *Riyasti Praja Mandal* and the Indian National Congress. The *Praja Mandal,* at its Conference held at Simla in 1931, adopted a resolution on Tenancy problems and the eviction of tenants by the *biswedars.* Even through their efforts the platforms of the political parties outside the Patiala State were effectively used for the promotion of peasants' cause. It will not be out of place if we repeat that the peasants' struggle in this region was patronized, in its early stages, by the *Praja Mandal* movement

8. Vaid, Chhajju Mal, "Tenant Movement" in *Punjab Peasant in Freedom Struggle* by Master Hari Singh, New Delhi, 1984, 242.
9. Prime Minister's Office File No. 564, *Patiala State Records,* PSA, Patiala.
10. *Ibid.*

with its rural background.[11] The rural population, mainly *Jat* Sikh peasantry, with their religious favour and war like temperament,[12] stuck to democratic social system based on the amalgam of Sikh, tribal and agrarian traditions.

Interestingly the early leadership formed a colourful spectrum. To cite an example, Sewa Singh Thikriwala, a *biswedar* and high official of the Patiala State was the first who emerged as a leader and represented the cause of the poor peasants/tenants.[13] He travelled a long way from social reforms[14] to voluntry surrender of his own mortgaged land to the tenants without any compensation. His sufferings and sacrifices for the *muzaras* and landless labourers and the depressed classes, enhanced his status and position, which lent strength to the movement which was greatly needed in its infant stage. He mobilized peasants and led their demonstrations and processions against the oppressive rule of the states' authorities, the rulers and the *biswedars.*

Bhagwan Singh Longowalia was a leading figure in organizing peasants/tenants. Though he was a petty landlord, he was an active member of the Punjab *Riyasti Praja Mandal* who, in particular, highlighted the problems of the tenants of Kishangarh and Gurthali. As a forceful speaker and journalist he raised his voice against the injustice of the *biswedars* to the poor tenants. He exhorted the tenants to form *muzara* Committees to voice their genuine and long standing grievances. He also assured them of his *Mandal's* support.[15]

---

11. The *Praja Mandal* Movement was then predominantly rural with rural leadership.
12. Conningham, J.D., *History of the Sikhs,* New Delhi, 1972, 12.
13. Thabal, Amrinder, *Sardar Sewa Singh Thikriwala,* Patiala : 1878, 8.
14. Walia, Ramesh, *Praja Mandal Movement in East Punjab States,* Patiala : 1972, 65; Sen, S.P. (*ed.*), *Dictionary of National Biography,* Vol. IV, Calcutta : 1974, 348.
15. Shaheedi Conference held at Anandpur Sahib, Prime Ministers' Office File No. 743, *Punjab State Records,* Punjab State Archieves, Patiala.

After some time, he came under the influence of Marxist ideology during his stay at Amritsar and Lahore.[16] In 1925, Maharaja Bhupinder Singh and Master Tara Singh signed a pact.[17] As a result of it, he parted with the Akali leadership and formed an alliance with the Hindu urban intelligentia and the Communist workers in Punjab. His sacrifice and courage became a symbol of the spirit of revolt for the peasants/ tenants.[18] He desired to see the extinction of feudal tyranny and introduction of peasants' reforms. Jagir Singh Joga was an other popular leader who mobilized the peasants and led their movements. He too came under the influence of leftist ideology and ultimately became a socialist.

The *Praja Mandal* Movement originally led by the *Jat* Sikh peasant leaders, attracted Hindu leaders like Brish Bhan, Des Raj, Narain Dutta, Shankar Lal, etc., and developed its roots in urban areas by the mid of 1930s. Previously it was restricted to rural areas. Influenced by socialist, all the leaders wanted abolition of *biswedari* system. The Sixth All India States people's Conference held at Ludhiana[19] from 15th to 17th February 1939 under the Presidentship of Jawahar Lal Nehru, was attended by peasants and leaders of all walks of life of Patiala State. For instance, Jangir Singh Phuguwalia, Harnam Singh Dharamgarh, Wazir Singh Daftriwala, Gian Singh, Sant Singh Pandhi, Diwan Singh and several others were present in this Conference.

The national leadership, because of the increasing influence of the leftist ideology, took special interest in the cause of the

16. Walia, Ramesh, *Praja Mandal Movement in East Punjab States*, Patiala : 1972, 134.
17. Faują Singh (*ed.*), *Eminent Freedom Fighters in Punjab*, Patiala : 1972, 76.
18. Oral History Cell File No. 48—Department of Punjab Historical Studies, Punjabi University, Patiala.
19. Secret Do letter No. F 41-Misc/48 dt., 2nd February, 1939, from the Secretary to the President for Punjab States, Lahore, to the Foreign Minister, Patiala Government, Prime Ministers' Office File No. 756, PSR, PSA.

peasants. It led to the formation of All India *Kisan Sabha* in 1936. This *Sabha* wanted to organize and prepare the peasants for their emanicipation from every form of exploitation. It also wanted to secure complete freedom from economic and political power for the peasants and workers and all other exploited classes.[20] The provincial *sabhas* like the Punjab *Kisan Sabha* were formed under the auspices of the All India *Kisan Sabha*. The Punjab *Kisan Sabha* was dominated by militant elements drawn from the earlier anti-imperialist movements in the states *i.e.*, the *ghadr* group, the Akali, the *babbar* Akali and the *Praja Mandal*.[21] On the call of the *Praja Mandal* the peasants formed their own *sabhas* and got them affiliated with the *tehsil Kisan Sabhas*.[22]

Now the tenants' leaders decided to organise a *muzara* war council. This council was to work under the general direction of the *Kisan Sabha* and to guide the tenants' movement. A state level convention of tenants representatives was called at village Jaithuke on March 16, 1939 by the prominent tenant leader Dharam Singh Fakkar. The convention set up the *muzara* war council with Narain Singh Bhadaur as President, Chand Singh as General Secretary and Dharam Singh Fakkar as Joint Secretary.[23] Its branches were set up at Budhlada, Buchho and Sehna.[24]

---

20. Desai, A.R. (*ed.*), *Peasant Struggle in India*, Delhi, 1982, 430.
21. Presidential address of Baba Gurmukh Singh—President *Kisan* Committee, at the Eight annual Conference of State *Kisan* Committee held at Jampur, September 21, 1946, Desh Bhagat Printing Press, Lahore, 16.
22. PSR, PM's Office File No. 746, PSA; Master Hari Singh, *op. cit.*, 244-245.
23. PSR, PM's Office File No. 756 and 5882, *Ijlas-i-khas*, File No. 2077 and 2266, PSA, Patiala.
24. Budhlada was in Hissar district (now in Bhatinda district), Buchho in Ferozepur district and Sehna in Ludhiana district. These places were conveniently situated at the outskirts of the Patiala State to conduct propaganda work in the adjacent state villages. Vide., *Ijlas-i-khas* File No. 2077, PSR, PSA, Patiala.

The *muzara* committees were to perform the following functions :

1. to help local committee to educate peasants and collect funs for the activities of the state committees;
2. to send workers to the *biswedari* villages to educate tenants on the lines of the manifesto of the committee;
3. to defend tenants in their legal battles against the *biswedari*;
4. to organize meetings of the *muzaras*;
5. to send *jathas* (deputations) of the muzaras to the higher officials of the state and the British Government to highlight the grievances of the muzaras; and
6. to print and distribute propaganda material in order to strengthen the peasants' struggle.

The *muzara* committee authorized Dharam Singh Fakkar to lead a delegation to meet the leaders of the All India *Kisan Sabha*. The delegation met Baba Rur Singh Churchak, President of the Punjab *Kisan Sabha*.[25] The *muzara* Committee came to be known as the *Kisan Muzara* Committee, thus identifying itself with broader peasant struggle.[26] As a result of the intensification of the struggle, many petty peasant workers joined the movement as local leaders. '*No batai*' compaign was also accelerated by the *kisan muzara* Committee. Many of them moved around the villages encouraging and mobilizing those who were hesitant to join.[27] Now, the Maharaja appointed a Commission[28] to enquire into the cause of dispute between the *biswedars* and occupancy tenants. Thus, it is apt that the

25. PSR, *Ijlas-i-Khas File No. 2077*, PSA, Patiala.
26. *Ibid.*
27. PSR, PM's Office File No. 1555—see confidential weekly Report from Inspector General of Police, Patiala, dated 28.7.1939, PSA, Patiala.
28. Mr. M.L. Raina, the Law Minister of the state headed this Commission.

peasants' movement in this region underwent a radical change. In its out look and programme of action, creating necessary conditions for the growth of the tenants' movement. As the *muzara* Committee wanted direct confrontation with the *biswedars*, the moderate and the loyalist leadership got isolated and discredited. It is during this period that we can draw distinction between the loyalists and the militant leadership. In fact the militant leaders got complete control over the *muzara* movement. Several radical leaders like Harnam Singh Dharamgarh, Jangir Singh Phaguwalia, Wazir Singh Daftriwala, Pritam Singh Gojran, etc. inspired the peasants/tenants and came forward to lead their struggle.

With the outbreak of the World War II on September 1, 1939, the states' authorities got an opportunity to crush the tenants' movement. Almost all the front line leaders of the movement were arrested and punished under Section 447 and 107 of the Indian Penal Code.[29] From the end of 1939 till the beginning of 1942 the movement continued at a slower pace and with low profile. The *muzara* workers felt discouraged with the arrest of Harnam Singh Dharamgarh, the prominent leader and the moving spirit of the Patiala *Kisan* Committee. In fact, the *muzara* workers were thrown into disarry.[30] Secondly, after the death of Sewa Singh Thikriwala, the *Praja Mandal* leadership was divided into two groups, one inspired by left wing ideology and the other by religious fervour. With the arrest of communist leaders, Master Tara Singh who had fallen into disrepute,[31] thought to exploit the situation to win over the leadership cadre and also build up mass support for the Akali's among the peasants. In 1940, several religious *dewans* were held at a number of places which were addressed by Master Tara Singh.[32] However, as a consequence of their new

---

29. PSR, PM's Office File No. 1559—CID Secret Abstract of Intelligence, dated 5.7.1940, PSA, Patiala.
30. *Ibid.*,—CID Secret Abstract of Intelligence dated 12.7.1940.
31. Master Tara Singh had earlier lost credibility due to his alleged loyalist attitude among the radical Akalis.
32. PSR, PM's Office File No. 745, PSA, Patiala.

activities, Ujjagar Singh Bhaura and his associates attracted the associates of Jagir Singh Joga—they were Jangir Singh Phaguwalia, Wazir Singh Daftriwala and Pritam Singh Gojran.[33]

Thus, polarization in leadership and political parties was further enhanced as a consequence of the position taken by the Akali *dal,* led by Master Tara Singh, in National politics on the side of the British in supporting the war efforts.[34] In this new situation, the Congress, the *Praja Mandal* and the Communists were on one side and the communal and pro-imperialist elements such as the Akalis, the Muslim League and the Unionists on the other.[35]

From the beginning of 1942, the peasants' struggle again began to gather strength and momentum, because many prominent Communist leaders like Sohan Singh Josh, Achhar Singh Chhina, Teja Singh Swatantar, etc., were released from jail on the understanding that they would collaborate with the Government in the war effort. This peculiar situation had risen after Russia had joined allies in the World War II. The Communists and the Akalis along with the princes of India were helping the British in their war efforts. Jagir Singh Joga, a Communist leader of Patiala State made a hollow claim that the Communist would launch the movement at suitable time to attain the rights of the peasants. He also asserted that they would not only halt the Government machinery but "time will tell whether we—the Communists or Master Tara Singh had his party have been leading the *Panth* on the wrong path.[36]

In 1942, the Communists organised a meeting at Bhangeli near Lahore. It was attended by prominent *Kisan* leaders. They decided to revive the *Kisan Sabhas* in the East Punjab States and maintain a close link between the *Kisan Sabhas* and the

33. PSR, PM's Office File No. 1560--see CID Secret Abstract of Intelligence, dated 12.7.1940, PSA, Patiala.
34. Walia, Ramesh, *op. cit.,* 155.
35. *Ibid.,* 156.
36. PSR, PM's Office File No. 565—CID Secret Abstract of Intelligence, PSA, Patiala.

Communist party.[37] Once again the Communist influence began to increase in this region. The reason for this was that they co-operated with rival Akali *Jatha* against the Akalis and led by Master Tara Singh. They also took part in religious congregations held by this group to condemn Master Tara Singh's anti-national and communal politics.[38] This projection of the communists as the militant upholders of the Akali tradition of relentless struggle against oppression was ideologically in mobilizing the tenants

It will not be out of place to state that the tenants' movement in the East Punjab States got inspiration from the freedom struggle and it was further intensified.[39] Under the influence of the Marxist leaders and leftist ideology, the *muzara* war council organized armed guards to protect the gains of the movement.[40] Even the three Units[41] of *muzara* war Council were assigned duties. Now, 'No *batai*' agitation spread from village to village rapidly in 1946-47, leading to many serious clashes between the *muzaras* and the *biswedars*. Armed guards were organized because the *biswedars* had organized armed bands of *goondas* to get their lands vacated which were forcibly occupied by the tenants and to effect their eviction. Secondly, at the national level the members belonging to the *Kirti* wing of the Communist Party decided to oppose the partition of India by adopting war methods. Teja Singh Swatantar along

37. PSR, *Ijlas-i-Khas*, File No. 2226, PSA, Patiala.
38. PSR, PM's Office File No. 565—CID Secret Abstract of Intelligence, dated 13.3.1942, PSA, Patiala.
39. Master Hari Singh, *op. cit.*, 248.
40. PSR, PM's Office case No. J-1 of 201 (1945)—file on Landlords Association, Patiala, PSA, Patiala.
41. First Unit comprising of Harnam Singh Dharamgarh, Giani Bachan Singh, Gurbachan Singh Rahi and Ghuman Singh covered Sunam area; Second Unit comprising of Arjan Singh Bhadaur, Chand Singh Bhadaur, Harnam Singh Gandasinghwala, Dulla Singh Jalaldiwala and Bachan Singh Khudi covered Barnala area and third Unit comprising of Dharam Singh Fakkar, Jagir Singh Joga, Arjan Singh Tamkot, Santa Singh Bajewala, and Sobha Singh covered Mansa area.

with the *Kirti* wing organized a Lal Communist Party for this purpose. In launching an armed struggle the tenants' struggle in the East Punjab States, which had become militant, offered ready allegiance to the Lal Communist Party in resisting *biswedari* oppression. Giani Bachan Singh of Sunam circle was made incharge of the armed wing which had about thirty five trained volunteers while Teja Singh Swatantar was in charge of the armed guards. These guards were organized for self defence and were not motivated to cause terror. Backed by the enthusiasm, of the tenants and inactivity on the part of administration, this small force of armed guards terrorised the *biswedars* who finally fled their villages.[42]

In 1947, the tenants' movement inspired by the communists became militant. Now, the tenants refused to pay *batai* and they forcibly occupied *biswedari* land. This led to violent clashes between the tenants and the *biswedars*. The latter resorted to armed assault on the tenants and pushed those to the courts who refused to pay *batai*.[43] Finding it an opportune time the communists organized their defence both inside and outside the courts. Supported by the Congress and the *Praja Mandal* leaders, the tenants' movement became so intense that it was compared with "an open revolution throughout the states like that of France".[44]

The Maharaja of Patiala, under the growing threat of growing violence with the independence of India imminent,

42. *All India States People's Conference* File No. 133-A, 1945-48 (Patiala State) NMML, New Delhi.
43. PSR, PM's Office File No. 565—CID Secret Abstracts of intelligence, dated 8.6.1945, 12.7.1945, and of August 1945; PM's Office Case No. 7-1, of 1945—Report sent by *biswedars* to the Government, PSA, Patiala.
44. PM's Office Case No. 1-1 of 2001 (1945)—File on Landlords Association, see letter dated 13.1.1947; PM's Office Case No. 1B-1-2 of 2000 (1945-46)—see CID Secret Abstracts of Intelligence, dated 27 July, 28 August, 21 September, 23 November, 1945 and 22 February and 29 March, 1946; also see Reports Sent in by *biswedars* to Government, dated 22 February, 1946, PSA, Patiala.

issued a *farman-i-Shahi* to solve and settle the tenants-*biswedars* dispute. However, the *muzara* War Council under the leadership of Dharam Singh Fakkar and Teja Singh Swatantar out rightly rejected this *farman-i-shahi*. They launced mass campaign to explain the pro-*biswedari* character of the farman through pamphlets, posters and conferences.[45] At this time India got independence but was partitioned into Indian Union and Pakistan. There was communal bloodshed and mass migration of minority population across the border. It took off the fire out of the movement. Thus for a ear, the peasants' movement was subdued.

For about a year there was stalemate due to the aftermath of India's position. However, the formation of Pepsu and the growth of many democratic political organizations gave the peasants' leadership an opportunity to voice their grievances. It brought into existence a number of new political organizations which viewed political, social and economic problems of the people from different prospective. The growth of such political organizations brought new polarization in the leadership of the peasants' struggle. Some of the urbanite Praja Mandal leaders such as Brish Bhan and Des Raj drifted towards the Congress while another group of rural leaders bened towards the *Akali Dal*. Popular among these rural leaders were Bhagwan Singh Denewalia and Wazir Singh Daftriwala. Col. Raghbir Singh formed a new *Lok Sewak Sabha* with a view to raising the economic and social status of the peasants and the depressed classes and to create and promote communal harmony.[46] Sunder Lal, the President of Patiala *Praja Mandal*, protected the Punjab Congress leaders against the activities of the *Lok Sewak Sabha* because it attempted to make a dent on the Akali and *Praja Mandal* parties, it naturally became their targets of criticism and condemnation. Now, the *Praja Mandal* submitted a memorandum to the state Ministry of the Government of India in which it accused the new organization

45. Master Hari Singh, *op. cit.*, 251.
46. *The Hindustan Times*, Delhi, April 3, 1948; Rattan Pal Singh, The Illustrated History of the Sikhs : 1947-78, Chandigarh, 1978, 25.

"propagating the programme of the ruler".[47] However, the *Lok Sewak Sabha* denied the charges and rejected them by saying that such statements were being made because it was gaining popularity and the communalists and communists were getting disturbed.[48] The span of existence of this new *Sabha* was very short. It ultimately got merged into the Congress on the eve of the first general elections in 1951. The reason for this merger was apt. The *Praja Mandal* was in great need of peasants' support which it had lost to the Akalis and the communists.

A large number of peasant leaders had come under the influence of the leftist ideology and began to or under the banner of the Punjab *Kisan Sabha* and Punjab *Kisan* Committee. These two rival peasants organizations were led by the Lal Communist party and the communist party of India respectively. A brief analysis of the perspective of these different types of leaders on peasants/tenants' problems would not be out of place.

The urbanite leaders of the state *Praja Mandal* organisation looked at the tenants' problem form the point of the view of simple tenancy reforms. Their outlook was almost the same as that of the Congress Party. They wanted an early solution of the tenants' problem but they were least interested in mobilizing the peasantry on revolutionary lines. But they were deeply interested in participating in the native politics of the East Punjab States. It is interesting to note that they proposed radical solution in form of complete abolition of *biswedari* system,[49] before the formation of the Pepsu; but after its formation, their attitude towards the peasants' problems underwent a sea change. Realising the value of the support of the *biswedars* in mobilizing votes during the election campaign, they were ready to accept them. However, they never wanted to loose the tenants instead desired to keep their old following among the tenants intact. They, therefore, wanted such a solution to the tenants'

47. *The Indian News Chronicle*, Delhi, April 10, 12, 1948.
48. *The Statesman*, Delhi, April 16, 1948.
49. *All India States People's Confernece Papers, op. cit.*

problem through which the interest of both the *biswedas* and the *muzaras* could be protected. Thus, their earlier opposition to the *biswedari* system got mild. Now, they proposed such reforms as would protect the interest of both the parties to the dispute. This makes clear why Brish Bhan and his group, who advocated radical land reforms, were viewed by the Congress leaders with the suspicion of hob-nobing with the communists.[50]

A large number of peasant leaders and activities owed allegiance to peasants' organization led by the two communist parties and look at the peasants' problems from radical prospective. It is interesting but significant to state, though the leaders of the rival communist parties indulged in an open propaganda against each other, yet they advocated the abolition of the *biswedari* without compensation. However, their tactics and lines of action were slightly different on the peasants' front. The Lal Communist Party[51] had a mass following among the tenants. It aimed at mobilizing the peasantry on revolutionary lines. It believed in the use of force. To achieve its end, this group designed to forge an alliance of the land workers, tenants, pro-peasants and middle peasants against the *biswedars*. Besides, the leadership of the Communist Party of India[52] disliked the tactics of the Lal Communist Party on the basis that its policies largely would benefit the rich peasantry. In support of their opinion its leadership gave this plea that the use of force would only tend to bring the *biswedars* and the Government together in suppressing the movement.

Teja Singh Swatantar, the founder of the Lal Communist Party was deeply involved in the *muzara* movement because

50. Walia, Ramesh, *op. cit.,* 185.
51. This party was formed in 1948 by Teja Singh Swatantar. It was a splinter group mostly belonging to the *Kirti* wing. Dharam Singh Fakkar, Jagir Singh Joga and Giani Bachan Singh were other important members of this Party.
52. The Communist Party of India comprised Master Hari Singh, Kartar Singh Baghi, Harnam Singh Chamak and Hira Singh Bhattal.

of its militant character. Under his direction there came into existence small band of armed men devoted to the cause of *muzaras* against the *biswedars*. The leaders of this party instilled a new life in the Pepsu *Kisan Sabha*. They attempted to forge an alliance of peasants, tenants and agricultural workers against the *biswedars*. The demands of the tenants-at-will and agricultural workers were also included in the programme of the agitation. The peasants were asked to put an end to the exploitation of agricultural workers by giving them their due share. Distribution of the common lands of villages among *kamins* and other exploited sections of the rural society was also demanded. But caste and community stood in the way of success.[53]

However, the leadership did not lose the courage as well as the hope. The village and *tehsil* level committees were re-organised; a new war council was formed and a volunteer crops was raised to help the *muzaras* in their struggle against the *biswedars* and the police.[54] Funds were raised for defending the tenants in the courts against false police cases; villages were grouped into clusters of six village each for conducting the agitation effectively. Vilage Kishangarh was the most important centre of the *muzara* movement. During the *kharif* season of 1948-49, 'No *batai*' operation was personally supervised by Comrade Chhajju Mal Vaid and Dharam Singh Fakkar of Dalelsinghwala.[55] A serious clash took place between the tenants and armed forces on March 16, 1948, resulting in the death of a police officer and six kisan workers including Dharam Singh Fakker were arrested and cases were registered against them. But all of them were acquitted and released in 1950 by the court through the efforts of the Kishangarh Defence Committee comprising Brish Bhan, Des Raj and Harnabs Lal. All these

53. *Ibid.*
54. Kishangarh, *The heroic Defence of His Land,* published by *Pepsu Kisan Sabha* (Bhatinda : Mittal Printing Press-n.d.), 49.
55. *The Tribune,* March 23, 1949, 3; Vaid, Chhajju Mal, Comrade Dharam Singh Fakkar : *Ik Jiwani—IkPresna,* Bhatinda : 1980, 13.

leaders were known for their left leaning in *Praja Mandal* organization.[56]

Thus the 'brave' and 'heroic' battle of Kishangarh peasants led to the burial of the *farman-i-shahi* of March 1947. It also led to the dissolution of Rarewala Ministry on November 18, 1949. The *farman-i-Shahi* was amended by the State Government and an other ordinance was issued on August, 15, 1949.[57] But this ordinance also failed to solve the tenancy problem in the Pepsu. Let it be noticed that throughout the period under review, the *Pepsu* Government was following a policy of stick and carrot in relation to the tenants' movement combining repression with concession to protect the interests of the *biswedars* to the extent it could be possible under the circumstances, the *Pepsu Kisan Sabha* and the *muzara* war council in a meeting held at Tamkot in September 1949 rejected the new ordinance. It was decided to launch struggle vigorously[58] as stress was laid on creating leadership in tenants' villages and setting up trained volunteers corps. Teja Singh Swatantar now wrote two pamphlets titled "Tenant Struggle for land in Pepsu and Attitude of Political Parties" and "Times for Akali *Dal* to take decision". The principal purpose of writing these pamphlets was to inspire and prepare the peasants/tenants to launch a fresh struggle against the states' government.

Under the guidance of comrade Gurcharan Singh Randhawa and Wadhawa Ram, who escaped from Ludhiana without trial and entered Pepsu, the peasants' movement became intense. Gurdial Singh Dala, Avtar Singh Banga, Surain Singh Khela and Inder Singh Murari were already working in Pepsu as leaders of volunteer squads, Giani Bachan Singh Bakshiwala, Ishar Singh Tamkot, Pirtha Singh Kishangarh, Kehar Singh Bakshiwala and Puraj Singh Siriwala were working as local squad leaders. All these leaders were working under

56. *Muzara Kisana De Mittar Kaun,* published by Tenants' Committee, Pepsu (Ludhiana : Civil and Military Press, 1949).
57. Rattan Pal Singh, *op. cit.,* 21.
58. Master Hari Singh, *op. cit.,* 257-58.

the guidance of Teja Singh Swatantar.[59] The police arrested a prominent peasant leader Chanchal Singh Chabha from the conference held in April, 1951 on the eve of *rabi* harvest. However, he was rescued by the organized volunteers from the clutches of the police.[60]

Under the new constitution of India, elections to the Pepsu Assembly were held in 1952 for the first time. There were three prominent tenant leader M.L.As—Giani Bachan Singh, Basawa Singh and Arjan Singh Bhadaur, who supported the United Front Ministry of Rarewalal. Let it be noticed that these three leaders were of communist leanings. Rarewala Ministry appointed a 7 member committee to suggest a solution of the agrarian problem within 3 months. At this time a big conference was held at Mansa under the chairmanship of Jagir Singh Joga. At this conference, *biswedars* of Talwandi Sabo, Khatriwala and Kharaksinghwala surrendered their lands in favour of tenants without compensation.[61] During its short stay the United Front Ministry drafted three bills. This ministry also facilitated the merger of two communist groups and with this merger the violent phase of the agrarian struggle came to an end.[62] When the United Front Ministry was dissolved, the Pepsu was placed under the President's rule which let loose repression of the peasants. The peasants were horrified and demoralized as well. The arena of the leaders fight for the cause of the tenants shifted from masses to the Legislature. They kept themselves busy in exacting more favourable terms in the form of tenancy legislation for the tenants. The communist members also pleaded the cause of the tenants in the Assembly. In the first session of the newly elected Legislative Assembly, Harbans Lal, A *Praja Mandalist,* and Giani Bachan Singh demanded the release of tenant leaders and the abolition of punitive police

59. *Ibid.,* 258-59.
60. *Ibid,* 260.
61. Gupta, C.L. Bhatinda the Storm Centre of People's Movement, in 21st National Conference. All India *Kisan Sabha,* Bhatinda, *Souvenir,* 35.
62. *The Tribune,* August 4, 1952, 8.

posts.[63] Giani Bachan Singh, a Communist M.L.A. criticised the Congress Government for having failed to solve the tenants-*biswedars* dispute without compensation.[64] He also narrated the sufferings of the tenants in the hands of the *biswedars.* He told the Assembly that the tenants were not satisfied with the existing laws. He also narrated the history of the *biswedari.* His motive behind all this was to touch the pulse of the members and to secure better deal for the peasants.

Baba Hira Singh Bhattal supported the resolution of abolition of landlordism. He urged the Government that no compensation should be given to the *biswedars* rather they should be forced to pay a penalty to tenants for illegally depriving the tenants of their right for a such long time.[65] The President, All India *Kisan Sabha,* Mr. Karyanand, in a press conference, criticized the United Front Ministry for the proposed agrarian reforms by them. The clause of compensation was also opposed by him because he held that the *biswedars* had already squeezed the tenants enough.[66]

The agrarian Bills introduced in the Assembly by the United Front Ministry to make cultivation and ownership coincide as far as possible. However, these Bills could be enacted during the President's rule in Pepsu, after the dissolution of the Assembly due to the suspension of the constitution.[67] On the other hand the peasants' movement was suppressed heartlessly during the President's rule from March, 1952 to March 1954. Many tenants' leaders were arrested and implicated in false cases. The police killed several innocent persons in fake encounters.[68] However, during this period, the

63. *Pepsu Legislative Assembly Debates, Official Report,* Vol. 1, S. No. 4, May 6, 1952, 85-88.
64. *Ibid,* Vol. I, No. 4, May 9, 1952, 152-53.
65. *Ibid,* 169.
66. (Press Conference was held in the Communist Parliamentary Office). *The Tribune,* November 25, 1952.
67. *Report on the Administration of Pepsu, from April 1, 1952 to March 31st,* 1953, Government Publication, 67-68.
68. *Election Menifesto to the Pepsu Communist Party,* Jullundhur Awami Printing Press, 1954, 7-8.

Government made an attempt to reform the existing tenancy laws in the States. Three important Acts were passed *i.e.,* The Pepsu Aboliion of *Ala Malkiat* Rights Act, 1953; The Pepsu Occupancy Tenants (Vesting of proprietary rights) Act and the Pepsu Tenancy and Agricultural Lands Act, 1953.[69]

The political situation in Pepsu became complex before 1954 elections because of a sudden change in the attitude of the *biswedars* and the Princes. They joined the Congress en bloc and left Akali Party in the wilderness. Now the chief of the Akali Party, Giani Kartar Singh, sought the co-operation from other political parties to defeat the Congress. However, the Congress won 37 seats in the elections of March, 1954.[70]

The Pepsu Tenancy and Agricultural Lands Act, 1953 was passed by the Pepsu Legislative Assembly. But the Communist Party and the local *Kisan Sabha* disapproved the clause creating distinction between occupancy and non-occupancy tenants. They did not agree to the payment of compensation.[71]

A demonstration was staged at Patiala on June 12, 1954 by over 700 peasants-members of the *Kisan Sabha*. It was led by the Octogenarian peasants' leader Baba Harnam Singh Dharamgarhia; local communist leader and five *Sanjha* members of the State Legislative Assembly. The demonstrators demanded the release of the detained MLA and stoppage of ejectment of tenants. The Pepsu agricultural Tenants (Temporary protection and Disability) Bill, 1954 was passed in the Assembly. The Communist MLAs opposed this Bill. Hira

---

69. *President Rule in Pepsu* (March 1953 to March 1954), published by Pepsu Government, 4-5.
70. *The Statesman,* New Delhi, 1, Columns 6-7, January 15, 1954; Rattan Pal Singh, *op. cit.,* 35 (The Akali Dal was divided between two groups of Sampuran Singh Ram and Pritam Singh Gojran, the latter owing allegiance to the *Shiromani Akali Dal* headed by Master Tara Singh). The Parties position : The Congress-37; The Right Wing Akalis-10; The left wing Akalis-2, The Communists-4; and Independents-7.
71. This distinction was created by the ruling class to divide the peasantry. *The Statesman,* New Delhi, June 6, 1954.

Singh Bhattal, leader of the *Sanjha Morcha* group in the Assembly charged the Government of supporting the *biswedars* and letting loose a reign of terror on the tenants and they were being ejected forcibly on large scale.[72]

The Pepsu *Kisan Sabha* in its annual session passed a resolution to stop the ejectment of tenants, reinstate the already ejected ones to grant occupancy rights to the tenants. The Sabha demanded ceiling on the *biswedars'* land and that the excess land be distributed among the landless. The resolution added that the Congress Assembly party inspite of protests by the *kisan Sabha* and others passed the Tenants Amendment Bill in December, 1954, withdrawing the right conferred on tenants-at-will by the Presidents' Act, 1953. The State Assembly again passed the main Act but withheld its operation for one more year.[73] The Communist MLAs Jagir Singh Joga, Dharam Singh fakkar, Baba Hardial Singh Bhattal and Arjan Singh Bhadaur all pleaded the cause of tenants and they made following proposals :

(a) Abolition of *biswedari* without any compensation;

(b) Ceiling on land holdings;

(c) Stoppage of ejectment;

(d) Granting of Occupancy rights to the tenants-at-will; and

(e) distribution of surplus land among the landless.

The proposal was sternly opposed by the treasury banches, mostly dominated by the big *biswedar*.[74] They favoured

72. *The Tribune*, 6, Column 8, June 13, 1954; *Pepsu Vidhan Sabha* Debates, Official repot, Vol. V, S. No.6, December 22, 1954 (Hardit Singh Bhattal, Jagir Singh Joga, Dharam Singh Fakkar and Arjan Singh-all the Communist leaders opposed the Bill).
73. The Tribune, April 17, 1955, 9, Column 6.
74. They were Raja Maheshinder Singh, Uncle of the *Rajparmukh* Col. Surindra Singh, a former ruler of Nalagarh State and brother-in-law of the *Rajparmukh, Nawab* of Malerkotla, Gen. Shivdev Singh, a former Chief Minister of Nabha State and one of the biggest landlords of the East Punjab States.

compensation and opposed ceiling on land holdings. The final situation that emerged was a compromise between the stand taken by the Communist leaders and the Government.

Hence, from the above discussion two major trends are discernible in the leadership of the peasants' movement in the East Punjab State. First, the peasant leaders who spearheaded the movement, sprang up from low rung land owning class and mainly the peasants with occupancy rights were given proprietary rights in 1953, the movement almost ceased to exist. The leaders joined some political party—the Akali Party or the Congress. The leaders were not idealist who wanted to reform the rural society on socialist lines. They were simply interested in acquiring proprietary rights in land. When they achieved this target they withdrew from the movement and began to consolidate their personal position socially and economically by joining some political party. The second trend is that the agricultural workers did not gain any thing from the struggle because the leaders did not advocate the rights of the tenants-at-will. These tenants-at-will were exploited socially and economically even by petty *biswedars*.

It would not be wrong to say that the leaders of the peasants' struggle were short-sighted. Their vision was parochial, their objectives limited, their strategy inadequate, their understanding of the problem shallow and their role in reforming the society was ineffective. As a result, they could neither indoctrinate the masses nor could they forge a worker-peasant alliance. They failed to achieve their objectives due to the fact that they considered themselves, especially after having obtained proprietary rights in 1953, as volunteers or activists of the political parties rather than of the struggling peasantry and those of the peasant movement.

The peasants' struggle was very violent and intense facing corresponding extent repression by the State and the *biswedars*. It is noteworthy to point out that its leadership though highly political could not act as mediator. Instead, the leaders led people to a direct confrontation with the Government because they compelled to do so by the community local leaders.

Representing highly cohesive and well knot *jat* dominated communities, they had very little political space to direct the movement into channels borrowed either by the political parties to which they belonged or the peasants themselves.

The peasant leaders in the East Punjab States were directed in their line of action by the programme and the policies of the political parties, the pressure of the peasants from below and the necessity of maintaining law and order by the State. Because of these factors we note that whereas the other political parties even after independence carried the struggle even to an open confrontration with the Government. However, the other political organizations, at no stage ingnored the interests of the peasants. Even the local leadership supported the Lal Communist Party in its struggle against the State and the *biswedars*. During the year 1952-53, the local leaders were compelled to take a line of action as desired by volatile rural communities and not as the political parties wanted. As a result, the movement became violent and militant, almost revolutionary in its character. So far as the peasants were concerned, they released that they had been ejected from their land by illegal means; no amount of oppression deterred them from the violent methods; while on the other hand the Government was unwilling to bear defiance of its legal and administrative authorities. At this stage, the radical among the leaders-both the communists and the *Praja Mandalists* captured the leadership of the peasants/tenants' movement. The moderate leadership was completely alienated from the tenants as it did not offer any radical line of action and radical programme. As they were discredited, they could not play any effective role till 1953. As most of the peasants with occupancy rights got their proprietary rights, the pressure was lessened and they withdrew from the movement. However, the politically motivated moderate leadership again became active especially for capturing political power. On the other hand, the radical among the leaders dominated the political scene in Pepsu during the period under review.

Evidently, the nature of leadership and its line of action is determined by the social backgrounds of the leaders. In other words its nature is closely related to the nature of society from which it emerges. Wherever the traditional social structure was intact, especially in the tribal and semi-agrarian tribal societies, as in the East Punjab States, so the struggle here was violent and intense and even radical. It was due to the fact that the communities were rightly or wrongly conscious of the legitimacy as well as genuineness of their demands. It too imparted radicalism to their leadership. It explains why the leaders were more radical in this part of the province than their counterparts outside the States. Moreover, radicalism of leaders was not related to the actual demands of the peasants/tenants or the ideology of the political parties to which they belonged. It was only a radicalism of action based on the peasants' awareness that their demands were just and legitimate. However, this awareness was confined to their basic demands and not aimed at reforms of the rural society. Therefore to achieve these demands they involved themselves in the long drawn struggle with the *biswedars* and the government. From this we may draw the conclusion :

(i) that during the movement the radical leadership failed to raise the awareness of the peasantry to a higher level transcending their immediate economic demands;

(ii) that political and ideological radicalisation of the leaders especially the Marxist leaders had no direct relationship with the awareness of the peasants. This tells why most of the leaders either left the struggle after 1953[75]or shifted their loyality to either the Congress Party or the Akali Party.

(iii) that most of these leaders as were drawn from a single socio-religious community, they did not develop the communal or sectarian outlook; and

(iv) that in the East Punjab States the peasants/tenants'

75. Giani Bachan Singh, Jangir Singh Phaguwalia, Achar Singh Chhina and a few others belonged to this category.

struggle did not proceed on any theoretical formulation or ideological compulsion.

Thus, the leaders who were supposed to have theoretical knowledge of the social action found their knowledge of no use as the nature of action was determined not by historic-economic situation as by the level of awareness of the community and its cohesion. That is why some scholars think that the political leadership especially that of the Marxist/ suffered from contradiction between their theory and practice. To conclude we may believe that the leadership of the peasants' struggle in these States was of an informal character which depended on personal traits. Moreover, such leadership required personal qualities of consistency, dedication, courage, commitment, understanding, and determination in organizing the mass movement, and in inspiring the peasants/tenants with courage and determination. On these ground they, undoubtedly, played a vital role in organising and leading the peasantry, and in infusing radicalism and dynamism in the peasants/tenants' struggle.

10 STRUCTURAL RELATIONSHIP AMONG PEASANTS, BISWEDARS AND THE GOVERNMENT

The peasants' movement was the outcome of relationship among peasants, *biswedars* and the government concerned. It, therefore, becomes imperative to explore its roots in the dynamics of relationship among these three parties. However, this relationship can be determined on the basis of the social structure which gives rise to peasants' problems. In this chapter, the social structure of the rural society will be discussed on the basis of the landholdings and their interaction among the different rungs within itself and with the government. Of course, it is not easy to formulate a pattern of relationship[1] among peasants, *biswedars* and the government in view of the varied agrarian social structure in terms of the land control and land use, but they can be socially categorized on the basis suggested by Daniel Thorner.[2]

Now, starting from the bottom, there were three types of income obtained from land in the form of rent, produce and the wages. So far as the rights were concerned, they were also of three kinds *i.e.,* proprietary, occupancy and share cropping. There is also evidence of the existence of absentee landlords the *khudkasht* and the tenants in the East Punjab States during the period of our study. The agrarian social system in this region during the period under review comprised the *biswedars* as the big landlords who enjoyed proprietary right in land and exploited the peasants by keeping the level of rent up and that of the wages very low. Some peasants had proprietary rights

1. Dhanagre, D.N., *Peasant Movement in India : 1920-1950,* (Delhi : 1968), 11.
2. Daniel Thorner, *The Agrarian Prospect in India,* (London : 1962), 4.

in lands, other had occupancy rights and still a large number had no rights at all.

While investigating the genesis of the peasants/tenants' movement in this part of the Punjab we should not be carried away by the western model which analyses the problem within the framework of colonial economy as the East Punjab States were mainly an agrarian society operating on feudal relationship, wherein the *biswedars* and the State tried to devour as much as possible the produce of peasants by force or by fraud. It gradually created a cleavage between the *biswedars* on the one hand and the peasants and tenants on the other. Thus, the aristocratic and autocratic state helped by the *biswedars* lived luxuriously on the labour of the peasants in particular and rural masses in general. Naturally with the influence of the nationalist movement and growing awareness, the peasants rose in arms against the states' authorities.

To understand clearly the nature of agrarian structure and the dynamics of mutual relationship during the period under review, it becomes essential to study the relationship between tenants and *biswedars* and tenants and government. Let it be noticed that the agrarian structure in this region before 1887 underwent no change and it has been safely presumed on the basis of the absence of evidence. The *biswedars* exercised their hold and enjoyed their share in the produce without making any claim to proprietary rights in land and without ejecting tenants from the land, the latter had been cultivating. Major Popham Young—the Settlement Commissioner of Patiala State, states that before the settlement of Punjab Tenancy Act of 1887, "the right of Occupancy was well recognized. But the relation between the tenants and landlords began to deteriorate because the landlords began to acquire the proprietary rights. There was no clear understanding either as to how these rights were acquired, or what they amounted to".[3] He further wrote that in

3. Major P. Popham Young, *Report on the Settlement of the Patiala State (1900-1908)* : Ajmer : Scottish Mission Industries Co. Ltd., 26.

several cases the proprietary rights were in dispute between the cultivating peasants and the *biswedars*, who claimed proprietary rights on account of descent from the founder, the state courts often favoured the *biswedars* and reduced the cultivators/tenants having proprietary rights, to the status of occupancy tenants. He further states that there had been a compaing of oppression and aggression on the part of several *biswedars*, leading to the eviction of cultivators having occupancy rights.[4] Even so the peasants, who approached civil courts for justice, were not very large as most of them being ignorant and uneducated were under the impression that their rights over land were just and permanent and they, therefore, should not be disturbed in their possession. Despite the fact that the peasants were not aware of their rights, nor were the rights well defined, the *biswedars* also never thought of ejection of peasants as long as they paid their rent.[5] However, on the commencement of the regular settlement, the *biswedars*, fearing that under the new settlement the tenants were going to be declared as landlords, began to shift them from one field to another to prevent them being declared as landlords, began to shift them from one field to another to prevent them being declared occupancy tenants of their holdings. Some peasants who had long been out of possession took advantage of the weakness of the *biswedars* and forcibly occupied the lands which they had seldom or never cultivated. It let to violent clashes between the tenants and the *biswedars*.[6]

The land tenure system of this region, being in a state of chaos and flux, was steadily tending to the adoption of the Punjab Tenancy Laws. This too led to evict tenants who were in possession of land for a long time. But the tenants felt that they had hereditary claim and as a result of it, several tenants marched to the cities and sought justice in the courts.[7] About

4. *Ibid.*, 27, (More details are given in the next chapter).
5. *Punjab State Gazetteer*, Vol. XVII, A Phulkian States Patiala, Nabha and Jind, Lahore, 45.
6. *Ibid.*
7. *Ibid.*

their rights as granted by law, the tenants were not only guided but helped by the lawyers. During the Settlement Operation, Mr. Young attempted to ascertain the position and define the rights of tenants throughout the States.[8]

The most significant cause which led to the deterioration of relation between tenants and *biswedars* was the insecurity of tenancies. When Mr. Young's regular Settlement was effected, it was noticed that the claims of tenants and *biswedars* were some times equally valid. The former felt more insecure as they were aware of the collusion between the *ahalkars* and the *biswedars*. They also knew that in case of dispute the *biswedars*. Would be helped by the *ahalkars*. Thus, they were forced to send petition to the British authorities who were the lords of their immediate masters. One such petition was sent to the Viceroy of India on February 13, 1937 by the tenants of village Kishangarh : "We had been declared the owners of our land since 1876 *Bikrami* but in 1923 the *Sardars*[9] of Kishangarh, the relations of *Maharaja* and other men of contact in state service made us declared unauthorised farmers and our crops are captured with the help of police every year since then."[10]

Another factor which deteriorated the relations between the tenants and the *biswedars* was the *thappa* and *kankut* system of revenue collection. The tenants fought a dogged battle for the abolition of these systems and finally succeeded in their objective in the later half of thirties.[11] Though the *kankut* system was abolished, the problem of exploitation of the tenants by the *biswedars* could not be solved as the existing *batai* system as no less exploitative. Supported by the Punjab *Riyasti Praja Mandal* and the Punjab *Kisan Sabha*, the tenants launched a struggle against the batai system with two slogans namely;

8. *Ibid.*, 27.
9. In fact, these *Sardars* were the *biswedars* who received proprietary rights from the *Maharaja*.
10. *Ijlas-i-Khas* File No. 1263-PSR, PSA, Patiala.
11. Vaid, Chajju Mal, "Tenant Movement" In Master Hari Singh's book, *Punjab Peasant in Freedom Struggle*, PPM, New Delhi, 1984, 241-242.

'Land to the tillers' and 'no *batai*'.[12] The 'no *batai*' agitation resulted in clashes between the tenants and the *biswedars.* A serious clash took place in village Qulla Hakimen, District Bassi on November 25, 1937 resulting in the death of two *muzaras* and nine injured. The Government's attitude was always pro-*biswedars.* So, the police force suppressed the agitation and the State Government passed new laws to prosecute the *muzaras'* leaders and workers too.[13] As a result of this policy, the relations between the tenants and the *biswedars* further deteriorated. As the *muzaras* were in a very large number, every political group was after enlisting them in its own ranks to simply increase numerical strength of the party.[14]

We have already discussed how the vast area passed on to the *biswedars* soon after the emergence of the state from within the State. The relatives and kinsmen of rulers secured land on the payment of the nazranas. During the period of crisis-internal as well as external-liberal land grants were accorded to the influential persons to win them over. From the revenues accruing to them they were supposed to maintain their troops ready for service.[15] There were several other factors which were also responsible for effecting the groups of land. According to the *Punjab State Gazetteer,*[16] it was a favourite plan of the Sikh government to carve out new estates, regardless of existing rights and plant new settlements on cultivated lands. Some times to plant a hostile colony in neighbourhood of a powerful feudatory.

It will not be out of place if it is recalled that a number of Indian princes participated in the upheaval of 1857 on the British side. The imperialists, therefore, decided not to annex

12. *Ibid.,* 244.
13. PSR, PM's Office File No. 6175, PSA, Patiala.
14. *Ibid.* (Extract from the secret Abstract of Ingtelligence No. XVIII, dated 19.6.1942 by Superintendent of Intelligence).
15. Lepel, H. Griffan, The Rajas of the Punjab, (Second Edition), London : 1863, 125-126.
16. *Punjab State Gazetteer, op. cit.,* 144.

the territories of Indian rulers to the British empire.[17] In fact, they sought an alliance with the entire feudal land owing case *i.e.,* both the prices and the landlords. So, the rulers of the East Punjab States and other feudal lords were given free hand in establishing the feudal rule because they too had helped the British in crushing the revolt. Thus the *biswedari* system in this region of the Punjab was established after the revolt.[18]

Now, the ahalkars (officials) and the *biswedars* collaborated throughout the region. In fact, they were one in torturing the tenants. The former tried to improve his contact with the *biswedar* and the latter tried to enhance his prestige and influence in the official camp. Their constantly increasing influence finally led to the issue of *hidayat* in 1872 from the *Maharaja,* making it compulsory for all occupancy tenants to pay rents in kind.[19]

Let it be noticed that Maharaja Bhupinder Singh of Patiala State was an upholder of the *biswedari* system during the period 1900-1938. He granted *jagirs* to a large number of persons as favours by way of materimonial alliance. Such persons were cruel to the peasants. We shall have a detailed account of the untold misery on the villagers, particular in Kishangarh and Rajomajra in the second half of the chapter. These two villages were the centre of the peasants' movement in the whole region of the East Punjab States.[20]

The peasants in the East Punjab States can be divided into two categories—one category of peasants comprised those who paid revenue directly to the State and also enjoyed proprietary rights. They were petty cultivators described as *khudkasht;* the other category of peasants called tenants had no proprietary

17. Enik Komarov, Content and Principal Forms of the Evolution of Agrarian Relations in India in the 19th Century, in *New Indian Studies,* by Soviet Scholars, USSR Academy of Sciences, No. 13, 1976, 41.
18. *Patiala Tenants on the March,* Issued by *Muzara* Committee, Progressive Publishers, Lahore (ND), 3.
19. Major F. Popham Young, *op. cit.,* 27.
20. PSR, *Ijlas-i-Khas,* File No. 2077, PSA, Patiala.

rights on land. They paid revenue to the *biswedars.* These tenants were of two categories-tanents with occupancy rights and tenants-at-will. Out of the total 3,620 villages in the erstwhile Patiala State, there were 784 villages where the institution of *biswedari* was in existence. In the rest of the villages numbering 2,836, the tenants were *khudkasht.*[21] They were as backward, poor and ignorant as the tenants in *biswedari* villages. But they were better off than the tenants in *biswedari* villages in as much as they paid revenue directly to the government according to fixed rates. But in the case of the tenants in *biswedari* villages where the government was not directly involved, the agents exploited them and the *biswedars* charged revenue not according to the same rulers. Even the States' authorities collaborated with the *biswedars* in the exploitation of the tenants. For a very long time the situation did not allow the tenants' movement to grow because of two reasons. Firstly, the passivity and ignorance of the cultivators and secondly, perhaps, the *biswedari* institution did not become that coercive in its early stage.

Moreover, before 1875, there was no settlement done between the *biswedars* and the tenants. It is, therefore, not easy to assess the rights of the tenants. Since tradition was dominant in this part of the region, it may further be presumed that the tenants believed that they had proprietary rights in land[22] because the village communities cultivated the land. The members of village communities cultivated the land in their possession on almost the same terms as recongised proprietors, though legally and in popular estimation, their belief in being proprietors of land and their claim was untenable.[23]

The Summary Settlement of 1875 was the first Act which served as a shock realization for the tenants because according to it, both the tenants and proprietors were promiscuously

---

21. *Census Report of Patiala States* : 1931 (Lahore : Civil and Military Gazettee Ltd.), 14; PSR, *Ijlas-i-Khas,* File No. 2077, PSA : Patiala.
22. *Punjab State Gazetteer, op. cit.,* 93.
23. *Ibid.,* 146.

entered as *assamis*[24] (cultivators). This was done mainly because there were no records available to indicate the rights of the tenants. The Settlement of 1875 and the Land Legislation following this settlement weakened the position of the tenants and strengthened that of the *biswedars.* Following the pattern prevailing in the British Punjab territories, the State Government passed a rule that a tenant cultivating a piece of land constantly for 30 years was to be declared as occupancy tenant.[25] However, practically this rule was not put into practice because in several cases, the tenants cultivating land for over thirty years were deprived of their rights and even the efforts to grant rights were obstructed.[26] On the other hand, the tenants had to pay a large number of cesses such as *khush hasiayat,* a tax of three *annas* per *bigha* for the pleasure of the *biswedars.*[27] One of the many taxes imposed on the tenants was *neonda* which was paid on the occasion of the marriage of royal princes or the sons or daughters of the *biswedars.* This was prevalent in the *Bahia* villages related to the Maharaja.[28] In 1934, a complaint was made by an evicted tenant at a public meeting held at Budhlada which stated :[29] "On the marriage of *Tikka Sahib* we were forced to pay *neonda* @ 5% of the land revenue. What relation do we have with the Maharaja? If he considers us his relatives, then why does he not pay *neonda* to us".

The rulers and their *ahalkars* had adopted a repressive policy and there was absolutely no check on them. As a result inefficiency and instability crept into the administration of these

24. *Ibid.*
25. *Ibid.*
26. *Ibid.*
27. Joga Jagir Singh's Statement, Oral History Cell, File No. 35, Punjab Historical Studies Department, Punjabi University, Patiala; also supported by Sh. Brish Bhan in personal interview.
28. The first village that the ancestors of the ruling family of Patiala founded was Mehraj in Bhatinda district and later on around this village 22 villages sprang up and constituted the *Bahia,* mostly the kinsmen of these villages were known as the supporters of Maharaja.
29. PSR, PM's Office, File Nos. 1155, 4516, PSA : Patiala.

states and the already provocative situation deteriorated further. At the same time, the British Government had been suppressing this movement since the beginning of the twentieth century. At least, in the princely states of the Punjab, the awakening had become conspicuous during 1920's and 1930's; and the people particularly the peasants clearly told the dictatorial regime and dictators that the movement could not have been subdued by resorting to repressive measures. As a result, the rulers of these states and their Government had fully realized that besides repressive policy, there was a strong need for such a policy by which people could be silenced by giving them some concessions—in other words, they decided to follow the policy of stick and carrot.

The imperialists were in a fix because they could neither give full backing to the dictatorial policy of the rulers of the Punjab states and their policy of repression and suppression, nor could they alienate themselves from them because on one hand, there was fear of revolt and on the other, the British had been enjoying the support of the native rulers since 1849 when the British had annexed Punjab. Thus, these problems were quite complicated and difficult, especially at the time when the proposal to form a confederation had been gaining strength.[30]

However, in 1932, ignoring the wishes of the people some instructions were published according to which the public meetings, religious *diwans,* conferences and procession were banned; and besides, the formation of new political societies was strictly banned.[31] Almost all; the important political leaders

30. For further details see the files of *Punjab States Records*-particularly in the Prime Minister's Office files of Patiala State PSA : Patiala.
31. Walia, Ramesh, *A Study of Praja Mandal Movement in the East Punjab States,* Patiala, 1974, p. 115 (Patiala, Nabha and Jind-states issued a common decree which was later known as *hidayat-88* as it was signed on 5th *Poh,* 1988-*Bikrami.* Patiala implemented it through a special *Firman-i-Shahi* of January 14, 1931 which remained in operation till 1946 and finally it was withdrawn—of course under the pressure of *muzaras* movement).

and leading workers were interned in 1931-32. Sewa Singh Thikriwala and Bhagwan Singh Longowalia were the chief among them. The former died in jail itself in January, 1935 after a hunger strike,[32] lasting for a long period. Though its details are cited in the preceding chapter, it is pertinent to point out here that it was the death of Sewa Singh that led to the creation of new political milieu in the princely states of East Punjab and the movement against the rulers of these states and their government gained strength due to this fact only. But the declaration of the royal decree and its implementation in January itself made the political activities in the states all the more difficult due to which the peasants' movement could not speedily forge ahead.

The *biswedars* of Patiala state particularly appeared to be exceedingly perturbed. They anticipated that the final decision of this long standing controversy was going to be made in favour of the *muzaras* by the commission appointed by the Maharaja of Patiala, a reference to which has already been made in the second chapter. Some big *biswedars* concluded that if the decision resulted in favour of the *muzaras* it would ruin the *biswedars* altogether and would mean another great trouble for the state administration because the *muzaras'* movement in the states formed a part and parcel of the *Kisan* Party in the British Punjab which was essentially communistic in character.[33]

Since the beginning of the peasants' movement, the *biswedars* had been standing like a rock in their way, as a result of which the peasants' agitation could not succeed in extending its activities in every region of the state. The *biswedars* also held that the States' administration ought not to have taken up this question, at least, during the war period. They further argued that since the same law pertaining to the rights of the tenants was in force in the British Punjab and no special

32. Waila, Ramesh, *A Study of the Praja Mandal Movement in the East Punjab States, Patiala,* 1974, (For details see its Chapters-III, IV & V), 117-120.
33. PSR, PM's Office Case No. 565/C of 1939, PSA : Patiala.

concession were being allowed to them *muzaras* there, why then any such steps should be taken in the state.[34] Moreover, the *biswedars* requested the *Maharaja* of Patiala not to accede to their (tenants) demands. Firstly, the tenants wanted rights from the *biswedars* and then they would refuse payment of revenue to the state. They also stated that in case the state Government did not concede to their rights, the *biswedars* would send a deputation to wait upon the viceroy.[35]

Just as the tenants were organising attacks on the *biswedars*, the *biswedars* thought of oranising attacks on them. The *biswedars* felt that they should recruit strong youths for this purpose. Their names would be kept secret and they would be expected to be on duty for all the 24 hours. The landlords, being the friends of police and other officials, since they were rich men, could very easily win over them, and use this force against the tenants' struggle.[36] When the campaign for non-payment of *batai* was launched by the tenants, the *biswedars* *sought* to eject them with due formality.[37] However, this rather strengthened the agitation because the tenants were not ready to accept this treatment.[38] Even if the *muzaras* of some village promised to pay batai according to the *girdawari* rule, the

34. File No. 1564, Basta No. 50, Case No. 565/C of 1940 (Part-III) Basta No. 173, Case No. 41/C of 1939, PSA : Patiala.
35. PSR, Basta No. 15, PSA : Patiala.
36. PSR, Basta No. 25, File No. 740, Case No. 773/C of 1936; Basta No. 15, File No. CB-1-2 (Po. CID), 1945-46, PSA : Patiala.
37. PSR, Case No. 565/C of 1939 (when the tenants absolutely stopped to pay our proprietors' shore, some *biswedars* approached the law-courts and got decrees for arrears of rent and ejected some from non-occupancy holdings) vide, Basta No. 135, Case no. 120, S.No.6157, PSA : Patiala.
38. The tenants fought their cases from the lowest to the highest courts; when they failed they either offered resistence or about themselves and let the *biswedars* take nominal possession of the land but as soon as the Government officials had departed, they resumed possession. Vide., PSR, S.No.6157, Basta No. 135, Case No. 120; Basta No. 50, File No. 1560, Case No. 565/C of 1939, PSA : Patiala.

mukhtiars (agents) of the *biswedars* did not like this attitude of the *muzaras* and they approached the state officials and the latter always favouring them ordered payment of *batai* to be made according to the *girdawari.* The *biswedars* on the contrary forcibly took away the crops (unthrashed) from the fields of the tenants with the help of police or hired *goondas.*[39] All sorts of atrocities were inflicted on the poor peasants. In fact, the *biswedars* did not treat the *muzaras* as human being, nor did the state government have any soft corner for them.[40] Thus, the poor peasants were badly tyrannized over by the *biswedars* but the latter failed to crush their agitation.

The *biswedars* too had their association to meet the challenge of the tenants' movement. Its leaders always sided with the state government. They always poisoned the ears of the *Maharaja* and also of the officials against the tenants' movement in the state.[41] It will not be out of place to cite some of the suggestions given by the *biswedars* to the states' authorities against the tenants' movement. These are as follows :

(a) The *zamindar sabha* requested the state' government to direct the police authorities to recover unlicensed and unauthorised arms from the villages of *biswedars.* The tenants had already launched attacks upon *biswedars.* If no immediate action was taken there was every possibility of wide-spread lawlessness. The *sabha* had already been informing the state officials of the intentions of the tenants and all the information had proved to be correct.

(b) The *zamindar sabha* viewed with great concern the speedy increase of dacoits, and murder cases due to the influence of communists and therefore called upon all its members to help the authorities in getting the dacoits arrested. The natural result of their help would be that the increased

39. PSR, S. No. 1553, File No. 565/C of 1939, PSA : Patiala.
40. *Ibid.,* also Basta No. 51, S. No. 1574, Case No. 565/C/1017-C, Basta No. 50, case No. 565/C of 1939, PSA : Patiala.
41. PSR, T.I. of 2001, PSA : Patiala.

power of the communists and the leaders of the tenants' movement would be smashed in a few days for ever.

(c) The *zamindar Sabha* requested the states governments to issue orders to district officers to carry out the provisions of *batai* under the existing law because the sabha found that the steps so far taken by these officers were inadequate and unsatisfactory;

(d) The *zamindar sabha* considered the murderous attack upon some of the *biswedars,* like Jaswant Sinh Jeji, as the direct out come of a deep rooted conspiracy by the tenants. The *sabha* therefore, had started collecting a fund called 'Gobindgarh Relief Fund' which was to be utilized to fight the oppression by tenants and communists against the *zamindars* during the course of the peasants' struggle;

(e) The *zamidnar sabha* considered the question of restoration of the properties of those wards who had attained the required age, and recorded its surprise that so many wards who had attained the age were not getting their estates. The sabha requested the states' authorities to take immediate steps in this direction;

(f) The *zamidnar sabha* expressed their resentment against the settlement report, submitted by the Settlement Commissioner, Popham Young. All the tenants of Patiala Villages were, upto the last settlement, tenants-at-will. But for the first time, the tenants were raised to the status of occupancy-tenants, never before known in the Patiala or any other state. This too was resented by the *biswedars.*[42]

However, the *zamindar sabha* in question had been existing for a long time. For some time its activities had become slow, but it did not become an inactive body. It was fully loyal to the Government. Keeping in view their position, it could not be suspected that the *zamindars* would oppose the administration at any time.[43] The states' Government, therefore,

42. *Ibid.,* Case No. 41/C of 1939, PSA : Patiala.
43. PSR, Basta No. 51, Case No. 565/C, PSA : Patiala; *Kalsia State Records,* File No. 35 of 1938, PSA : Patiala.

were whole-heartedly supporting the states' *biswedars* against the rightful cause of the *muzaras*.[44] Consequently, the *biswedars* joined hands with the government and began to work against the tenants.

Moreover, there was throughout the states a strong offensive and defensive alliance between the official (*ahalkar*) and *biswedars* classes. The *ahalkar* who was not a biswedar generally contrived to become one, and the *biswedar* found that it was necessary to obtain a footing in the official camp. It was the influence of the *zamindars*' class which led to the issue of a '*hidayat*' from the supreme authority in the Patiala state making it incumbent upon all occupancy tenants to pay rents in kind.[45] Here, let us be clear that the *biswedars* always tried to crush the mounting peasants' agitation. This is cited in the following pages.

The states administrative machinery always backed the *biswedars* in their moves against the tenants and their struggle. The government started arresting the political workers and many peasants were prosecuted and the tenants were strictly checked from participating in the political conferences as well as the religious *diwans*—where political issues were discussed at length. Besides, the police reinforcements were sent to the villages by the rulers to enable the *biswedars* to realise *batai* and other dues.[46] The police and the *biswedars* openly unleashed atrocities upon the peasants with a view to crushing the peasants/ tenants' movement. Punitive police stations were

44. *Kalsia State Records,* File No. 25 of 1938, PSA : Patiala.
45. *Kalsia State Records,* File No. 35 of 1938, PSA : Patiala.
46. PSR, PM's Office File No. 1547-1554 (CWR from I.G. Police, Patiala March 29, April 20, May 1, 19 & 31, June 2 & 9, 1939. The S.P. Barnala proudly recounted how he got the tenants of Kishangarh, Pharwahi and Chakrian to start paying *batai* by using threats of beatings and confiscations and arrests. Vide., File on Correspondence regarding anti-*biswedars* 'movement', see in it D.O. letter No. 199/C of 2.5.1939 from the S.P. Barnala to the IGP Patiala. For this see PSR, PM's Office File No. 2077, PSA : PTA.

set up at several villages such as Kishangarh, Qilla Hakim, Rajomajra, etc. Actually, these villages were considered to be the most notorious centres of peasants' stir as well as the most disturbed and the worst areas.[47]

In the preceding chapter we have discussed in detail that the *muzaras* occupied the lands of many *biswedars* and also clashes between the *biswedars* and *muzaras* broke out when the henchmen of some *biswedars* carried away the harvest from the disputed lands in some villages. As a result, the government had to take a serious note of these developments as the situation was worsening day by day.[48] However, the government had realized that it was neither practical nor easy to send the large police forces to help collect *batai* every time.[49] There was no enduring solution to the problem of deploying the police for the collection of *batai*. On the other hand, the strict measures taken by the police keeping in view the need of the hour did not yield the desired results and effects. So much so that Maharaja Mohinder Bahadur was happy at this development and he had firmly made up his mind not to take deterrent steps to check the peasants' movement at every cost.[50] But this desire could not be fulfilled owing to the incidents which occurred at that time. Meanwhile the revenue Minister informed the Prime Minister that he had given orders for the realization of the

---

47. PSR, PM's Office File No. 1554 (CWR from IGP—Patiala of April 20, 1939), PSA : Patiala.
48. PSR, PM's Office File No. 2077—This file is related to anti-*biswedari* movement—See in it, confidential letter No. 733-H of April 4, 1939 from the private secretary to Mohinder Bahadur, the Maharaja of Patiala to the revenue Minister Patiala and a Message of, May 14, 1939 from IGP-Patiala to the Private Secretary to the *Maharaja* of Patiala, reporting on a conference, attended by the Revenue Commissioner, *nazims* and the S.P.S. held to discuss the *Muzaras'* movement, PSA : Patiala.
49. PSR, PM's Office File No. 5804 (see letter No. 1089/C of August 18, 1939 from the Revenue Minister to the Prime Minister of Patiala State-file is related to 'Kishangarh affairs') PSA : Patiala.
50. *Ibid.*, (See letter No. 67/C of May 3, 1939 from Secretary to the Prime Minister of Patiala States).

amount spent on punitive police and had ordered that the amount was to be realised at any cost even by auctioning the properties of the peasants. Consequently, it was ordered to realise the amount even by disposing of the household of the peasants and even by auctioning their proprietorship rights.[51]

On September 26, 1935 the Revenue Minister convened a high level meeting which was attended by Law Minister, Agriculture Minister, Revenue Minister, I.G. Police, *nazim*, S.P. and several other important officials. The views were exchanged on the peasants and *muzaras'* movement currently in progress. Finally, it was decided to deploy 200 additional policemen to check this movement and to keep a strict watch over its leaders. The persons who attended this meeting[52] had already perceived that the *biswedars* were the creation of the state government and had been consistently helping the administration in the states. There was a class of sycophants which always endorsed the rulers' policies so it was they duty of the administration to provide them security against the *muzaras.* This fear was also expressed at the meeting that if this rising tide was not checked immediately, it would assume the shape of a massive peasants' struggle.[53]

---

51. PSR, PM's Office File No. 1553 (CWR of September 29, 1939); File No. 2077—file regarding correspondence about 'anti-*biswedari* movement' (see in it confidential letter No. 1515/C of Sep., 17, 1939 from the Revenue Minister of the Patiala state and also notes of proceeding of the Conference, File No. 2077 relates to the correspondence relating to 'Anti-*biswedari* movement') Vide., PSR, PM's Office File No. 2077, PSA : Patiala.
52. PSR, PM's Office File No. 2077 (Reference to '*Kisan* Movement is obviously to a movement that was led by the communists); also see note by the *Maharaja* Mohinder Bahadur of October 5, 1939 on the proceedings of the Conference held on September 26, 1935, PSA : Patiala.
53. PSR, PM's Office File No. 1553 (see CWR from I.G. Police-Patiala of October 10, 1939 and also see Secret DO letter No. 6655/67-C of October 3, 1989-from I.G. Police-Patiala to various S.P.s Patiala to various S.P.s Patiala State), PSA : Patiala.

As a result, a decree was issued to suppress this tide and to effectively implement the government's policies. Cases were filed against the peasants only at the request (asking) and the complaint of the *biswedars*.[54] In addition to it, additional policemen were recruited in large number and the S.P. issued orders to keep in readiness the reports against the leading revolutionaries and their leaders so that if the need arose the cases could be filed against them firmly.[55] Notwithstanding all these efforts of the administration, the collection of *batai* continued to be a problem and headache for it.[56]

A conference of the police officers was held at Patiala on October 23, 1938 in which the S.P. deliberated with the *nazims* and at the conclusion of the conference some changes were also introduced in the methods of containing the peasants' struggle. Firstly, a harsh policy was adopted to keep the disillusioned and disappointed workers aloof from this movement and to contain them; secondly, the policy of forging an agreement between the *muzaras* and the *biswedars* and to maintain peace, was also adopted. In addition to it, the *biswedars* were pressurized to be soft in their dealings with the *muzaras* and not to collect exorbitant land revenue or *batai*. The peasants were also instructed not to occupy the lands of the *biswedars* forcibly and to respect their authority.[57] The *nazim* of Barnala

---

54. PSR, PM's Office File No. 1553, (CID Secret Abstracts of Intelligence of October 11 and 20, November 3 and 10, 1939 and also see CWR from IG Police, Patiala of October 27, 1939), PSA : Patiala.
55. *Ibid.*, (CID Secret Abstracts of Inteligence of November 3 and 10, 1939) also see undated letter—probably written some time in December by the District *nazim* (Barnala) to the Prime Minister Patiala State. *Vide.*, PSR, PM's Office File No. 2077—File on correspondence regarding Anti-*biswedari* movement, PSA : Patiala.
56. PSR, PM's Office File no. 1547 (CWR from I.G., Police of August 12, 1938), for details also see file No. 655, 1931, PSA : Patiala.
57. PSR, PM's Office File No. 2077, (It is related to the Correspondence regarding anti-*biswedari* movement), PSA : Patiala.

got the optimum success in implementing these policies. But it was evident that the deployment of greater number of policement had the advantages of its own but the situation could take a serious turn which could pose obstacle in the next session at the time of collection of *batai* if the report of the Enquiry Commission was not submitted by that time. Till now the *batai* was collected on all the occasions on individual assurance to the peasants that the Enquiry Commission was very expeditiously looking into their problem, grievances and demands and that the report of the commission was impending.[58]

It was not the state government alone which was trying to put down the peasants' movement but it also had the fully support of the *biswedars* and they were constantly goading the government on to crush this movement. The *biswedars* had become active since the very start of the movement and had started thinking deeply about the results of this movement and its repercussions on the lots of the *biswedars*. Consequently, giving the assurance of remaining faithful to, the Maharaja the *biswedars* put their weight behind the state government. Now the state government and the *biswedars* pooled their efforts and took harsh measures to prevent the meetings from being held and if at all the meetings were held to disrupt them, especially those meetings in which the problems and demands of the peasants were likely to be put before the people.[59]

In 1938 when this movement gathered momentum, the *biswedars* again started discussing with the government the possibility and methods of suppressing it. In the first few months of 1939, when the peasants adopted a violent and aggressive attitude and refused to pay *batai*, the *biswedars* competed with one another in sending telegrams to the government, demanding the police assistance and asked for protection on the plan that their lives and properties were in danger. It was also demanded that the strongest possible action

---

58. *Ibid.*
59. *The Tribune* (Lahore), June 21,1939.

be taken against the extremist peasants.[60] The *biswedars* expressed their gratitude to the *Maharaja* and the state government when they resorted to the oppressive policy of crushing the peasants' movement. They started sending the letters of thanks and congratulation to the state government and vehemently assured the government of their support and faithfulness.[61]

The *biswedars* became all the more vigilent when the leaders of the peasants' struggle decided to spread it far and wide by hectic propaganda; it was decided to send a *jatha* of the peasants and workers to Simla to call upon the British Resident. In 1939, a land owner association was formed in Patiala States; the main objective of which was to safeguard the rights and the interest of the *biswedars*.[62] In its very first meeting, some resolutions were passed and one of these resolutions read that the *biswedars* had decided to assist the government in stemming the tide of false propaganda by the peasants workers and it was also resolved to check the masses from joining the movement under the influence of the propaganda campaign launched by the peasants. Another resolution stated that they would extend whole-hearted cooperation to the government to crush the peasants' movement and to liquidate the misguided and mischievous elements.[63] The speakers in this meeting also clearly stated that they were prepared to give all sorts of facilities to the peasants and redress all their grievances on the condition that the peasants pay full *batai* in time without any resistance or opposition.[64]

60. *Ibid.*
61. *Ibid.*, (Biswedars of Kotduna, Karamgarh, Talwandisabo, Chakrian, Nagalkurd, Pharwahi, Dalelshinghwala, etc. were present) vide., VID Secret Abstract of Intelligence of July 7, 1939 given in PSR, PM's Office File No. 1555, PSA : Patiala.
62. Landlords' Association was also known by two other names- *biswedar* committee and *zamindar* committee. See CID Abstracts of Intelligence of July 7, 1939—PSR, PM's Office File No. 1555, PSA : Patiala.
63. *Ibid.*, (See Secret Abstract of Intelligence of August CID 4, 1939), PSA : Patiala.
64. *Ibid.*

As the situation turned from bad to worse, *biswedars* also after the formation of their association started calling meetings to take decision on taking a collective step against the mounting tenants' agitations. One such meeting was convened by the *biswedars* on June 23, 1939 at Mansa in Barnala district. The *biswedars* of all those villages which had come under the deep impact of the peasants' movement attended this meeting. The Secretary of the meeting prepared a poster of the grievances and the demands of the *biswedars*. Rupees one hundred each were collected from all of them to raise fund so that such posters, pamphlets and other hand bills could be released in the future also and the rising tide of the peasants' and *muzaras'* movement could be stemmed.[65] It was also decided to check the false propaganda campaigns launched by the *mazaras* in different parts of the states and to condemn their misdeeds. On July 26, 1939, a meeting of 30 *biswedars* coming from different parts of the states was held at Bhatinda under the banner of *zamindara* committee. This meeting discussed changing policies of the peasants tenants struggle and the situation which had resulted from the appointment of Enquiry Commission.[66] This meeting constituted a committee comprising 50 *biswedars* which was to present the case of the *biswedars* and their arguments before the commission. It was also decided to collect Rs. 2000/- for this work.[67]

Another decision that was taken was to request the Maharaja of Patiala to include the Revenue Minister of the State in the Commission and also to appoint two advisers—one for the *biswedars* and the other for the *muzaras* so that they could prove them right before the Commission.[68] After three days, 12

65. *Ibid.*
66. *Ibid.*, (around this time, another poster was published by the *biswedars* of Bhatinda condemning the lawlessness caused by the *muzaras*. It was duly circulated—see Secret Abstract of Intelligence of July 21, 1939).
67. PSR, PM's Office File No. 2077—It relates to correspondence regarding anti-*biswedari* movement—PSA : Patiala.
68. *Ibid.*

biswedars gathered at the residence of the Revenue Minister-who himself was a *biswedar.* All of them unanimously decided to put an end to the mischievous propaganda being carried on by the *muzaras* by taking harsh measures so that the peasants' movement might not flare up.[69] But instead of coming to an end, this movement went on becoming stronger and the *biswedars* were totally frustrated.

In a letter to the Maharaja of Patiala, the President of the *zamindara sabha* of Barnala district wrote to him about the *muzaras* meetings held in his district and informed him that the peasant workers and their leaders not only denounced and opposed the *biswedars* in these meetings but also strongly censored the administration of the Patiala Maharaja in particular and the rulers of other states in general.[70] He also informed him that the condition of *biswedars* had become very critical owing to the deteriorating economic condition of the masses and the denial of their share to them by the peasants. Very soon, it would become difficult for the *biswedars* to pay revenue and other taxes to the government. Keeping in view the approaching *kharif* harvest, he asked the Maharaja to issue directive to the revenue and police officials that they must maintain law and order and provide the requisite help to both sides without any prejudice and to retain the rights which they enjoyed at that time without any hestitation.[71] But the condition of the *biswedars* turned from bad to worse. In September 1939, the I.G. Police observed that it had become hard for the *biswedars* to live in the villages safely and also to keep their property intact.[72]

---

69. *Ibid.*, (He too pointed out that the tenants had interpreted the appointment of the Enquiry Commission as a triumph of their agitation and further that it means to stoppage to all *batai* till the Commission gives its decision).
70. PSR, PM's Office File No. 1553, (CWR from I.G. Police, Patiala of September 29, 1939), PSA : Patiala.
71. *Ibid.*, (CID Secret Abstract of Intelligence of October 22, 1939).
72. *Ibid.*

A meeting of the *biswedars* was convened in the Barnala district on October 19, 1939. Another note similar to the previous one was prepared, *Biswedar* Chhattar Singh Kishangarhia deplored the fact that as the peasants had become so powerful that they had defied their masters and ceased to fear the revenue and police officials; the *biswedars* must organize themselves and pressurize the administration and the rulers to take some steps for the security of the *biswedars* and to crush the growing strength of them *muzaras*. He also expressed his doubts if the *biswedars* would ever get *batai* again.[73] The *biswedars* also decided to see the Maharaja of Patiala collectively and to present before him their grievances.[74] Thus, a cataclysmic change could be discerned in the political field, for till a few months back the *biswedars* were only content to send telegrams to the *Maharajas* or to seek their help by complaining against the peasants in writing, without moving out of their villages.

However, now in changed circumstances, they could not remain passive as their lives and property were in danger. So they were determined to crush the *muzaras* as well as their stir. Moreover, they had firmly made up their mind to send a deputation to the rulers of Patiala. The *muzaras'* movement had greatly weakened the *biswedars* due to which they could leave themselves entirely to the Governments patronage. But even in these circumstances they were keen to give an evidence of their faithfulness to the state government by depositing the land revenue with it despite the fact that they had not been getting *batai* for a long time. So the state government was also pressurised to confer a special position upon the *biswedars* so that they might be able to properly act as the just mediators between the government and the peasants. Moreover, the rights

73. *Ibid.*, (CWR from I.G. Police, Patiala of December 16, 1939); *The Tribune*, November 29-30, December 1, 1939; Fortnightly Reports for the Second half of November, 1939—Home Political, File, 18.11.1939, NAI, New Delhi.
74. PSR, PM's Office File No. 1553 (CID Secret Abstracts of Intelligence of November 3,17 and 24 December 1, 8 and 15, 1939) PSA : Patiala.

and privileges of the *biswedars* should at least be regarded as equal to the rights and privileges of the peasants.

Now, a new policy was adopted to check unrest and the peasants' struggle in the villages. The policy involved the strains of reforms, agreement with the peasants and crushing the rebels with a heavy hand. On one hand the resident refused to see any *jatha* on the plea that unless the Report of the Enquiry Commission was submitted, he was not ready to entertain any deputation nor was he willing to see any.[75] On the other the States' administration clamped IPC 144 so that no demonstration or *jalsa* could be held by the peasants. Presently, this policy started showing its results and effects as gradually the news of the collection of greater quantum of *batai* started dropping in.[76] By the end of December, 1939, it was gathered that 80% to 85% of *batai* had been collected. The arrears stood in the names of only those peasants and *muzaras* who were still away from their villages—those who had run away from Patiala state to the region of British Punjab; they had mostly started living at Budhlada.[77] Actually these peasants and *muzaras* had gone there to escape from the oppression of the *biswedars* and the administration of the state. The state records clearly indicate that in most of the villages, the movement for non-payment of *batai* had been fizzling out or at least been weakening simply due to the repressive policy of the state administration and the highhandedness of the *biswedars*, who had been backing the state government since the beginning of the peasants' struggle.

Here, it is worth noticing that the Maharaja appointed an Enquiry Commission just to pacify the agitating peasants and not to find any permanent solution of the problem. Thus, there

75. *Ibid.*, (CWR from I.G. Police, Patiala of December 22, 1939 and January 4, 1940; CID Secret Abstract of Intelligence of December 22, 1939.
76. PSR, PM's Office File No. 763 (CID Secret Abstract of February 3, 1942), PSA : Patiala.
77. Ibid., (CID Secret Abstracts of February 15 and 18, 1942).

was no hope of an early settlement as the state government adopted the policy of keeping the peasants aloof from the villages plagued with political unrest and checking the political leaders from reaching those villages. However, the peasants' agitation continued and now it was found that the *muzaras* were having illicit arms in several villages. As a result, the S.P. Barnala issued an order to seize their arms as it was done at the time of emergency.[78]

After some time a deputation of five *muzaras* from Takhatpura village of district Ferozepur went to Lahore on January 15, 1942. It was to call upon the Resident. However, its members were told that the resident *Sahib* was reaching Patiala on February 7, 1942 to decide their case.[79] Subsequently 50 *muzaras* reached Patiala on February 6 to see the Resident but the latter returned to Lahore without having a word with them. When some peasants again went to Lahore to see him, they were informed that the Resident had asked the foreign Minister of Patiala State to look into their grievances and problems.[80] In the meantime, the rumours were rampant that the *biswedari* system had been abolished in 27 villages. As a result of this, a deputation of 5 rebel *muzaras* which was on tour, reported that it had gained remarkable success in raising the funds and getting the local help for revising the *muzaras'* movement in the district of Barnala and Sunam. This deputation included

78. PSR, PM's Office File No. 1565, Basta No. 50, Case No. 386, Basta No. 18, File No. 221/4-7775, PSA : Patiala.
79. Faridkot State Records, File Nos. 23 and 27 (Confidential diaries of District Magistrate No. 2920-21), the *muzaras* of village Kishangarh had reached Patiala on June 29, 1939. They were bent up to reach Khandaghat. The Prime Minister as well as the Revenue Minister instructed the I.G. Police to see that these people were sent back to their village at every cost) *Vide.*, PSR, PM's Office File No. CB-1-2 (2001), CID Police (1944-45), Basta No. 13, PSA : Patiala.
80. Basta No. 85, S. No. 1263, File Nos. M/3-22/40; 221/4-7745, Patiala : 7775, PSA : Patiala.

Dalelsinghwala and Dharam Singh Fakkar,[81] the renowned Communists and peasant workers. In March 1942, about 12 *muzaras* tried to call upon the *Maharaja* of Patiala but without any success. Their despair notwithstanding, they tried to stop the Maharaja's car but the police foiled all their effots.[82] Hence, the state administration as well as the *Maharaja* remained absolutely indifferent to the peasants' problems and always made efforts to suppress their stir with a strong hand.

However, by this time, the state government had exhausted all its political and other sources and the administration had no new policy or method to end this movement. As we have already stated, the government had been fully aware that the communists had started organizing the *muzaras'* movement anew and owing to it there was every hope of the beginning of a fresh movement.[83] Now, the state government could think of only one way of crushing this movement and solving this problem *i.e.,* the communal forces should be backed under the leadership of master Tara Singh and the policy to completely crush this stir should be followed. Thus, the rulers of the states issued strict orders not to allow any outsider to hold any meeting in any of the states and not to give a long rope to the *muzaras'* movement. If at all it began it must be crushed immediately.[84] The IG-Police passed instructions to the S.P. to identify all the political leaders and activities at the earliest and

81. All the *biswedars* in the States had become *biswedars* by having given the hands of their daughters to the *Rajas* and the real owners of land had become *muzaras* and *kamins.* Vide PSR, Basta No. 13—Police CID, CB-1-2 (2001), PSA : Patiala.
82. What happened in Sunam? Fire was opened, females were dishonoured and even were asked to loosen their nalas : This was a kind of zulam. The rulers and their Ahalkars wanted that the *muzaras* should yield *batai,* when the poor fellows were, in fact, starving. When they refused to, pay *batai,* they were prosecuted under section 423. Vide Basta No. 50, File Nos. 1565; 19281-23-C, PSA : Patiala.
83. File No.—42/C of 1939, PSA : Patiala.
84. PSR, Confidential 17, Case No. T-1 of 2001, PSA : Patiala.

to take action against them according to the Defence of India Act.[85]

The S.P. Barnala extended his full co-operation in this matter and also gave the plea that unless the states were kept free from the political leaders coming from outside and the permission was granted to hold the meetings in the jurisdiction of the states, the *muzaras* movement could not be suppressed rather there would always be a possibility of this movement assuming dangerous peoprations.[86] Only the Superintendent of CID had perceived the importance of the policies and methods adopted till 1939. He had rightly anticipated the outcome of the peasants' movement when it was only in its infancy. His recommendations culminated into the policy adopted by the end of 1939 and according to this policy while the peasants were to be provided help and facilities, the political parties which were trying to strengthen the *muzaras'* movement were to be crushed. An official report disclosed that it was felt by the officials of the police department that both the *biswedars* and the peasants should be kept within their limits. It was imperative to provide them true justice at low cost and in a simple manner.[87] To realize this goal, it was recommended that a Board be constituted, consisting of three high officials, who were to be taken from the revenue, judicial and police departments, and it should be equipped with the requisite police force. It was to tour every *biswedari* village and having given hearing to the leaders and workers of different parties regarding their disputes, give its decision there and then, basing on facts and after satisfying them before responsible village *panchayat* officers and get it acted upon at the spot.

---

85. PSR, Basta No. 85, S. No. 1263, File No. 221/4-7775, PSA : Patiala, Basta No. 50, File No. 1565, PSA : Patiala.
86. PSR : Basta No. 180, Case No. 189/C (see Final Report of the settlement of Patiala State (1900-1908), submitted by Popham Young), PSA : Patiala.
87. Vaid., Chhajju Mal, '*Pepsu Muzarain Da Ghol Ten* Communist Party', Souvenir, issued by the CPI on January 26, 1976.

Thus, the cases pending for a long time started being decided. Moreover, now the *muzaras* had no need of going to the cities for getting their disputes settled or for filling the cases. Thus, they were delivered of both extravagance and their problems. Another function of this Board was to effect a compromise between the *biswedara* and the *muzaras* through peaceful means and mutual agreement. When a number of *muzaras* were rendered homeless they joined one or the other agitation.[88] We come to know from the situation of that time that the district authorities were not adopting any such measures as might resolve the disputes or differences between the *biswedars* and the *muzaras* through peaceful settlement rather they were forcibly collecting the *batai* only with the help of the police or revenue officials.[89]

This report very clearly criticized the government and its higher officials for not having taken any step to suppress the *muzaras'* movement or to pacify the *muzaras*. Finally, it emphasised that it was the most pressing demand of the time that the administration should take measures to enable officers to pacify the people, particularly the *muzaras* by exercising their influence and the officers should take such steps to maintain law and order as may make the *muzaras* start paying *batai* to the *biswedar* voluntarily. There is hardly any need to mention here that this appeal did not cut much ice and the governments of the princely states continued to function as before. For instance, the states' governments continued the policy of confiscating the properties of the communists and some other peasant activists-particularly those who had been propagating the cause of the peasantry and also provoking the *muzaras* to keep their stir alive. Moreover, whenever any deputation went to meet the *Maharaja* and his Prime Minister, they emphatically

88. Master Hari Singh, '*Punjab Wich Kirsani Lehar* (in Panjabi), Souvenir, issued by the CPI on January 26, 1976.
89. The Pepsu Tenancy and Agricultural Land Act, 1955, Section 9, p. 15; Vaid, Chhajju Mal, '*Pepsu Muzarian Da Ghol Ten* Communist Party', Souvenir, issued by the CPI, on January 26, 1976.

asked the *muzaras* to return to their villages and also tried to convince them that they would be soon intimated about the decision of the Government regarding their problems and demands.[90] In other words, the states' administration remained indifferent to them.

On the other hand, the states' administration was fully aware of the complication that might arise from the activities of the *biswedars,* so the Maharaja expressed his views and attitude to the challenge thrown to the state authorities by the *biswedars* (discussed in detail in the preceding chapter). A strong warning was given to the Chairman of *zamindara sabha* against the formation of *darauli jatha* as it could create some fresh problems for the state. No such act would be tolerated and the architect of such a *jatha* would be liable to severe punishments according to the state laws. Obviously, the *biswedars* had transgressed their limits and no government, though only nominal one, could tolerate that any section of the society should openly flout the state laws or do anything against the interests of state. The state was not in favour of rewarding the loyalty of the *biswedars* wholly in deference to their wishes. Therefore, when the *biswedars* threatened or tried to take the law in their own hands, the state government had to intervene and the *biswedars* were told in unambiguous terms that they too were nothing but the subject of the state. However, it does not mean that the peasants' movement was seen with sympathy and kind eyes.

Any movement for the liberation of suffering masses was described by the state as the reason and its advocates were punished through all meas. No wonder the tenants' movement was described by the authorities of the East Punjab States as an open challenge and against the law. The tenants wanted to introduce the progressive principles in the government by the elimination of the *zamindars* entirely from the village polity in contravention of their recorded and traditional rights.

---

90. PSR, PM's Office File No. 763 (CID Secret Abstract of Intelligence of February 15, 1942), PSA : Patiala.

When the movement reached its climax the situation became quite serious and it could not be trifled with. The *biswedars* in the states were as much the bulwark of administration as the tenants. The latter were, however, more dependable and thoroughly loyal and any movement to crush them could only lead to a very serious dislocation of administration. The state wanted to curb the rising tide and had given power to police even to resort to firing if and when it was necessary. Firing was resorted to at various places at the time of the *muzaras'* agitation.[91] It was ordered that all the ring leaders must furnish heavy security. The Government policy was to take hold of the ring-leaders, who were instigating and also leading their morchas against the *biswedars* system and the states' authorities as well. But the government was helpless in taking hold of them.

Now, stray cases of politically active individuals were reported in Faridkot, Kapurthala and Kalsia states, but prompt action by the authorities forestalled any organised movement. The entry of newspapers was banned in time and suspected characters were ousted from the states. *Kisan* conferences were not allowed to take place and even the *jathas* of the tenants bound for the conferences were checked at the places of starting by the government.[92] Those who resisted were thrown into jails and the police even registered false cases under section 424 IPC against the tenants, thus causing them unnecessary harassment.

If at all the states' governments were compelled to probe into some clashes between the *biswedars* and the *muzaras,* they instead of ordering a judicial enquiry under the government of India Act, appointed some personal friends of the ruler.[93]

91. *Ibid.,* (CID Secret Abstracts of Intelligence of February 21, and March 2 and 21, 1942).
92. PSR, PM's Office File No. 770 (see letter from Hari Sharma, Private Secretary to the Maharaja to Colonel S. Gurdial Singh Dhillon, I.G. Police, Patiala of August 3, 1942, Conveying His Highness' orders), PSA : Patiala.
93. PSR, PM's Office File No. 1573, (see margin note by I.G. Police on CID Secret Abstract of Intelligence of June 6, 1942) PSA : Patiala.

Consequently, the *muzaras* boycotted the enquiry and the problem remained unsolved. It is interesting to note that new taxes were levied and old taxes enhanced according to the whims and fancies of the land revenue authorities and that several other hardships were caused to the ryots in this connection. The state government in connection with the peasants/tenants movement decided :

(i) Legal action should be taken against those who were inciting the *muzaras* for the non-payment of *batai* to the *biswedars*;

(ii) Such persons as were visiting the tenants and might thereafter visit them with the intention of inciting them not to pay *batai* due from them should be stopped from doing so and counter propaganda should be started by the district officials, police and revenue officers with the help of such *biswedars* as could be depended upon for the purpose;

(iii) When any *muzara* refused to pay *batai*, although it was a rightful due according to the revenue records and the past practice action should be taken against him under the Tenancy Act;[94]

(iv) Revenue, Civil and Criminal laws should be promptly and strongly enforced and sections 107/151 Cr.P.C. might be freely used against the agitators and the efforts should be made to arrest the professional agitators and a list of such *muzaras* should be drawn up.

(v) Punitive posts in the villages affected by this movement were set up and it was to be watched by the district officials that the *muzaras'* movement must be stopped.[95]

The *muzaras*, who had fled for life into the British territory, were arrested by the state police with the assistance of their

94. *Ibid.*, (See CID Secret Abstract of Intelligence of July 27,1942).
95. *Ibid.*, (See Extract from CID wing of the police of June 19, 1942 under the head '*muzaras*' movement).

British Counterpart. If any one resisted the police, he was prosecuted and subjected to so much torture that he became unconscious. Besides, the administration had so far refused to acknowledge the *Kirti Kisan Sabha* as a representative body and held that they represented only a very small minority of mischief-mongers.[96]

The position, in brief, is that it was for the *darbar* to take all necessary measures to deal with the situation within the state. As for the situation in British India districts surrounding the states, the Punjab Government was being kept informed of the position as reported from time to time by the *darbar* and it was for the government to decide upon the action to be taken.[97]

Besides the heavy and oppressive taxes imposed by the *biswedars*, of course, with the tacit approval of the states' authorities, the method and practice of land revenue collection *i.e.*, the *batai* system was defective as well as oppressive. Due to lack of basic facilities and also in terms of security, an average tenants led a life of misery, drudgery and frustration. As mentioned earlier, Maharaja Bhupinder Singh was an upholder of *biswedari*; during his reign, the condition of the tenants further deteriorated consequently it led to a gap between the tenants and the government. Its reason was obvious. Their results were not care to, nor could they engage in costly affairs of filing suits in the courts. After his death, the young Maharaja Yadvindra Singh tried to win the confidence of the peasantry. He appointed three commissions in 1939, in 1945 and 1946 which were to settle the long standing dispute between the tenants and the *biswedars*. However, the attempts of these commissions to settle the disputes between the tenants and the

96. It is naturally a reference to those *muzaras* who had to flee their villages and homes to escape the tyranny of the police and the states' officials.

97. PSR, PM's Office File No. 1573, (CID Secret Abstract of Intelligence of June 19, 1942); Case No. CB-1-2 of 2000, (CID Secret Abstract of Intelligence of January 12,1945), PSA : Patiala.

biswedars proved absolutely futile. Again, the Maharaja's attempt to resolve the issue by partitioning holdings between the *biswedars* and tenants through *farman-i-shahi* also fell through.

At the very outset of 1948, the peasants' position *vis-a-vis* the government remained materially unchanged. However by this time, the tenants had become fully aware of their rights and they were equally prepared to fight for the protection of such rights. After the formation of the Pepsu, the government issued *farman-i-shahi* to resolve the issue[98] but the tenants outrightly rejected the royal order thinking that it was meant to divide the peasants.[99] However, after the formation of a popular ministry, the government peasants' relationship underwent a radical change. The popular government with Gian Singh Rarewala as Chief Minister, who was responsive to the tenant problem, was keen to solve the tenant problem especially because of the serious clash between the tenants and the police at the village Kishangarh.[100] Rarewala's interim Ministry attempted to amend the *farmain-i-shahi* by issuing various ordinances with a view to transforming feudal lords into capitalist landlords. But his ministry could not overcome the pressure of the feudal clash. In fact, for some political reasons, the Congress Party tried to secure solid social base of the landlords.[101] Thus, when we view the peasant-government relationship in the context of the newly emerging political structure, we see that the political parties having an eye on power could not afford to alienate the landlords but at the same time they desired to see the tenants peaceful as an administrative necessity. However, the efforts on the part of

98. Report on Agrarian Reforms in Pepsu; Government of India, Ministry of States, 1952, 10.
99. Kishangarh, 'The Peasants' Heroic Defence of His Land' published by Pepsu Kisan Sabha (Bhatinda, Mittal Printing Press Ind.), 31.
100. *Ibid.*, 36-37.
101. Some Aspects of Agrarian Question CPI Publication, Delhi 1958, 2.

the government to formulate legislation appear half-hearted, at the most a kind of compromise completely ignoring the cause of the tenants-at-will.

The agrarian grievances of the occupancy tenants appeared in the form of the peasants' movement in Pepsu. The movement was led by the middle class peasants because their political organisation was backed by the poor non-occupancy tenants whose economic aspirations led them to political conferences and agitations against the *biswedars*. The co-operative endeavour of occupancy and non-occupancy tenants saved the movement from splitting at the bottom and in maintaining the traditional social relationship between them. During 1948-1953, the peasants' movement became mighty because of the structural dependence of the tenants-at-will on the occupancy tenants in their political agitation against the *biswedars* as well as the state government. This phenomenon also explains the reason as to why the peasants meetings and conferences were well attended and resistance to the pressure of the *biswedars* was offered. Moreover, the tenants forcibly occupied lands which were cultivated by the landlords.[102] During this period the demands of the peasants ranged from the abolition of the *biswedari* to the non-payment of compensation.[103]

The triangular relationship among the government, the *biswedars* and the peasants is really worth noting as we withness three dimensions of this relationship. One tenants supported by the Communist Party of India and the Akalis demanded radical change in the agrarian structure not only in the region but of India.[104] Two, the *biswedars* compelled the Government to secure the payment of compensation and increase in their holding. Three, the Congress Party was not against compensation but was anxious to solve the problem by

102. Kishangarh, The Peasants' Heroic Defence of His Land, published by Pepsu Kisan Sabha (Bhatinda, Mittal Printing Press (nd.) 49-50, The Tribune, October 27, 1950.
103. For details see the text of the 3rd Chapter.
104. *The Tribune,* April 9, 1952.

abolishing *biswedari* to which it was committed.[105] At first, the state government suppressed the peasants' movement ruthlessly but after some time, as the political pressure was gradually mounting and as the peasants' agitation was causing considerable anxiety, it recognised the proprietary rights of the occupancy tenants. The cause of the poor non-occupancy tenants remained unresolved and was left to be solved in the future.

The nature and character of the peasants' struggle underwent a radical change after 1953 while the rights of middle class peasants were accepted. Now, the middle class peasants left the movement as they were sufficiently satisfied with the *ala-malkiat* rights. Consequently, the non-occupancy tenants backed by the communists continued their struggle till 1956. During this period, we withness a sort of understanding between the government and the *biswedars* and the government and the Middle class peasantry. The communist leaders and those of local *kisan sabhas* did not favour a distinction between occupancy and non-occupancy tenancy tenants.[106] They worked hard to realise their slogan 'Land to the tillers' and saved the poor tenants from ejection at the hands of the *biswedars*. The government which suffered from inner contradictions, on the one hand, passed legislation to save the tenants from eviction while on the other it adopted a policy favourable to the *biswedars*. The class character of the movement emerging at this stage displays a change in their mutual relationship. As opposed to the communists' propaganda and their hold on the non-occupancy tenants, the Congress began to find its base in the middle class peasants who had been given proprietary rights in 1953. The *biswedars*, realising that they were fighting a losing battle, collaborated with the ruling party to get the favour which the government could concede to them against the tenants-at-will. In the

105. Phulwari (Amritsar), February 1951, 39(An article by the General Secretary, Kisan Sabha, Patiala Union).
106. *The Statesman* (New Delhi), June 6, 1954.

emerging pattern of relationship, the society can be split into two parts *i.e.,* the Congress the right wing Akalis and the rich peasantry on the one side, the poor non-occupancy tenants on the other. The former factions were politically organised and they were favourite of the state authority. They had enough sources but even them they could not obstruct the demands of the non-occupancy tenants. They could of course, delay the passing of the legislation that too for a period of three years. This of course, helped the *biswedars* in ejecting the tenants, selling their land and transferring them in the names of their relatives. Undoubtedly, the government provided temporary protection to the tenants from eviction by passing the Pepsu Agricultural Tenants (Temporary Protection and Disability) Act 1954. But several communist leaders such as Jagir Singh Joga, Hardit Singh Bhattal, Dharam Singh Fakkar and Arjan Singh along with *Sanjha morcha* members, Ch. Albel Singh and Dhanna Singh Gulshan and even Congress member Nihal Singh opposed the bill on the ground that the Act did not provide proper protection to the tenants. They believed that the act provided protection to the landlords at the cost of the tenants.[107] The issue created a sharp split in the Congress party but the Act was finally passed in October, 1956. It was hailed by the Chief Minister of Pepsu as the one which solved the problems of tenants-at-will.[108] However, the details aptly show that the *biswedars* stood to gain by the Act because large areas were still under their control in the form of *benami* land. Most of the tenants were not benefited because the land available to them on compensation was not sufficient, nor were they in a position to pay compensation which was fixed at a very high rate. Though on papers the *biswedari* was abolished, large tracts of land were still held by the *biswedars.* This led to bitterness between the tenants and the *biswedars.* After the merger of Pepsu, the Punjab government did not pass any legislation to amend the situation. Nevertheless, the year 1956 was significant

107. *The Statesman* (New Delhi), March 3, 1953.
108. Pepsu Vidhan Sabha Debates, Vol. IX-B, S. No. 15, October 10, 1956.

because the *biswedari* was legally abolished in the Pepsu though illegally it continued to exist, but in a restricted form. The occupancy tenants acquired proprietary rights and a large number of non-occupancy tenants also acquired similar rights. As a result, the tenants movement became weak because the problem of tenants-at-will existed to a limited degree.

Change in the relationship among the peasants, the biswedars and the government made the peasants' struggle militant in character. Before 1938, the autocratic government of the Maharaja and the selfish *biswedars* conspired to bring down the peasants with occupancy rights and tenants-at-will. The peasant struggle was growing by leaps and bounds under the influence of the freedom struggle and the Akalis' agitation. After some time, under the pressure of National and Local forces and the revolutionary ferment, the Maharaja of Patiala tried to effect a compromise. After the country became independent the relationship underwent a further change as there was a competition among the political parties to capture power. The communists with revolutionary ideology led the peasants against the government and the *biswedar* while the Congress with its declared policy and responsibility for establishing law and order adopted repressive methods. With status, influence and economic power, the *biswedars* wanted to derive as much benefit as possible from the government. They by adopting foul and fair means salvaged their position as far as they could. The peasants in this region were yet at the stage of semi-agrarian structure of the society. By virtue of this characteristic fact, it was less stratified and more cohensive and solid than the peasants' society of central Punjab. The tenants in this region, having no civil liberties, resorted to strong, militant, revolutionary but united struggle, which in term of militancy approximated revolutionary situation. They were led by petty middle class peasants lacking revolutionary ideology. Despite the fact that the communists made efforts to impart ideological orientation to the peasant, they failed and succumbed to the pressure from below. This, there was hardly any revolutionary and leftist ideology to guide the peasants.

As a result, when their demands were conceded in 1953, the bottom of the movement went off and the peasants' struggle collapsed without leading to any radical transformation in the relationship among the peasants, the *biswedars* and the government except the upper middle peasants took the place of the *biswedars* and naturally the upper middle peasantry included the erstwhile *biswedars*.

11 CONCLUSION

Now, let us try to prepare the balance sheet of the achievements as well as the weaknesses of the struggle launched in wake of the peasants' and *muzaras'* problems in the East Punjab States. Undoubtedly, the foundation of their struggle was very strong and it had a very old and historical background. It has also the most powerful and militant struggle ever led by the Communists. Even today, their party proudly claims credit for it. However, the participation and involvement of other political organizations such as : the *Praja Mandal*, the Congress, the Akalis, the *Kisan* Committees, etc. was equally significant. In fact, the people of all shades remained closely connected with the problems, demands, and above all the struggle of the peasants and the *muzaras*.

The personal despotic rule of the *Maharajas* of Patiala and other Punjab States stood in the way of the reforms introduced to modernize the administrative machinery. The States' laws were personal decrees of the rulers. An elected legislatures and free press were unknown to the States. The people were burdoned with unnecessary taxes. In fact, the financial and administrative set up were rusty and of medieval pattern. The lower peasants and the village manials were leading a life of miserable poverty, while the upper class agriculturists and feudal lords, on the other hand, lived in comfort and luxury. Moreover, the agrarian structure of the states also left much to be desired. Nearly 90% of the people lived in the rural areas, who were generally illiterate, traditional in outlook and superstitious. Most of them had to work hard to just make both ends meet. The authorities made little efforts to ameliorate the lot of general peasantry. As a result, there was a growing incidence of two fold alienation in the rural society, that of the lower and middle peasants from the upper peasantry on the one hand and from the state on the other. The inevitable, if limited, impact of westernization and commercialisation was another important factor that contributed to the break-up of the traditional society.

The backward and stagnant nature of agriculture and irrigation in this region, provided no hope to the tenants. Of course, some steps were taken by the states' authorities to modernize agriculture such as the setting-up of Department of Agriculture, a model farm and an agricultural training institute. Also, the cultivators were encouraged to use better implements and improve the quality of their livestock. But, modernization had no impact on the backward agriculture and irrigation system in this region. The co-operative credit facilities were monopolized by influencial *biswedars*. The state was indifferent to the interests of the ordinary and poor peasantry. Only one-sixth soil was under canal irrigation. Draughts occurred frequently. The peasants could not afford the costs of sinking *pacca* wells. This further aggravated the existing dichotomy between the lower peasantry and the states' authorities.

The Regular Settlement was effected in the first decade of the present century under the direction of Popham Young, the Settlement commissioner of Patiala State. Assessment was made on scientific basis and five-eighth of the net produce was fixed as the State share. Despite the sincere efforts of Mr. Popham Young to improve land revenue administration, the settlement effected by him had some drawbacks also. His special concessions to the *biswedars* were highly objectionable. Instead of improving the *lambardari* system, he introduced another class of rural revenue collectors, popularly known as *zaildars*. Even during the draught period, the state demanded its share of revenue. The *muzaras* were denied the facility of credit. Sometimes, the *biswedars* were imposed as proprietors on actual tillers of land. It continued well into the twentieth century. The peasant proprietors felt agitated due to high land revenue rate and other burdens imposed on them. However, as a class they had closer affinities with the lower peasantry.

They were destined to play an active but significant role in the peasants' struggle. The worst sufferers were the lower peasants or the tenants—the occupancy tenants and the tenants-at-will, in the British ruled Punjab. The Punjab Tenancy Act, though promulgated in the late 12th century, was never applied seriously. The tenants frequently claimed proprietary status, as they felt that they were the earliest cultivators, and that the *biswedars* had come much later.

Besides insecurity of tenure, the tenants were forced to pay kind rent to the *biswedars.* The kind rent rate (*batai*) was generally heavy but the worst was the *kankut* system—the share of *biswedars* from standing crops. The middle and lower peasants were alienated from the *biswedars* and they resented the role of the rulers and also of the British Government. In fact, the peasants and the tenants had come a long way in their struggle against the repression of the states, exploitation by the *biswedars* and the protection as well as the help given by the British to the rulers of these states. There had been a conviction among the peasants and the *muzaras* that the *biswedars,* the rulers and the British regime had been giving a raw deal to them for a very long time. There had been a time when the rulers could not be persuaded to receive a deputation of the peasants and the *muzaras* of their leaders. Even their petitions which carried their genuine demands were not received by the authorities of these states. They were being denied their legitimate rights and inherited position. When they contrasted their position with the one they had been enjoying in the past, they felt a strong urge to recreate the image of a new world. Consequently, the valiant struggle, which had started soon after the formulation of the *Praja Mandal* organization, continued till 1945, when the *Maharaja* of Patiala in particular and the other rulers in general made efforts to solve their problems. But they failed to satisfy them. As a result, the struggle was again launched which continued till 1947, when the peasants and the *muzaras* bravely faced the firing at Naraingarh, displaying their unity and strength. However, the heavy firing failed to suppress their movement. The struggle continued, though after a brief interval, and lasted till 1949, when tanks and armoured vans were taken out in Kishangarh to terrorise them and make their leaders yield.

However, as we have already discussed in the main text of this work, the first signs of tension between the tenants/ peasants and the *biswedars* appeared in the last quarter of the nineteenth century when the Punjab tenancy laws were introduced in the state. Regular Settlement did not do justice to the cultivators of long standing. The middle and lower peasants raised their voice against *nazool, begar, kush haisiyat, neonda, muzarat* and hateful *shikar* laws. The *mukthars* let loose their wrath on the poor tenants and the peasants. Basic acquisitive urge was also one of the causes of discontent among the peasants. The occupancy tenants aspired to be proprietors while the tenants-at-will, the occupancy tenants.

The peasants'/tenants' discontent worsened during the depression of 1929 when the prices of agricultural produce suddenly increased and the state demanded land revenue at the same rate. The *Praja Mandal* consisted mainly of peasants and so naturally they raised their voice against the exploitation of the peasants/tenants by the *biswedars.* It almost identified itself with the peasants' movement. The period 1928-1938 witnessed the birth of *Riyasti Praja Mandalists* who were influenced by leftist ideas. In 1937, there was a violent communist inspired *biswedar—muzaras* clash in the village Qilla Hakiman. A Constitutional Reforms Commission was appointed by *Maharaja* Bhupinder Singh but it did not submit its report because the *Maharaja* died soon after. During 1938-48 when the Patiala state was ruled by Maharaja Yadvindra Singh, the peasants' movement was organised. This was decidely the most vigorous phase of the movement except or the brief period of world war-II, when the Government found excuse in war in suppressing the movement. In 1939, the State *Kisan* Committee transformed into the radical and militant *muzara-kisan* Committee. The *muzara* war council was set up in 1945 which launched the consistent *muzara* agitation. It forced the ruler to abolish the *biswedari* system in 1947. The award of redistribution of land between the *biswedars* and the tenants in the ratio 1 : 2 was not acceptable to the latter. The independence of India on 15th August, 1947, of course, upset the programme of the peasants' movement.

We are aware of the fact that in July 1948, Pepsu consisting of the East Punjab States was formed. With this the peasants' unrest and movement was again launched. However, the peasants/tenants were not inspired by any ideology. The tenancy legislation from 1947 to 1956 shows that after the peasants had secured certain rights through these legislations and the abolition of the *biswedari,* the movement almost came to a, halt. On the basis of the recommendations of five Enquiry Commissions, one *Shahi Farman* (1947) one Ordinance in 1949 (which was further amended in 1959 and 1951), three Acts in 1953 (out of these Acts, the Pepsu Tenancy Act of 1953 was further amended in 1956) were passed to solve the tenancy problem in the States. But the *biswedars* in collaboration with officials obstructed the operation of these Acts. The tenants had to pay compensation and leave some land for the self-cultivation of the *biswedars.* In spite of the sincere efforts of the *Lal* Communist Party leaders, the movement failed to survive.

It is worth-noticing that the leadership left no stone unturned in organizing the peasants/tenants into cohesive groups in terms of caste, class and landholding. They upheld and promoted their interests. The lower middle class also produced leaders who showed flair for politics and ambition to obtain and maintain leadership. The peasant leaders maintained link between the masses and central leadership. But it would not be wrong to say that the leaders of the peasants' struggle lacked idealism and they had no vision of reformation of rural society on progressive lines. They thought of land problems in terms of peasant proprietors. The agricultural workers gained nothing from the struggle. The middle class peasantry continued to exploit them socially and economically. Though endowed with qualities of courage, dedication and determination, the leaders failed to act as mediators. Convinced of their demands being just and legitimate, the highly organised and motivated peasants put so much of pressure from below than they were carried away by the current primarily due to its non-hegemonic character.

The participation and contribution of the peasants is mainly determined by the circumstances and environment in which he is placed. It is, therefore, essential to analyse and comprehend the structural relationship which sets the parameters of a peasants' struggle. The peasant in this region was poor, ignorant and he too was exploited by the *biswedars*. As we know, necessity is the mother of invention, forced by the tyranny of the *biswedars* and the States' officials, they forged unity in the form of peasants' movement. However, he was related to his community with strong kinship ties which created a kind of unity for the action of movement. This was mainly due to the fact that particularly, in the Patiala State there were few internal differences among the peasants. They were one in their struggle against exploitation and highhandedness of the state as well as the *biswedars*. The notable example of the brave and heroic struggle of the peasants against the tyranny of *biswedars* was found in Qilla Hakiman, Rajomajra and Kishangarh. Here, their action forced the authority to think seriously of solving the agrarian problems.

The *biswedar* was powerful big landlord and generally not belonging to the same community of the village. In most of the villages, he was an outsider and a relative of the high state official. Moreover, the *biswedars* in the ereswhile Patiala State and Pepsu were mostly high officials and members of legislative Assembly; so they had close rapport with the authority.

The Congress ministry despite its best intentions could not implement its policy of abolition of *biswedari* in the East Punjab State. Between 1948 to 1954, there was political instability in Pepsu and because of such political instability and upheaval, the peasants' cause was bound to suffer. The peasants movement was ill-organised with this structural relation, the peasants' struggle tended to be half-backed, ill-organised as peasants of all the states could not be fully associated with the struggle. Only the tenants of the Communist dominated areas came forward to fight for their just rights. The Communists also failed to build a permanent base in these areas. Of course, these tenants were not fired by the socialist revolutionary ideas or egalitarian vision of Marx and Lenin. They wanted the Communists to help them in fulfilling their desire to own land. They were not interested in building up a participatory egalitarian and just social order. Once their aspirations were fulfilled, they left the communists in the lurch. The communists could not win a single seat in the Patiala State in the general election to the Punjab State Assembly in 1957.

Despite the fact that the peasants' movement was intense, it suffered from various limitations. Leadership to the peasants' struggle was provided by the communist party which was divided into two groups—The Lal Communist Party and Communist Party of India. This was a great set back for the peasants' movement. The peasants could not put up a united front against the *biswedars* and the Government. Even merger of the communist groups later on did not help the peasants' movement to grow. The second hurdle in the way of their struggle was that all sections of peasants were not unanimous in their fight against exploitation. The tenants had no ideology to inspire them. When their material ends were achieved they withdrew from the struggle. In the third phase of the movement (1948-1953) when the Occupancy tenants acquired their proprietary rights, they withdrew from the struggle. The special tenants such as in Faridkot and Kapurthala States were also given the proprietary rights through an ordinance without compensation. Only the non-occupancy tenants were left to carry on the struggle. The third obstacle which stood in the way of the tenants was the influence and strength of the *biswedars* on the officials to recover dues from the *muzaras.* The *biswedars* got the implementation of the Pepsu Tenancy and Agricultural Land Act of 1953 postponed upto 1954. This period of three years was utilized by the *biswedars* for *benami* transactions. The fourth hindrance in the progress of the peasants' struggle was that it was not wide spread. It was restricted to the communist dominated regions of Bhatinda,

Mansa, Barnala and Sunam. Lastly, the leaders of the peasants' movement never worried about the landless labourers. As a result, they could not mobilize and integrate them with the peasants'/tenants' struggle.

Influenced by the external factors, this mighty struggle had roots in the region which shaped its nature and character. It was based on the local problems confronted by the peasants. Like most of the peasants' struggles, it was to a certain extent conventional and conservative because the basis of its mobilization was both ethnic and peasant, the former denoting social and the latter economic aspects of the rural society. It aimed at ending the exploitation of the *biswedars* by restoring the traditional rights of the peasants over the soil they had been cultivating for the last many generations and for which they had been deprived by the *biswedars.* It was especially an effort of the peasants to obtain the rights legitimated by tradition rather than conferred by the political authority.

Throughout the period under review, the Government followed a repressive policy and left no stone unturned to crush the movement. Still the peasants and the *muzaras* valiantly continued their long drawn struggle though with some convenient intervals. It is obvious that the struggle could be continued merely because the peasants and the *muzaras* enjoyed full support of the different political parties. Moreover, they were being exploited to such an unbearable degree that they would not permit themselves to be exploited any more.

Now, a question arises whether the peasants and the *muzaras* succeeded in their principal objective. So far as they were concerned, their answer would naturally be 'yes', because they had no other desire than becoming owners of the lands that had been confiscated from their ancestors. However, it was not the limitation of their vision alone; for even the leftists, whose theoretical vision encompassed the setting up of atleast a socialist society and for whom 'land to the tiller' was only a minimum programe—a mere bourgeois task—in reality rarely envisaged anything beyond. Let us be very clear that socialist here did not simply mean development; but it also meant that every peasant should own a piece of land for cultivation. Moreover, the communists of the Punjab having their roots in the self-cultivating peasant proprietors of the Central Punjab already held this belief. The Russian experience had also been viewed in the same spirit.

The example to illustrate this perspective was available especially in Patiala state where the *Kisan* Committee, at its peak during the course of *muzara'* struggle, when the communists had a complete hold on it, threatened the *kamins* (landless labourers and the servants in the villages) that if they did not boycott the *biswedars*, they would be banished from their villages or, at least they would have to lose their wages. It was, in fact, an astonishing treatment for the people who had pledged to serve the proletariat, the urban as well as the rural people. It might have been a hasty step, but the absence of any programme for the rural poor was evidence enough in itself that that perspective was biased. Nor did their participation in the *muzaras'* movement force them to challenge or question this perspective. The *muzaras*, from our limited evidence on this question (it is available to us if we see Patiala State Records, Prime Ministers' Office File No. 6157—that nearly 20 *muzaras* of Qilla Hakiman cultivated land that varied from 20 to 200 *bighas* and averaged at 80 *bighas*) appeared to be fairly substantial tenants. The truth that before the Settlement was made, they owned the land which they now cultivated as occupancy tenants, or that there were occupancy tenants who were holding the land as tenants-at-will, indicates in this direction.

Moreover, their capacity to resist their repression for along time indicates that they were enough sound financially. They had a desire to be the land owners and they had been given the impression that—if not in reality, at least as right—they were either the land owners or the occupancy tenants. Their own perspective, therefore, was in the nature of the land owning peasants. Perhaps, the *biswedars* who had warned the government that there might be a revolution on the lines of the 'French Revolution'—though contrary to their wishes—was not much ill founded. Similar weaknesses were visible in understanding the nature of the British rule. It was believed that the British Punjab territory was definitely in a better condition as there the people had the duly elected institutions and they enjoyed civil liberties. There the burden of the land revenue, *abiana* and other taxes was not much. The farmers got remunerative prices for their produce. While the comparison between the Punjab States and the neighbouring British territory for political purposes is undeniable, it tended to go much further. Many speakers, therefore, in the Conferences and the posters stressed their demand that they wanted nothing more than what their counterparts in the British territory had been enjoying. They, indeed, worked to inspire the masses and bring the *muzaras* and the peasants into action. They, in reality, strengthened the idea that they did not demand or want more than what their counterparts in the British Punjab region actually enjoyed. The limited nature of civil liberties, the very high revenue and the *abiana* against which the peasants of the Punjab had been agitating, the unrepresentative nature of the Councils and the Assemblies and above all the whole of the nationalistic criticism of the British rule was never brought home to the peasants and the *muzaras* of the princely states of the Punjab. As a result, even the contents of the nationalistic ideology presented before the peasants and the *muzaras* of this region were diluted badly. Even the connection between the existence of the British rule and the survival of the Princely order was not clearly brought out.

Undoubtedly, the British were looked upon as the supreme power and the princes as their subordinates. There was complete truth in the people's saying or belief that they were the slaves of slaves. The deputations, which went to see the political agent or the British resident, are to be seen as attempts to get the British to put pressure on the rulers and to make them realise that the British had helped them to maintain autocratic rule, but the British would help them no longer. However, this point was not adequately expressed. This was, in reality, a serious weakness, for without it, no real unity in struggle between the people of the British Punjab and the princely states of the Punjab could be built. This was probably one reason why the Indian states joined the independent union at a very low pace and indeed a big push was needed from above to complete the composition of the Indian Union.

Further, no emphasis was laid on the connection between the maintenance of the *biswedari* system and the existence of Princely rule. At one level, when the States' repressive policy was intensified; and the rulers gave support to the *biswedars*, fingers were raised against it. But the criticism was very mild. At another level, the rulers were appealed in their capacity as heads of the States to intervene and protect the *muzaras* and the peasants from the *biswedars* as well as from the highhandedness of the *ahalkars*. It strengthened their claim that they were the real fountain heads of justice to different sections of the society. In this way, keeping in view their own interests, the rulers' efforts to stabilize their despotic rule and also the *biswedars'* desire to maintain their rights—an identity of interests came to light during the period of serious crisis. It proved how the two were working in close association. It posed a serious threat to the existence of the states where the rulers put all their force at the back of the *biswedars*—This aspect was also not given due attention. Instead it was often lost sight of.

The peasants and the *muzaras'* struggle led by the communists in the Punjab states certainly lacked courage and strength, especially against the Akalis and other communal forces—the forces which helped the rich capitalists *biswedars* against the *muzaras* and the poor peasantry. As stated earlier in the second part of the second chapter, their (communists) sharp attack on the communal minded Akalis and also their efforts to present themselves as the successor to the militant Akalis gave a significant push to the peasants and the *muzaras'* movement, but that attack could not go any further, nor could it show the social basis of communalism as well as its own ideology. Hence, the argument centred round the communal and non-secular framework. However, it is noteworthy to state that they only criticsed the Akalis led by Master Tara Singh for being more inclined towards compromise and collaboration with the reactionary conservative and even anti-national forces. They claimed to be more honest than the Akalis; they were better in sense, because they were better fighters against the oppression and exploitation of the government and *biswedars* respectively. They too claimed that they had been fighting like old Akalis (who were considered to be militant and loyal to the *Panth*-those Akalis who had struggled for the reforms of Gurdwaras—for details see Chapter-III) for the unity and liberation of the society.

But emphasis on the personal dishonesty, hypocrisy and such other matters diverted the attention from the deep roots of communalism causing destruction. This evel could not be stamped out until its root was attacked, which was the whole notion of the existence of separate interests of different communities. It was not astonishing that the communists by 1945 had started supporting the demand of a separate Muslim Pakistan. And, a section of the Punjab communists also began to sympathise with the demand of a separate Sikh homeland. But, that was probably done to oppose the move of creating a separate Muslim Pakistan. Another serious drawback of the communists' failure to attack the Akalis communal approach was that it confined their appeal only to the Sikh peasantry. Of course, it enhanced the power of the appeal, but it had its own dangers.

While discussing the communal issue, it may be stated that the states' authorities could use the communal forces to their own advantage, because in the mind of the common people, there was a confusion between the Akalis on one hand and the Communists and the *Praja Mandalists* on the other. This confusion had arisen because the workers, who were holding leftists ideology, kept themselves completely aloof from the Akalis. However, it is interesting to note that this confusion persisted in their own minds also. Consequently, when Master Tara Singh openly helped the *Maharaja* of Patiala and the British imperialists, he could rally behind him a large number of Sikh peasants and the *muzaras* who still considered the Akalis to be the militant fighters. But, ultimately, when faced with problem of choosing between the Akalis, the *Praja Mandalists* and the Communists, they realized that the secularism of the Akalis was only skin deep.

Thus, the weakness that had appeared in challenging the ideological basis of the communal politics too left its imprint on this movement. It particularly influenced the states' politics. It was clearly visible when after the liberation of the country, the Maharaja of Patiala as well as the other rulers with the help of the Akalis opposed the integration, and got Pepsu formed. They, in fact, had realised the use of communal forces in their favour. That was the factor why they had a soft corner not only for the Akalis, but for the *Rashtriya Swayam-Sewak Sangh* (RSS) and such other elements which sided with them. Consequently, they threw their lot with the representatives of such politics in 1948, when the Indian democracy posed a great threat to the existence of the states; they were clearly told that the Western democracy did not suit the contemporary situation and that the Eastern democracy (may be called autocracy) was to be established.

Only the *biswedars* could remain untarnished from the Communal influence, as they felt a sense of security by the presence of their representatives within the administration and the active state support which had been extended to them to protect their interests in the earlier stages of the peasants' and the *muzaras'* struggle. But they failed, in good time, to make the transition to a subtler ideological expression of their class interests and politics. In this, they had yet much to learn from the *zamindars* of the British Punjab, who were leading the Unionist Party, which used not only the Communal and Caste identities (The muslim *zamindars* hailed from the West Punjab while the *Jat zamindars* from the East Punjab) but also with the help of the British bureaucrats, developed a new identity around the moneylenders, traders, etc., putting the rural and urban interests in clash. Consequently, they succeeded in dividing the rural society in different sections and forming a separate rural society in different section and forming a separate rural block which the *zamindars*, the peasants and the *muzaras* could join, and it stood in the way of the rising peasants' and the *muzaras'* movement. *Biswedars*, however, could not use communalism for their benefit. Nor could they produce any such ideology as would further their own concept and thereby safeguard their interest. At the most they could only form an association, pressurise the rulers and give a threat to form an armed force; they too showed that they had begun to learn the techniques of warefare. They also tried to win over the sympathies of the leaders of the right wing. However, they could never 'come to the stage in the politics of the day'.

An interesting thing presented by the tenants' movement was who along with the Communists should lead the movement. Being in a position of leadership and successfully leading the movement, the Communists in these states were free from those weaknesses from which their comrades in the British Punjab suffered. These weaknesses sprang from the groupism in the party. These Congressmen in the Punjab also suffered from the same weakness. The Communists luckily were non-sectarian in their approach. They worked equally well with the militant Akalis, the *Praja Mandalists* and the Congressmen. Their closest association, however, was with Brish Bhan who was leading the *Praja Mandalists*: so much so, when the Congress and the Communists separated formally, Brish Bhan and his associates continued helping the Communists, particularly in the states. It was clear from the election of Jagir Singh Joga as the President of the Patiala *Praja Mandal* in 1948, and the formation of the defence Committee by the lawyers of the *Praja Mandal* Organisation in the case of Kishangarh in 1949. The polarization between the loyalists and the communal elements on the one hand, and the forces of secularism, nationalism and communalism on the other hand, which led to a united front of left and democratic elements, came into existence though this was not verbalised in theory. It took place as a result not of manipulative tactics of factional intrigue but of participation in actual mass politics and achievement of ascendancy within.

Now, we are entering the end of the balance sheet of the peasants'/tenants' movement. With its militant approach, sacrifices, bravery and success this movement did not remain a limited economic struggle of the Punjab peasants; it went beyond the *biswedari* territory of the states and joined hands with the *kisan* movement in the neighbouring British Punjab areas. It managed to get both help and opportunities for political and ideological advancement for the future.

It means a powerful wave was kindered from adopting different methods of struggle and exhibiting their power. To substantiate, it may be observed that all the sections of peasantry as well as the political groups took keen interest in this struggle of the peasants and the *muzaras*. This movement could not be prevented from learning a valuable lesson of non-sectarian approaches and associating with it. As a result, even after 1949, the peasants and the *muzaras* continued with more vigour their struggle and ultimately they succeeded in forcing the rulers to redress their genuine grievances.

However, on the other hand, it was strongly obstructed from achieving a greater legitimacy and integration and as a result it remained confined to the level of a political organization, or to the level of leadership—at the most to the level of political activists. It remained far away from its real programme and objectives. It can be said about it that in the non-*biswedari* area, no campaign of non-tax was ever launched and the governments' demand in respect of the rate of land revenue and water rate was never opposed by any of the leaders. Had the leaders taken just a step in the direction of the non-payment of *batai*, the struggle would have become a part of the *muzaras* movement in the Punjab states and pressurized the government to accept their demand.

The Punjab *kisan* Committee which on behalf of the communist Party, guided the peasants and the *muzaras'* movement in the British domain as well as in the states, failed to gather much help from outside the states on the lines of the *morchas* like the Lahore *kisan morcha* of 1939-39 or like the *jathas* sympathizing with the British areas. In fact, no *sabha* is on record where the Punjab peasants offered their help to the *muzaras.* The British political agent expressed his views to the Lahore deputation in 1939 : "No body in Lahore paid any attention towards it". The peasants in their individual capacity did help the *muzaras,* addressed the *muzaras* conferences and even tried to get their grievances redressed by mediating between them and the rulers, but no practical solidarity was built. The impact of the movement did not go beyond the communists, peasants and the *Praja Mandalists.* For instance, no congress leader as far as we know, ever referred to this movement in public. It is believed that Subhash Bose showed interest in this movement, but it is also doubtful. As far as the leaders were concerned, it became their wont to refer to a leader of national stature so that they could make an image of their own on the local or provincial level. The lack of interest in the movement on the part of the national leaders was not only their weakness but it also weakened their political perspective. However, its failure to become a part of national movement can be explained. Essentially it remained a narrow movement in its perspective. Its political interests could neither develop politically, nor could they be explained fully. Its significance was never revealed to the nationalists outside the Princely states of Punjab; if at all it was, that was confined only to a limited circle. However, the movement could not remain completely aloof from the national movement as this powerful movement was opposed to the tyranny and highhandedness of the *biswedars* in collaboration with the political power. It was mobilized on ethenic and local grounds in order to end exploitation of the *biswedars* and to restore the rights of the peasants over their land. It was bound to draw strength from the latter and in turn give strength to it.

Of course, the peasants and the *muzaras* had to pass through a long struggle; they won back their rights which had been lost by their ancestors; they became owners of the land which they had been cultivating. It is true that development was also made, not because of the social planning or the revolutionary reorganization of the agrarian structure, but because of the green revolution and Nehru's five Year Plans.

However, the tenants failed to acquire the land promised to them.

Nevertheless, it will be a mistake to under-rate these movements. They brought about a rapport between the anti-*biswedar*, anti-*rajshahi* and anti-imperialist forces and it strengthened the growing awareness among the various sections of the society, particularly the peasantry that they should fight a united and organized battle. At the same time, these movements succeeded in creating an awareness among the peasants, the *muzaras*, workers and youngmen to launch a meaningful struggle against exploitation landlordism and imperialism. Moreover, the activities of the leftists and the congress socialists, the *Praja Mandlists* and the Akalis derived their strength from the prevailing agrarian unrest and they succeeded in encouraging anti-imperialist elements and traditions and also in creating an atmosphere for opposing the political authority of the rulers of these states as well as of the British bureaucracy. Further, so far as the peasants' and *muzaras* movement in these states is concerned, it was against the allies of the rulers; the allies of the British, the *biswedars*, and consequently gave birth to the feelings of national solidarity along with anti-feudalism.

It is not less important to take notice of the fact that the leadership of these movements always co-operated with the Indian National Congress and created an awakening in this region of the country. In short, the peasants' struggle in this part of the country was also to oppose such policies as could hinder India's achievement of freedom and to promote the programmes and policies which could help achieve this end.

Above all, the peasants' organisations, particularly these led by the left nationalist leaders, provided a wider outlook to the Congress and Communists programme through their hold criticism, continuous propaganda and mighty agitation. It was this movement which gave birth to the leftist and socialist ideologies in the Punjab, and at the same time created a leftist wing in the Indian National Congress having sympathies with these movements. The left programme was a step ahead of the

Congress programme and the leadership of this struggle made efforts to give a socialistic orientation to the Congress programme and also the Communists'. Its real object was to make them more militant organisations and to enlist its ideological support in their fight against landlordism, exploitation and also imperialism. Finally, the experience of the peasants' and tenants' struggle in the Princely states of East Punjab during the period under review revealed the potentialities of rural upsurge against the said evils *i.e.*, feudalism, exploitation, capitalism and imperialism.

APPENDICES

APPENDIX-I

Revised schedule of occupier's rates beginning from 1924 leviable on the areas irrigated in the Patiala territory from the Patiala state distributaries and water courses on the Sirhind and Western Jamuna canals

		Rates per Kacha Bigha	
Class	*Crops*	*Sirhind Canal Rs/ A.P*	*Western Jamuna Canal Rs. A. P*
(1)	*(2)*	*(3)*	*(4)*
I.	Sugarcane (except on *kharif* channels) water nuts, and annual charge for gardens & orchards to be assessed in *rabi* season.	3 - 2 - 0	3 - 2 - 0
II.	Sugarcene on *kharif* channels	2 - 1 - 4	2 - 1 - 4
III.	Rice	1 - 12 - 0	1 - 12 - 0
IV.	Wheat, barley and oats (except *kharif* channels), maize, cotton, vegetables (except turnips) indigo & other dyes tobacco, poppy, spices & drugs.	1 - 6 - 0	1 - 06 - 0
V.	Oilseeds (except *rabi* oil-seeds on kharif channels) melons, fibres (other than cotton) and all crops not otherwise specified.	1 - 2 - 0	1 - 2 - 0
VI.	*Rabi* oilseeds, wheat, barley and oats on *kharif* channels, gram, field peas and beans, lentils and pulses.	1 - 0 - 0	1 - 0 - 0

(Contd...)

(Contd...)

(1)	*(2)*	*(3)*	*(4)*
VII.	*Jowar, bajra,* grass which has received two or more waterings	0 - 14 - 0	0 - 14 - 0
VIII.	*(a)* Watering for ploughing not followed by a cropin the Same succeeding harvest.	0 - 5 - 0	0 - 5 - 0
	(b) Homp, indigo, and *guara,* ploughed in as green manure before September 15.	0 - 5 - 0	0 - 5 - 0
	(c) Village and District Board Plantations :		
	Any number of waterings *kharif*	0 - 5 - 0	0 - 5 - 0
	On watering in *rabi*	0 - 5 - 0	0 - 5- 0
	Two or more waterings in *rabi*	0 - 10 - 0	0 - 10 - 0
	(d) Grass-a single watering in *kharif* or *rabi.*	0 - 5 - 0	0 - 5 - 0

Note 1 : Grass, given two or more waterings falls under class VII.

Note 2 : Gram, when sown mixed with wheat or barley in a field, will be charged @ of Rs. 1-3-0 per *kacha bigha*.

Source : Patiala Gazette (Patiala), 7 May 1924.

APPENDIX-II

Prices of Agricultural Produce in the Main Patiala State Mandis, At the End of June-October 1940

	Narnaul	*Gobindgarh*	*Mansa*	*Barnala*	*Narwana*	*Sunam*
(1)	*(2)*	*(3)*	*(4)*	*(5)*	*(6)*	*(7)*
Wheat	-	13	14	14	-	14
Barley	-	18	19	19	-	18
Gram	-	12	13	13	-	13
Mustard	-	9	9	9	-	7
Gur	-	8	8	7	-	7
Rice	-	4 -10	3-10	4 -10	-	4 -10
Maize	-	16	13	15	-	15
Ind. corn	-	8	10	10	-	12
Millet	-	12	12	12	-	12
Moth, Mung	-	8	9	10	-	10
Mung	-	8	7	9	-	7
Mah	-	8	8	8	-	7
Ghee	-	12	12	12	-	12
Wheat	10	11	11	12	-	12
Barely	16	18	18	18	-	17
Gram	11	11	12	12	-	12
Mustard	8	10	9	8	-	8

(Contd...)

(Contd...)

(1)	(2)	(3)	(4)	(5)	(6)	(7)
Gur	10-12	11	12	12	-	11
Rice	6-8	4-10	3-9	4-8	-	4-10
Maize	14	16	17	18	-	16
Ind.corn	19	16	13	13	-	14
Millet	17	18	19	19	-	17
Moth	13	12	12	15	-	10
Mung	8	8	11	8	-	7
Mah	9	9	9	9	-	8
Cotton	7	7	7	7	-	10
Ghee	12	13	13	13	-	10

Contd...... Appendix II)

APPENDIX-II

Prices of Agricultural Produce in the Main Patiala State Mandis, At the End of June-October 1940

	Dhuri	*Sirhind*	*Patiala*	*Rajpura*	*Srinagar*	
(8)	*(9)*	*(10)*	*(11)*	*(12)*	*(13)*	*(14)*
Wheat	13	16	14	15	14	
Barley	18	17	18	16	18	
Gram	12	13	11	14	12	
Mustard	8	8	7	8	7	26.6.1940
Gur	8	7	7	9	6	
Rice	6-10	4 -10	4 -10	7-10	8	
Maize	14	13	13	12	14	
Ind. corn	10	12	16	14	13	
Millet	10	-	11	10	11	
Moth, Mung	10	9	10	9	7	
Mung	8	7	6	7	7	
Mah	8	7	7	6	6	
Ghee	12	11	12	12	14	
Wheat	12	11	12	12	14	
Barely	-	14	16	16	16	
Gram	-	10	11	11	10	

(Contd...)

(Contd...)

(8)	*(9)*	*(10)*	*(11)*	*(12)*	*(13)*	*(14)*
Mustard	-	8	8	8	7	25.12.1940
Gur	-	11	11	11	7	
Rice	-	4-10	4-10	4-10	4-9	
Maize	-	14	15	15	16	
Ind.corn	-	13	16	16	16	
Millet	-	-	-	13	13	
Moth	-	14	13	9	9	
Mung	-	8	8	8	7	
Mah	-	8	8	8	7	
Cotton	-	7	6	6	7	
Ghee	-	11	11	12	12	

Source : Patiala Gazette (Patiala) June, 1940 & 25 December, 1940.

APPENDIX-III

Patiala State-Five Yearly Prices of Agricultural Produce, Per Maund, for Years 1920-1940

Crops	*Months & Annual*	*1920 Rs. A.P*	*1925 Rs. A.P.*	*1930 Rs. A.P.*	*1935 Rs. A.P.*	*1940 Rs. A.P.*
(1)	*(2)*	*(3)*	*(4)*	*(5)*	*(6)*	*(7)*
Wheat	June	7/3/6	7/9/2	12/8/-	16/-/-	14/1/3
	December	6/12/-	6/1/2	19/2/4	14/10/1	11/01/3
	Annual	6/15/1	6/13/2	15/8/2	15/5/-	12/8/3
Barley	June	10/9/2	11/12/-	17/6/4	25/9/3	17/8/-
	December	8/10/3	9/2/5	13/11/3	22/14/2	16/6/2
	Annual	9/9/5	10/7/2	15/9/-	24/3/5	16/15/1
Gram	June	8/4/-	11/8/5	10/1/3	21/3/1	12/8/-
	December	7/4/4	8/10/1	14/6/4	19/11/3	11/1/3
	Annual	7/12/2	9/9/3	12/8/-	20/7/2	11/12/4
Mustard	June	4/1/2	4/14/1	5/4/-	7/11/1	8/-/-
	December	3/3/3	4/1/2	7/4/-	7/7/1	8/3/1
	Annual	3/10/2	4/9/4	6/4/-	7/9/1	8/1/3
Gur	June	5/6/2	4/10/4	5/5/2	7/6/3	7/6/2
	December	3/3/3	4/8/4	7/4/3	8/15/-	10/9/3
	Annual	4/4/5	4/9/4	6/4/5	8/2/4	8/15/4

(Contd...)

(Contd...)

(1)	(2)	(3)	(4)	(5)	(6)	(7)
Rice	June	3/9/4	4/14/-	5/1/2	4/2/4	5/3/1
	December	2/9/4	4/14/3	8/14/4	4/9/-	4/7/4
	Annual	3/1/4	4/14/1	7/-/-	4/5/5	4/13/2
Maize	June	11/8/3	10/8/-	15/7/1	26/9/3	13/9/3
	December	9/6/2	10/6/2	28/14/4	22/11/3	15/9/3
	Annual	10/7/2	10/7/1	22/2/5	24/10/3	14/9/3
Cotton	June	4/1/2	2/4/-	5/10/-	7/8/5	7/14/1
	December	4/13/2	3/5/4	8/11/1	6/7/1	7/-/-
	Annual	4/7/2	2/10/5	7/2/3	7/-/-	7/7/-
Bajra	June	8/5/4	9/8/-	8/8/-	18/12/2	11/3/3
	December	7/-/4	7/8/-	23/12/4	16/11/1	16/4/4
	Annual	7/11/1	8/8-	16/2/2	17/11/4	13/12/-

Source: Patiala Gazette (Patiala).

APPENDIX-IV
Nature of Debt Burden of Landholders

District	No. of land holders	Area of land	Amount of assessed land revenue	Without Mortgage		Under Mortgag	
				Area of land	Revenue	Area of land	Rave
(1)	(2)	(3)	(4)	(5)	(6)	(7)	(8)
Bassi	59836	9 03 488	13 24 187	7 36 706	10 47280	1 66782	2814
Narnaul	31 744	709532	454567	561464	373029	148068	8153
Patiala	33672	830669	620129	602350	427614	228319	192515
Barnala	110463	1849677	1325961	1262091	890331	587586	419610
Sunam	74965	1382167	1008101	1243448	882214	138719	125887
Kohistan	9923	84539	54024	57717	35942	26823	1808
Total	310603	5760072	4786969	4463775	3657930	1296297	11190

(Contd...)

APPENDIX-IV
Nature of Debt Burden of Landlorders

	Amount of Debt			Causes				
District	*Secured of land*	*Unsecu-red*	*Total*	*Marriage*	*Previous debts*	*Domestic expenses*	*Purchase of land*	*Purchase of agricultural impliments*
(9)	*(10)*	*(11)*	*(12)*	*(13)*	*(14)*	*(15)*	*(16)*	*(17)*
Bassi	2510255	7757273	30267498	5168423	7333435	60174476	4122007	6826017
Narnaul	2189027	4038370	6227307	1773097	2398270	1391108	278810	386001
Patiala	1782964	4100301	15883266	3979879	3839188	41,84273	2307879	1578040
Barnala	396265	12084081	39481046	5071122	19978518	779301	2993248	3644856
Sunam	818694	14627417	36446111	4836774	1228134	5120640	2564108	1643255
Kohistan	989706	3909437	5809143	2481333	224601	1302623	1339171	55815
Total	7687581	465416880	124204461	23310699	46019341	26609482	18105285	14629654

Source : Census Report of Patiala State for 1941.

APPENDIX-V
Distribution of State Officers

Executive & Revenue	Total	Head Quarter	NIZAMATS				
			Karam-Garh	Barṇala	Amargarh	Pinfore	Narnaul/ Mohindergarh
Diwan	1	1	-	-	-	-	-
Revenue Assistants	6	6	1	1	1	1	1*
Tehsildars	18	18	4	4	3	4	2
Naib-Tehsildars	17	17	4	3	4	4	2
Village Revenue Staff Office	22	22	5	4	4	5	4
Kanugoes (including Naib Sadar Kanugoes)							
Field Kanungoes	49	49	14	11	11	9	4
Patwaris	810	803	232	191	179	141	62
Village Officers	2623	3	742	678	625	384	191
Zaildars	257	257	64	64	53	43	33
Lambardars	9491	-	2627	1861	2190	1717	1076

*One attached to Sadr Mal Office.

Source : Punjab State Gaztteers, Volume XVII s, Phulkian States.

APPENDIX-VI

Firman-i-Shahi

(Number 2, dated Motibagh Place, Patiala, the 19th of May, 1946)

A dispute has existed for a long time between the *biswedars* and tenants of village Rajomajra in Sunam district regarding their rights to the land in their possession and their status *vis-a-vis* each other. This question has been the subject of several enquiries from time to time extending over a period of nearly 70 years, but unfortunately the matter has not been settled finally so far. We, therefore, appointed a Commission, vide one *Ijlas-i-khas* order number 30 dated the 4th September 1945, to make an exhaustive enquiry into the whole case, giving the parties full opportunity of presenting their respective view points, and recording both documentary and oral evidence. This Commission submitted its report to us on 4-12-1945 which we considered at a special meeting of our Cabinet at which we presided on 16-4-1946.

Certain points which required further elucidation were referred back to the Commission who have now submitted their supplementary report on 23-4-1946, which we considered at a further special meeting of the Cabinet under our Presidency on 29-4-46.

In the two reports the Commission dealt very fairly and sufficiently exhaustively with all the aspects of this dispute, and after giving our due consideration to the recommendations of the Commission and the discussions held in our Cabinet thereon, we have come to the decision that it would be equitable and fair to both the sides and in common interest that their respective rights and status *vis-a-vis* each other should be clearly defined, and are accordingly pleased to order as follows :

1. The biswedars of Rajomajra shall be treated as *Malikan-i-Ala* and the tenants as *Malikan-i-Adna*, the land revenue being payable by *Malikan-i-Adna*, and a surcharge of one *anna* on the rupee being collected from them along with the land revenue.

2. The *Malikan-i-Ala* shall receive this surcharge of one *anna* per rupee to be recovered from the *Malikan-i-Adna* with the land revenue at the time of every harvest.

3. The *Malikan-i-Ala* shall be the owners of all the land in the village and the *Malikan-i-Adna* full proprietors of the land in their possession subject to the payment of the surcharge as

the share of *Malikan-i-Ala,* but not liable to eviction on failure to pay it.

4. The *Malikan-i-Adna* shall be entitled to introduced tenants with reference to the *Malikan-i-Ala* who, shall have no right to interfere in the management of the cultivation of the proprietary lands of the village.
5. The *Malikan-i-Adna* shall have the right to sink wells in their lands of which they will be considered the proprietors.
6. The proprietary rights to the holdings of issueless *Malik-i-Adna* shall vest in *Malikan-i-Ala*.

Maharaja Dhiraj Mahendra Bahadur.

Source : Patiala Gazettee (Patiala), 2 June, 1946, pp. 109-10.

APPENDIX-VII

Patiala and East Punjab States Union Abolition of Biswedari Ordinance, 2006, BK. Ordinance. No. XXIII of 2006 B.K.

Amended by Pepsu Ordinance No. XXXVI of 2006 and Pepsu Act No. IV of 2007

An

Ordinance to amend and consolidate the law regarding abolition of occupancy tenures and settlement of disputes between occupancy tenants and landlords as contained in Farman-i-Shahi No. 6, dated the 11th of March, 1947.

Whereas His Highness Shri 108 Maharajadhiraj Mahendra Bahadur of Patiala state promulgated Farman-i-Shahi No. 6, dated, Motibagh Palace, Patiala, the 11th of March, 1947, with a view to the restoration in the erstwhile Patiala State of amicable relations between the landlords and their occupancy tenants, and removing the causes of disputes between them and providing for apportionment of lands between the landlords and their occupancy tenants in the ratio of one-third and two-third in the case of occupancy rights under section 5 of the Tenancy Act and two-fifth and three-fifth in the case of occupancy rights under section 6 and 8 of the said Act.

And whereas it is expedient to amend and consolidate the law as contained in the aforesaid Farman-i-Shahi and in the interest of peace and good government to abolish the occupancy tenures in the Patiala and East Punjab States Union in the light of the aforesaid Farman-i-Shahi and to provide for other ancillary matters.

Now, therefore, in exercise of the powers conferred by the proviso to paragraph (2) of Article X of the Covenent entered into by the Rules of the East Punjab States as amended by Article 1 of the supplementary Covenant, the Rajpramukh is pleased to make and promulgate the following Ordinances :

PART-I

PRELIMINARY

1. Short title, extent and commencement : (1) This ordinance may be called the Patiala and East Punjab States Union Abolition of Biswedari Ordinance, 2006. (2) It extends to the whole of the Patiala and East Punjab States Union. (3) It shall come into force on the date of its publication in the official Gazette.

2. Definitions : (1) In this Ordinance, unless there is anything repugnant in the subject or context :

(a) "arrear of land revenue" means land revenue which remains unpaid after the date on which it becomes payable upto the notified dates

(b) "arrear of rent" means rent which remains unpaid after the date on which it becomes payable upto the notified date;

(c) "Financial Commissioner" means any person appointed by the Government to perform the functions and exercise the powers of Financial Commissioner under this Ordinance;

(d) "Government" means the Government of the Patiala and East Punjab States Union;

(e) "holding" means a share of part of an estate held by one land-lord as defined in clause (h) of jointly by two or more such landlords;

(f) "land" means land which is not occupied as the site of any building in a town or village and is occupied or has been let for agricultural purposes or for purposes subservient to agriculture or for pesture, and includes the sites of buildings and other structures on such land;

(g) "landlord" means an owner of land in which a tenant has or establishes immediately before the notified date a right of occupancy under either section 5 or section 6 or section 7 or section 8 of the Tenancy Act in force in the Union and includes a joint Hindu family and a limited owner;

(h) "notified date" means, in respect of an estate or group of estates; such date as may, by notification in the official Gazette, be appointed by the Partition Commission for carrying out the purposes of this Ordinance;

(i) "occupancy tenant" means a tenant who immediately before the notified date :

(i) has a right of occupancy in pursuance of either section 5 or section 6 of the Punjab Tenancy Act, 1887, inforce in the Union; or

(ii) has established or establishes a right of occupancy in pursuance of either section 7 or section 8 of the said Act, in any land owned by a landlord;

(j) "Partition Commissioner" means the officer appointed as such by the Government for performing the duties and functions assigned to him under this Ordinance, and includes the Assistant Partition Commissioner appointed under sub-section (1) of Section 6;

(k) "prescribed" means prescribed by rules made under this Ordinance;

(l) "Union" means the Patiala and East Punjab States Union.

(2) The expression "estate", "land revenue" and "tenant" shall have the meaning respectively assigned to them in the Punjab Land Revenue Act, 1887, inforce in the Union.

(3) Certain persons deemed to be occupancy tenants despite dispossession—Where any person who was an occupancy tenant within a period of seven years before the 11th March, 1947, (the date of the promulgation of the Farman-i-Shahi) has been dispossessed or deprived of his right to the occupation of the holding for non-payment of rent in execution of a decree against him, be shall, for the purposes of this Ordinance and subject to the provisions thereof, be deemed to be an occupancy tenant on the date of the Commencement of this Ordinance.

Provided that he shall not be deemed to be an occupancy tenant if before the first day of January 1951 he does not deposit in the tehsil treasury the decretal amount for the realization of which he was dispossessed or deprived.

Explanation : Occupancy tenant includes his heirs and successors-in-interest.

4. Abolition of occupancy tenures and determination of future rights and interest. Notwithstanding anything contained in the Punjab Tenancy Act, 1887, or in any other law for the time being, in force in the Union on and with effect from the notified date and save as otherwise expressly provided in this Ordinance :

(a) No tenant shall have and claim a right of occupancy under either section 5 or section 6 or section 7 or section 8 of the aforesaid Act or under any other law in any land held by him under a landlord;

(b) All rights and interests created in or over any holding before the notified date shall be regulated and determined in the manner laid down in this Ordinances;

(c) The relationship of landlord and occupancy tenant in any holding shall, as between them be extinguished and the holding shall, subject to the provisions of section 11, be partitioned by the Partition Commission between them in such manner and proportion and on such terms as are provided in this Ordinance.

PART-II

Appointment and functions of officers and Government, determination of compensation and division and transfer of holdings.

5. Appointment and function of Partition commissioner : (1) As soon as maybe after the commencement of this Ordinance, the Government shall appoint a Partition Commissioner to carry out the purposes of this Ordinance including partition operations in holdings, assessment of compensation ad settlement of disputes between the landlords and their occupancy tenants. (2) The Partition Commissioner shall be subordinate to the Government and shall be guided by such instructiosn in consistent with the provisiosn of this Ordinance, as the Government may from time ot time issue.

6. Appointment of Assisting Officers : (1) The Partition Commissioner may, with the approval of the Government, appoint as many Assisting Partition Commissioner as he thinks necessary for assisting him in carrying out the functions and duties assigned to him under this Ordinance. (2) Any lawful order of an Assistant partition Commissioner shall be deemed to be the order of the Partition Commissioner unless modified by the latter.

7. Powers of Control of the Government—The Government shall have power :

(a) to give effect to the provisions of this Ordinance and in particular to exercise control and superintendence over the Partition Commissioner;

(b) to issue instructions for the guidance of the Partition commissioner; and

(c) to concel or revise any of the orders, acts or proceedings of the Partition Commissioner other than those in respect of which an appeal lies under this Ordinance.

8. Determination of holdings : (1) As soon as may be after the commencement of this Ordinance, the Partition Commissioner may suo motu and shall on application, enquire and determine whether or not any holding in any village or estate in his jurisdiction is a holding within the meaning of this Ordinance.

(2) Before holding the enquiry the Partition Commissioner shall cause to be published in the village or estate in the prescribed manner, a notice requiring all persons whether as landlord or occupancy tenant or otherwise claiming an interest in the said holding to file before him statements of their interests.

(3) The Partition Commissioner shall than bear the parties and afford to them a reasonable opportunity of adducing all such evidence either oral or documentary as they may desire and shall thereafter give his decision in writing.

(4) *(a)* Any person aggrieved by a decision of the Partition Commissioner under sub-section(3) may; within thirty days from the date of the decision, appeal to the Financial Commissioner. *(b)* Where any such appeal is preferred, the Financial Commissioner shall cause to be published in the prescribed manner, a notice requiring all persons who have applied to the Partition Commissioner under sub-section (1) or filed before him statements under sub-section (2) appear before the financial Commissioner, and after giving them a reasonable opportunity of being heard, give his decision. *(c)* The decision of the Financial Commissioner on appeal under this sub-section shall be final and shall not be liable to be called in question in any court or before any authority.

(5) No decision of the Partition Commissioner under sub-section (3) or of the Financial Commissioner under sub-section (4) shall be invalid by reason of any defect in the form of the notice referred to in sub-section (2) or sub-section (4) as the case may be, or the manner of its publication.

(6) Every decision of the Financial Commissioner and subject to such decision, if any, every decision, of the Partition Commissioner under this section shall be binding on all persons claiming an interest in the holding concerned notwithstanding any such person not having preferred any application or filed any statement or adduced any evidence or appeared or participated in the proceedings before the Financial Commissioner or the Partition Commissioner as the case may be.

9. Declaration of shares of occupancy tenant and landlord in a holding. The Partition Commissioner shall determine and declare the respective shares of the landlord and the occupancy tenant in a holding which shall be :

(a) in the case of occupancy tenant, three-fourth of the entire holding, and

(b) in the case of the landlord, one-fourth of the entire holding :

Provided that :

(a) where the occupancy tenant pays only cash rent; or

(b) where the occupancy tenant pays rent in kind which is less than one fourth of the produce of the holding, the respective shares of the landlord and the occupancy tenant shall be determined in accordance with the rules made in this behalf by the Government.

Provided further that where in respect of any holding the occupancy tenant does not pay to the landlord anything over and above the land revenue and rates and cesses thereon, he shall be entitled to the entire holding.

10. Option to occupancy tenant to acquire share of landlord : The occupancy tenant shall be notice issued by the Partition Commissioner be given an option to purchase the share of the landlord in the holding, which has been declared under section 9, on payment of such total compensation as may be payable by the occupancy tenant under section 14.

11. Consequences of exercise of option by occupancy tenant : (1) If the occupancy tenant within fifteen days of the receipt of the notice issued under section 10 consents in writing to the purchase of the share of the landlord, the entire holding shall on deposit of compensation as required by section 14 be transferable to the occupancy tenant.

(2) If the tenant does not agree to the purchase of the landlord's share or the Partition Commissioner does not receive his consent within the period specified in sub-section (1), the occupancy tenant shall be entitled to the transfer to him of only such share of the holding as is declared by the Partition Commissioner o be his share under the preceding section.

(3) The occupancy tenant shall as from the notified date, in respect of the holding or part thereof transferable to him under sub-section

(1) or sub-section (2), as the case may be the full owner thereof for all intents and purposes to the exclusion of the landlord.

(4) If the occupancy tenant :

(a) elects not to acquire that part of the holding declared under section 9 to be the share of the landlord; or

(b) fails to deposit the amount of compensation payable to the landlord as required by section 14, the landlord shall as from the notified date be the full owner of that part of the holding to the exclusion of any rights therein of the occupancy tenant.

12. Determination of compensation : (1) Where the occupancy tenant elects to purchase the landlords' share of the holding, the Partition Commissioner shall proceed to determine the amount of compensation payable to the landlord in respect of his share of the holding in accordance with such rules as may be made in this behalf by the government.

(2) *(a)* Any person aggrieved y an order of the Partition Commissioner under sub-section (1) may, within thirty days from the date of the decision, appeal to the financial Commissioner. *(b)* Where any such appeal is preferred the Financial Commissioner shall cause to be published in the prescribed manner, a notice requiring the landlord or, as the case may be, the occupancy tenant to appear before him, and after giving the parties a reasonable opportunity of being heard, shall give his decision. *(c)* The decision of the Financial Commissioner on appeal under the sub-section shall be final and shall not be liable of be called in question in any court or before any authority.

(3) No decision of the Financial Commissioner under sub-section shall be invalid by reason of or any defect in the form of notice referred to in that sub-section or manner of its publication.

(4) Every decision of the Financial Commissioner and subject to such decision, if any, every decision of the Partition Commissioner under this section shall be binding on all persons claiming an interest in the holding concerned, notwithstanding any such person not having appeared or participated, in the proceedings before the Financial Commissioner or the Partition Commissioner as the case may be.

13. Period within which deposit to be made : (1) If any occupancy tenants elects to acquire under section 11 the landlord's share of the holding he shall deposit in the tehsil treasury within a period of three

months from the date of notice issued in this behalf by the Partition Commissioner the amount of total compensation determined by the said officer.

(2) The Government may in any special case for reasons to be recorded in writing extend the period prescribed in sub-section (1) by not more than three months.

14. Total Compensation payable by occupancy tenant (1) The total compensation payable by the occupancy tenant shall be compensation determined under section 12, the value of buildings assessed under Section 23 and the arrears of rent, if any. (2) Where any landlord has obtained against the occupancy tenant a decree for arrears of rent in respect of the holding, such amount shall form a part of total compensation payable to the landlord under sub-section (1).

15. Division of holding-where the tenant :

(a) elects not to acquire the share of the landlord in any holding or,

(b) elects to acquire but fails to deposit the total compensation within the prescribed or extended period, the Partition Commissioner shall, as soon as may be, proceed to divide the holding between the occupancy tenant and the landlord in accordance with their respective share declared under section 9.

16. Manner of payment and period of claims : (1) The total compensation deposited by an occupancy tenant in the tehsil treasury may be paid in such manner as may be prescribed. (2) The Partition Commissioner shall cause to be published in the village or estate in the prescribed manner, a notice requiring all persons claiming an interest in the total compensation in respect of any holding to file before him statements of their claims within a period of six months from the date of publication of the notice. (3) Any claim for payment of compensation or part thereof which is not made to the Partition Commissioner within the time specified in sub-section (2) shall cease to be enforceable.

17. Reference to civil court : Where any dispute arises between persons claiming, compensation under the preceding section the Partition commissioner shall require them to refer their claims to a civil court for adjudication.

18. Payment of compensation : (1) Where there is no dispute

between the claimants as to their respective shares in compensation the Partition Commissioner shall make payment to them in accordance with their respective shares. (2) In the case of dispute the Partition Commissioner shall pay the compensation to the claimants in accordance with the adjudication of the civil court under section 17.

19. Forfeiture of compensation to Government. If no person claims payment of compensation within a period of six months specified in sub-section (2) of section 16, the compensation shall forfeit to the Government.

20. Compensation to be deposited in bank in case of minors—where the landlord is a minor the Partition Commissioner shall cause the compensation to be deposited in the bank of Patiala or in any post office savings bank and shall direct the payment of interest thereon to the guardian of the minor.

21. Arrear of land revenue to be deducted : The arrears of land revenue, if any, shall be deducted by the Partition Commissioner form the total amount of compensation payable to the landlord.

PART III

MISCELLANEOUS

22. Conflict between Farman-i-Shahi and this Ordinance : The provisions of the Farman-i-Shahi 6 dated, Motibagh Place, Patiala the 11th of March, 1947, in so far as they are repugnant to the provisions of this Ordinance shall, to the extent of the repugnancy, be void.

23. Building on the holding constructed by landlord : Where there are any buildings on any holding constructed by the landlord or at his expense :

(a) the value of such buildings shall also be assessed by the Partition Commissioner with reference to the notified date and shall form a part of the total compensation payable to the landlord, or

(b) where the occupancy tenant elects not to pay the compensation the Partition Commissioner may, while partitioning the land, give due consideration to the claim of the landlord to such building.

24. Sham-i-Lat : Where under the provisions of this Ordinance the holding or any part thereof is transferred absolutely to the occupancy tenant, the rights of the landlord in the sham-i-lat shall as

from the notified date devolve on the occupancy tenant to the extent of the transfer without payment of any compensation in respect thereof.

25. Supplementary powers of Financial Commissioner and Partition Commissioner : The Financial Commissioner and the Partition Commissioner shall have all the powers of a civil court under the code of Civil procedure, 1908, in force in the Union for the purpose of administering oaths, taking evidence on oath, and of enforcing the attendance of witnesses and compelling the production of documents and material objects, and the Financial Commissioner and the Partition Commissioner shall be deemed to be Civil courts for the purposes of section 5 and of Chapter XXV of the Code of Criminal Procedure in force in the Union.

26. Jurisdiction of civil courts barred : No civil court or any other authority shall have jurisdiction to settle, decide or deal with any question which is, by or under this Ordinance, required to be settled, decided or dealt with by the Government or the Financial Commissioner or the Partition Commissioner.

27. Bar of certain suits and proceedings : (1) No Suit or other proceeding shall lie against the Government for any act done or purporting to be done under this Ordinance or any rule made there under. (2) No officer or servant of the Government shall be liable in respect of any such act in any civil or criminal proceeding, if the act was done in good faith in the course of the execution of the duties or the discharge of the functions imposed by or under this Ordinance.

28. Exemption from registration and payment of stamp : No instrument or document executed or made in pursuance of the provisions of this Ordinance or the transfer of any holding under this Ordinance shall be liable to registration or payment of stamp thereon, notwithstanding any law in force in the Union.

29. Power to make rules : (1) The Government may make rules to carry out the purposes of this Ordinance. (2) In particular and without prejudice to the generality of the foregoing provision, such rules may provide for :

(a) all matters expressly required or allowed by this Ordinance to be prescribed;

(b) the procedure to be followed by the Financial Commissioner and the Partition Commissioner in the discharge of their duties and functions;

(bb) the manner of determining the respective shares of the landlord and the occupancy tenant under the first provisor to section 9;

(bbb) the manner of determining compensation payable by the occupancy tenant to the landlord under sub-section (1) of section 12;

(c) the manner in which the compensation is to be deposited by the occupancy tenant in the tehsil treasury;

(d) the manner in which the compensation is to be paid to the landlord;

(e) fees, if any, to be paid on applications or petitions under this ordinance;

(f) transfer of proceedings from one Assistant Partition Commissioner to another;

(g) method of publishing notices.

30. Power to consolidate holdings dealt with under this Ordinance : Notwithstanding anything contained in the Patiala Consolidation of Holdings Act, 2003, and subject to the provisions of this Ordinance, the Consolidation Officer shall be competent to undertake suo motu the consolidation of holdings in any estate or sub-division of an estate after any holding comprised therein has been under this ordinance either partitioned or wholly assigned to the occupancy tenant.

Source : Patiala and East Punjab States Union Government Gazette, October 8, 1950.

APPENDIX-VIII

Area and Number of Tenants-at-Will Having No Land of Their own Paying Rent at Different Rates

District	*At Land Revenue Rate*		*Rent in Cash*		*Fixed Rent*		*Rent in Kind ½*		*Rent in Kind 1/3*	
	Area	*No. of Tenants*	*Area*	*No. of Tenants*	*Area*	*No. of Tenants*	*Area*	*No. of Tenants*	*Area*	*No. of Tenants*
(1)	*(2)*	*(3)*	*(4)*	*(5)*	*(6)*	*(7)*	*(8)*	*(9)*	*(10)*	*(11)*
1. Barnala	316	173	3,217	345	...	...	7,825	,111	8,386	1,016
2. Bhatinda	2	10	19,214	2,290	...	...	15,406	2,337	12,288	1,223
3. Fatehgarh Sahib	...	...	3,521	489	...	...	3,139	421	8,921	1,079
4. Kandaghat	11	6	1,437	168	...	...	821	94	153	33
5. Kapurthala	...	...	7,137	1,271	...	...	16,629	3,419	...	...
6. Mahendra-garh	...	...	41,028	7,136	79	16	9,928	2,080	1,998	401
7. Patiala	...	...	24,059	3,150	...	...	43,328	6,389	56,645	4,721
8. Sangrur	142	48	2,545	332	...	...	1,513	215	38,175	4,921
Total	471	237	102,159	15,181	79	16	99,389	16,086	126,556	13,394

(Contd....)

(Contd..)

APPENDIX-VIII (Contd....)

Area and Number of Tenants-at-Will Having No Land of Their own Paying Rent at Different Rates

District	*Rent in Kind 1/4*		*Rent in Kind 2/5*		*Rent in Kind 1/5*		*Mixed Rent*	
	Area	*No. of Tenants*	*Area*	*No. of Tenants*	*Area*	*No. of Tenants*	*Area*	*No. of Tenants*
(12)	*(13)*	*(14)*	*(15)*	*(16)*	*(17)*	*(18)*	*(19)*	*(20)*
1. Barnala	49	6	1,788	273	2,631	150	...	...
2. Bhatinda	825	81	1,678	141	43	4	...	...
3. Fatehgarh Sahib	4	2	3,009	442	...	...	969	126
4. Kandaghat	...	...	...	...	...	...	...	...
5. Kapurthala	...	...	...	...	...	...	...	...
6. Mahendragarh	10	2	254	36	...	...	...	...
7. Patiala	12,849	1,230	11,858	1,933	3	1	...	...
8. Sangrur	11,163	1,457	81	19	82	15	...	...
Total	24,900	2,778	18,668	2,844	2,759	170	969	126

Total area under tenants-at—well 375960

Number of tenants-at-well—50838

Source : Report on Agrarian Reforms in Pepsu, 1952, p. 83.

APPENDIX-IX

District	No. of Holdings	Under one acre	1 acre & above but under 3 acres	3 acres & above but under 5 acres	5 acres & above but under 10 acres	10 acres & above but under 15 acres	15 acres & above but under 20 acres	20 acres & above but under 25 acres	25 acres & above but under 50 acres	50 acres & above
Barnala	97,435	8,502	12,971	16,246	25,419	17,660	7,836	4,881	3,239	881
Bhatinda	66,399	8,989	7,979	6,367	10,321	7,471	6,381	4,876	11,023	5,892
Fatehgarh Sahib	38,699	7,482	5,626	5,322	6,687	5,272	4,130	775	2,067	1,338
Kandaghat	42,950	5,251	5,821	4,679	9,543	5,305	3,716	5,970	2,533	132
Kapurthala	68,721	32,624	13,808	6,386	7,420	3,384	1,736	1,139	1,415	809
Mahendragarh	59,284	6,404	8,355	8,217	10,529	7,818	5,911	4,320	5,119	2,611
Patiala	72,223	15,887	14,205	8,689	10,512	7,463	5,490	3,945	4,142	1,890
Sangrur	77,703	10,195	10,768	8,532	12,335	9,691	7,894	5,707	8,607	3,972
Total :	523,414	92,434	79,533	64,438	92,768	63,864	43,094	31,613	39,045	17,525

Sources : Pepsu-Report on Agrarian Reforms in Pepsu, June 1952, p. 84.

APPENDIX-X

Registeree No.S.P.141

PATIALA AND EAST PUNJAB STATES UNION

GAZETTE EXTRAORDINARY

Published by Authority

Vol. Patiala Tuesday	October 14, 1954	
No. 7	Asauj 28,1011	No. 106
	G.N.S. 485	

GROUP C

PART III-SECTION I

THE PEPSU AGRICULTURAL TENANTS (TEMPORARY PROTECTION AND DISABILITY) ORDINANCE 1954,

(ORDINANCE NO. 6 OF 1954)

Promulgated by the Rajpramukh in the Fifth year of the Republic of India.

AN

ORDINANCE

to provide for the temporary protection from ejectment of and the imposition of certain disabilities on agricultural tenants.

Whereas the legislative Assembly of the Patiala and East Punjab States Union is not in Session and the Rajpramukh is satisfied that circumstances exist which render it necessary for him to take immediate action.

Now therefore, in exercise of the powers conferred by clause (I) of Article 213 read with Article 238 of the Constitution, the Rajpramukh is pleased to promulgate the following Ordinance :

1. Short title, extent and commencement : (1) This Ordinance may be called the PEPSU agricultural Tenants (Temporary Protection and Disability) Ordinance, 1954. (2) It extends to the whole of the State of Patiala and East Punjab States Union. (3) It shall come into force at once.

2. Definitions : In this Ordinance, unless the context otherwise requires :

(a) "the Act" means the Patiala and East Punjab States Union Tenancy and Agricultural lands Act, 1953 (President's Act 8 of 153);

(b) all words and expression used and not delined but defined in the Act shall have the meanings assigned to them in the Act.

3. Protection of tenants from ejectment on ground of personal cultivation-Not-withstanding anything contained in the Act, no decree or for the ejectment of a tenant as defined in cause (k) of sub-section (II) of Section 2 of the Act on the ground that the land comprising his tenancy is required by the landowner for his personal cultivation, shall be passed or if passed shall be executed, for a period of one year from the commencement of this Ordinance.

4. Disability of tenants to acquire proprietary rights : Notwithstanding anything contained in the Act, no tenant as defined in Section 20 of the Act shall, for a period of one year from the commencement of this Ordinance, be entitled to acquire from his land owner in respect of the land comprising his tenancy the right, title and interest of the landowner in such land.

5. Postponement of proceedings : If any proceedings :

(a) for the ejectment of a tenant on the ground of personal cultivation or

(b) for acquisition by a tenant of proprietary rights in the land comprising his tenancy under Chapter IV of the Act,

are pending on the date of commencement of this ordinance, they shall be postponed for a period of one year from such commencement.

YADVENDRA SINGH
RAJPRAMUKH

HARBAKHSH SINGH
Legal Rememberancer and
Secretary to Government
Law Department

BIBLIOGRAPHIC NOTE

Numerous sources pertaining to the subject under study are available, though scattered. Of these, the Prime Minister's Office files and the *Ijlas-i-Khas* files, available at the Punjab State Archives, Patiala, are most valuable in so far as these files contain a detailed information on virtually all aspects of the study. These files contain a detailed information on the origin and growth of peasants struggle. These files also contain CID reports, tenants/peasants petitions, various reform commissions correspondence, reports, pamphlets, posters and newspapers clippings. These are most useful to ascertain the reaction and response of the peasants, *biswedars* as well as the official view-point of the State authorities.

Pepsu Legislative Assembly Debates and later Pepsu *Vidhan Sabha* Debates, Pepsu Government Gazettes, Ordinances, Notifications, Acts, Bills, Reports on Agrarian reforms, Administration reports, census reports of Patiala and Pepsu, Young Settlement Report, New Paper Files, News Diarly files and other government publications on Pepsu are the valuable original published sources material available in PSA, Patiala Files of the Maharaja Bhupinder Singh History Section at the Punjab State Archives constitute another primary source of a similar character. This section is specially useful in the understanding of the administration and personality of Maharaja Bhupinder Singh. There are a few files pertaining to the land revenue system and the *muzaras* struggle, it suffers from the same handicaps as the Prime Minister's and *Ijlas-i-Khas* Files.

Another significant source of information is the official State organ-the weekly Patiala Gazette, a more or less complete serial of the paper covering the period 1910-1948 is available at the Punjab State Archives. It throws light on various aspects of the state administrative structure, events, State ceremonies, visits of dignitaries, prices of agricultural produce and irrigation etc. It helps to give valuable insight into the nature of land revenue cases and especially the litigation between the *muzaras* and the *biswedars*.

The Records of the Chamber of Princes preserved at the Punjab State Archives, supply only a scantly but important information about the activities and administrative measures of the State authorities, having a socio-economic bearing. By shifting these documents one may discerned dichotomy between the pretensions and actual performance of the State rulers.

Perhaps the most complete set of extent data on the Patiala State are the decennial census Reports of the State (for years 1901, 1911, 1931, 1941, 1951). Apart from throwing light on general census topics, these reports also contain notes on contemporary socio-economic conditions. Their immense value in determining agricultural occupational stratas is somewhat undermined by frequently changing categorization.

Administration Reports of the State available at the Punjab State Archives are also the most valuable primary sources for this study. But the historical value of these reports is diminished by the eagerness of the authorities to present a more rosy than real picture of the State Administration. Some conspicuous gaps in these reports may be viewed as another failing, a limitation of this course.

The Punjab State Gazetteers Volume XVIIA, and Major Popham Young's Settlement Report constitute one solid block of source-material on the agrarian conditions in the State. Put together, the two sources give deep insight into the evolution of the land revenue administration and the land tenure system of the State. The former helps one knit the agrarian fabric of the State by supplying copious information about the nature of agricultural operations, the crop patterns, soil conditions, implements used in agricultural and irrigation etc. And the Settlement Report, which was the first and the last of its kind for the State, gives precious details of the new land revenue set up and tenurial system introduced by Young on existing pattern in the British Punjab.

Foreign and Home Department Proceedings of Government of India, available at the National Archives of India, New Delhi, supplement the primary source-material preserved at the Punjab State Archives. One goes through the foreign and Home Proceedings with a hope that in reporting about the administration of the States to their high-ups, the British officials would be objective, but on perusal of these documents such a hope is belied. The officials seldom projected a correct picture of the conditions in the State. This, however, does not imply that no complaints against the rulers were registered. There is evidence to suggest that such complaints were received and put on records, but the files which possibly contained all the valuable details about such complaints are not traceable.

All India States People's Conference (AISPC) papers and All India Congress Committee papers and files also provide a valuable information on the subject. From this emanates highly useful information regarding the tenants' struggle and the attitude and thinking of the Conference towards the States and the Princes—information which is seldom acquired from other sources.

Contemporary newspapers and the Reports on the native newspapers (available at the National Archives of India) have yielded invaluable information for the study. The news items, articles and editorials contained in these contemporary newspapers represent view-point other than official, and as such these are of immense value in the understanding of public opinion on the agrarian problem. It may, however, be observed that in spite of a large number of contemporary newspapers consulted, the information yielded on the subject is not as much as one would have expected or desired. This may be explained by the fact that there were restrictions imposed on the press in the State by authorities and that the newspapers operating from outside evinced comparatively little interest in the affairs of the State.

The files containing the interview with the eminent persons possessing the knowledge of the movement conducted by the Oral History Cell, The Punjab Historical Studies Department, Punjabi University, Patiala, Provide first hand information of the tenants movement. These interviews have proved beneficial in filling some gaps and reconstructing the historical moniac.

With regard to the secondary sources, their paucity is implicit in the fact there is not a single research-oriented published work bearing on the agrarian system of the Princely States of the region, much less of the Patiala State. The book that comes nearest to this subject is Ramesh Walia's *Praja Mandal Movement in East Punjab States.* But it touches only the fringe of the agrarian problem in as much as it is essentially a study of the political movement of the people in the East Punjab States, including Patiala. In the absence of any secondary source giving concrete information, a large number of books had to be consulted to yield fragmentary information on various aspects of the study.

BIBLIOGRAPHY

PRIMARY SOURCES : UNPUBLISHED

Proceedings of the Finance Department : 1915-30 and 1934-38;
Proceedings of the Home Department : 1920-40;
Proceedings of the Home Department (Political) : 1919-47;
Proceedings of the Department of Revenue and Agriculture : 1900-04;
Proceedings of Government of India, 1900-1948.
Foreign Department, Political Consultations.
Foreign Department, Internal A and Internal B.
Foreign Department, General A and General B.
Foreign Department, Establishment Proceedings.
Foreign Department, Revenue Proceedings.
Foreign Department, Secret and Secret X.
Files on the Workers' and Peasants' Parties;
Gurmukhi Exhibit;
Punjab and UP Speeches;
Statements of the Punjab Communists (especially of R.S. Nimbkar and others) involved in the case :
Abdul Majid, Sohan Singh Josh and Kedar Nath Sehgal.
(Available at Nationa Archives of India, New Delhi).

Punjab States' Agency Records (Political) : 1928-33;
Punjab States' Agency Records (General) : 1922-36;
Punjab State Records : Prime Ministers' Officer Files :
256, 317, 372, 380, 541, 542, 544, 547, 548, 549, 552, 553, 555, 556, 563, 564, 566, 568, 569, 578, 608, 609, 613, 623, 624, 630, 639, 642, 644, 653, 654, 655, 667, 669, 670, 672, 675, 685, 689, 690, 692, 697, 698, 700, 702, 703, 710, 713, 715, 724, 727, 729, 730, 733, 734, 737, 738, 742, 744, 745, 746, 747, 749, 750, 752, 756, 763, 767, 770, 772, 787, 847, 900, 936, 1101, 1155, 1544, 1546, 1547, 1550, 1553, 1554, 1555, 1559, 1560, 1561, 1562, 1563, 1573, 1574, 1583, 1650, 1860, 1945, 6157, 2077, 5804, 2226/100, 238/SPC,CaseNo.565/C of

1934-44, 565/C,CB-1-2 of1944-45, CB-1-2 of 1945-46, T-I of 1945, G-2165,4516, 4531, 5271, 5445, 5446, 5567, 5582, 5640, 5675, 5982, 6849, 10176,10189, 10213, 10227, 10473, 10710.

Ijlas-i-Khas Files Nos :

446, 645, 652, 1261, 1263, 1264, 1684, 1938, 1943, 1946, 1947, 1952, 1953, 1956, 1957, 1963, 1964, 1965, 1968, 1974, 2022, 2077, 2193, 2197, 2207, 2221, 2226, 2242.

Official Records of the Patiala States 1900-1948.

Chamber of Princes Record, 1921-1947.

Chamber of Princes' Records, File-CAS/L-9 (Subscersive movements from across the border) Press Clippings pertaining to the states and the Political movements;

Proceedings of the Punjab States Council Meetings held at Lahore on 17th-18th March, 1940 and at Simla on 30th-31st March, 1943;

Nabha State Records : Confidential Meetings Files-82-B, 49-C, 62-C, 337;

Kalsia State Records : Confidential Files—1, 2, 132, 164;

Kapurthala State Records : Files- A-1, M/3-14, M/3-39.
(Available at Punjab State Archives : Patiala)

Punjab Legislative Council Debates, Proceedings, 1920-1945, Vols VI-XXIV.

Published Reports :

Annual Administration Reports of Patiala State for the years :
1920-21, 1929-30, 1932-33, 1938-39, 1939-40, 1940-41.

Annual Administration Reports of Nabha, Kapurthala, Faridkot and Kalsia States for the period 1911-39;

Annual Reports of the Canals in the Punjab : 1919-20.
(Available at Central State Library, Patiala)

Census Reports of Patiala State for the years :
1901, 1911, 1921, 1931, 1941, 1951.

Final Report of the Settlement of the Patiala State
(A.D. 1900-1908)

Patiala in Years 1910-1921, During the reign of His Highness Maharaja Bhupinder Singh.

PEPSU Administration Reports for the years 1948-1955.

PEPSU Census of India 1951.

Report of Ministry of Law and Justice of Patiala for 1935-36.

Reports on Administration of Punjab and its Dependencies for the years 1900-1921.

Financial Commissioner Office, Pepsu, Revenue Department,

Punjab Civil Secretariat, Chandigarh, File No. R.D. 26 (74) C/52.

Punjab Legislative Assembly Debates, Proceedings, 1937-40, Vol. I-XX.

Abhyankar, G.R., and Trivedi Manishanke S., *Report of the States Peoples'* Conference, Bombay Session : 1928;

Annual Administration Reports of the East Punjab States and Khalsa States : 1919-36;

India in 1921-22 (Calcutta : 1922);

India in 1925-26 (Calcutta : 1926).

India in 1927-28 (Calcutta : 1928);

All India States People's Conferences Papers.

File Nos :

1, 53, 54, 55, 89, 90, 91, 108, 118, 132, 133, 133-A, 134, 138.

All India Congress Committee Papers.

File Nos :

13/1948-49, G-6/1939, C-16/1946-49, IG.49/1947-48, G-52/1929-29, 84/1931-47.

(Available at Nehru Memorial Museum Library, Teen Murti House, New Delhi)

Ministry of Home Affairs.

File No. 17/33-Judi-Pepsu Tenancy.

Ministry of States.

File Nos 3(39)-P/49, 3(85)-P/49, 9(16)-P/49, 13(20)-P/50 14(77)-P/50, 55-P/50, 3(21)-P/51, 5(54)-PA/51, 7(40)-s/51. 1(238) J/52, 1(284)-J/52, 1(284)-J/52, 1(75)-J/52, 1(52) J/52, 3(23)-PA/52, 17(10)-PA/52, 17(16)-PA/52, 55-J/52, 17(38) H (P)-53, 1(135) J/S/Sect, 2(6)-P, 3(10) P (G), 2 (13)-P, 3(6)-P, 3(79)-P(S), 3(7)-P, 3(84)-P.

(Available at National Archives, of India, New Delhi)

Government Gazetteers :

Imperial Gazetteer of India Provincial Series Punjab, Volume II, Calcutta, 1908.

Punjab district Gazetteers, Ludhiana District 1904,

Part A, VOLUME XV A, Lahore, 1907.

Punjab States Gazetteers, Malerkotla State, 1904, Volume XV A, Lahore, 1988.

Punjab States Gazetteers-Phulkian States, Patiala Jind and Nabha, 1904, Volume XVII A, Lahore, 1909.

Punjab States Gazetteers-Phulkian States, Patiala Jind and Nabha, Volume XVII B, Lahore, 1913.

Miscellaneous Abstracts, Reports, Acts etc :

Chamber of Princes, Record of Chamber of Princes Relating to Constituent States of PSPSU (Printed and Mss.).

Government of India, Indian States Committee 1928-29 Report, Calcutta, 1929.

____________________, *Indian States Today,* New Delhi, 1946.

Government of India, Land Revenue Policy of the Indian Government, Calcutta, 1902.

____________________, *Memoranda on Native States for the years :* 1909-1912, 1915, 1921, 1934-1937, Calcutta and Delhi.

____________________, *Statistical Abstract for British India : with Statistics Available relating to certain Indian States for the years 1930-40.* Calcutta and Delhi

__________________, *White Paper on Indian States,* Delhi 1948.

Patiala State Government, Patiala's Pround Record as Britain's Friend and Ally, Patiala, 1929.

Pepsu Government, Facts about Pepsu, Patiala, 1952.

__________________, *Pepsu Abolition of the Malkiyat Rights Act, 1954,* Patiala, 1954,

__________________, *Pepsu Agricultural Tenants (Temporary Protection and Disability) Act, 1954,* Patiala, 1955.

__________________, *Pepsu Land Acquisition Act. 1954,* Patiala, 1955.

__________________, *Pepsu Occupancy Tenants (Vesting of Proprietary Rights) Act 1954,* Patiala, 1954.

__________________, *Pepsu Since Inauguration, Patiala 1951.*

__________________, *Pepsu Tenancy and Agricultural Lands Act 1955,* Patiala, 1955.

__________________, *President's Rule in Pepsu (March 1953 to March 1954),* Patiala, n.d.

__________________, *Quarterly Bulletin of Statistics : July to September 1951,* Patiala, 1952.

__________________, *Report on the Inquiry into Rural Indebtedness Problem in Pepsu,* Patiala, 1954.

Punjab Government, Punjab Government Records, Records of Ludhiana Agency, Volume II, Lahore, 1911.

__________________, *Punjab Press Abstracts, 1916-1924.*

__________________, *Selection from the Native Newspapers Published in the Punjab, 1900-1916.*

Punjab States Agency, List of Ruling Princes, Notables and Principal Officials, Delhi, 1938.

Census Report of Patiala State-1941, Patiala, Bhupendra State Press.

Census Report of Pepsu-1951, Vols. I to VIII, Patiala : Buhpendra State Press.

Facts about Pepsu, Patiala : Directorate of Information and Public Relations, Pepsu, 1953.

Kishangarh, the Peasants' Defence of His land, Published by Pepsu *Kisan Sabha,* Sangrur, Bhatinda, Mittal Printing Press (N.D.).

Land to the Tiller, Directorate of Information, Pepsu, Patiala, 1953.

Patiala and East Punjab States Union, Since Inauguration, Patiala. Directorate of Information and Public Relations, Pepsu (N.D.).

Patiala De Muzarian De Ghol Te Thuada Farz, (Punjab), Lahore : Published Secretary Muzara Committee, Riyast Patiala, 1947.

Patiala and East Punjab States Union-Historical Background, Patiala : Archives Publication, 1951.

Patiala Tenants on the March, issued by Muzara Committee, Lahore : Progressive Publishers, (N.D.).

Pepsu Plans for Prosperity, Patiala, Directorate of Information & Public Relations, Pepsu, 1953.

Proceedings and Resolutions of All India Kisan Sabha. Amritsar, 1956.

Pepsu, Legislative Assembly Debates, Official Report, Patiala, Published By Pepsu Legislative Assembly Secretariat :

——— 1952, Vol. I, Part I, S. No. 1 to 13.

——— Vol. II, Part I, S. No. 1 to 7.

——— Part II, S. No. 1 to 7.

Pepsu Vidhan Sabha Debates, Official Report-1954 :

——— Vol. III, S. No. 1 to 13.

——— Vol. IV, S. No. 1 to 11.

——— Vol. V, S. No. 1 to 10.

1955;

——— Vol. VI, S. No. 1 to 23.

——— Vol. VII, S. No. 1 to 5.

——— Vol. VIII, S. No. 1 to 5.

1956;

____________ Vol. IX, S. No. 1 to 21.

____________ Vol. IX A, S. No. 1 to 4.

____________ Vol. IX B, S. No. 1 to 15.

Quarterly Bulletin of Statistics : July to September, 1951 Patiala : Bureau of Economics and Statistics, 1952.

Report on the Administration of Patiala State, 1929-30, Patiala, Bhupendra State Press,

________________________ 1932-33.

________________________ 1938-39.

________________________ 1939-40.

________________________ 1940-41.

Report on the Administration of Patiala and East Punjab States Union, From 1st of April 1951 to 31st March, 1952.

Report on the Administration of Patiala and East Punjab States Union, From 1st April 1952 to 31st March, 1953, Printed at the Bank of Patiala Press.

Report on the States Re-organisation, Commission, 1955, Government of India Publication.

Report on Agrarian Reforms, Pepsu, Government of India, Ministry of States, June, 1952 (C.S. Vinkatachar Committee).

Report on Agrarian Reforms in Pepsu, 1952, Pepsu Government (Dara Singh Committee).

Report of the Congress Agrarian Reforms Committee, Published by the All India Congress Committee, New Delhi, 1951, (Second Edition).

Report on the Progress of the State Five Year Plan-1954-55, Pepsu Government Publication.

Report of the Inter Departmental Secretaries, Committee, Pepsu First Five Years Plan, Government Publication (ND.)

PEPSU GOVERNMENT PUBLICATIONS :

Tenancy Ordinances/Legislation and Acts :

Farman-i-Shahi, March 11, 1947.

The Patiala and East Punjab States Union Abolition of Occupancy Tenures and Settlement of Land Disputes Ordinance No. XXIII, 2006, B.K. (1949).

The Pepsu Amendment Abolition of *Biswedari* Ordinance No. IV of 2007 B.K. (1950).

The Patiala and East Punjab States Abolition of *Ala-Malkiat* Rights Act, 1953, Patiala : Bhupendra Press, 1953.

The Pepsu Occupancy Tenants (Vesting of Proprietary Rights) Act, 1953, Patiala, Bhupendra Press, 1953.

The Pepsu Tenancy and Agricultural Act, 1953, Patiala, Bhupendra Press, 1953.

The Pepsu Occupancy Tenants (Vesting of Proprietary Rights) Act, 1954, Published by Authority, 1954.

The Pepsu Land Acquistion Act, 1954, Published by Authority, 1954.

The Pepsu Tenancy and Agricultural Lands Act, 1955, Patiala : Bhupendra State Press, 1955.

The Pepsu Tenancy and Agricultural Lands (Amendment) Bill, 1955, Published by Authority, 1955.

The Pepsu Tenancy and Agricutlural Lands (Second Amendment) Act, 1956, Published by Authority, 1956.

The Pepsu Code of Laws, Vol. II, Patiala : Bhupendra State Press, 1951.

The Punjab Tenancy Act (XVI of 1887) Printed at the Wazir-i-Hind Gas Press, Amritsar, 1907 (Third Edition).

The Punjab States Gazetteers, Vol. XXII-A, Phulkian States Patiala, Nabha, and Jind, Lahore : Civil and Military Gazette Press, 1931.

The New Tenancy legislation in Pepsu, directorate of Information, Pepsu, Patiala, 1953.

What the President has done—For Pepsu-During the Last six months-March-August 1953, Patiala : Bhupendra State Press, 1953.

Young, F. Popham, Final Report of the Settlement of the Patiala State (A.D. 1900-1908) Ajmer : Soottiah Mission Industries Co. Ltd., 1909.

Non-Official Documents, Files and Polomics :

All India Congress Committee Papers Files (Available at Nehru Memorial Museum and Library, New Delhi).

All India States Peoples Conference Papers Files (Available at Nehru Memorial Museum and Library, New Delhi.

All India States Peoples Conference, Congress Policy towards States, Bombay, 1938.

__________________, *Indictment of Patiala : Patiala Enquiry Report,* Bombay, 1930.

__________________, *Memorandum Presented to Indian States Committee,* London, 1928.

__________________, *Presidential Address to the Sixth Session of the All India States Peoples Conference, J. L. Nehru,* Ludhiana, 1939.

__________________, *Report of Bombay Session, 17th, 18th of December 1927,* Bombay, 1928.

All Parties Conference 1928, Report of the Committee appointed by the Conference to Determine the Principles of Constitution of India, Allahabad, 1928.

Harbans Lal, *Report on Punjab States, Patiala, 1947.*

Lok Sewak Sabha, Memorandum to Ministry of States, Patiala, 1948.

Shiromani Gurdwara Parbandhak Committee Papers (Available at Sikh Reference Library, Amritsar).

Standing Committee Patiala State *Praja Mandal,* Memorandum presented to the Prime Minister, Patiala State on 16th December, 1946, Patiala, 1946.

The British Crown and the Indian States : An outline Sketch presented to the Indian States Committee on behalf of the Standing Committee of the Chamber of Princes, London, 1929.

Contemporary Newspapers and Periodicals : (available at Dwarka Das library, Chandigarh/Sikh Reference Library,

Amritsar and Special Collections Section of Punjabi University, Library, Patiala).

Akali, Lahore, 1920-1922, 1937-1941.

Akali Patrika, Lahore, 1920-1922, 1936-1938.

Akali Te Pardeshi, Amritsar, 1922-1930.

Asli Qaumi Dard, Amritsar, 1929-1939.

Safar Ghar, Amritsar, 1924-1926, 1928-1930.

Desh Dardi, Amritsar, 1933.

Faton, Amritsar, 1907, 1928-33, 1935-1940.

Gargaj, Akali, Amritsar, 1922.

Gursewak, Amritsar, 1936-1937.

Heera, Amritsar, 1938.

Khalsa Samachar, Amritsar, 1900-1947.

Khalsa-Te-Khalsa Advocate, Amritsar, 1903-1905, 1916-1947.

Kirpan Bahadur, Amritsar, 1928-1931.

Kirpan Bahadur Te Sangat, Amritsar, 1927-1928.

Malwa Gazette, Amritsar, 1927-1928.

Nawan Jug, Lahore, 1933.

Panch Khalsa Samachar, Amritsar, 1924-1929.

Panth Sewak, Amritsar, 1915-1922.

Patiala Gazette, Patiala, 1911-1948.

Punjab Amritsar, Amritsar, 1906-1908, 1938-1940.

Sher Khalsa, Lahore, 1929-1930.

The Daily Jathedar, Amritsar, 1922.

The Riyast, Delhi, 1928-1948.

Newspapers and Journals :

Kirti (Panjabi), and *Kirti Lehar* (Panjabi) : February 1926 to November, 1939 (The Copies of *Kirti* and *Kirti Lehar* are available in Bhai Mohan Singh Vaid Section : Library, Panjabi University,

Patiala; Desh Bhagat Yadgar Hall Library, Jullundhur NMML, Teen Murti, New Delhi (Micro-Film), National Archives of India, Library-Prescribed Literature Section).

Hind Samachar : 1920-45;

The Tribune, Lahore : 1920-55 (Microfilm) NMML, Teen Murti, New Delhi;

Daily Nawan Jamana (Panjabi) selected issues;

Weekly Sada Yug (Panjabi), selected issues;

National Front (Weekly Newspaper of the CIP)

Vol. I, Nos 1 to 5 (Feb 13, 1938 to Feb 5, 1939);

Vol. II, Nos 1 to 33 (Feb 12, 1939 to Dec 17, 1939).

The Communist : The Official Organ of the CPI Section of the CI-Some Selected Issues of the years 1935 to 1938, Vol. I of each year and years 1939-41, Vol. II of each year and also Vol. III of 1941;

Communist International (Journal of the CI) Selected Issues : May, 1919 to April, 1928;

The Congress Socialist : Organ of the All India Congress—Socialist Party : Vol. I, No. 1 & 2, 1934; Vol. I, Nos. 7, 8, 10 to 12, 1935);

The Punjab Past and Present (various issues), issued by the Historical Research Department : Panjabi University, Patiala.

The Panjabi (Lahore), 1907;

Reports on the Native Newspapers (Panjabi); 1920-40 (of a few years missing).

(Available at NAI, New Delhi).

Private Papers of Individuals.

Prithvi Singh Azad Papers;

Sir Sunder Singh Majithia Papers;

Sri Ram Sharma;

Gokul Chand Narang;

Bhai Jodh Singh;

Zaheer Shri Sajjad;

AISPC-Papers;

Linlithgow Papers;

Indian News-Papers : 28.2.1935 to 26.12.1936;

Zetland Papers : Private Papers of second Morquis of Zetland, Secretary of State for India : 1935-40;

India Office Library Records, London, A.P. Hume Collections : *Papers of A.P. Hume, Indian Civil Services :* 1927-47;

Oral Evidence :

(i) Oral History Cell, Punjab Historical Studies Department, Punjab University, Patiala

Person	*Oral History Cell File No.*
Brish Bhan	-
Bhaura, Bhan Singh	-
Daftriwala, Wazir Singh	41
Gojran, Pritam Singh Ex-MLA Pepsu	4
Jeji, Harchand Singh	10
Joga, Jagir Singh Ex-MLA Pepsu	20
Kushdeva Singh, Dr.	50
Kothala, Pritam Singh	33
Lal Singh, Dr.	63
Malik, Hardit Singh Ex-Prime Minister Patiala State	-
Phugawalia Jangir Singh Ex-MLA Pepsu	55
Parshad, Diwan Niranjan	3
Rarewala, Gian Singh Ex-Chief Minister Pepsu	68
Tirath Singh Advocate	-

News Diary Files, Punjab State Archives Patiala

Pamphlets, Posters, Magazines and Weekly or Monthly newspaper files, Bhai Mohan Singh Vaid Section, Panjabi University Library and Historical Studies, Department, Panjabi University, Patiala.

Jounrnals and Periodicals :

All India Kisan Sabha, Souvenir, Bhatinda, Session-1973.

Bengal Past and Present, Calcutta, Vol. XCII-I, Jan-June 1973.

Journal of Punjab University Historical Society, Lahore, Vol. N-2, 1935.

Journal of Regional History, Amritsar, Vols. I, 1980; II, 1981.

Patiala Post, Patiala, Nos. Nov. 1943-Dec. 1943, Dec. 1943-Jan. 1944, Jan. 1944-Feb. 1944, May 1944-June 1944, June 1944-July 1944, July 1944-Aug. 1944, April 1946-May 1946, July 1946-Aug. 1946.

Proceedings Indian History Conference :

4th Session, Lahore, 1940; 9th Session, Patna, 1946;

14th Session, Jaipur, 1951; 18th Session, Calcutta,

1955; 20th Session, Vallabh Vidya Nagar, 1957;

23rd Session, Aligarh, 1960; 25th Session, Poona,

1963; 26th Session, Ranchi, 1964; 28th Session,

Mysore, 1966; 29th Session, Patiala, 1967; 32nd Session; Jabalpur, 1970.

Punjab Past and Present, Panjabi University, Patiala, a Vols.

VI-I, April 1970; VII-I, April 1973, VIII-II, October 1974; X-II, October 1976; XIII-I, April 1979; XIV-I,

April 1980; XV-I, April 1981; XVII-I, April 1983; XIX-II, October, 1984.

'Sangrama Share Panjah Vareh', *Souvenir,* Communist Party of India, 1976.

Studies in History, Jawaharlal Nehru University, New Delhi, Vols. I and II, 1981; IV-I, January-June 1982 and Vol. II, January-June, 1986.

Unpublished Thesis

Barrier, N.G., Punjab Politics and the disturbances of 1907, Duke University, 1966—in Microfilm.

Bhan, Prem Narayan, 'Revenue Policy of the Punjab during the time of Lord Dalhousie', Punjab University, Lahore, 1938.

Dhilion, Gurdarshan Singh, 'Character and Impact of the *Singh Sabha* Movement on the History of the Punjab', Panjabi University, Patiala, 1972.

Gajrani, S.D., 'Some Aspects of Agrarian problems and the role of Peasantry in freedom Struggle in Punjab', Guru Nanak Dev University, Amritsar, 1981.

Gursharan Singh, 'Akali Movement and Phulkian States (Upto 1938)', Panjabi University, Patiala, 1967.

Harcharan Singh, 'British Policy towards the Phulkian States', Panjabi University, Patiala, 1980.

Kaloka, Gagandeep, Rural Leadership in *Praja Mandal* Movement in Punjab (1927-47), Panjabi University, Patiala, 1983.

Jaspal Kaur, 'Tenant Movement in Patiala State', Panjabi University, Patiala, 1967.

Lata, Prem, 'Pepsu *Vidhan Sabha'*, Panjabi University, Patiala, 1976.

Maljinder Kaur, 'Administration of Maharaja Bhupinder Singh of Patiala 1900-1938', Panjabi University, Patiala, 1978.

Mohan, Kamlesh, 'Militant Nationalism in the Punjab', Guru Nanak Dev University, Amritsar, 1980.

Purie, Suresh, 'Ministry in Pepsu', Punjabi University Patiala, 1976.

Raja Ram, The Impact of the First World War on the Punjab, Punjab University, Chandigarh.

Rao, S. N., 'Cis-Sutlej Sikh States 1800-1849', Punjab University, Chandigarh, 1953.

Sharma, Inderjit, 'The Land Revenue Administration in the Punjab between 1849 and 1901', Punjab University,Chandigarh, 1974.

Sukhwant Singh, 'Agricultural Development in the Punjab Plains 1849-1947', Guru Nanak Dev University, Amritsar, 1979.

Persons Interviewed Personally :

Brish Bhan, Ex-Chief Minister, Pepsu, Chandigarh.

Dara Singh Advocate, Ex-Revenue Minister, Pepsu, Chandigarh.

Giani Bachan Singh, Ex-MLA Pepsu, Village Bakshiwala, Distt. Sangrur.

Jagjit Singh (Comrade) College Road, Sangrur.

Joga, Jagir Singh, Ex-MLA, President Punjab Kisan Sabha, Joga.

Majhail S. Ishar Singh, Arjun Nagar, Patiala.

Mann, Bhupinder Singh, Ex-Finance Minister Pepsu, Sirhind.

Master Hari Singh, Ex-MLA and Ex-General Secretary, Punjab *Kisan Sabha,* Chandigarh.

Murori, Inder Singh, a prominent Kisan workers during the Muzara Movement, Sirhind.

Pt. Kishori Lal (Comrade), Jullundhur.

S. Sohan Singh Josh (Comrade) New Delhi.

Sunder Lal Advocate; Ex-President; Patiala *Praja Mandal,* Patiala.

Swaran Singh Bir (Comrade) Village Bir, District Bhatinda.

Vaid Chhajju Mal, Secretary All India *Kisan Sabha,* Delhi.

Vidyarthi, Davinder Singh Dr., Sikh History Research Department, Khalsa College, Amritsar.

SECONDARY SOURCE

Books (English)

Abdul Latif : *Industrial Punjab* (Calcutta : 1911).

Abhedanand Swamy : *India and Her People* (Calcutta : 1963).

Abraham, Francis : *Dynamics of Leadership in Village India* (Allahabad : Indian International Publication, 1974).

Adhikari, G. : *Documents of History of the Communist* Party of India,Vol. I & II (PPH, New Delhi : 1972 & 1974 respectively).

Aggarwal, O.P. : *The Punjab land Revenue* (Act XVIII of 1887), 8th Ed., (Delhi : 1975).

Ahluwalia, M.L. : *Kukas : The Freedom Fighters of the* Punjab (Bombay : 1965).

Ahmad, Muzzaffar : *The Communist Party of India and Its* Formation Abroad (Calcutta : 1962). *Myself and the Communist Party of India :* 1920-29 (Calcutta 1970).

Ahmad Zahir : *Dust and Dawn in Village India* (London : 1965). *Communist Challenge Imperialism from Dock* (Calcutta : 1967).

Ahmad, Z.A. : *The Agrarian Problem in India* (Lahore : 1936).

Alakh Dhari : *Economic Possibilities of Kapurthala* (Punjab : 1921).

Alexander, K.C. : *Peasant Organization in South India* (New Delhi, Indian Social Institute, 1981).

Allen, G.C. : *The Economic Development of India,* 3rd Edition, (London : 1939).

Anderson, G. : *British Administration in India* (London : 1923).

Anderson, J.D. : *Customery Law of Muzzafargarh District* (Lahore : 1925). People of India (Cambridge : 1913).

Anstey, V. : *The Economic Development of India* (London : 1939).

Antonova, K. : *A History of India* (Moscow : 1978).

Apter Devid E. : *Ideology and Discontent* (New York : The Free Press, 1964).

Arvind Dass, V. Nila Kant : (*ed.*) *Agrarian Relations in India,* (New Delhi : Manohar Publications, 1979).

Aulakh, Jagjit Singh : *Ikk Jiwan-Ikk Itihas (Panjabi)* n.d.

Babbar, Sunder Singh : *Babbar Akali Lehar* (Amritsar : 1961)

Dukhi Mansha Ram : *Jiwan Bhai Sahib Mohan Singh Vaid (Panjabi)* (Amritsar : n.d.).

Gurbux Singh : *Manzil Dis Pai (Panjabi)* (Ludhiana : 1969).

Gurcharan Singh : *Ankhi Surma (Panjabi)* (Hoshiarpur : 1950).

Babar Akali Lehar (Punjabee), (Hoshiarpur : 1950).

Makhsuspuri, Sunder Singh : *Babbar Akali Lehar,* 2nd Edition *(Panjabi)* (Amritsar : 1970).

Panchhi Pritam Singh : *Ghadr Ki Gunj Aur Kamaghata Maru Ka Romanch* (Delhi : 1961).

Puri, Sahib Chand : *Ahalkari Sazshan* (Phulkian Samachar Publication, Patiala, n.d.).

Sainsara Gurcharan Singh : *Oh, Vee Din San (Panjabi)* (Ludhiana : 1965).

Ujjagar Singh : *Amar Saheed Sewa Singh Thikriwala (Panjabi)* (Patiala : 1970)

Baba, Karam Singh (*ed.*) : *Abhinanadan Granth* : 86th Birth Commemoration Vol Baba Kharak Singh Abhinandan Committee, New Delhi.

Badon-Powell B.H. : *The Land Systems of British India* (Delhi : Oriental Publishers, 1974).

Bajwa, Fauja Singh : *A Brief Account of the Freedom Movement in Punjab* (Patiala : Panjabi University, 1972).

Eminent Freedom Fighters of Punjab, Patiala (Panjabi University, 1972).

Kuka Movement (Delhi : 1965);

Who is Who : Punjab Freedom Fighters (*ed.*) (Patiala : 1975).

Banerjee, G.L. : *Dynamics of Revolutionary Movement in India : Housekeeping of Revolution in Russia and India* (Calcutta : 1970).

Banga Indu : *Agrarian System of the Sikhs, Late Eighteenth & Early Nineteenth Century* (Delhi : 1978).

Rangal, Jogesh Chandra : *Peasant Revolution in Bengal* (Calcutta : Bharathi Library Publishers, 1953).

Benerjee, Himadri : *Agrarian Society of the Punjab, 1849-1901 :* (New Delhi : Manohar Publications).

Barrier, N.G. : *The Punjab Alienation of Land Bill of 1900* (Monograph : Duke University, 1966).

Punjab Politics and Disturbances of 1907 (Microfilm, NMML, New Delhi).

Beoli, B.P.L. : *Monstrous Rule in Faridkot* (Delhi : nd).

Beteille, Andre : *Studies in Agrarian Social Structure* (Delhi : Oxford University Press, 1949).

Bhalla, G.S. & Talib, B.D.: *Agrarian Structure and Peasant Movement in Punjab,* New Delhi : Centre for the Study of Regional Development School of Social Sciences, Jawaharlal Nehru University.

Bhattacharyya, D.A.: *Concise History of Indian Economy* 1950-1950, (New Delhi, 1979).

Blunt, Sir Edward : *Caste System in Northern India* (Madras : 1931).

Social Service in India (Madras : 1931).

An Introduction to Some Social and Economic Problems of the Indian People (London : 1938).

Blyn, G.: *Agricultural Trends in India*: 1891-1947 (Philodelphia : 1966).

Bose, A.C.: *Indian Revolutionaries*: Abroad, 1905-1922 (Patna : 1971).

Rose, Atindra Nath : *Social and Rural Economy of Northern India,* 2 Vols. (Calcutta, 1967)

Bose Manjula : (*ed.*) *Land Reforms in Eastern India* (Planning Form, Jadavpur University, 1981).

Bose, Nemi Sadloan : *The Indian National Movement* – An Outline (Calcutta : 1965).

Bowles, Cherter : *Who Owns the Land* (New Delhi : Albion Press, 1964).

Burns, W.: *Sons of Soil,* Studies in India, Cultivator (Delhi, 1941).

Brij Narain : *The Agricultural Workers and the Punjab Land Revenue Committee* (Lahore : 1939).

Brij Narain : *India In Crisis* (Allahabad : 1934).

Economic Structure of Free India (Lahore : 1946).

Rational View of Life: *Punjab Socialist Party* (Lahore : n.d.).

Cab, G.D.H. : *Communism and Social Democracy : 1914-31 Part I* (London : 1931).

Calvert, H.: *The Wealth and Welfare of the Punjab* (Lahore : 1936).

Carr, E.H.: *The Bolshevik Revolution : 1917-23, Vol III* (Lahore : 1966).

Cartwnight : *Drawin and Zander* Arvin (*ed.*), Groups Dynamics : Research and Theory, Evanston Illionis, Row Paterson.

Caveeshar, Sardar Singh : *Sikh Politics* (Delhi : 1950).

Non-Violent Non-Cooperation (Lahore : 1934).

Chadha, T.R. : *A Study of the Communist Movement in the Punjab* (Gaziabad : 1954).

A Study of the Communist Movement in the Punjab (Gaziabad : 1954).

Champakalashmi : *The Economic and Social Life of the Peasantry in the Deccan in the 19th Century,* (Hyderabad (MD).

Chandra, Bipan : *The Rise and Growth of Economic Nationalism in India* (PPH, Delhi : 1977).

Nationalism and Colonalism in India, (New Delhi, 1979).

Chaudhary, M.K. : (*ed.*), *Trends of Socio-Economic Change in India : 1871-1961* (Simla, 1969).

Chaudhary, Rai : *Leftist Movements in India 1917-47* (Calcutta, 1975).

Chaudhary, S.B. : *Civil Disturbances during the British Rule in India (1765-1857)* (Calcutta : World Press, 1955).

Chaudhary, Sukhbir : *Peasants' and Workers Movement in India 1905-29* (PPH, Delhi : 1971).

Growth of Nationalism in India : 1919-20, Vol. II (Delhi : 1973).

Chosmeaux Jean : *Peasant Revolts in China 1940-1949* (London : Thomas and Hudson, 1973).

Chudgar, P.L. : *Indian Princes Under British Protection* (London : 1929).

Chhabra, G.S. : *Social and Economic History of the Punjab (1849-1901)* (Jullundhur : S Nagin & Co., 1962).

Clarke John : *The Sikhs* (Oxford : 1946).

Cohen, S.P. : *Indian Army : Its Contribution to the Development of a National* (Berkeley : 1971).

Crooke, W. : *Natives of Northern India* (London : 1907).

Darling, M.L. : *The Punjab Peasant in Prosperity and Debt* (London : 1925).

Rusticus and Loguitur or the Old Light and the New in the Punjab Village (London : 1930).

Darling, M.L. : *Wisdom and Waste in the Punjab Village* (London : 1934).

At Freedom Doors' (London : 1949).

Dutt, Romesh : *The Economic History of India, Vols. I and II,* (Delhi, 1976) Third reprint, first published London, 1906).

Dutt, R.S. : *India Today* (Bombay, 1947).

Datta, Dvijadan : *Land Laws in India* (Bombay : D.E. Taraposewala and Sons and Co. 1931).

Dayanand, Swami : *Hand Book of the Arya Samaj* (nd.).

Deol, G.S. : *The Role of the Ghadr Party in the National Movement* (Jullundhur : 1969).

Sardar Bhagat Singh (Patiala : 1978).

Desai, A.R. : *Peasant Struggle in India* (*ed.*).

(Bombay : Oxford University Press, 1979).

Desai A.R. : *Rural Sociology in India* (Bombay : Popular Prakashan, 1979, first Published in 1961).

Desai, A.R. : *Rural India in Transition* (Bombay : Popular Prakashan, 1979, First published in 1961).

Desai, A.R. : *Social Background of Indian Nationalism* (Bombay : Popular Prakashan, 1966).

Dewan Raj Kumar : *Modern Kapurthala and Its Makers* (Kapurthala Government Publication : n.d.).

Dewan Jermani Dass : *Maharaja : Lives and Loves and Intrigues of Indian Princes* (Bombay : 1969).

Driver, Pershotam : *Problems of Zamindari and Land Tenure Reconstruction in India* (Bombay : New Book Company Ltd., 1949).

Dube, Leela : *Studies on Leadership in Village India, "in Emerging Pattern of Rural Leadership in Southern Asia* (Hyderabad : National Institute of Community Development, 1965).

Dube, S.C. : *The Indian Village* (London : Rutledge, 1965).

Engels, F. : *The Peasant War in Germany* (London, 1969).

Farooqi, Z.A. : *British Relations with the Cis-Sutlej States 1809-1923* (Lahore, 1941).

Fithe, Venneth, : *Twilight of the Maharajas* (London, 1956).

Fortos, Rosita : *India of the Princes,* 1939.

Fox, Sir Cyril : *Economic Mineral Resources of Patiala State and Their Industrial Possibilities* (Patiala, 1946).

Fuller, J. Bamptyloke : *The Empire of India* (London : 1913).

Fix, Richard G. : *Kin Clan Raja and Rule-State Hinterland Relations in Pre-industrial India* (Berkeley : University of California, Press, 1971).

Frykenberg, Robert, Fric (ed) : *Land Control and Social Structure in Indian History* (Madison, University of Wisconsin Press, 1969).

Gadgil, D.R. : *The Industrial Evolution of India in Recent Times 1887-1939* (Delhi, 1973 Fifth Edition, first published in 1924).

Ganda Singh : *History of Gurdwara Shaheed Ganj (Amritsar : 1936); Some Confidential Papers of the Akali Movement* (Amritsar, SGPC, 1930-Edited).

Pepsu : A Historical Background (Patiala : 1952).

Gandhi, M.K. : *The Indian States' Problems* (Ahmadabad : 1941).

Gandhi, M.K. : *Collected Works of Mahatma Gandhi* Vols. XVI, XLI, XLII (Ahmedabad : 1965, 1970 & 1971 respectively).

Gangula, N.N. : *The Indian Peasant and His Environment* (London : 1935).

Gauba, K.L. : *Pathology of Princes (Lahore : 1930-Famous Trials for Love and Murder* (Delhi : 1967).

Ghoshal, V.N. : *Agrarian System in Ancient India* (Calcutta : Saraswat Library, 1973, Reprint of 1929, Edition).

Gokal Chand : *A Biographical Sketch of his Highness Maharaja Bhupinder Singh, with a brief History of the State* (Patiala, 1911).

Giani Nahar Singh : *History of Freedom Movement in India* (Amritsar : 1950).

Griffin Lepel : *The Rajas of the Punjab* (Patiala, 1970 reprint, first published, London, 1873).

Griffin Lepel : *Chiefs and Families of Note in the Punjab*, 2 Vols. (Lahore, 1909).

Griffin Lepel : *The Minor Phulkian Families* (Patiala Language Department, Punjab, 1970).

Griffith, M. : *India's Princes* (London, 1894).

Gulati, K.C. : *The Akalis Past and Present* (New Delhi, 1974).

Gupta, Hari Ram : *A History of the Sikhs*, Vol. I (Simla 1952).

Gupta, Hari Ram : *Presidential Address, 18th Session of Punjab History Conference* (Patiala, 1983).

Gupta, S.C. : *Indian Agrarian Structure, A Study of Evolution* (New Delhi, 1966).

Gurdwara Reform Movement and the Sikh Awakening (Jullundur : 1922).

Habib, Irfan : *The Agrarian System of Mughal India* (Bombay, Asia Publishing House, 1963).

Hambhin, Robert (*ed.*) : *Leadership and Crisis in Leadership in India* (New Delhi : Asia Publishing House 1967).

Handa, R.L. : *History of the Freedom Struggle in Princely States* (New Delhi : Central News Agency).

Harbans Singh : *Faridkot and Its Rulers*, Published by the Chairman, Faridkot State Publicity Committee.

Historical Backgound of Pepsu, A Pepsu State Government Publication.

Harbans Singh and Jagjit Singh : *Singh Sabha Lehar in Punjab : 1949-1960* (Ludhiana : 1962).

Hari Singh, Master : *Agricultural Workers Struggle in Punjab* (New Delhi : People's Publishing Hose, 1980).

Hari Singh, Master : *Agrarian Scene in British Punjab*, Vol. I (New Delhi, Peoples Publishing House, 1983).

Hari Singh, Master : *Punjab Peasant in Freedom Struggle*, Vol. I (New Delhi : People's Publishing House, 1984).

Hayland, John S. : *Indian Crisis*—The Background (London : 1943).

Hobabawm, E.J., Ashok, Raj, K.N. And Sachs, Iqnacq : *Peasants in*

History and Essays in Honour Kula, Witold, Mitra *of Daniel Thorner* (Delhi, Oxford : University, Press, 1980).

Hussain, Khalifa, S.M. : *A Short Account of the Principle Charitable and Administrative Acts of His Highness Shree Mahendra Singh of Patiala* (Calcutta, 1875).

Hussain, Khalifa, S.M. : *Tarikh-i-Patiala* (English Trans. Khalifa Saadat Hussain, Mss., PSA).

Ilbetson, Denzil : *Punjab Castes* (Patiala 1970 repring, first published in 1883).

Jadhave, Khashorao B. and Motta, V.D. : *Indian States* (Baroda, 1920). *Indictment of Patiala* published by the General Secretaries, Bombay : *The Indian States' People's Conference, 1930* — published by the General Secretaries, Bombay : The Indian States' People's Conference : *Indian States' Committee Report,* London : Printed and published by His Majesty's Stationery Office, 1929.

Indian States Today, New Delhi : Publication Bureau Government of India, 1948.

Indian States, Calcutta : Central Publication Branch, 1928.

Jagjit Singh, Maharaja : *My Tour of the World,* Lahore : Pioneer and Civil and Military Gazettee, 1929.

Jeoffery M. Paige : *Agrarian Revolution Social Movements and Export Agriculture in the Under-developed World* (London : Collier Macmillian Publishers, 1978).

Jeoffery, Robin (*ed.*) : *People, Princes and Paramount Power : Society and Politics in the Indian Princely States* (New Delhi, 1978).

John, Lord : *The Maharajas* (London, 1972).

Jones, Kenneth W. : *Arya Daram* (New Delhi, 1976).

Josh, Bhagwan Singh : *Communist Movement In Punjab : 1926-47* (Delhi : 1980).

Josh, Bhagwan Singh : *Land Reforms Indian Trends and Perspectives* (New Delhi : Allied Publishers, 1975).

Kapil Kumar : *Peasants in Revolt Tenants, Landlords, Congress and Raj In GUBH,* 1886-1922 (New Delhi : Manohar Publications, 1984).

Karunakaram, K.P. : *Religious and Political Awakening in India* (Meerut : 1965).

Kay, Sir Gecil : *Communism in India* : Unpublished documents from NAI, 1919-24 *ed.,* By Subodh Roy (Calcutta : 1971).

Kenneth Jones : Communism in the Punjab.

Kossinger, Tom G. : *Vilyat Pur* 1848-1968 (New Delhi, 1979).

Khan, Abdul Majid : *A Short History of Patiala State* (Patiala, 1940).

Khushwant Singh : *A History of the Sikhs,* 2 Vols. (Delhi, 1977 reprint, first published Princeton, 1963).

Khushwant Singh and Satinder Singh : *Ghadar* (New Delhi, 1966).

Khusro, A.M. : *Economic and Social Efforts of Jagirdari Abolition and Land Reforms in Hyderabad.* R.P.C. Project Report (Delhi : Atma Ram and Sons, 1958).

Kohli, Sita Ram : *Patiala and East Punjab States Union* - (A Leaf from their History, The Jyoti, Government Ranbir College, Sangrur, 1951).

Kotevsky, G. : *Agrarian Reforms in India* (New Delhi, 1964).

Kirpal Singh : *Life of Maharaja Ala Singh and His Times* (Amritsar, 1954).

Kulkarni, V.B. : *The Future of Indian States* (Bombay, 1944).

Kumar, Shive : *Peasant Uprisings Before First World War* (Meerut, 1979).

Lethe, A.B. : *Problems of Indian States* (Poona, 1930).

Landsbarger, Menry A. (*ed.*) : *Rural Protest, Peasant Movement and Social Change,* (New York, Macmillan, 1974).

Lassewell, d Harofed and Kaplan Abraham : *Power and Society : A Framework for Political* Inquiry (New Haven : Yalo University Press, 1950).

Lee Liarner, Sir William : Native States of India (London : 1954).

Leo-Warner, William : *The Native States of India* (London : 1910).

Leigh, M.S. : *The Punjab and the War* (Lahore : 1922).

Lenin, V.I. : *Capitalism and Agriculture* (New York : International Publishers, 1945).

Lewis Oscar : *Village Life in Northern India* (New York : Vintage Book, A Division of Random House, 1950).

Lefebvre, George : *The Great Fear of 1789 : Rural Panic in Revolutionary France* (London : New Left Books, 1973).

Loomis, P. Charles and Beagle, Allam : *Rural Social System* (New York : Prentice Hall, 1950).

Lothian, Arthur Cunnigham : *Kingdoms of Yesterday* (London : 1951).

Low, Sir Sydney : *The Indian States and Ruling Princes* (London : 1920).

Lumby, E.W.R. : *Transfer of Power in India, 1945-47* (London : 1954).

Macmun, Sir George : *The Indian States and Princes,* (London : 1975).

Malleson, G.B. : *Historical Sketch of Indian States* (London : 1875).

Mehta, K.K. and I.K. : *The Pepsu Tenancy and Agricultural Lands Act* (Chandigarh, nd.).

Malaviva, H.D. : *Land Reforms in India* (New Delhi : All India Congress Committee, 1955).

Mathur, K.S. : *Leadership in Rural India* (L.P. Vidyarthi, Bombay : Asia Publishing House, 1967).

Mao Tse-Tung : *Selected Works* (London : Co., Harper and Row, 1955).

Marx, Karl : *Pre-Capitalist Economic Formations* (London : Lowerance and Wishart, 1964).

Mehta, Shive Rattan : *Emerging Pattern of Rural Leadership* (New Delhi, Wiley Eastern Private Ltd., 1972).

Menon, V.P. : *The Story of the Integration of Indian States* (Bombay, Orient Longmans Ltd., 1956).

Metcalf, Thomas R : *Land Landlords and British Raj* (Delhi, 1979).

Mishra, G.P. : *Some Aspects of Change in Agrarian Structure* (New Delhi, Sterling Publishers, 1977).

Mittal, S.C. : *Freedom Movement in the Punjab : 1905-29* (Delhi : 1977).

Mohammed Hussain : *An Attack on the Police Administration of Punjab Native States* (Umbala : Royal Medical Hall Press, 1893).

Mohinder Singh : *The Akali Movement* (Macmillion, Delhi : 1979).

Moreland, M.H. : *The Agrarian System of Muslim India* (Allahabad : Central Book 1929, Delhi : Oriental Book Publishers, 1968, Reprint).

Moore, Jr. : *Social Origins of Dictatorship and Democracy—Land and Peasant in the Making Modern World* (London : Ponguin, 1970).

Moghe, K.B. : *The Indian States in relation to the British Crown and British India* (Bombay, 1928).

Mosley, Leonard : *Last Days of British Raj,* (London : 1967).

Moogy, Ajit K. : *The Paramount Power and the Princely States of India 1858-1881*(Calcutta, 1979).

Mukherjee, H.C. : Congress and the Masses (Calcutta : 1945).

Mukherjee, H. and Mukherjee, Uma : *Growth of Nationalism in India (1857-1905)* (Calcutta : 1957).

Rural India, Peasants Poverty, Its Causes and Cure (Allabhabad : n.d.).

Rural Reconstruction (Allahabad : 1946).

Mukherjee, Karuna : *Land Reforms* (Calcutta : H. Chatterjee and Co. Ltd., 1952).

Mukherjee, Radha Kamal : *Land Problems of India* (London, Longman Green, Col. Ltd.).

Nahar Singh : *Development in Sikh Politics : 1900-11* (Delhi : 1965).

Gooroo Ram Singh and the Kuka Sikhs : Rebels against the British Power in India : Documents, 1863-71 (Delhi : 1965).

Namboodiripad, E.M.S. : *Agrarian Reforms—A Study of the Congress and Communist Approach* (New Delhi, Peoples Publishing House, Pvt. Ltd, 1956).

Nanda, B.R. (Ed) : *Socialism in India* (Delhi : Vikas Publication, 1972).

Narahari Kaviraj : *Peasant Uprising in Bengal* (PPH : Delhi : 1972).

Naroji Dada Bhai : *Poverty and British Rule in India,* (Delhi : 1969).

Narang, G.C. : *Brief History of Malerkotla State* : 1914-18 (Lahore : 1920).

Natrajan, L. : *Peasant Uprisings in India (1850-1900)* (Bombay, Peoples Publishing House Ltd. 1953).

Nehru, J.L. : *Presidential Address to the Sixth Session of the All India States 'Peoples' Conference* (Ludhiana : 1939).

Nicholson, A.P. : *Scraps of Paper India's Broken Treaties, Her Princes and the Problem* (London : 1930).

Nihal Singh : *The Kings Indian Allies, The Rajas and Their India* (London : 1916).

Ojha, Ghaneshwar : *Land Problem and land Reforms-A Study with Reference to Bihar* (New Delhi, Sultan Chand and Sons, ND).

Oza, Keval Ram C. : *Indian States in Free India* (Bombay, 1947).

Pande, Ram : *Land Reform and Social Change,* (Jaipur : Shodhak, 1983).

Pannikar, K.M. : *Indian Princes in Council,* (London : 1936) *Patiala Census Report for 1931,* (Lahore : Printed at the Civil and Military Gazettee Press).

Pannikar, K.M. : *An Introduction to the Study of the Relations of the Indian States and the Government of India,* (London : 1927).

Panthasanathy, O.G. Prasada Rao S. : *Importance of Land Reforms in Andhra Pradesh* (Calcutta : Scientific Book Agency, 1969).

Patel, G.D. : *The Indian Land Problem and Legislation* (Bombay : N.M. Tripathi Ltd., Law Publishers, 1954).

Panikar, K.N. (*ed.*) : *National and Left Movements in India* (New Delhi, Vikas Publishing House Pvt. Ltd., 1980).

Phillips, Barnards : *Sociology : Social Structure and Change* (London : Macmillan Company, 1969).

Phillips, Barnards : *Progress in Land Reforms : Analysis of Replies by Government to a United Nation* (Overtionaire, New York : United Nations, Department of Economics Affairs, 1954).

Panikkar, K.M. : *The Indian Princes in Council : A Record of the Chancellorship of His Highness the Maharaja of Patiala 1926-31 and 1933-36* (London : 1936).

Panikkar, K.M. : *British Diplomacy in North India : A Study of the Delhi Residency 1803-1857* (New Delhi, 1968).

Panikkar, K.M. (*ed.*) : *National and Left Movement in India* (New Delhi : 1900).

Pettigrew, Joyco : *Robber Noblemen* (New Delhi, 1978).

Phadnis, Urmilla : *Towards the Integration of Indian States 1919-1947* (Bombay, 1968).

Pillai, D. Devadas : *Rajahs and Prajas* (Bombay : 1976).

Punjab Government : *Land of the Five Rivers* (Patiala : 1970-Reprint).

Punjab District Gazetteers, Vol. XVA, *Ludhiana District and Malerkotla State* Lahore : Civil and Military Gazettee Press, 1904.

Punjab States Gazetteers, Vol. XVIA, *Faridkot State,* Lahore : Civ il and Military Gazettee Press, 1907-Vol VII A, Kalsia State, Lahore : *op. cit.,* 1904-Vol XVII A, Phulkian States Patiala, Nabha and Jind, Lahore : *op. cit.,* 1904.

Raghovan, S.R.S. : *Indian States and Indian Polity* (Bangalore, 1931).

Raghubir Singh : *Indian States and the New Agency.*

Raise Your Voice against Landlord-Police Terror in Andhra Pradesh, (Marxist Book Agency (Pvt.) Ltd., Calcutta (N.D.).

Range, N.G. : *Revolutionary Peasants* (Delhi : Amrit Book Co., 1949).

Randhawa, M.S. : *A History of Agriculture of India,* 3 Vols. (New Delhi : 1983).

Rai, Satya M. : *Panjabi Heroic Tradition 1901-1947* (Patiala : Panjabi University, Patiala).

Revolutionary Terrorist Movement in the Punjab.

Raj Kumar Sardar : *Modern Kapurthala and Its Maker* (Lahore : Kapoor Arts Printing Works, n.d.).

Raja Ram : *The Jallianwala Bagh Massacre* (Punjab University, Chandigarh : 1969).

Ramusack, Barbara : *The Princes of India in the Twilight of the Empire Dissolution of a Patron Client System 1914-1939* (Columbus : 1978).

Raghavan, S.R.S. : *Indian States and Indian Polity* (Bangalore, 1931).

Raghubir Singh : *Indian States and the New Regime* (Bombay, 1938).

Randhawa, M.S. : *A History of Agriculture of India,* Vols. (New Delhi, 1983).

Ranga, N.G. : *Revolutionary Peasants,* (Delhi : 1949).

Range Iyer, C.S. : *India in Peace or War* (London : 1930).

Rasul, M.A. : *History of All India Kisan Sabha* (Calcutta : 1974).

Ray, Mihir K. : *Princely States and the Paramount Power 1958-1876* (New Delhi : 1981).

Rao, M.S.A. : *Social Movements in India,* Vol. I and II (New Delhi, Manohar Publications, 1978).

Rasul, M.A. : *History of All India Kisan Sabha* (Calcutta : Book Agency Pvt. Ltd., 1974).

Raychaudhari, Tapan (ed) : *Contribution to Indian Economic History* Vol. I & II (Calcutta : 1960 & 1963 respectively).

Ray Jhankhande : *Bhartiya Kranti Kari Andolan : Ekk Vishleshan in Hindi* (PPH, Delhi : 1974).

Roberts, W. and Kartar Singh : *A Text Book of Punjab Agriculture* (Lahore, 1947).

Rosa, H.A. : *Glsossary of the Tribes and Castes of Punjab and North West Frontier Province,* Vol. II (Patiala, 1970 reprint, first published in 1883).

Rothermund, Diotmer : *Government, Landlord and Peasant in India : Agricultural Relations Under British Rule 1865-1935* (Wiesbandon, 1970).

Rao, Prasada N. : *Land Reforms Under Congress Raj* (1950).

Roy, pradipted (*ed.*) : *The Characteristics of Emergent Leaders in Leadership in India* (IP Vidyarthi, New York : Asia Publishing House, 1967).

Saini, B.S. : *Social and Economic History of the Punjab : 1901-39* (Ess Ess Publishers, Delhi, 1975).

Sardesai, S.G. : *India and the Russian Revoltion* (New Delhi : 1967).

Sanderson, Dwight : *Leadership for Rural Life* (New York : Association Press, 1940).

Saraswati Sahajan and (Swami) : *Abolition of Zamindari : How to Achieve it* (Patna : Orient Press, 1945).

Sastry K.R.R. : *Indian States And Responsible Government* (Allahabad : 1939).

Sayana, V.V. : *The Agrarian Problems of Madras Province* (Madras, The Business Week Press, 1949).

Sen, D.K. : *Indian States* (London : 1930).

Sen, Bhawani : *Evolution of Agrarian Relations in India,* (New Delhi, Peoples Publishing House, 1962).

Sen, Bhawani : *Indian Land System and Land Reforms* (Delhi, People's Publishing House, 1935).

Sen, Sunil : *Agrarian Relations in India, 1793-1947* (New Delhi : People Publishing House, 1979).

Sen, Sunil : *Peasant Movements in India, Mid Nineteenth and Twentieth Centuries,* (Calcutta : 1982).

Sen, S.P. (*ed.*) : *Dictionary of National Biography,* Vol. IV (Stoz) (Calcutta : Institute of Historical Studies, 1974).

Sheo, Kumar Lal (*ed.*) : *Sociological Perspectives of Land Reforms,* (New Delhi : Agricole Publishing Academy, 1982).

Siddiqi, Majid Hayat : *Agrarian Unrest in North India,* (New Delhi : Vikas Publishing House Pvt. Ltd., 1978).

Shanin, T. (*ed.*) : *Peasants and Peasant Societies* (Middlepex, 1976).

Sharma, Hari : *Princes and Paramountcy* (New Delhi, 1978).

Sharma, R.S. : *Ancient India* (Delhi, 1977).

Shree Baba Ala Singh : *Anniversary Celebration Committee, Shree Baba Ala Singh Ji* (Patiala, n.d.).

Singh, Ganda : *Patiala and East Punjab States Union, Historical Background* (Patiala, Archives Department, 1951).

Singh, Ganda : *Bibliography of Pepsu* (Patiala Archives Department, 1951).

Singh, Gur Rattan Pal : *The Illustrated History of the Sikhs 1947-78* (Chandigarh : Akal Printmatics, 1979).

Singh, Mohinder : *The Depressed Classes : Their Economic and Social Conditions* (Bombay : Hindkitabs, 1947).

Singhal, M.L. : *The Patriot Prince* (Ludhiana : 1961).

Sinha, Sasadhar : *Indian Independence in Perspective* (Bombay : 1964).

Sircar, D.C. : *Land System and Feudalism in Ancient India* (Calcutta University, 1966).

Sita Ram Singh : *Nationalism and Social Reforms in India 1885-1920* (Delhi : 1968).

Sitaramaya Pattabhai : *History of the Indian National Congress,* Vols. I & II, (Bombay : 1947).

Sinha Sirdhar : *Indian Independence in Prospective* (Bombay : 1964).

Srinivas, M.N. : *Social Change in Modern India* (Barke Rey, University of California Press, 1966).

Steve Jones, Joshi P.C. Miquel Murmis (editors) : *Rural Poverty and Agrarian Reforms* (New Delhi : Allied Publishers Pvt. Ltd., 1982).

Strokes, E. : *The Peasants and the Rajas Studies in the Agrarian Society, and Peasant Rebellion in Colonial India* (Cambridge University Press, 1978).

Subhani, Akhtar : *My Ruler* (Maharaja Yadavindra Singh of Patiala, Lahore, 1940).

Suri, V.S. : *Punjab Ke Lok Geeton Main Azadi Ki Goonj* (Jullundhur : Daily Partap : 1956).

Syed, Abdoolah : *Memorandum of the Life and Character of His Highness the Maharaja Mahender Singh, Sovereign of Patiala* (London : 1872).

Syed Mohammad Hussain : *Tarikh-i-Patiala* (Amritsar : 1877).

Syngal, Munna Lal : *Patriot Prince or the Life Story of Maharaja Ripudaman Singh of Nabha who Died a Martyr* (Ludhiana : 1961).

Talib, Gurbachan Singh : *Sardar Sewa Singh Thikriwala* (Patiala : 1971).

Tandon, Prakash : *Punjabi Century 1857-1947* (London : 1961).

Tara Chand : *History of the Freedom Movement in India* : Vol. III, (Publication division, Delhi : 1972).

Teja Singh : *The Gurdwara Reform Movement and Sikh Awakening* (Jullundhur : 1943).

Thornburn, S.S. : *The Punjab in Peace and War* (Language Department, Patiala : 1970).

Thorner, Deniel : *The Shaping of Modern India* (New Delhi : 1980).

Thorner, Deniel : *The Agrarian Prospect in India* (Delhi : 1956). Land and Labour in India (London : 1962).

Thorner, Daniel and Malice Treveskis, Hugh Kennedy : *The Land of Five Rivers—An Economic History of the Punjab from the Earliest Times to the Year of Grace 1890* ((Oxford 1928).

Trevaskis, H.K. : *Land of the Five Rivers :* An Economic History of the Punjab from the Earliest times of the Year of Grace-1890, (London : 1928).

Trevaskis, Hugh Kennedy : *Punjab of Today :* An Economic Survey of the Punjab in Recent Years 1890-1925, 2 Vols., n.p. 1931.

Trilochan Singh : *Our Leader Today* (Maharaja Yadavindra Singh of Patiala) (Patiala, 1948).

Vable D. : *The Arya Samaj Hindu Without Hinduism* (Delhi : 1983).

Wasti, Syed Razi : *Lord Minto and Indian Nationalist Movement,* Oxford, 1967.

Whitcombe, Elizabeth : *Agrarian Conditions in Northern India,* (New Delhi : 1971).

Vidyarthi, L.P. (*ed.*) : *Leadership in India* (Bombay : Asia Publishing House, 1967).

Walia, Ramesh : *Praja Mandal Movement in East Punjab States* (Patiala, Panjabi University, 1972).

Wilson, John : *Introduction to Social Movements* (New York : Basic Books Inc. 1973).

Wolf, Eric : *Peasant Wars of the Twentieth Century* (London : Feber and Feber, 1971).

BOOKS IN PANJABI

Amar, Ajzib Singh : *Riasat Patiala Di Ik Bhadur Devi* (Patiala : 1944).

Amar, Ajzib Singh : *Riasat Patiala Te Sikh Itihas* (Patiala 1944).

Amar, Ajzib Singh : *Sarkar Hind Di Vidhayak Nitite Sarkar Patiala,* (Patiala, 1945).

Ashok, Shamsher Singh : *Punjab Dian Lehran,* (Dhuri, n.d.).

Ashok, Shamsher Singh : *Patiala Raj Bhawan Pustakalya* (Patiala : 1946).

Ashok, Shamsher Singh : *Patiala-Pati Maharaja Amar Singh Di Var* (Patiala : 1944).

Atma Singh : *Patiala Shahi Gharane Dian Surbeer Devian* (Lahore : 1936).

Atma Singh : *Patiala Union Raj ate Navin Lehran* (n.p. 1956).

Atma Singh : *Shairiac ate Patiala Union Da Sankhep Itihas* (n.p.n.d.).

Attar Singh : *Twarikh Sidhu Bararan* (Panjabi Translation), (Calcutta, 1934).

Avtar Singh : *Din Diharey Rattan* (Published by the author).

Bachan Singh : *Patiala Union Da Itihas Te Shariat,* (Patiala, 1932).

Bajwa, Fauja Singh and Gurnek Singh : *Praja Mandal Andolan Riasat Faridkot,* (Patiala, 1976).

Balwant Singh : *Sidhu Bararan Da Itihas, Malwa Da Sankhep Itihas* (Gumti Kalan, 1956).

Bhaura, Ujjagar Singh : *Kaumi Jeewan, Sardar Sewa Singh Thikriwala* (Ludhiana, n.d.).

Fauja Singh & Gurnek Singh : *Praja Andolan Riyast Faridkot* (Patiala : Panjabi University, 1976).

Gurcharan Singh : *Jeewan Sardar Sewa Singh Thikriwala* (Patiala, Panjabi University, Patiala).

Giani Gian Singh : *Twarikh Guru Khalsa,* (Patiala 1970 reprint).

Giani Kehar Singh : *Praja Malerkotla Dee Dard Kahani* (Amritsar : Desh Dardi Press (N.D.).

Giani Partap Singh : *Akali Lehar Da Itihas* (Singh Bros, Amritsar : 1951).

Moti, Prem Singh : *Khalsa Raj De Usariye, Ludhiana,* 1982 reprint.

Jaswant Singh (*ed.*) : *Master Tara Singh Jeewan Sangharsh Te Udesh,* (Amritsar, 1972).

Jus, Jaswant Singh : *Baba Ram Singh Namdhari,* (Amritsar, 1962).

Jus, Jaswant Singh : *Desh Bhagat Babe,* (Jullundhur, 1975).

Josh, Sohan Singh : *Akali Morchian Da Itihas,* (Delhi : 1972).

Lal Singh, Gianai : *Punjab Di Veer Parampara,* (Patiala : 1971).

Lal, Kanhya : *Tarikh-i-Punjab* (Panjabi Transalation), (Patiala : 1968).

Maftoon, Diwan Singh : *Had Sitian,* (Delhi : 1959).

Mohinder Singh : *Sardar-i-Azam* (Amritsar, n.d.).

Nahar Singh, Giani : *Azadi Dian Lehran* (Ludhiana : 1960).

Narain Singh : *Kujh Aaap Bitian Kujh Jag Bitian,* (Delhi : 1966).

Nath, Shiv : *Bhulle Visre Lok* (Amritsar : 1976).

Nath, Shiv : *Upholia Varka,* (Amritsar : 1979).

Niranjan Singh : *Jeewan Yatra Master Tara Singh,* (Amritsar : 1968).

Sahanara, Gurcharan Singh : *Ghadar Party Da Itihas,* (Jullundhur : 1961).

Seetal, Sohan Singh : *Pepsu Da Itihas,* (n. p. 1952).

Seetal, Sohan Singh : *Sikh Mislan,* (Zira : 1961).

Shergill, Kartar Singh : *Rajomajre De Biswedar* (Patiala : Cresent Press (N.D.).

Vaid, Chhajju Mal : *Comrade Dharam Singh Fakkar-Ik Jeewanee Ik-Parena,* (Bhatinda : 1980).

Vaid, Chhajju Mal : *Kisanan Muzarian De Mittar Kaun.*

Visakha Singh : *Malwa Itihas,* Vol. II, (Kishanpura Kalan (nd).

Tara Singh, Master : *Meri Yaad* (Amritsar : 1945).

Varsola, Swaran Singh : *Visphot Tone Bahad,* (Amritsar).

INDEX

E

F

G

H

M

T

Z